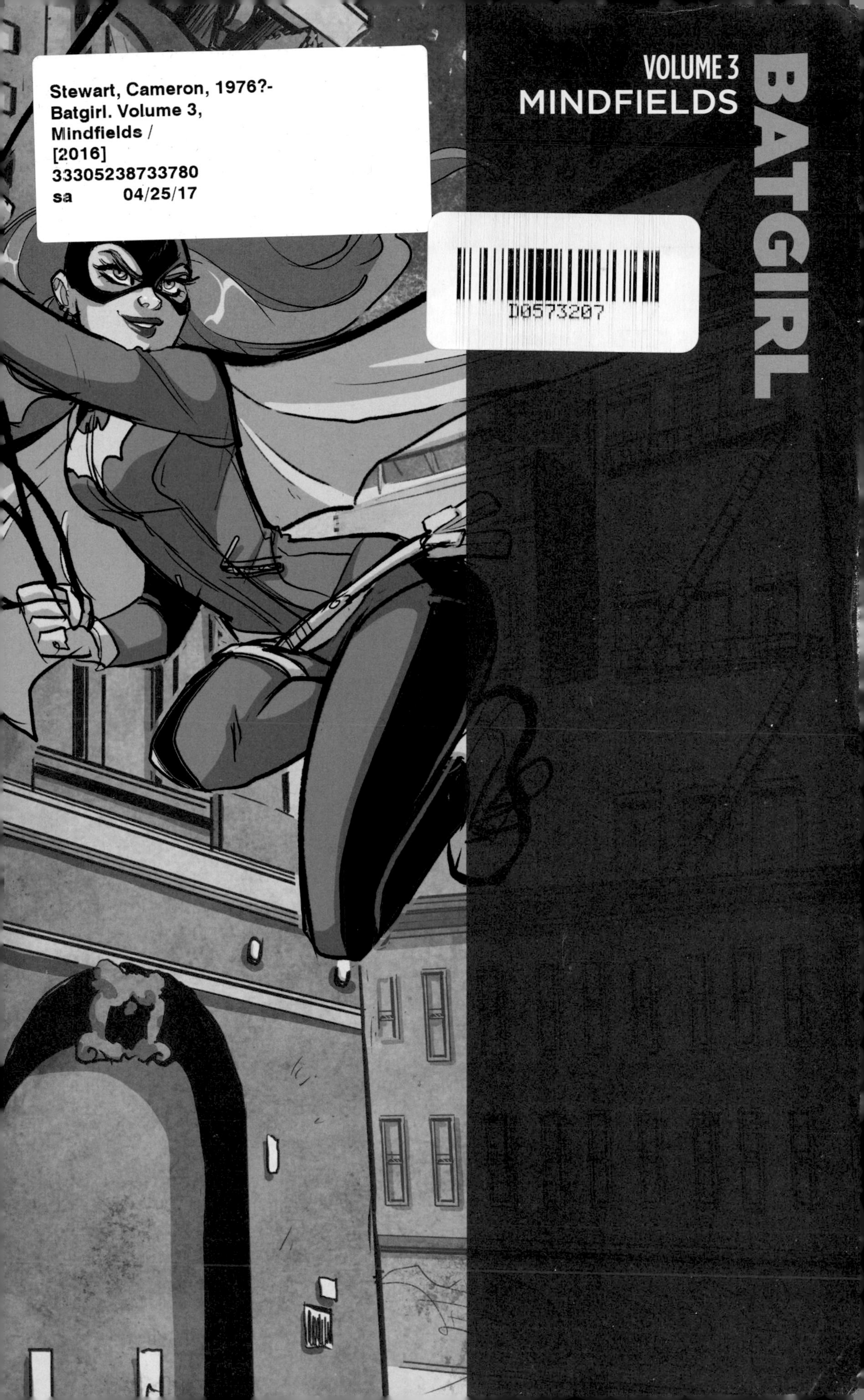

BATGIRL

VOLUME 3
MINDFIELDS

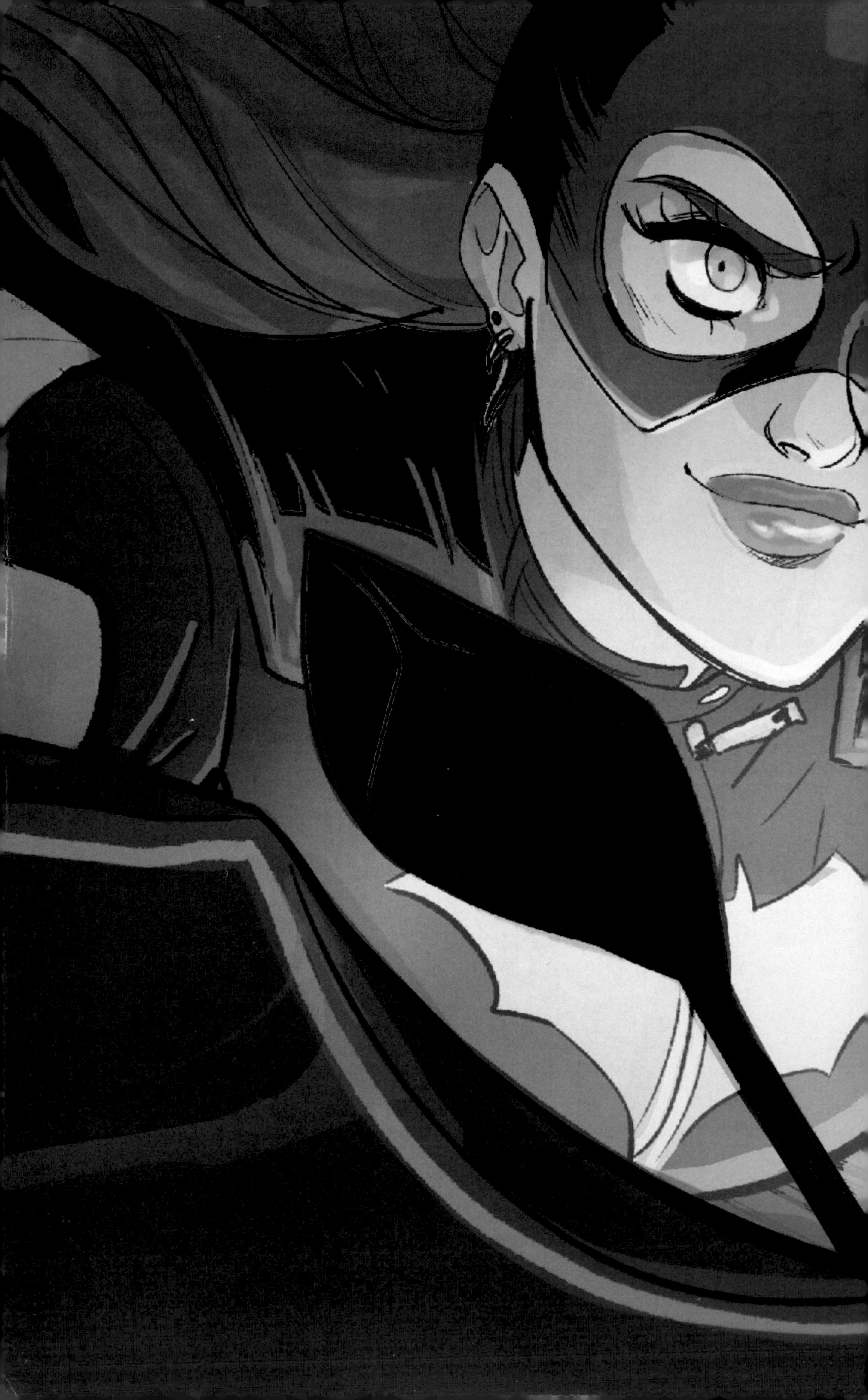

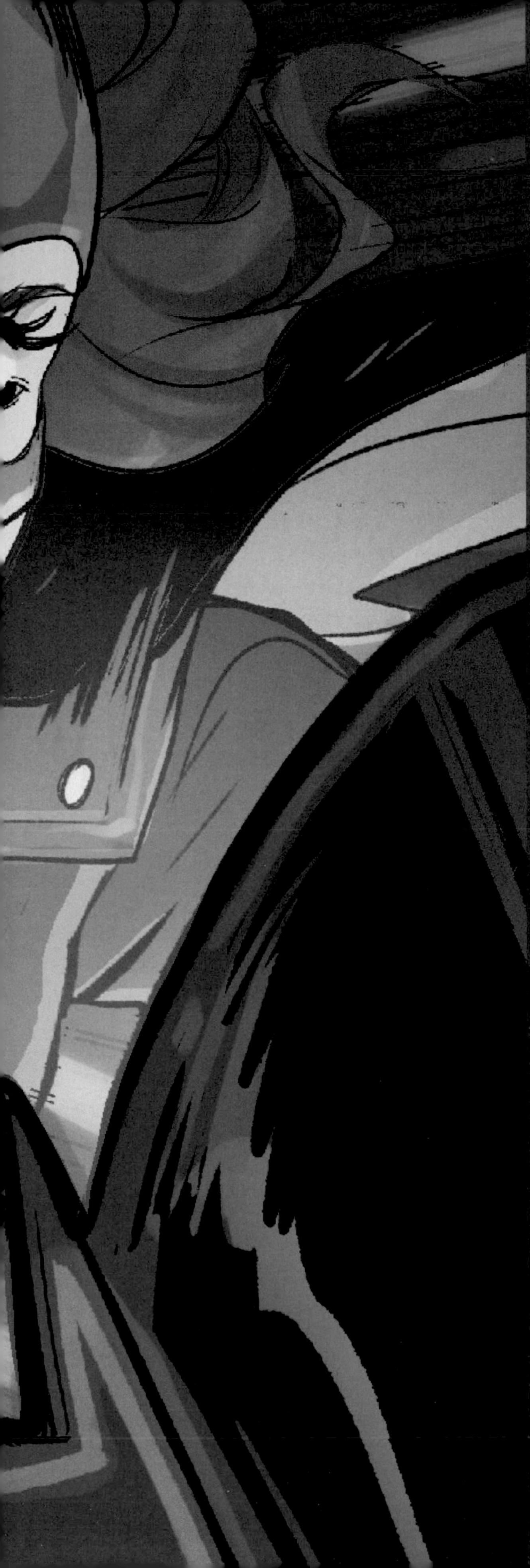

BATGIRL

VOLUME 3
MINDFIELDS

WRITTEN BY
CAMERON STEWART
BRENDEN FLETCHER

ART BY
BABS TARR
BENGAL
ELEONORA CARLINI
MORITAT
HORACIO DOMINGUES
ROGER ROBINSON
MING DOYLE
JAMES HARVEY
JOHN TIMMS
MINKYU JUNG
ROB HAYNES
CAMERON STEWART

COLORS BY
SERGE LAPOINTE
BENGAL
LEE LOUGHRIDGE
JAMES HARVEY

LETTERS BY
STEVE WANDS
JARED K. FLETCHER

COLLECTION COVER ART BY
BABS TARR

BATMAN CREATED BY
BOB KANE
WITH **BILL FINGER**

SPOILER CREATED BY
CHUCK DIXON
AND **TOM LYLE**

CHRIS CONROY Editor – Original Series
DAVE WIELGOSZ Assistant Editor – Original Series
JEB WOODARD Group Editor – Collected Editions
ROBIN WILDMAN Editor – Collected Edition
STEVE COOK Design Director – Books
DAMIAN RYLAND Publication Design

BOB HARRAS Senior VP – Editor-in-Chief, DC Comics

DIANE NELSON President
DAN DIDIO and JIM LEE Co-Publishers
GEOFF JOHNS Chief Creative Officer
AMIT DESAI Senior VP – Marketing & Global Franchise Management
NAIRI GARDINER Senior VP – Finance
SAM ADES VP – Digital Marketing
BOBBIE CHASE VP – Talent Development
MARK CHIARELLO Senior VP – Art, Design & Collected Editions
JOHN CUNNINGHAM VP – Content Strategy
ANNE DEPIES VP – Strategy Planning & Reporting
DON FALLETTI VP – Manufacturing Operations
LAWRENCE GANEM VP – Editorial Administration & Talent Relations
ALISON GILL Senior VP – Manufacturing & Operations
HANK KANALZ Senior VP – Editorial Strategy & Administration
JAY KOGAN VP – Legal Affairs
DEREK MADDALENA Senior VP – Sales & Business Development
JACK MAHAN VP – Business Affairs
DAN MIRON VP – Sales Planning & Trade Development
NICK NAPOLITANO VP – Manufacturing Administration
CAROL ROEDER VP – Marketing
EDDIE SCANNELL VP – Mass Account & Digital Sales
COURTNEY SIMMONS Senior VP – Publicity & Communications
JIM (SKI) SOKOLOWSKI VP – Comic Book Specialty & Newsstand Sales
SANDY YI Senior VP – Global Franchise Management

BATGIRL VOLUME 3: MINDFIELDS

DC Comics, 2900 West Alameda Ave., Burbank, CA 91505
Printed by RR Donnelley, Owensville, MO, USA. 7/22/16. First Printing.
ISBN: 978-1-4012-6269-3

Library of Congress Cataloging-in-Publication Data is available.

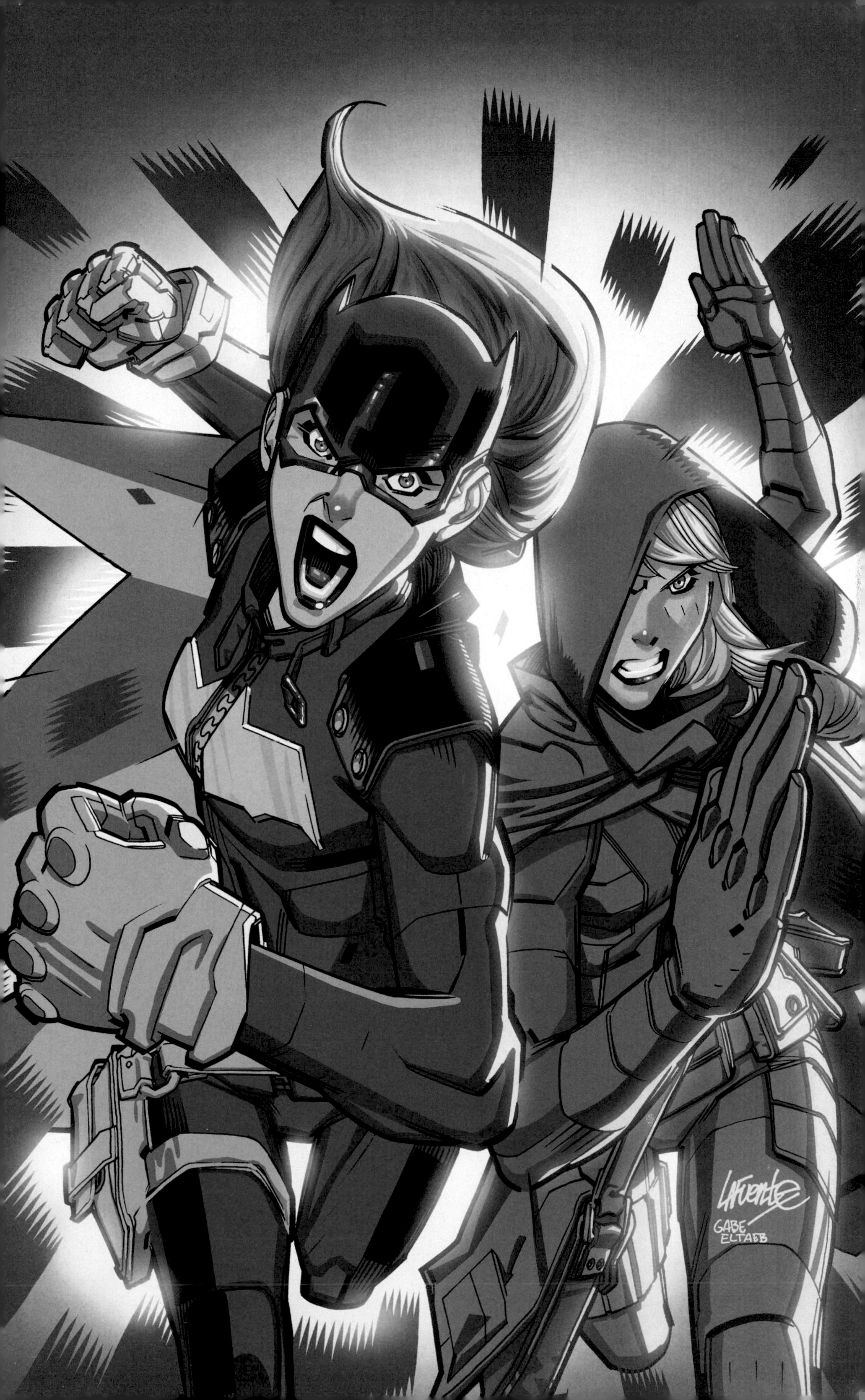
LAFUENTE
GABE
ELTAEB

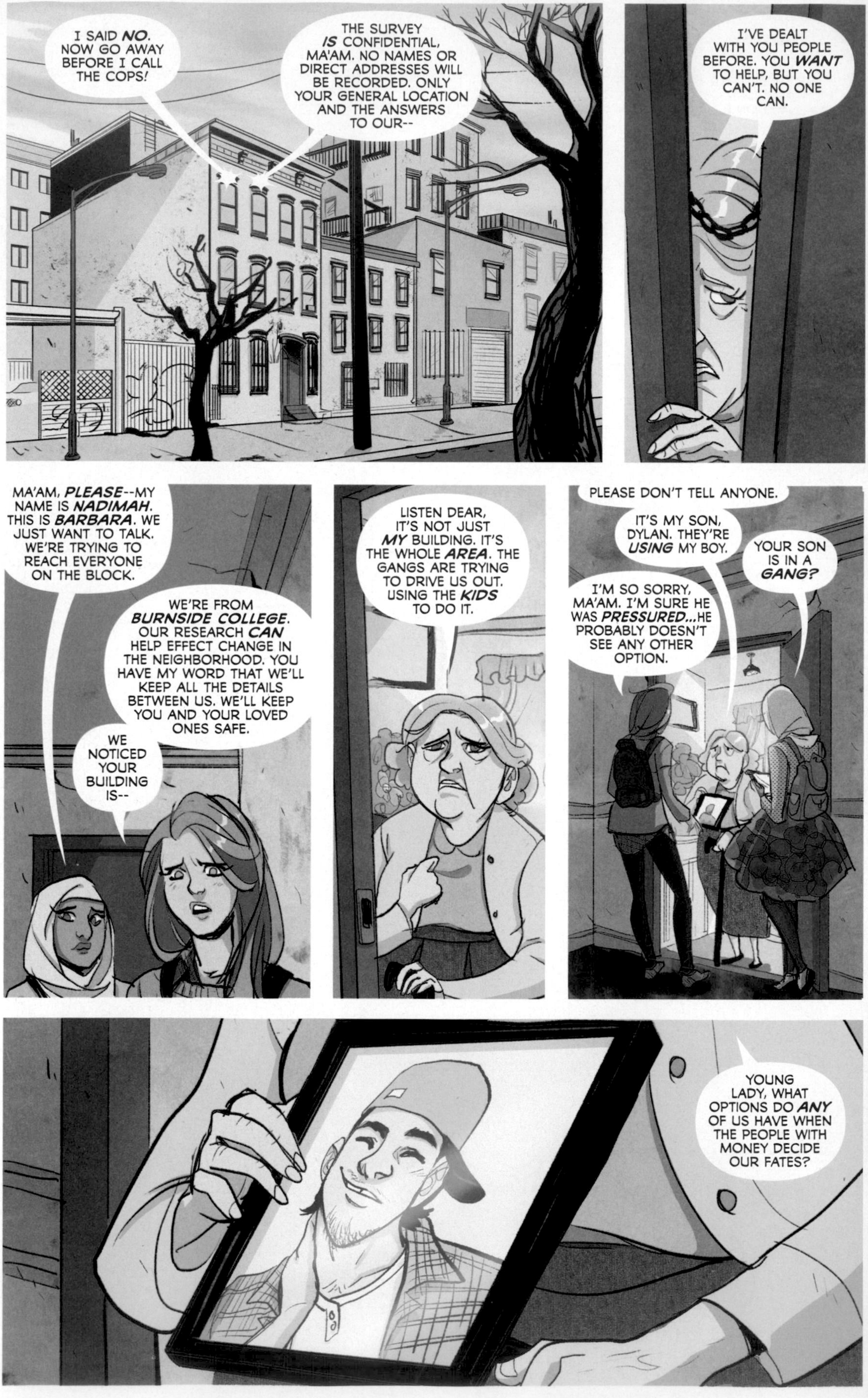
I SAID NO. NOW GO AWAY BEFORE I CALL THE COPS!
THE SURVEY IS CONFIDENTIAL, MA'AM. NO NAMES OR DIRECT ADDRESSES WILL BE RECORDED. ONLY YOUR GENERAL LOCATION AND THE ANSWERS TO OUR--
I'VE DEALT WITH YOU PEOPLE BEFORE. YOU WANT TO HELP, BUT YOU CAN'T. NO ONE CAN.
MA'AM, PLEASE--MY NAME IS NADIMAH. THIS IS BARBARA. WE JUST WANT TO TALK. WE'RE TRYING TO REACH EVERYONE ON THE BLOCK.
WE'RE FROM BURNSIDE COLLEGE. OUR RESEARCH CAN HELP EFFECT CHANGE IN THE NEIGHBORHOOD. YOU HAVE MY WORD THAT WE'LL KEEP ALL THE DETAILS BETWEEN US. WE'LL KEEP YOU AND YOUR LOVED ONES SAFE.
WE NOTICED YOUR BUILDING IS--
LISTEN DEAR, IT'S NOT JUST MY BUILDING. IT'S THE WHOLE AREA. THE GANGS ARE TRYING TO DRIVE US OUT. USING THE KIDS TO DO IT.
PLEASE DON'T TELL ANYONE.
IT'S MY SON, DYLAN. THEY'RE USING MY BOY.
YOUR SON IS IN A GANG?
I'M SO SORRY, MA'AM. I'M SURE HE WAS PRESSURED...HE PROBABLY DOESN'T SEE ANY OTHER OPTION.
YOUNG LADY, WHAT OPTIONS DO ANY OF US HAVE WHEN THE PEOPLE WITH MONEY DECIDE OUR FATES?

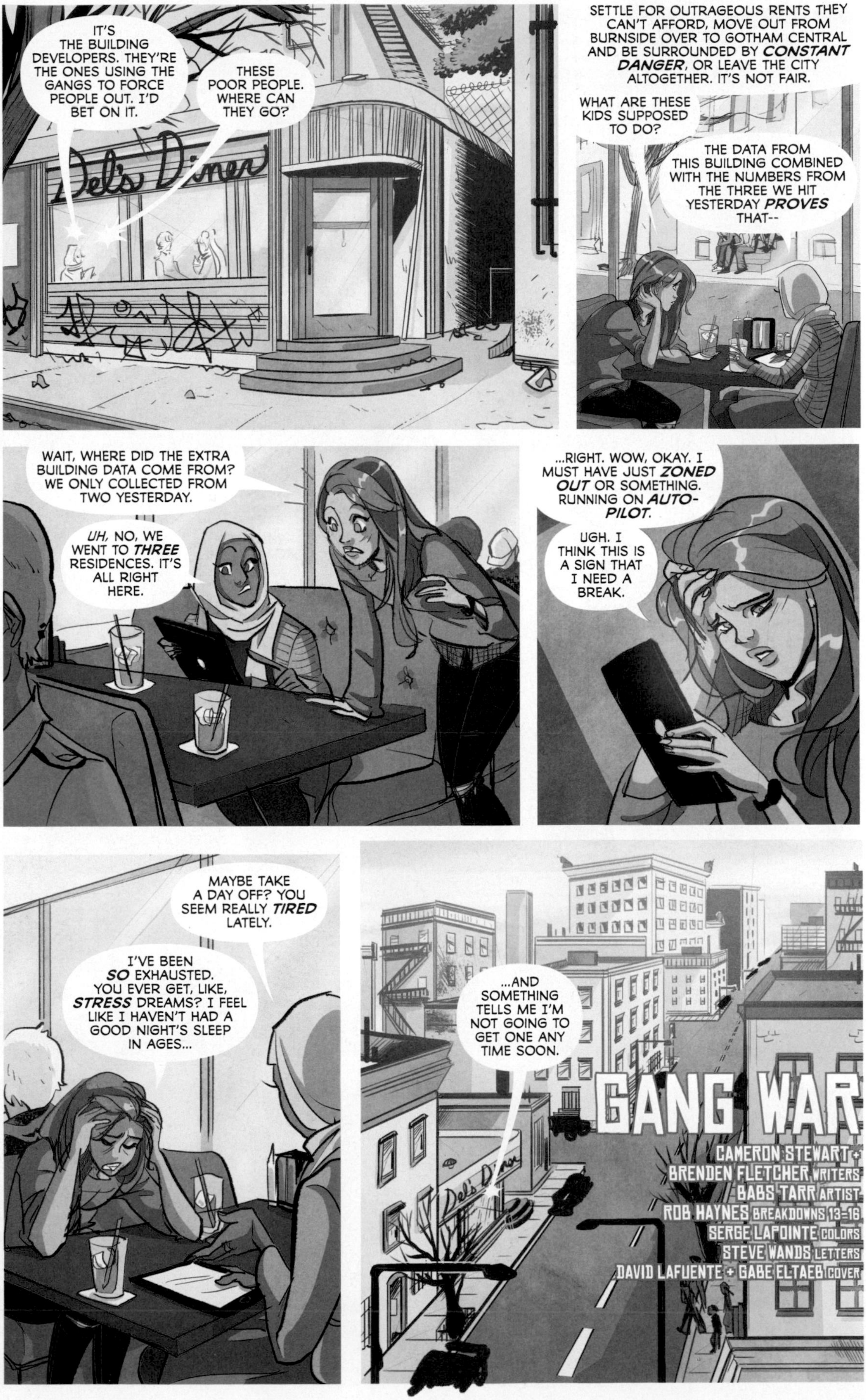
IT'S THE BUILDING DEVELOPERS. THEY'RE THE ONES USING THE GANGS TO FORCE PEOPLE OUT. I'D BET ON IT.
THESE POOR PEOPLE. WHERE CAN THEY GO?
Del's Diner
SETTLE FOR OUTRAGEOUS RENTS THEY CAN'T AFFORD, MOVE OUT FROM BURNSIDE OVER TO GOTHAM CENTRAL AND BE SURROUNDED BY *CONSTANT DANGER*, OR LEAVE THE CITY ALTOGETHER. IT'S NOT FAIR.
WHAT ARE THESE KIDS SUPPOSED TO DO?
THE DATA FROM THIS BUILDING COMBINED WITH THE NUMBERS FROM THE THREE WE HIT YESTERDAY *PROVES* THAT--
WAIT, WHERE DID THE EXTRA BUILDING DATA COME FROM? WE ONLY COLLECTED FROM TWO YESTERDAY.
UH, NO, WE WENT TO *THREE* RESIDENCES. IT'S ALL RIGHT HERE.
...RIGHT. WOW, OKAY. I MUST HAVE JUST *ZONED OUT* OR SOMETHING. RUNNING ON *AUTO-PILOT*.
UGH. I THINK THIS IS A SIGN THAT I NEED A BREAK.
MAYBE TAKE A DAY OFF? YOU SEEM REALLY *TIRED* LATELY.
I'VE BEEN *SO* EXHAUSTED. YOU EVER GET, LIKE, *STRESS* DREAMS? I FEEL LIKE I HAVEN'T HAD A GOOD NIGHT'S SLEEP IN AGES...
...AND SOMETHING TELLS ME I'M NOT GOING TO GET ONE ANY TIME SOON.
Del's Diner
GANG WAR
CAMERON STEWART +
BRENDEN FLETCHER WRITERS
BABS TARR ARTIST
ROB HAYNES BREAKDOWNS 13-16
SERGE LAPOINTE COLORS
STEVE WANDS LETTERS
DAVID LAFUENTE + GABE ELTAEB COVER

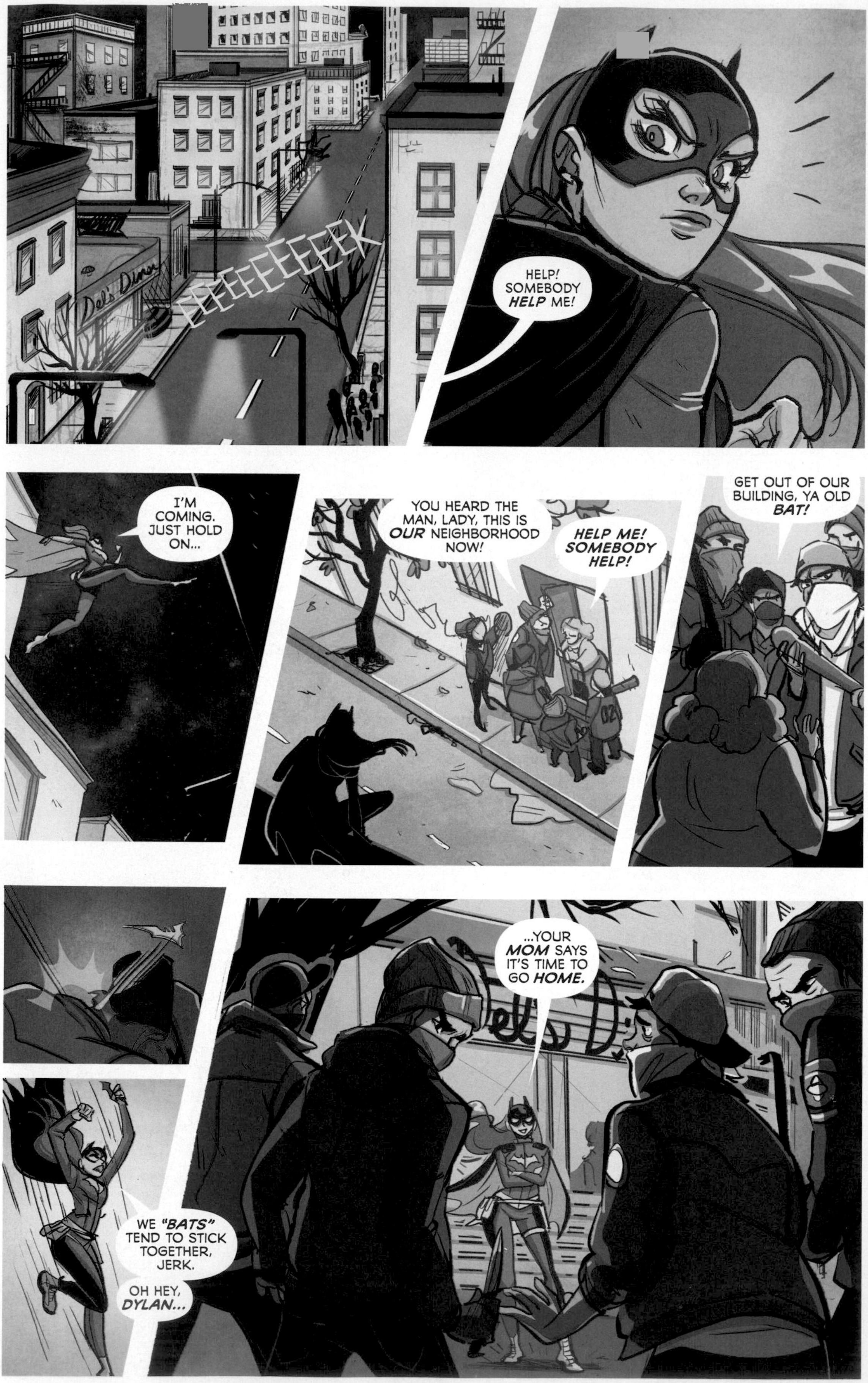
EEEEEEEEEEK
HELP! SOMEBODY HELP ME!
I'M COMING. JUST HOLD ON...
YOU HEARD THE MAN, LADY, THIS IS OUR NEIGHBORHOOD NOW!
HELP ME! SOMEBODY HELP!
GET OUT OF OUR BUILDING, YA OLD BAT!
WE "BATS" TEND TO STICK TOGETHER, JERK.
OH HEY, DYLAN...
...YOUR MOM SAYS IT'S TIME TO GO HOME.

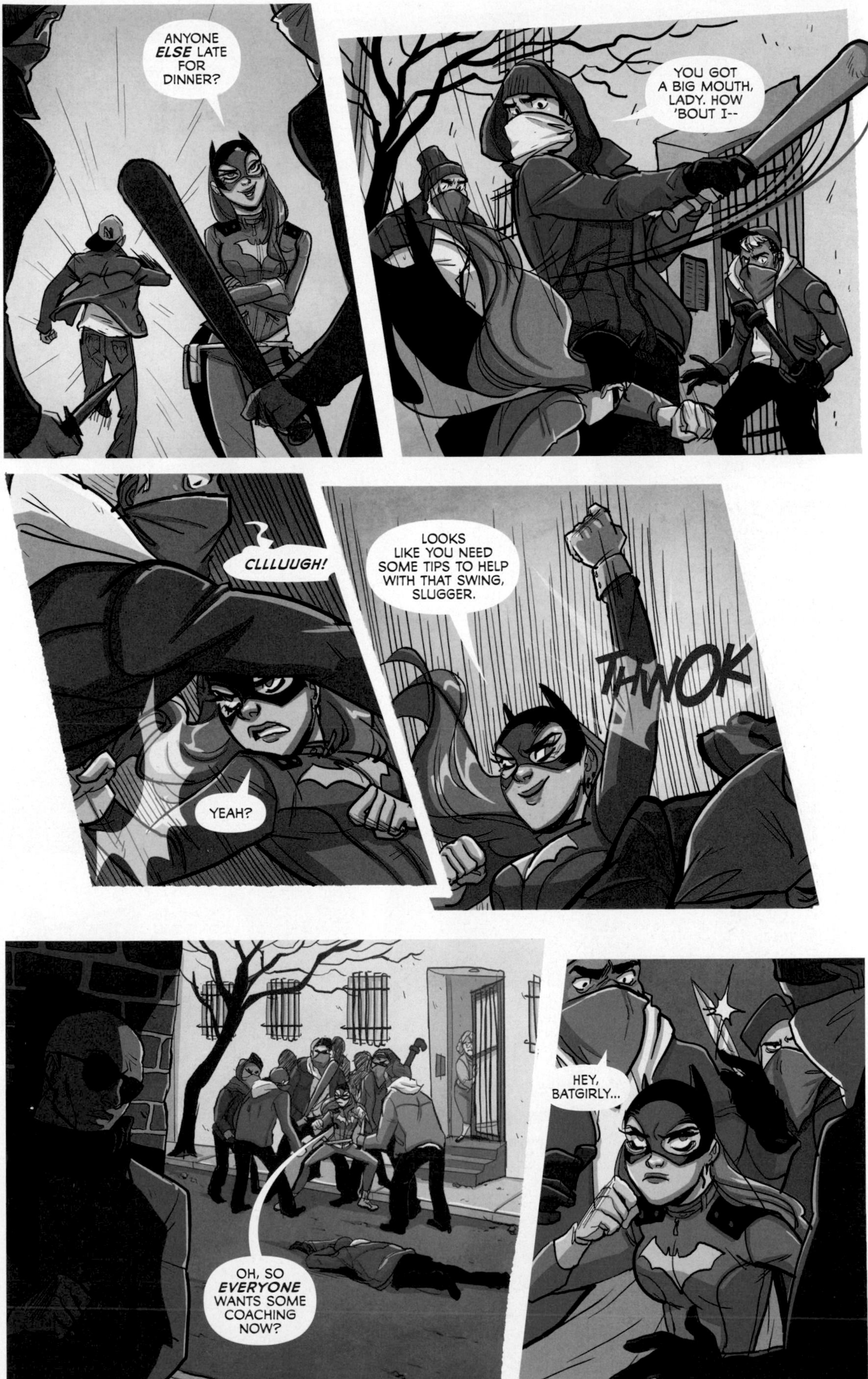
ANYONE ELSE LATE FOR DINNER?
YOU GOT A BIG MOUTH, LADY. HOW 'BOUT I--
CLLLUUGH!
YEAH?
LOOKS LIKE YOU NEED SOME TIPS TO HELP WITH THAT SWING, SLUGGER.
THWOK
OH, SO EVERYONE WANTS SOME COACHING NOW?
HEY, BATGIRLY...

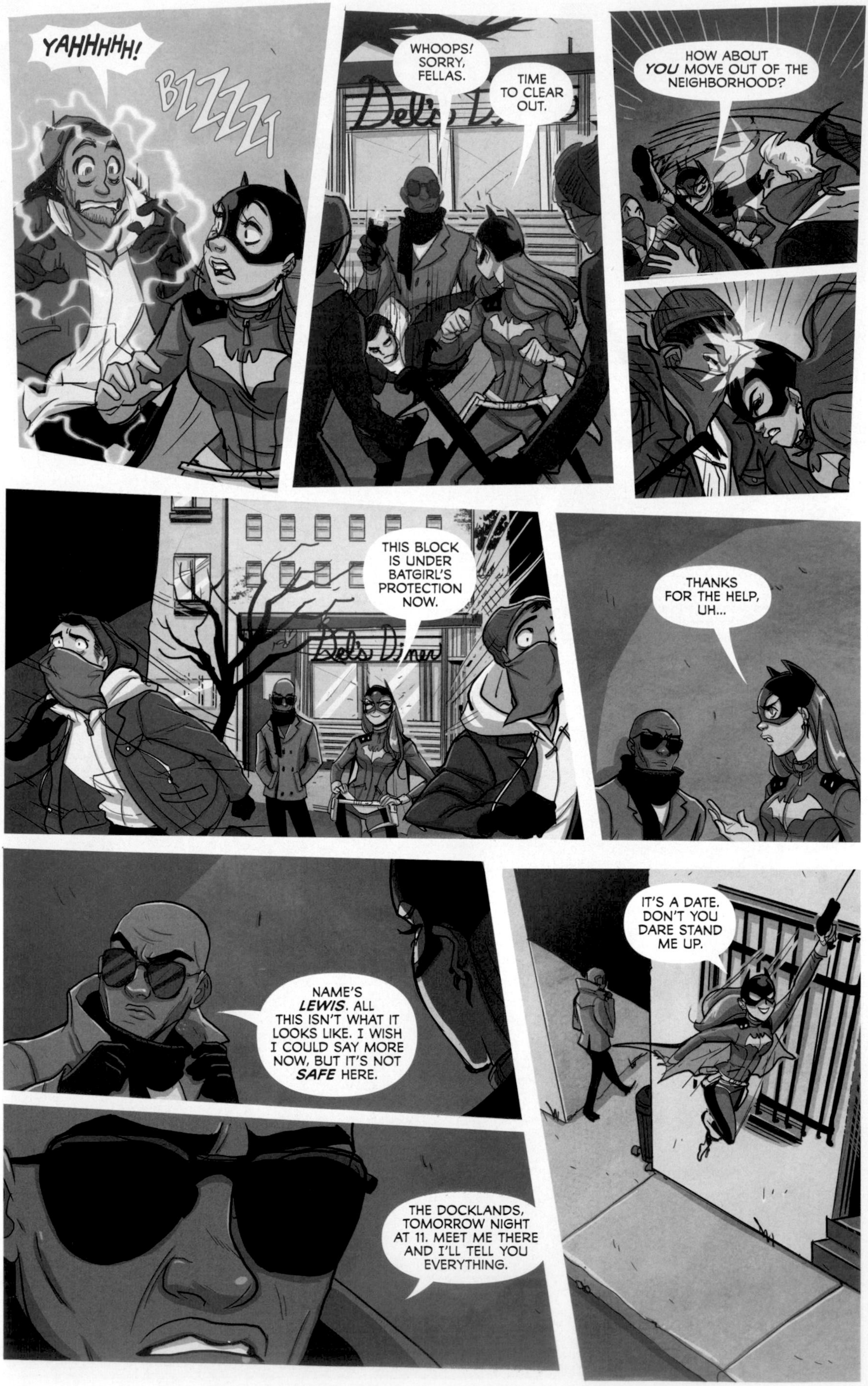
YAHHHHH!
BZZZZT
WHOOPS! SORRY, FELLAS.
TIME TO CLEAR OUT.
HOW ABOUT *YOU* MOVE OUT OF THE NEIGHBORHOOD?
THIS BLOCK IS UNDER BATGIRL'S PROTECTION NOW.
THANKS FOR THE HELP, UH...
NAME'S *LEWIS*. ALL THIS ISN'T WHAT IT LOOKS LIKE. I WISH I COULD SAY MORE NOW, BUT IT'S NOT *SAFE* HERE.
THE DOCKLANDS, TOMORROW NIGHT AT 11. MEET ME THERE AND I'LL TELL YOU EVERYTHING.
IT'S A DATE. DON'T YOU DARE STAND ME UP.

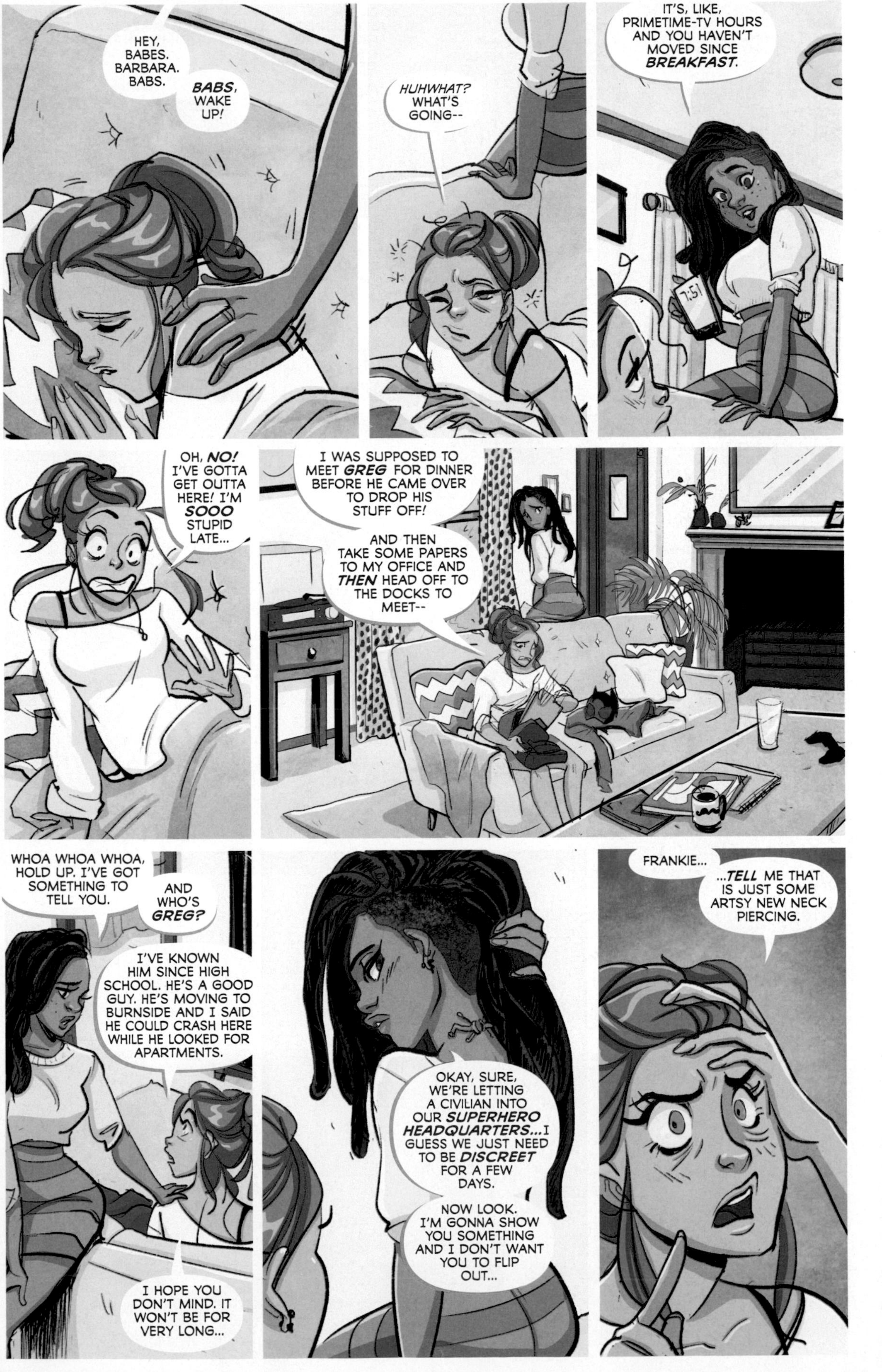
HEY, BABES. BARBARA. BABS.
BABS, WAKE UP!
HUHWHAT? WHAT'S GOING--
IT'S, LIKE, PRIMETIME-TV HOURS AND YOU HAVEN'T MOVED SINCE BREAKFAST.
7:51
OH, NO! I'VE GOTTA GET OUTTA HERE! I'M SOOO STUPID LATE...
I WAS SUPPOSED TO MEET GREG FOR DINNER BEFORE HE CAME OVER TO DROP HIS STUFF OFF!
AND THEN TAKE SOME PAPERS TO MY OFFICE AND THEN HEAD OFF TO THE DOCKS TO MEET--
WHOA WHOA WHOA, HOLD UP. I'VE GOT SOMETHING TO TELL YOU.
AND WHO'S GREG?
I'VE KNOWN HIM SINCE HIGH SCHOOL. HE'S A GOOD GUY. HE'S MOVING TO BURNSIDE AND I SAID HE COULD CRASH HERE WHILE HE LOOKED FOR APARTMENTS.
I HOPE YOU DON'T MIND. IT WON'T BE FOR VERY LONG...
OKAY, SURE, WE'RE LETTING A CIVILIAN INTO OUR SUPERHERO HEADQUARTERS...I GUESS WE JUST NEED TO BE DISCREET FOR A FEW DAYS.
NOW LOOK. I'M GONNA SHOW YOU SOMETHING AND I DON'T WANT YOU TO FLIP OUT...
FRANKIE...
...TELL ME THAT IS JUST SOME ARTSY NEW NECK PIERCING.

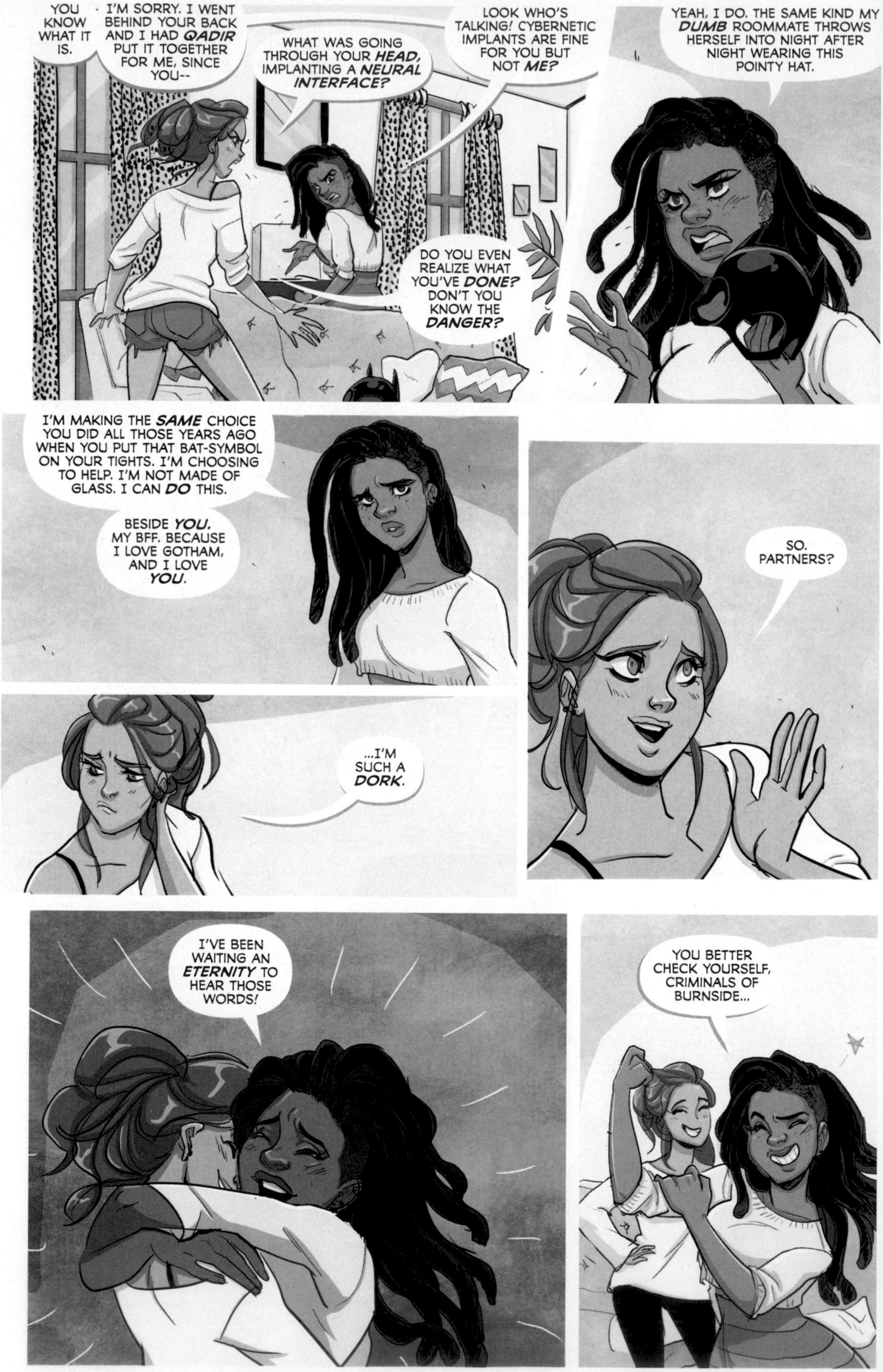

YOU KNOW WHAT IT IS.
I'M SORRY. I WENT BEHIND YOUR BACK AND I HAD QADIR PUT IT TOGETHER FOR ME, SINCE YOU--
WHAT WAS GOING THROUGH YOUR HEAD, IMPLANTING A NEURAL INTERFACE?
LOOK WHO'S TALKING! CYBERNETIC IMPLANTS ARE FINE FOR YOU BUT NOT ME?
DO YOU EVEN REALIZE WHAT YOU'VE DONE? DON'T YOU KNOW THE DANGER?
YEAH, I DO. THE SAME KIND MY DUMB ROOMMATE THROWS HERSELF INTO NIGHT AFTER NIGHT WEARING THIS POINTY HAT.
I'M MAKING THE SAME CHOICE YOU DID ALL THOSE YEARS AGO WHEN YOU PUT THAT BAT-SYMBOL ON YOUR TIGHTS. I'M CHOOSING TO HELP. I'M NOT MADE OF GLASS. I CAN DO THIS.
BESIDE YOU. MY BFF. BECAUSE I LOVE GOTHAM, AND I LOVE YOU.
...I'M SUCH A DORK.
SO. PARTNERS?
I'VE BEEN WAITING AN ETERNITY TO HEAR THOSE WORDS!
YOU BETTER CHECK YOURSELF, CRIMINALS OF BURNSIDE...

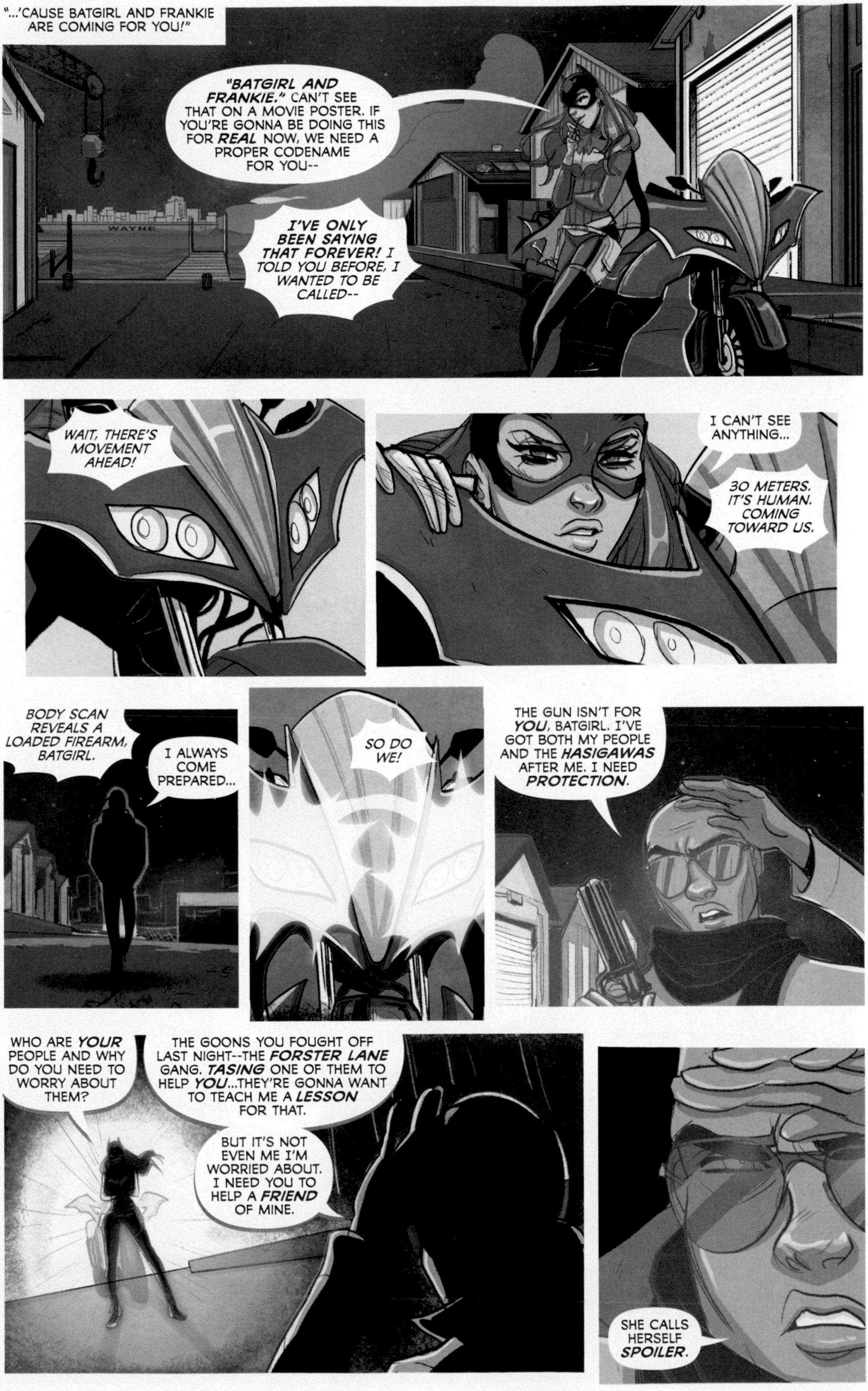
"...'CAUSE BATGIRL AND FRANKIE ARE COMING FOR YOU!"
"BATGIRL AND FRANKIE." CAN'T SEE THAT ON A MOVIE POSTER. IF YOU'RE GONNA BE DOING THIS FOR REAL NOW, WE NEED A PROPER CODENAME FOR YOU--
I'VE ONLY BEEN SAYING THAT FOREVER! I TOLD YOU BEFORE, I WANTED TO BE CALLED--
WAYNE
WAIT, THERE'S MOVEMENT AHEAD!
I CAN'T SEE ANYTHING...
30 METERS. IT'S HUMAN. COMING TOWARD US.
BODY SCAN REVEALS A LOADED FIREARM, BATGIRL.
I ALWAYS COME PREPARED...
SO DO WE!
THE GUN ISN'T FOR YOU, BATGIRL. I'VE GOT BOTH MY PEOPLE AND THE HASIGAWAS AFTER ME. I NEED PROTECTION.
WHO ARE YOUR PEOPLE AND WHY DO YOU NEED TO WORRY ABOUT THEM?
THE GOONS YOU FOUGHT OFF LAST NIGHT--THE FORSTER LANE GANG. TASING ONE OF THEM TO HELP YOU...THEY'RE GONNA WANT TO TEACH ME A LESSON FOR THAT.
BUT IT'S NOT EVEN ME I'M WORRIED ABOUT. I NEED YOU TO HELP A FRIEND OF MINE.
SHE CALLS HERSELF SPOILER.

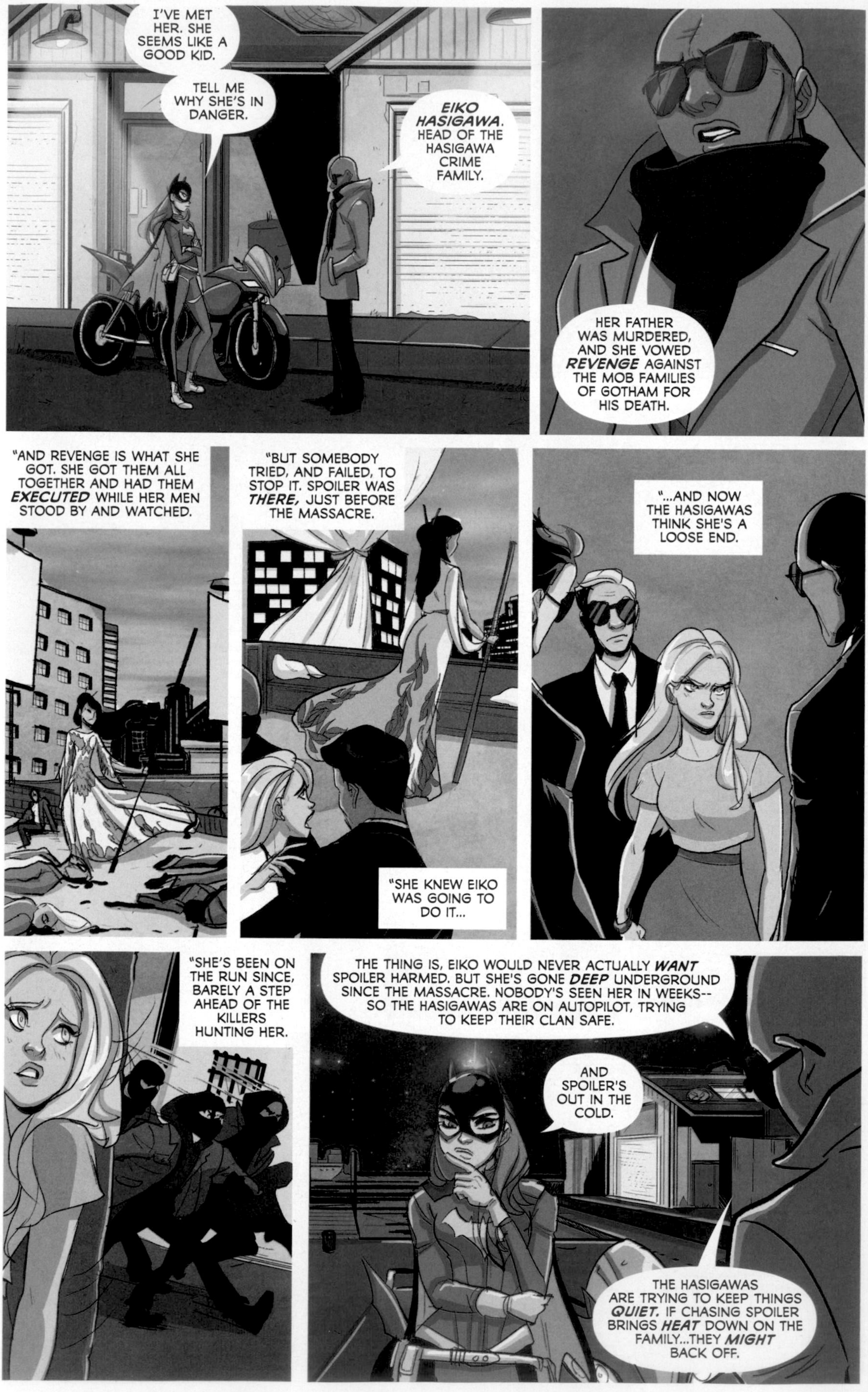
I'VE MET HER. SHE SEEMS LIKE A GOOD KID.
TELL ME WHY SHE'S IN DANGER.
EIKO HASIGAWA. HEAD OF THE HASIGAWA CRIME FAMILY.
HER FATHER WAS MURDERED, AND SHE VOWED REVENGE AGAINST THE MOB FAMILIES OF GOTHAM FOR HIS DEATH.
"AND REVENGE IS WHAT SHE GOT. SHE GOT THEM ALL TOGETHER AND HAD THEM EXECUTED WHILE HER MEN STOOD BY AND WATCHED.
"BUT SOMEBODY TRIED, AND FAILED, TO STOP IT. SPOILER WAS THERE, JUST BEFORE THE MASSACRE.
"SHE KNEW EIKO WAS GOING TO DO IT...
"...AND NOW THE HASIGAWAS THINK SHE'S A LOOSE END.
"SHE'S BEEN ON THE RUN SINCE, BARELY A STEP AHEAD OF THE KILLERS HUNTING HER.
THE THING IS, EIKO WOULD NEVER ACTUALLY WANT SPOILER HARMED. BUT SHE'S GONE DEEP UNDERGROUND SINCE THE MASSACRE. NOBODY'S SEEN HER IN WEEKS-- SO THE HASIGAWAS ARE ON AUTOPILOT, TRYING TO KEEP THEIR CLAN SAFE.
AND SPOILER'S OUT IN THE COLD.
THE HASIGAWAS ARE TRYING TO KEEP THINGS QUIET. IF CHASING SPOILER BRINGS HEAT DOWN ON THE FAMILY...THEY MIGHT BACK OFF.

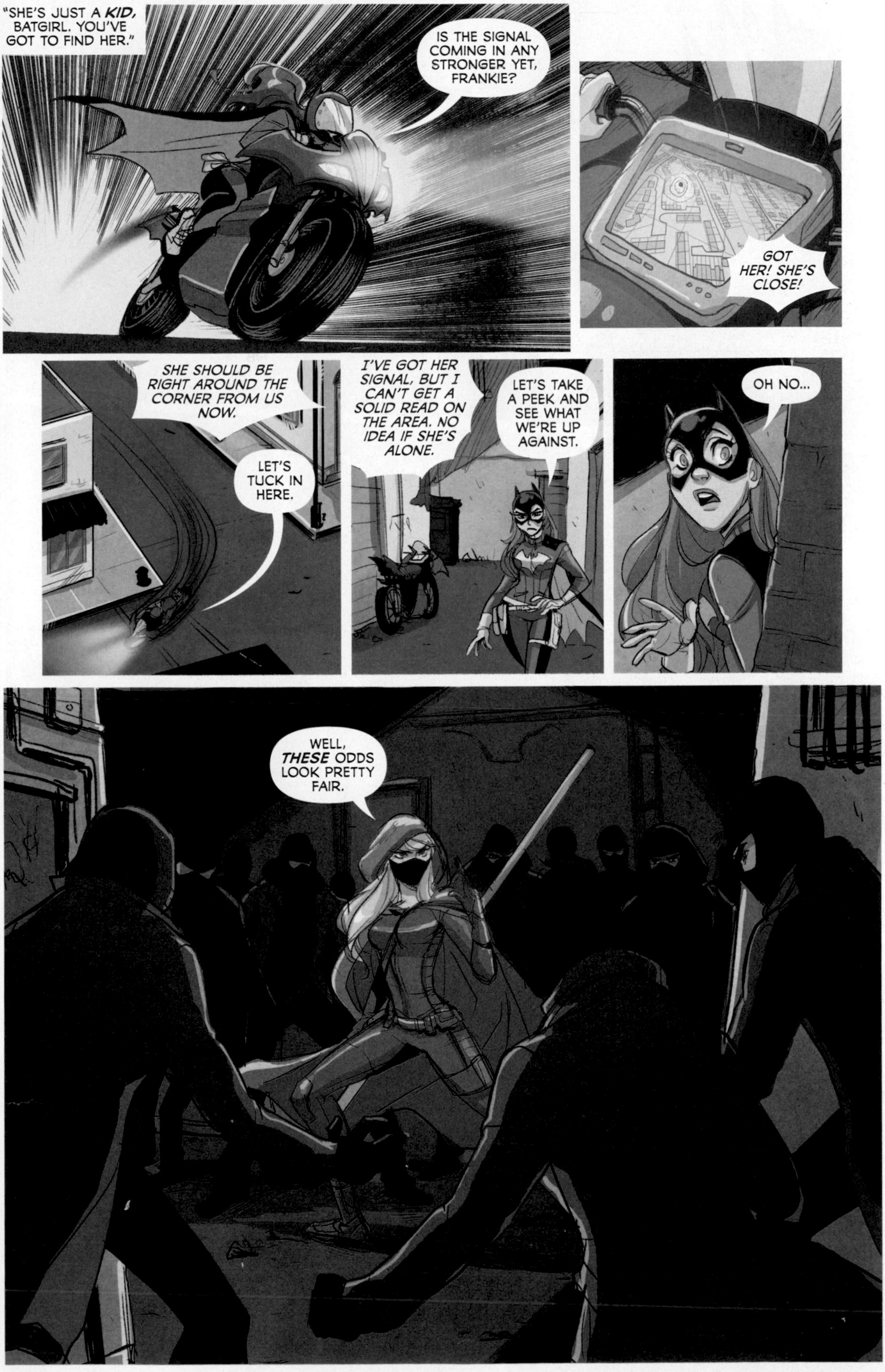
"SHE'S JUST A KID, BATGIRL. YOU'VE GOT TO FIND HER."
IS THE SIGNAL COMING IN ANY STRONGER YET, FRANKIE?
GOT HER! SHE'S CLOSE!
SHE SHOULD BE RIGHT AROUND THE CORNER FROM US NOW.
LET'S TUCK IN HERE.
I'VE GOT HER SIGNAL, BUT I CAN'T GET A SOLID READ ON THE AREA. NO IDEA IF SHE'S ALONE.
LET'S TAKE A PEEK AND SEE WHAT WE'RE UP AGAINST.
OH NO...
WELL, THESE ODDS LOOK PRETTY FAIR.

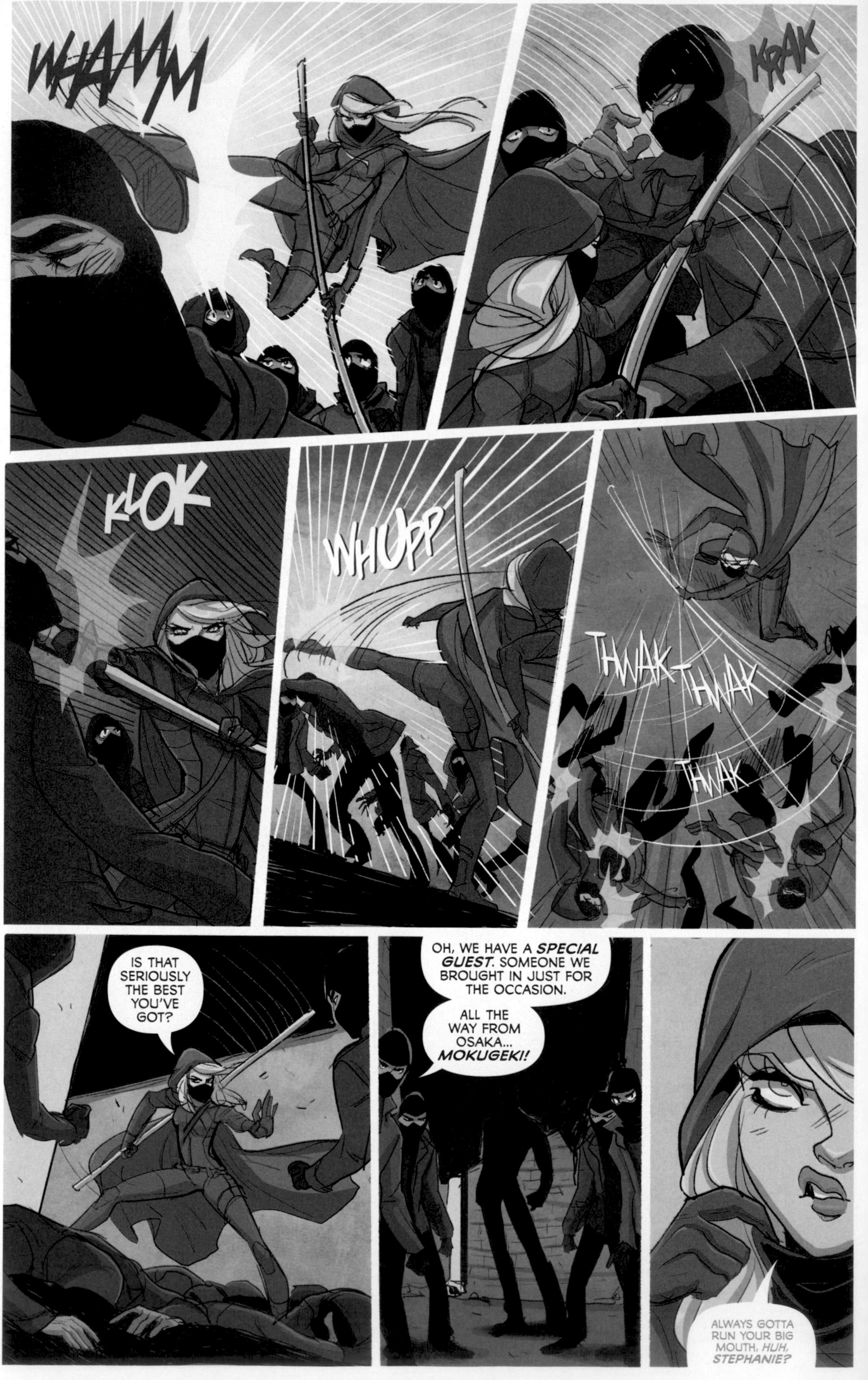
WHAMM
KRAK
KLOK
WHUPP
THWAK THWAK
THWAK
IS THAT SERIOUSLY THE BEST YOU'VE GOT?
OH, WE HAVE A SPECIAL GUEST. SOMEONE WE BROUGHT IN JUST FOR THE OCCASION.
ALL THE WAY FROM OSAKA... MOKUGEKI!
ALWAYS GOTTA RUN YOUR BIG MOUTH, HUH, STEPHANIE?

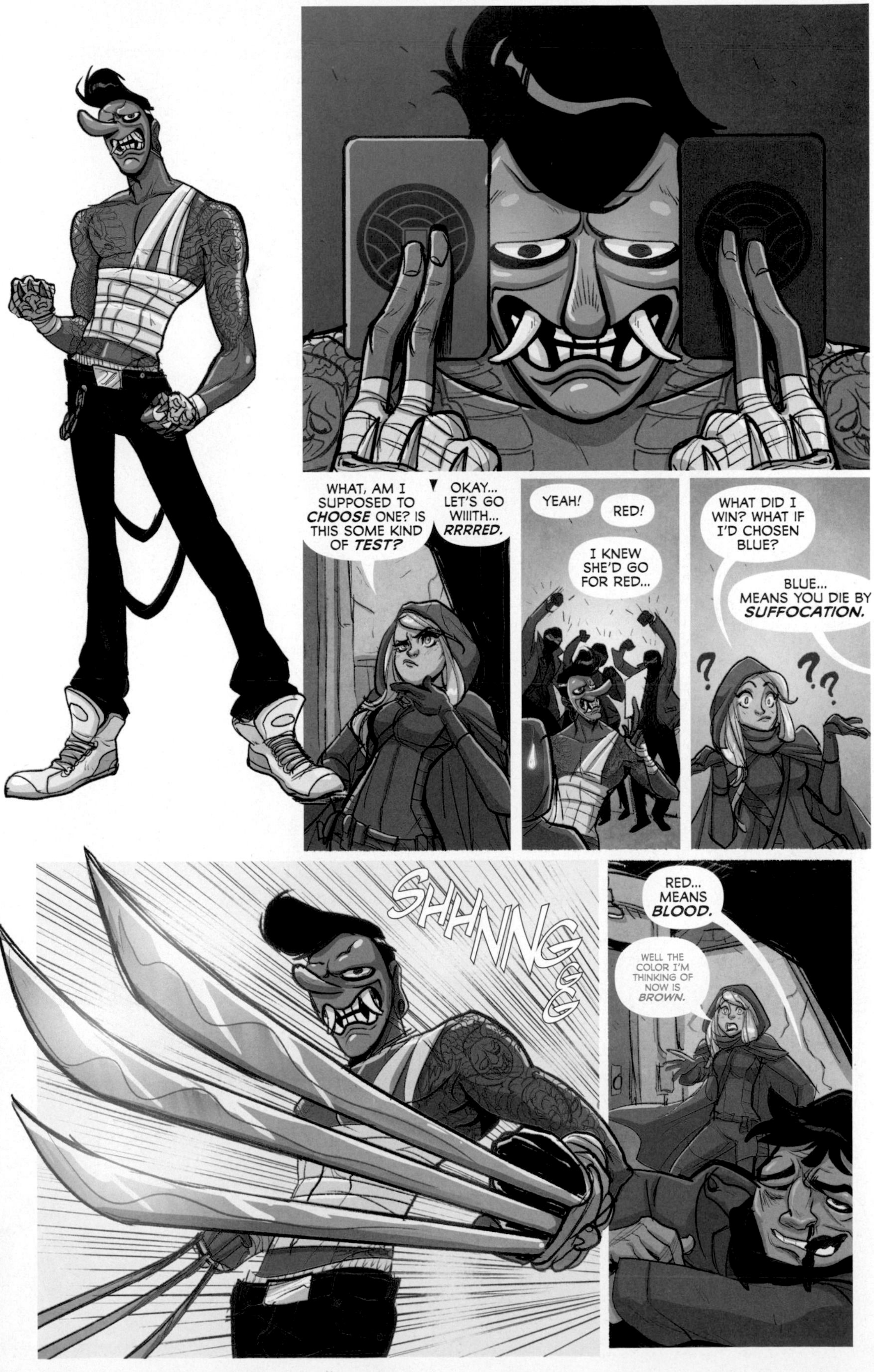
WHAT, AM I SUPPOSED TO CHOOSE ONE? IS THIS SOME KIND OF TEST?
OKAY... LET'S GO WIIITH... RRRRED.
YEAH!
RED!
I KNEW SHE'D GO FOR RED...
WHAT DID I WIN? WHAT IF I'D CHOSEN BLUE?
BLUE... MEANS YOU DIE BY SUFFOCATION.
SHHNNGGG
RED... MEANS BLOOD.
WELL THE COLOR I'M THINKING OF NOW IS BROWN.

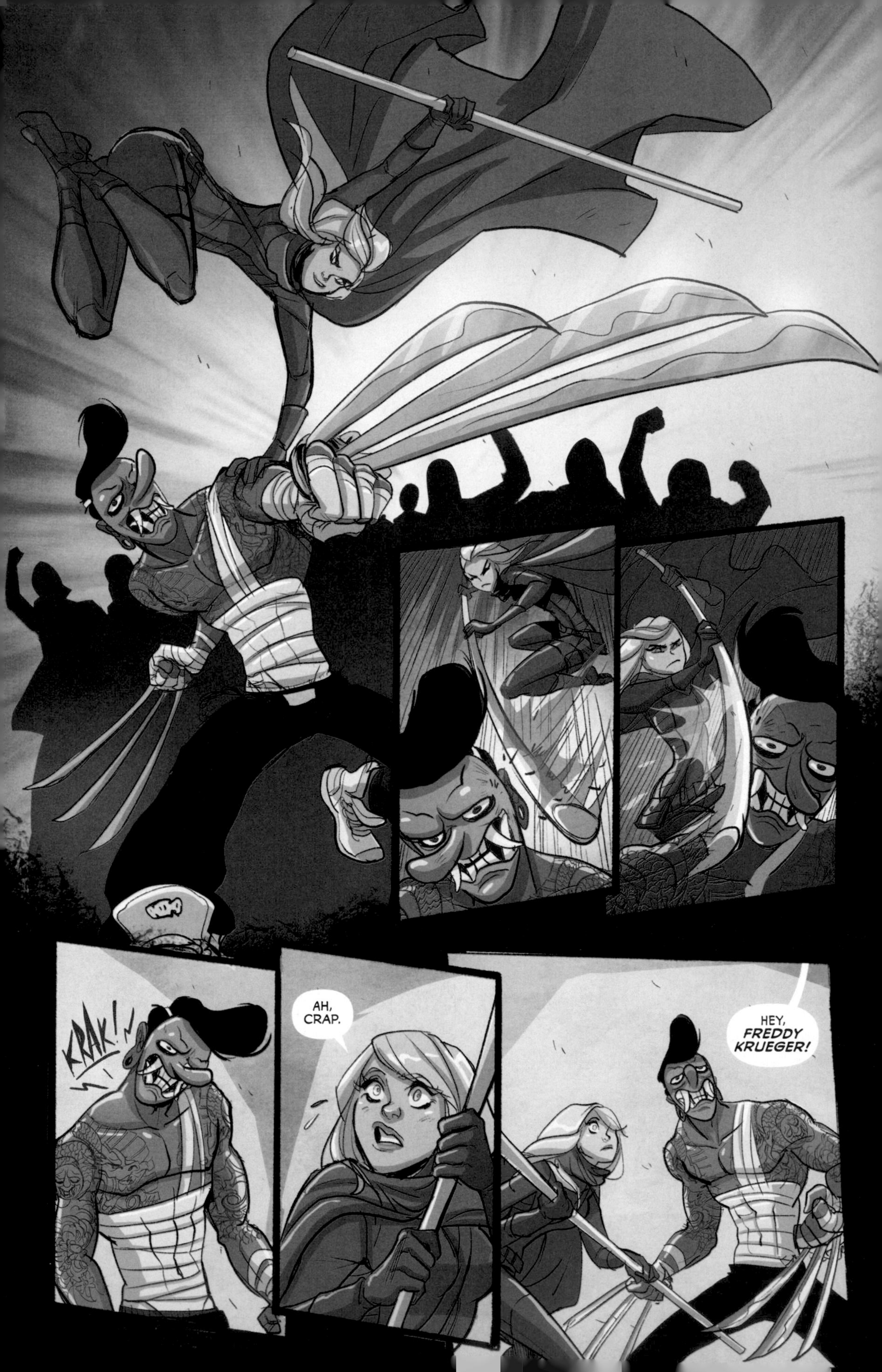
KRAK!
AH, CRAP.
HEY, FREDDY KRUEGER!

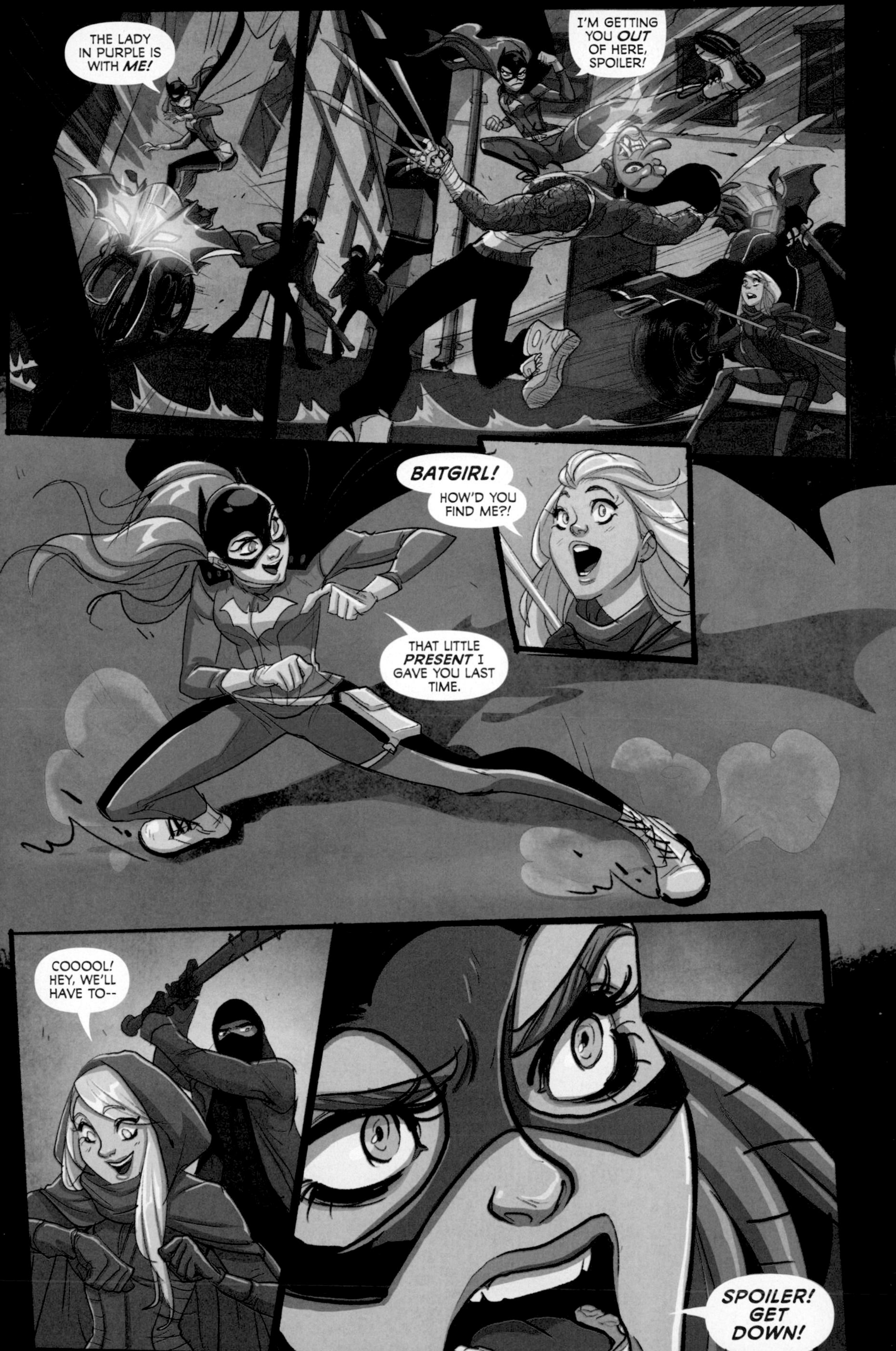
THE LADY IN PURPLE IS WITH ME!
I'M GETTING YOU OUT OF HERE, SPOILER!
BATGIRL! HOW'D YOU FIND ME?!
THAT LITTLE PRESENT I GAVE YOU LAST TIME.
COOOOL! HEY, WE'LL HAVE TO--
SPOILER! GET DOWN!

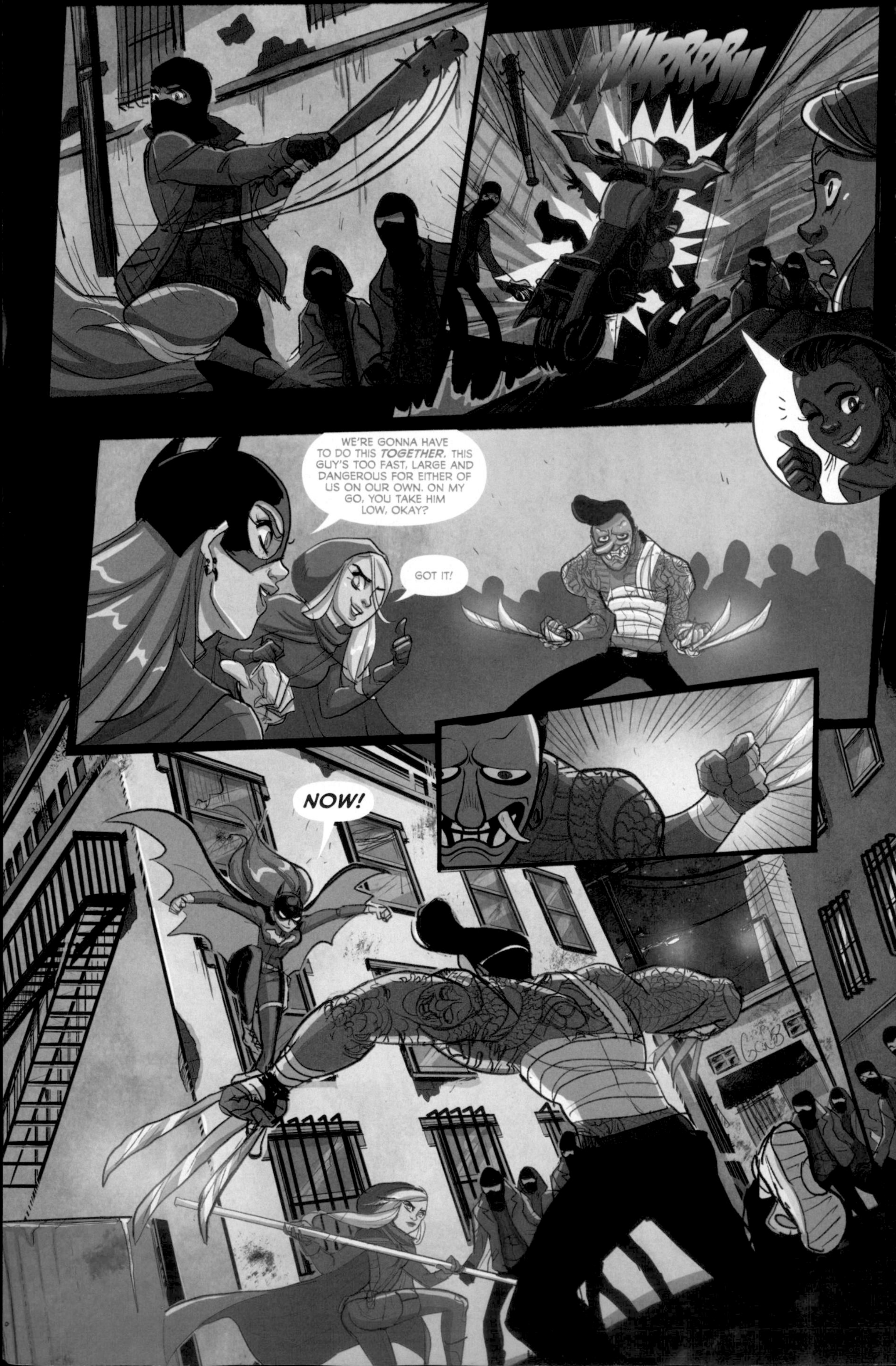
WE'RE GONNA HAVE TO DO THIS *TOGETHER.* THIS GUY'S TOO FAST, LARGE AND DANGEROUS FOR EITHER OF US ON OUR OWN. ON MY GO, YOU TAKE HIM LOW, OKAY?
GOT IT!
NOW!

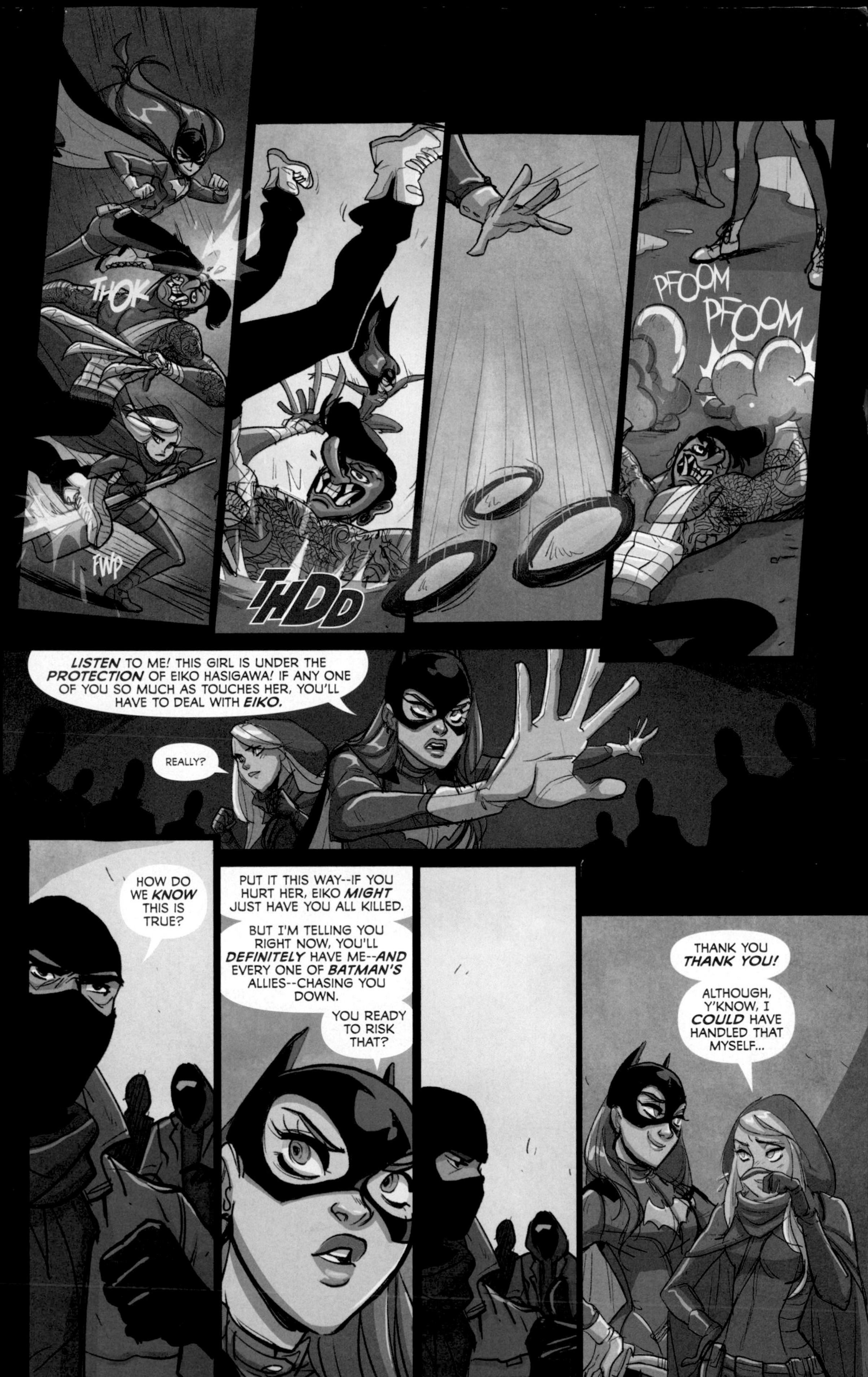
THOK
FWP
THDD
PFOOM
PFOOM
LISTEN TO ME! THIS GIRL IS UNDER THE PROTECTION OF EIKO HASIGAWA! IF ANY ONE OF YOU SO MUCH AS TOUCHES HER, YOU'LL HAVE TO DEAL WITH EIKO.
REALLY?
HOW DO WE KNOW THIS IS TRUE?
PUT IT THIS WAY--IF YOU HURT HER, EIKO MIGHT JUST HAVE YOU ALL KILLED.
BUT I'M TELLING YOU RIGHT NOW, YOU'LL DEFINITELY HAVE ME--AND EVERY ONE OF BATMAN'S ALLIES--CHASING YOU DOWN.
YOU READY TO RISK THAT?
THANK YOU THANK YOU!
ALTHOUGH, Y'KNOW, I COULD HAVE HANDLED THAT MYSELF...

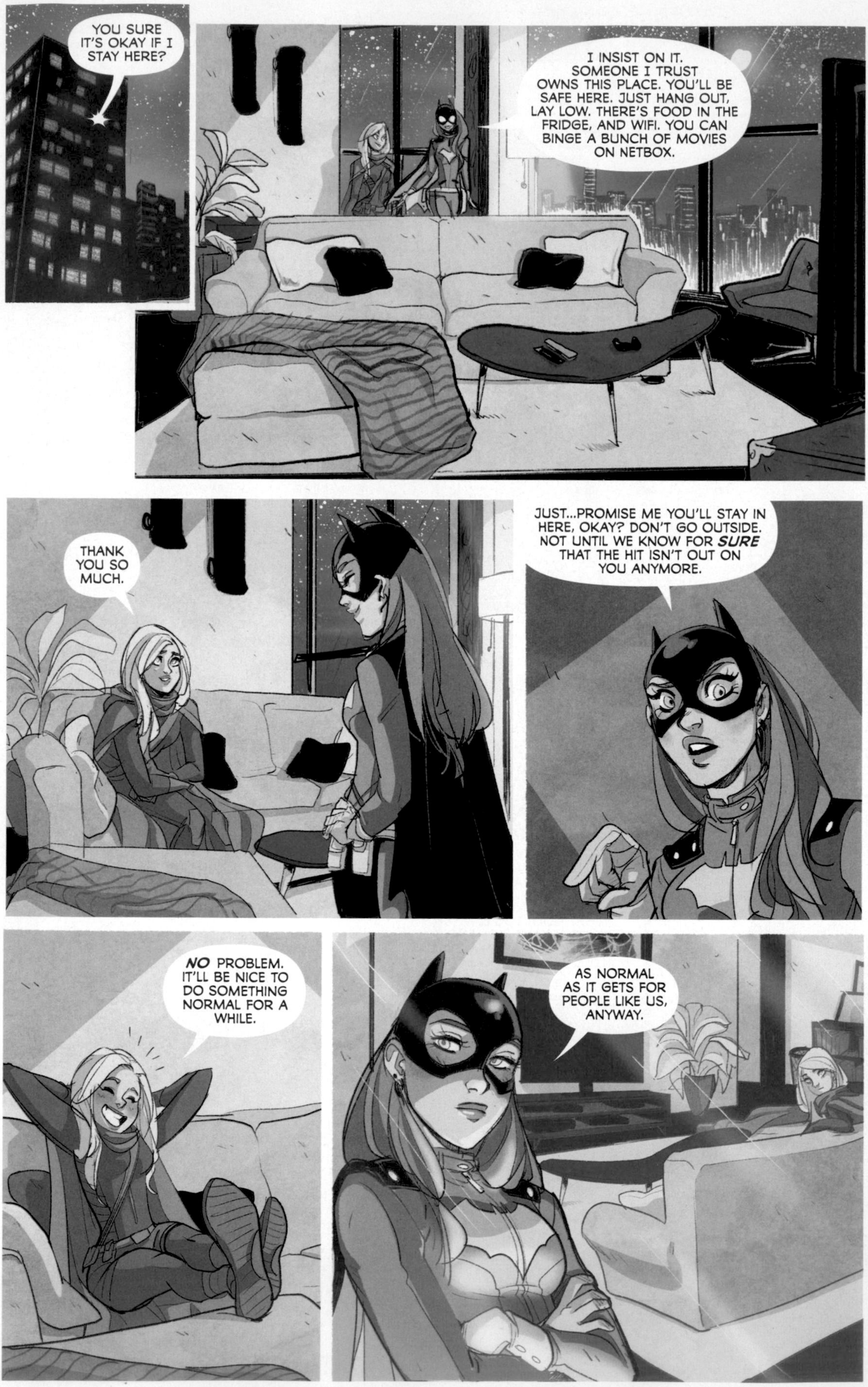
YOU SURE IT'S OKAY IF I STAY HERE?
I INSIST ON IT. SOMEONE I TRUST OWNS THIS PLACE. YOU'LL BE SAFE HERE. JUST HANG OUT, LAY LOW. THERE'S FOOD IN THE FRIDGE, AND WIFI. YOU CAN BINGE A BUNCH OF MOVIES ON NETBOX.
THANK YOU SO MUCH.
JUST...PROMISE ME YOU'LL STAY IN HERE, OKAY? DON'T GO OUTSIDE. NOT UNTIL WE KNOW FOR *SURE* THAT THE HIT ISN'T OUT ON YOU ANYMORE.
NO PROBLEM. IT'LL BE NICE TO DO SOMETHING NORMAL FOR A WHILE.
AS NORMAL AS IT GETS FOR PEOPLE LIKE US, ANYWAY.

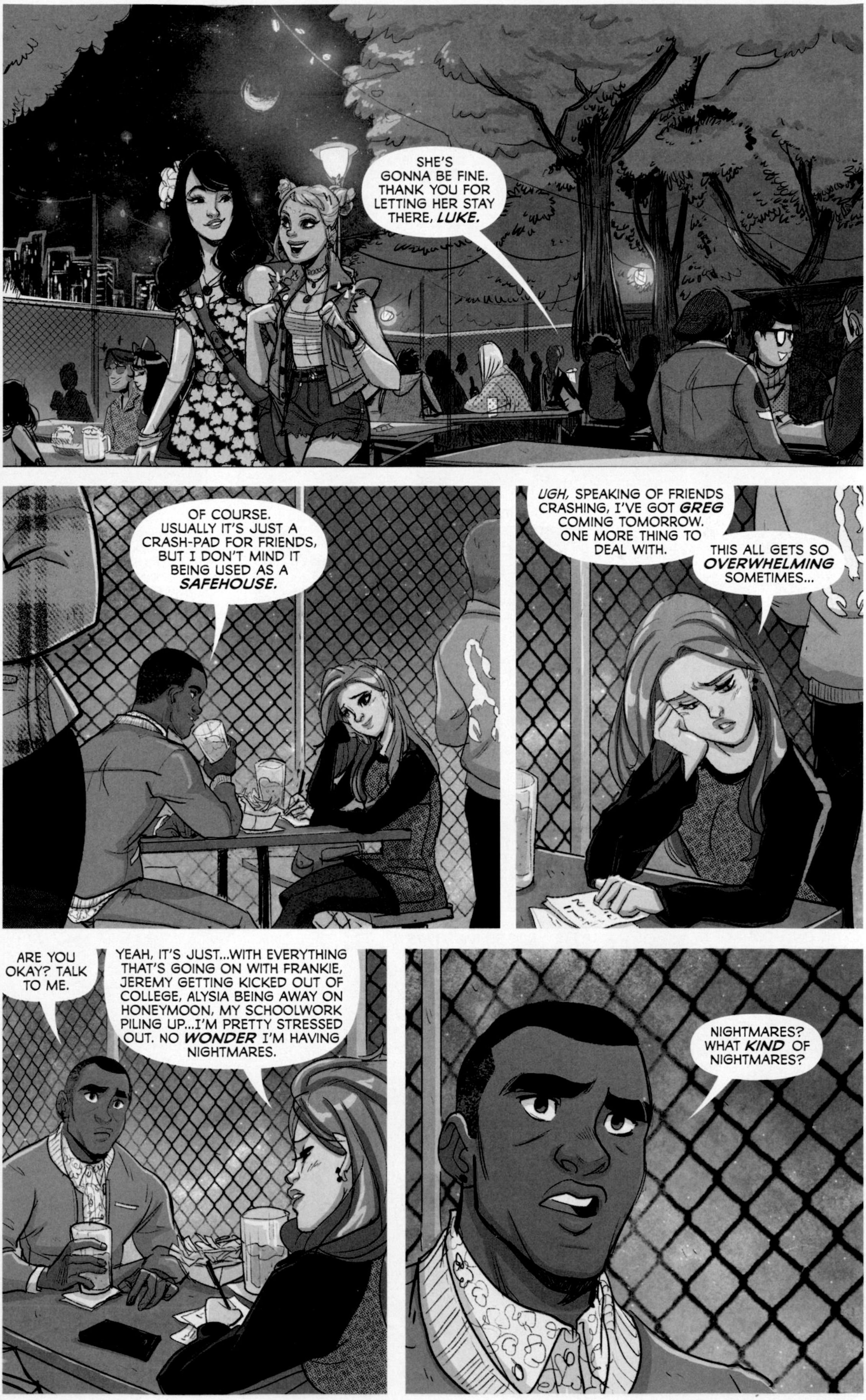
SHE'S GONNA BE FINE. THANK YOU FOR LETTING HER STAY THERE, *LUKE.*
OF COURSE. USUALLY IT'S JUST A CRASH-PAD FOR FRIENDS, BUT I DON'T MIND IT BEING USED AS A *SAFEHOUSE.*
UGH, SPEAKING OF FRIENDS CRASHING, I'VE GOT *GREG* COMING TOMORROW. ONE MORE THING TO DEAL WITH.
THIS ALL GETS SO *OVERWHELMING* SOMETIMES...
ARE YOU OKAY? TALK TO ME.
YEAH, IT'S JUST...WITH EVERYTHING THAT'S GOING ON WITH FRANKIE, JEREMY GETTING KICKED OUT OF COLLEGE, ALYSIA BEING AWAY ON HONEYMOON, MY SCHOOLWORK PILING UP...I'M PRETTY STRESSED OUT. NO *WONDER* I'M HAVING NIGHTMARES.
NIGHTMARES? WHAT *KIND* OF NIGHTMARES?

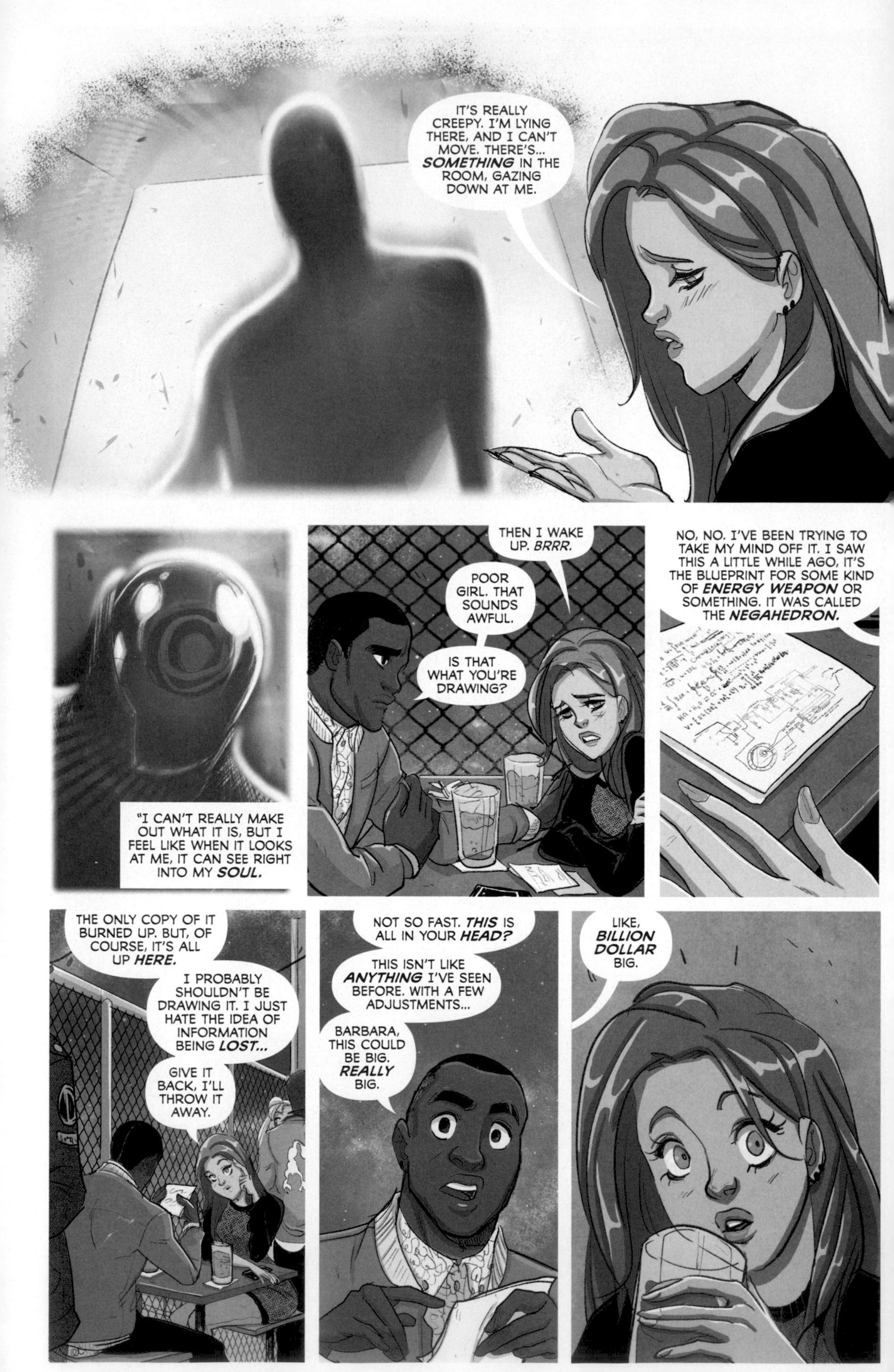
IT'S REALLY CREEPY. I'M LYING THERE, AND I CAN'T MOVE. THERE'S... SOMETHING IN THE ROOM, GAZING DOWN AT ME.
"I CAN'T REALLY MAKE OUT WHAT IT IS, BUT I FEEL LIKE WHEN IT LOOKS AT ME, IT CAN SEE RIGHT INTO MY SOUL.
THEN I WAKE UP. BRRR.
POOR GIRL. THAT SOUNDS AWFUL.
IS THAT WHAT YOU'RE DRAWING?
NO, NO. I'VE BEEN TRYING TO TAKE MY MIND OFF IT. I SAW THIS A LITTLE WHILE AGO, IT'S THE BLUEPRINT FOR SOME KIND OF ENERGY WEAPON OR SOMETHING. IT WAS CALLED THE NEGAHEDRON.
THE ONLY COPY OF IT BURNED UP. BUT, OF COURSE, IT'S ALL UP HERE.
I PROBABLY SHOULDN'T BE DRAWING IT. I JUST HATE THE IDEA OF INFORMATION BEING LOST...
GIVE IT BACK, I'LL THROW IT AWAY.
NOT SO FAST. THIS IS ALL IN YOUR HEAD?
THIS ISN'T LIKE ANYTHING I'VE SEEN BEFORE. WITH A FEW ADJUSTMENTS...
BARBARA, THIS COULD BE BIG. REALLY BIG.
LIKE, BILLION DOLLAR BIG.

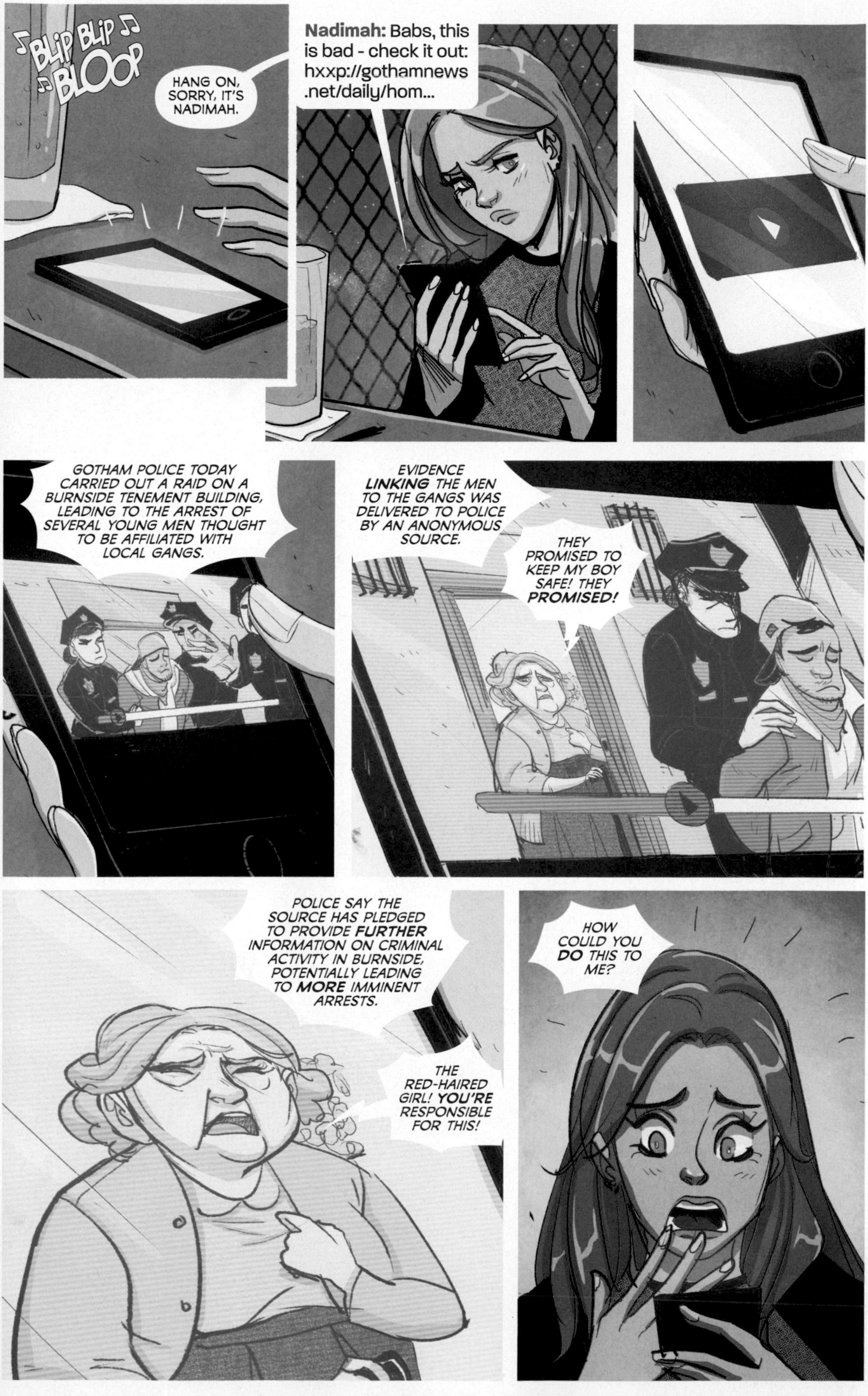
BLIP BLIP
BLOOP
HANG ON, SORRY, IT'S NADIMAH.
Nadimah: Babs, this is bad - check it out: hxxp://gothamnews.net/daily/hom...
GOTHAM POLICE TODAY CARRIED OUT A RAID ON A BURNSIDE TENEMENT BUILDING, LEADING TO THE ARREST OF SEVERAL YOUNG MEN THOUGHT TO BE AFFILIATED WITH LOCAL GANGS.
EVIDENCE LINKING THE MEN TO THE GANGS WAS DELIVERED TO POLICE BY AN ANONYMOUS SOURCE.
THEY PROMISED TO KEEP MY BOY SAFE! THEY PROMISED!
POLICE SAY THE SOURCE HAS PLEDGED TO PROVIDE FURTHER INFORMATION ON CRIMINAL ACTIVITY IN BURNSIDE, POTENTIALLY LEADING TO MORE IMMINENT ARRESTS.
THE RED-HAIRED GIRL! YOU'RE RESPONSIBLE FOR THIS!
HOW COULD YOU DO THIS TO ME?

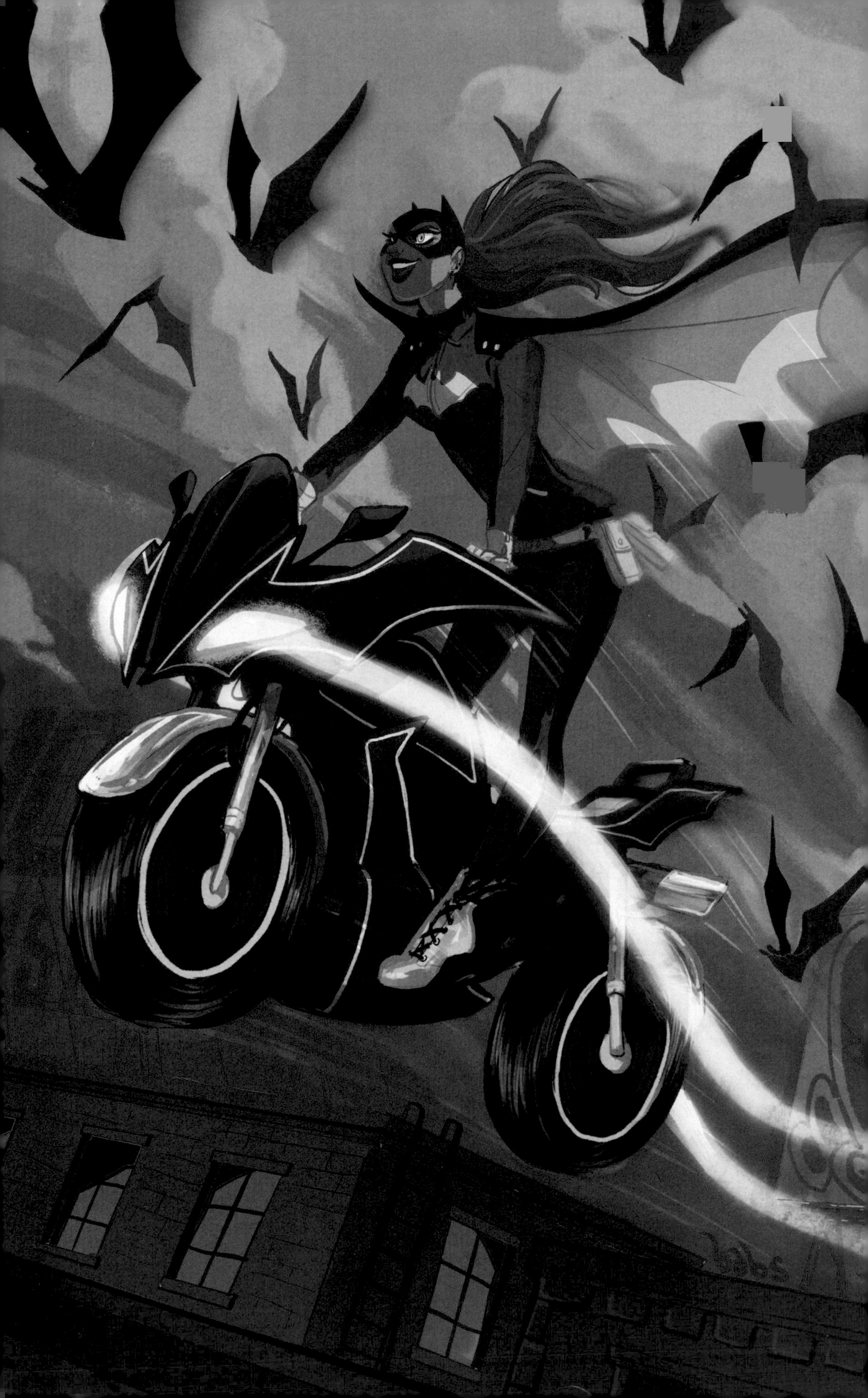

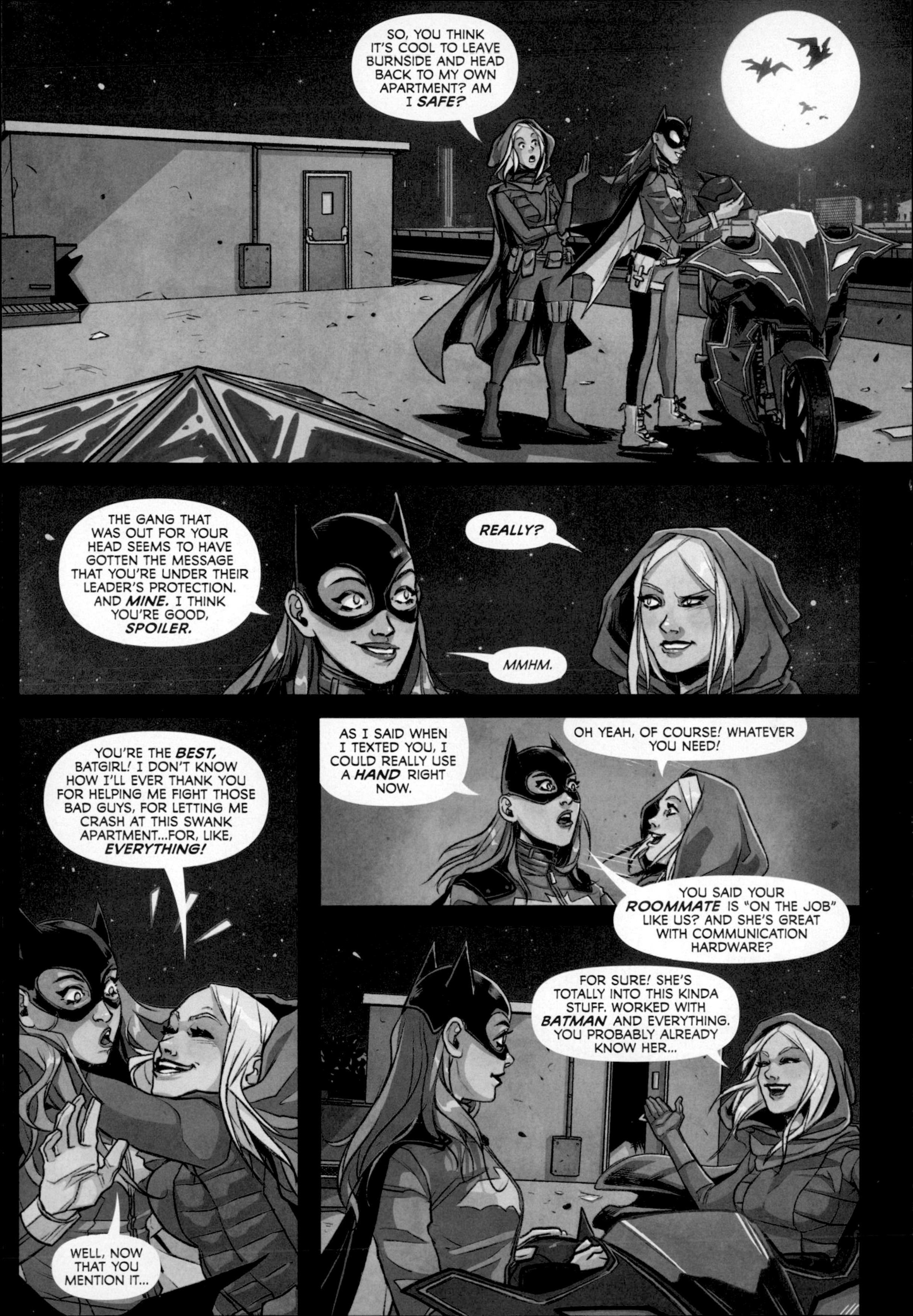
SO, YOU THINK IT'S COOL TO LEAVE BURNSIDE AND HEAD BACK TO MY OWN APARTMENT? AM I *SAFE?*
THE GANG THAT WAS OUT FOR YOUR HEAD SEEMS TO HAVE GOTTEN THE MESSAGE THAT YOU'RE UNDER THEIR LEADER'S PROTECTION. AND *MINE.* I THINK YOU'RE GOOD, *SPOILER.*
REALLY?
MMHM.
YOU'RE THE *BEST,* BATGIRL! I DON'T KNOW HOW I'LL EVER THANK YOU FOR HELPING ME FIGHT THOSE BAD GUYS, FOR LETTING ME CRASH AT THIS SWANK APARTMENT...FOR, LIKE, *EVERYTHING!*
WELL, NOW THAT YOU MENTION IT...
AS I SAID WHEN I TEXTED YOU, I COULD REALLY USE A *HAND* RIGHT NOW.
OH YEAH, OF COURSE! WHATEVER YOU NEED!
YOU SAID YOUR *ROOMMATE* IS "ON THE JOB" LIKE US? AND SHE'S GREAT WITH COMMUNICATION HARDWARE?
FOR SURE! SHE'S TOTALLY INTO THIS KINDA STUFF. WORKED WITH *BATMAN* AND EVERYTHING. YOU PROBABLY ALREADY KNOW HER...

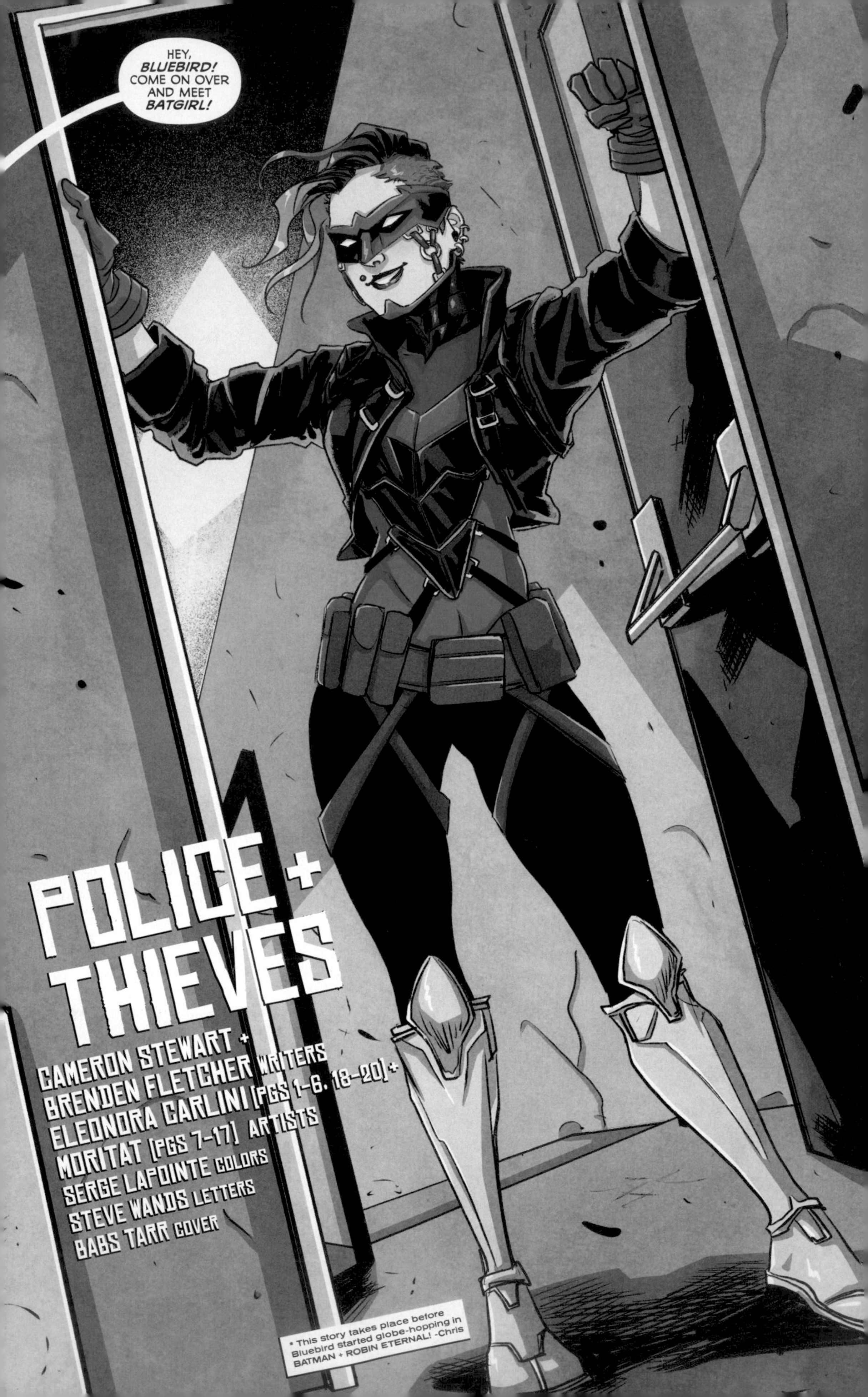
HEY, BLUEBIRD! COME ON OVER AND MEET BATGIRL!
POLICE + THIEVES
CAMERON STEWART + BRENDEN FLETCHER WRITERS
ELEONORA CARLINI [PGS 1-6, 18-20] + MORITAT [PGS 7-17] ARTISTS
SERGE LAPOINTE COLORS
STEVE WANDS LETTERS
BABS TARR COVER
* This story takes place before Bluebird started globe-hopping in BATMAN + ROBIN ETERNAL! -Chris

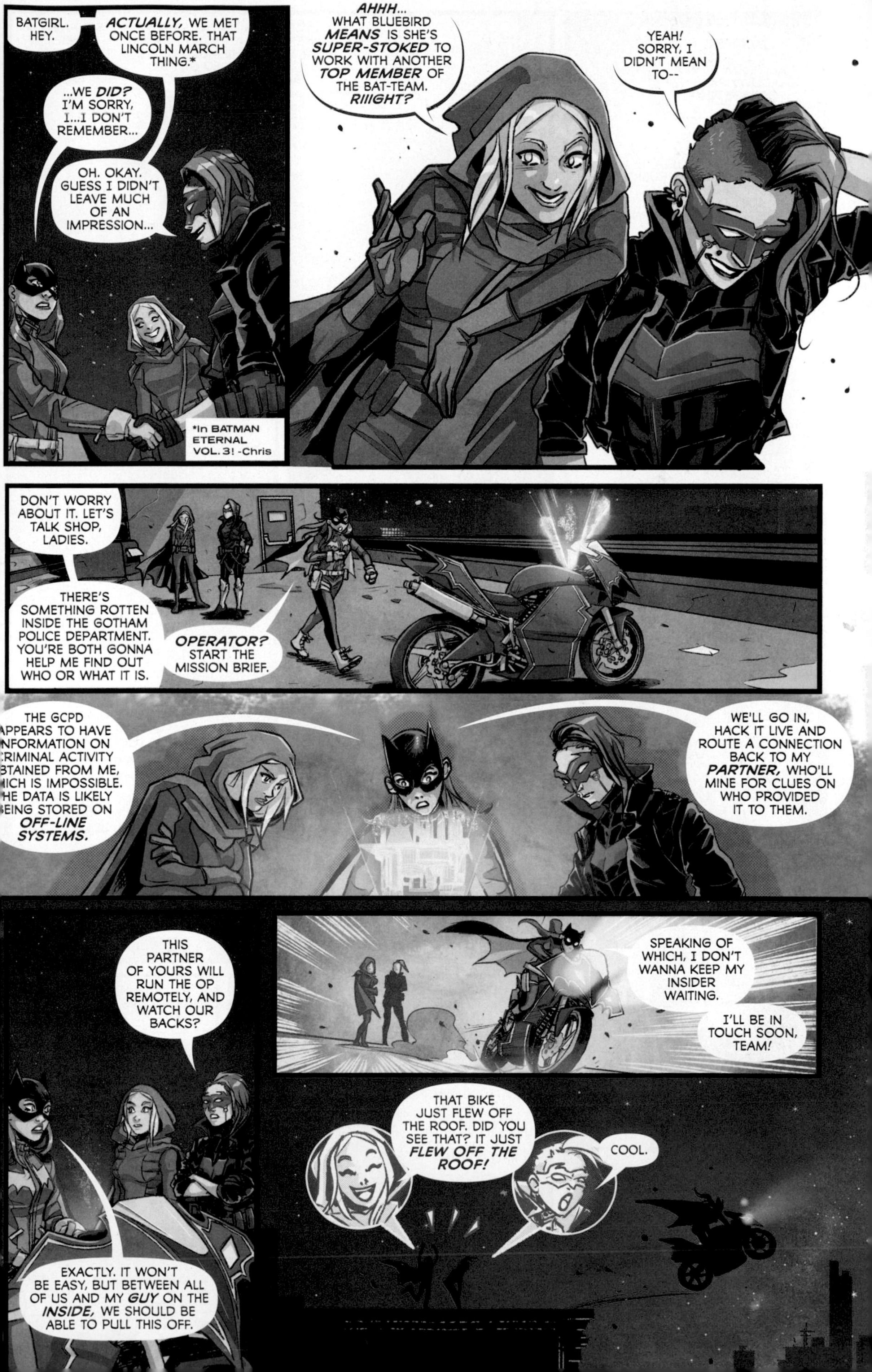
BATGIRL. HEY.
ACTUALLY, WE MET ONCE BEFORE. THAT LINCOLN MARCH THING.*
...WE DID? I'M SORRY, I...I DON'T REMEMBER...
OH. OKAY. GUESS I DIDN'T LEAVE MUCH OF AN IMPRESSION...
*In BATMAN ETERNAL VOL. 3! -Chris
AHHH... WHAT BLUEBIRD MEANS IS SHE'S SUPER-STOKED TO WORK WITH ANOTHER TOP MEMBER OF THE BAT-TEAM. RIIIGHT?
YEAH! SORRY, I DIDN'T MEAN TO--
DON'T WORRY ABOUT IT. LET'S TALK SHOP, LADIES.
THERE'S SOMETHING ROTTEN INSIDE THE GOTHAM POLICE DEPARTMENT. YOU'RE BOTH GONNA HELP ME FIND OUT WHO OR WHAT IT IS.
OPERATOR? START THE MISSION BRIEF.
THE GCPD APPEARS TO HAVE NFORMATION ON RIMINAL ACTIVITY BTAINED FROM ME, ICH IS IMPOSSIBLE. HE DATA IS LIKELY EING STORED ON OFF-LINE SYSTEMS.
WE'LL GO IN, HACK IT LIVE AND ROUTE A CONNECTION BACK TO MY PARTNER, WHO'LL MINE FOR CLUES ON WHO PROVIDED IT TO THEM.
THIS PARTNER OF YOURS WILL RUN THE OP REMOTELY, AND WATCH OUR BACKS?
EXACTLY. IT WON'T BE EASY, BUT BETWEEN ALL OF US AND MY GUY ON THE INSIDE, WE SHOULD BE ABLE TO PULL THIS OFF.
SPEAKING OF WHICH, I DON'T WANNA KEEP MY INSIDER WAITING.
I'LL BE IN TOUCH SOON, TEAM!
THAT BIKE JUST FLEW OFF THE ROOF. DID YOU SEE THAT? IT JUST FLEW OFF THE ROOF!
COOL.

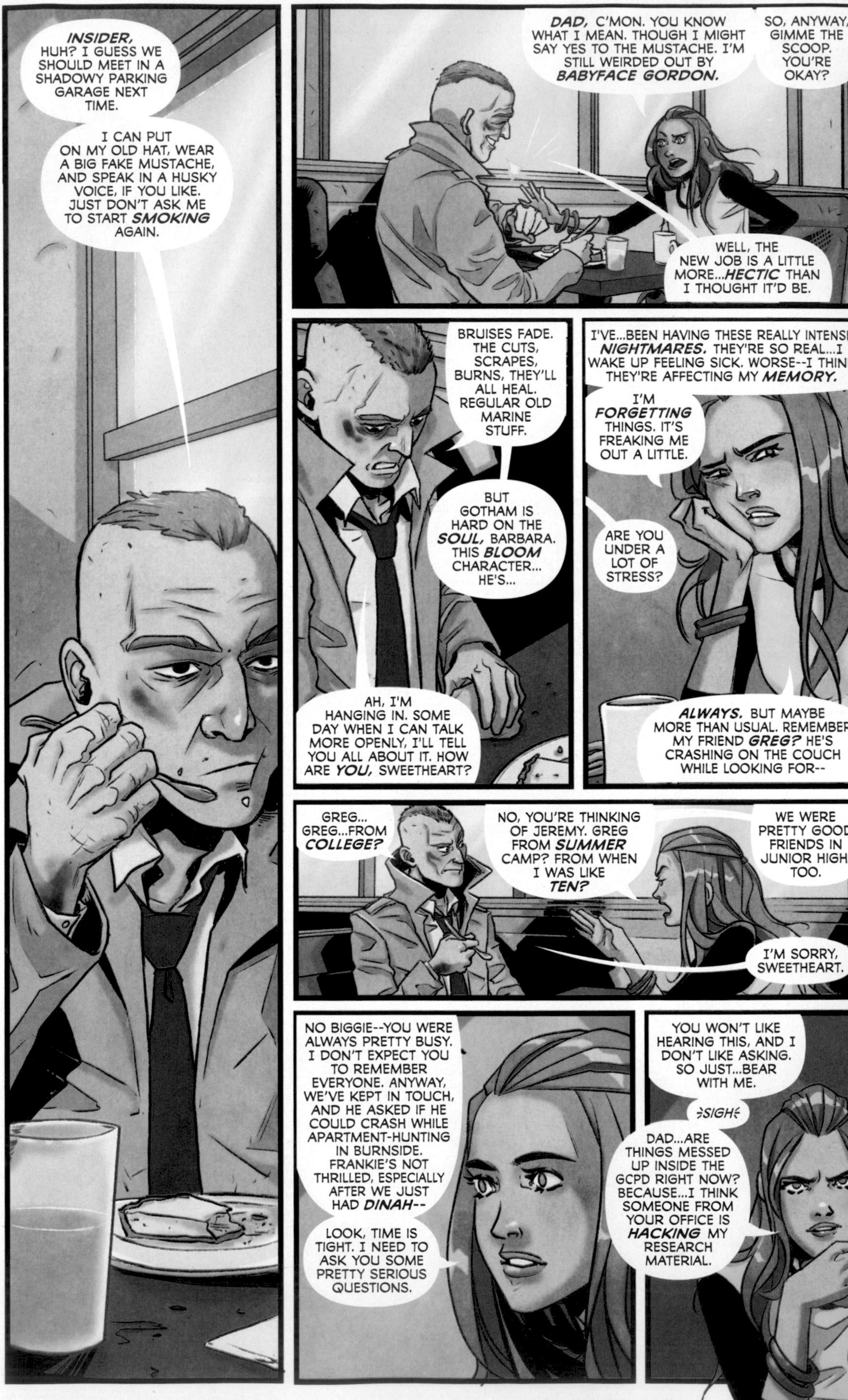
INSIDER, HUH? I GUESS WE SHOULD MEET IN A SHADOWY PARKING GARAGE NEXT TIME.
I CAN PUT ON MY OLD HAT, WEAR A BIG FAKE MUSTACHE, AND SPEAK IN A HUSKY VOICE, IF YOU LIKE. JUST DON'T ASK ME TO START SMOKING AGAIN.
DAD, C'MON. YOU KNOW WHAT I MEAN. THOUGH I MIGHT SAY YES TO THE MUSTACHE. I'M STILL WEIRDED OUT BY BABYFACE GORDON.
SO, ANYWAY, GIMME THE SCOOP. YOU'RE OKAY?
WELL, THE NEW JOB IS A LITTLE MORE...HECTIC THAN I THOUGHT IT'D BE.
BRUISES FADE. THE CUTS, SCRAPES, BURNS, THEY'LL ALL HEAL. REGULAR OLD MARINE STUFF.
BUT GOTHAM IS HARD ON THE SOUL, BARBARA. THIS BLOOM CHARACTER... HE'S...
AH, I'M HANGING IN. SOME DAY WHEN I CAN TALK MORE OPENLY, I'LL TELL YOU ALL ABOUT IT. HOW ARE YOU, SWEETHEART?
I'VE...BEEN HAVING THESE REALLY INTENSE NIGHTMARES. THEY'RE SO REAL...I WAKE UP FEELING SICK. WORSE--I THINK THEY'RE AFFECTING MY MEMORY.
I'M FORGETTING THINGS. IT'S FREAKING ME OUT A LITTLE.
ARE YOU UNDER A LOT OF STRESS?
ALWAYS. BUT MAYBE MORE THAN USUAL. REMEMBER MY FRIEND GREG? HE'S CRASHING ON THE COUCH WHILE LOOKING FOR--
GREG... GREG...FROM COLLEGE?
NO, YOU'RE THINKING OF JEREMY. GREG FROM SUMMER CAMP? FROM WHEN I WAS LIKE TEN?
WE WERE PRETTY GOOD FRIENDS IN JUNIOR HIGH, TOO.
I'M SORRY, SWEETHEART.
NO BIGGIE--YOU WERE ALWAYS PRETTY BUSY. I DON'T EXPECT YOU TO REMEMBER EVERYONE. ANYWAY, WE'VE KEPT IN TOUCH, AND HE ASKED IF HE COULD CRASH WHILE APARTMENT-HUNTING IN BURNSIDE. FRANKIE'S NOT THRILLED, ESPECIALLY AFTER WE JUST HAD DINAH--
LOOK, TIME IS TIGHT. I NEED TO ASK YOU SOME PRETTY SERIOUS QUESTIONS.
YOU WON'T LIKE HEARING THIS, AND I DON'T LIKE ASKING. SO JUST...BEAR WITH ME.
SIGH
DAD...ARE THINGS MESSED UP INSIDE THE GCPD RIGHT NOW? BECAUSE...I THINK SOMEONE FROM YOUR OFFICE IS HACKING MY RESEARCH MATERIAL.

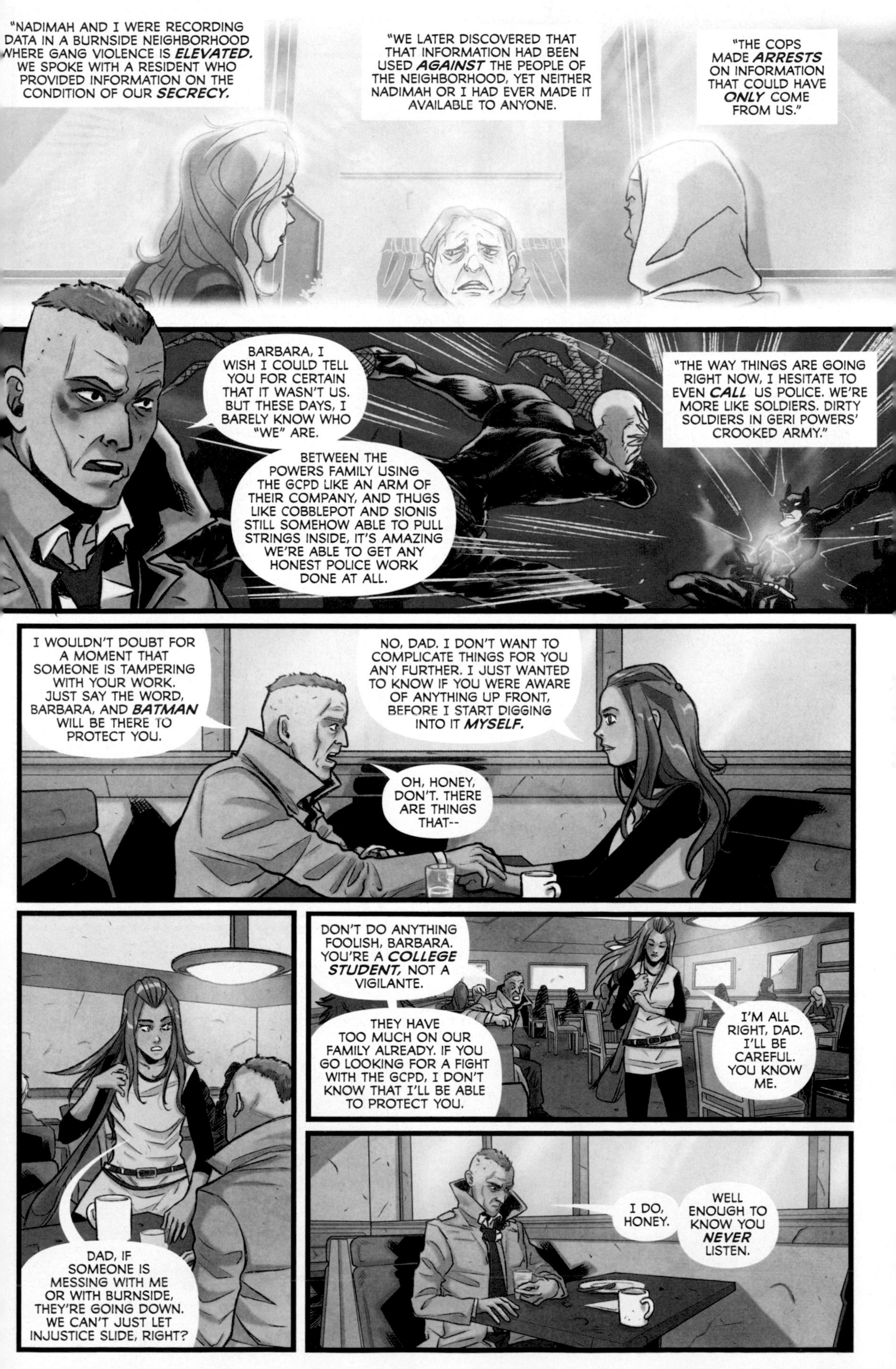
"NADIMAH AND I WERE RECORDING DATA IN A BURNSIDE NEIGHBORHOOD WHERE GANG VIOLENCE IS ELEVATED. WE SPOKE WITH A RESIDENT WHO PROVIDED INFORMATION ON THE CONDITION OF OUR SECRECY.
"WE LATER DISCOVERED THAT THAT INFORMATION HAD BEEN USED AGAINST THE PEOPLE OF THE NEIGHBORHOOD, YET NEITHER NADIMAH OR I HAD EVER MADE IT AVAILABLE TO ANYONE.
"THE COPS MADE ARRESTS ON INFORMATION THAT COULD HAVE ONLY COME FROM US."
BARBARA, I WISH I COULD TELL YOU FOR CERTAIN THAT IT WASN'T US. BUT THESE DAYS, I BARELY KNOW WHO "WE" ARE.
BETWEEN THE POWERS FAMILY USING THE GCPD LIKE AN ARM OF THEIR COMPANY, AND THUGS LIKE COBBLEPOT AND SIONIS STILL SOMEHOW ABLE TO PULL STRINGS INSIDE, IT'S AMAZING WE'RE ABLE TO GET ANY HONEST POLICE WORK DONE AT ALL.
"THE WAY THINGS ARE GOING RIGHT NOW, I HESITATE TO EVEN CALL US POLICE. WE'RE MORE LIKE SOLDIERS. DIRTY SOLDIERS IN GERI POWERS' CROOKED ARMY."
I WOULDN'T DOUBT FOR A MOMENT THAT SOMEONE IS TAMPERING WITH YOUR WORK. JUST SAY THE WORD, BARBARA, AND BATMAN WILL BE THERE TO PROTECT YOU.
NO, DAD. I DON'T WANT TO COMPLICATE THINGS FOR YOU ANY FURTHER. I JUST WANTED TO KNOW IF YOU WERE AWARE OF ANYTHING UP FRONT, BEFORE I START DIGGING INTO IT MYSELF.
OH, HONEY, DON'T. THERE ARE THINGS THAT--
DAD, IF SOMEONE IS MESSING WITH ME OR WITH BURNSIDE, THEY'RE GOING DOWN. WE CAN'T JUST LET INJUSTICE SLIDE, RIGHT?
DON'T DO ANYTHING FOOLISH, BARBARA. YOU'RE A COLLEGE STUDENT, NOT A VIGILANTE.
THEY HAVE TOO MUCH ON OUR FAMILY ALREADY. IF YOU GO LOOKING FOR A FIGHT WITH THE GCPD, I DON'T KNOW THAT I'LL BE ABLE TO PROTECT YOU.
I'M ALL RIGHT, DAD. I'LL BE CAREFUL. YOU KNOW ME.
I DO, HONEY.
WELL ENOUGH TO KNOW YOU NEVER LISTEN.

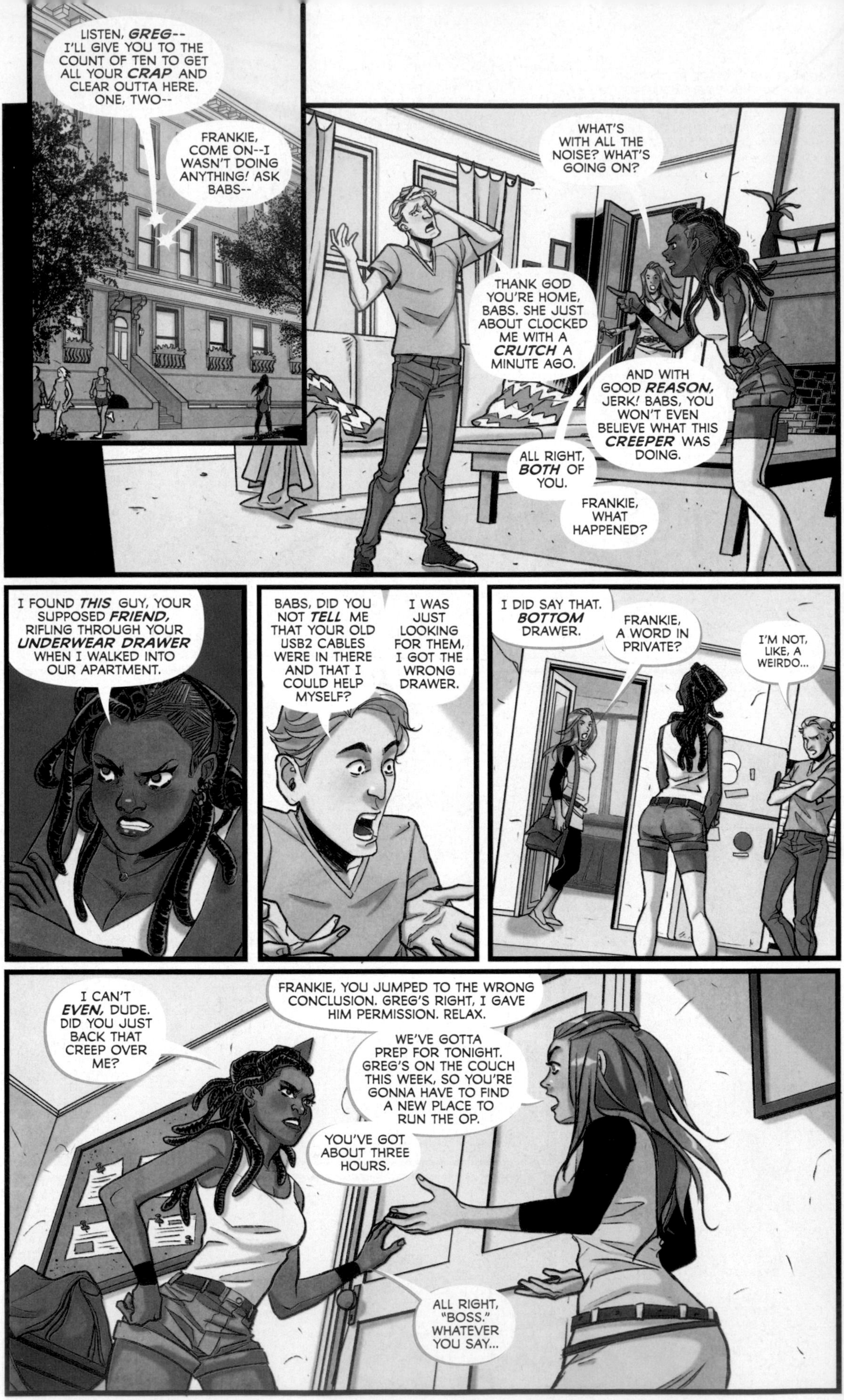
LISTEN, GREG-- I'LL GIVE YOU TO THE COUNT OF TEN TO GET ALL YOUR CRAP AND CLEAR OUTTA HERE. ONE, TWO--
FRANKIE, COME ON--I WASN'T DOING ANYTHING! ASK BABS--
WHAT'S WITH ALL THE NOISE? WHAT'S GOING ON?
THANK GOD YOU'RE HOME, BABS. SHE JUST ABOUT CLOCKED ME WITH A CRUTCH A MINUTE AGO.
AND WITH GOOD REASON, JERK! BABS, YOU WON'T EVEN BELIEVE WHAT THIS CREEPER WAS DOING.
ALL RIGHT, BOTH OF YOU.
FRANKIE, WHAT HAPPENED?
I FOUND THIS GUY, YOUR SUPPOSED FRIEND, RIFLING THROUGH YOUR UNDERWEAR DRAWER WHEN I WALKED INTO OUR APARTMENT.
BABS, DID YOU NOT TELL ME THAT YOUR OLD USB2 CABLES WERE IN THERE AND THAT I COULD HELP MYSELF?
I WAS JUST LOOKING FOR THEM, I GOT THE WRONG DRAWER.
I DID SAY THAT. BOTTOM DRAWER.
FRANKIE, A WORD IN PRIVATE?
I'M NOT, LIKE, A WEIRDO...
I CAN'T EVEN, DUDE. DID YOU JUST BACK THAT CREEP OVER ME?
FRANKIE, YOU JUMPED TO THE WRONG CONCLUSION. GREG'S RIGHT, I GAVE HIM PERMISSION. RELAX.
WE'VE GOTTA PREP FOR TONIGHT. GREG'S ON THE COUCH THIS WEEK, SO YOU'RE GONNA HAVE TO FIND A NEW PLACE TO RUN THE OP.
YOU'VE GOT ABOUT THREE HOURS.
ALL RIGHT, "BOSS." WHATEVER YOU SAY...

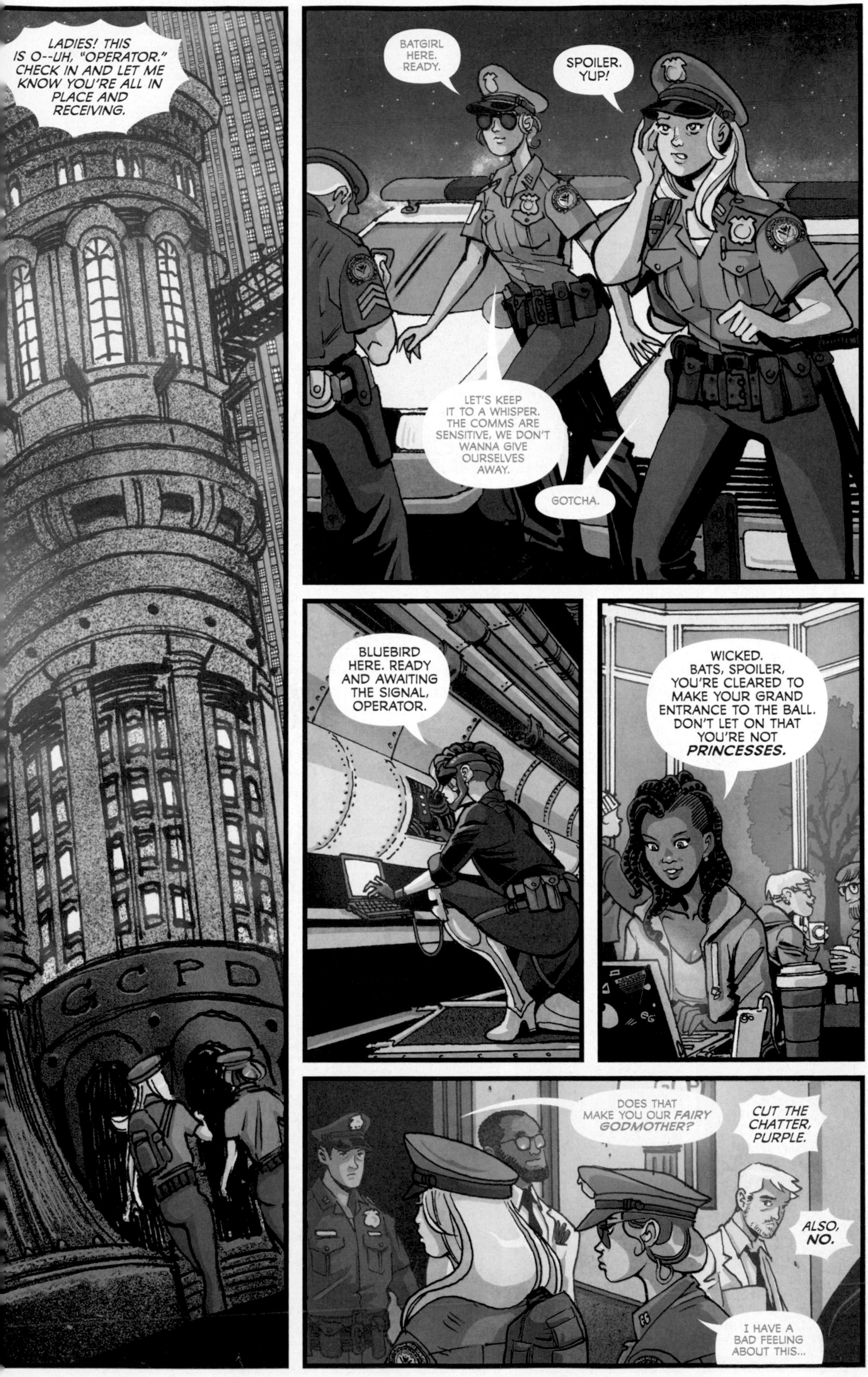
LADIES! THIS IS O--UH, "OPERATOR." CHECK IN AND LET ME KNOW YOU'RE ALL IN PLACE AND RECEIVING.
GCPD
BATGIRL HERE. READY.
SPOILER. YUP!
LET'S KEEP IT TO A WHISPER. THE COMMS ARE SENSITIVE, WE DON'T WANNA GIVE OURSELVES AWAY.
GOTCHA.
BLUEBIRD HERE. READY AND AWAITING THE SIGNAL, OPERATOR.
WICKED. BATS, SPOILER, YOU'RE CLEARED TO MAKE YOUR GRAND ENTRANCE TO THE BALL. DON'T LET ON THAT YOU'RE NOT PRINCESSES.
DOES THAT MAKE YOU OUR FAIRY GODMOTHER?
CUT THE CHATTER, PURPLE.
ALSO, NO.
I HAVE A BAD FEELING ABOUT THIS...

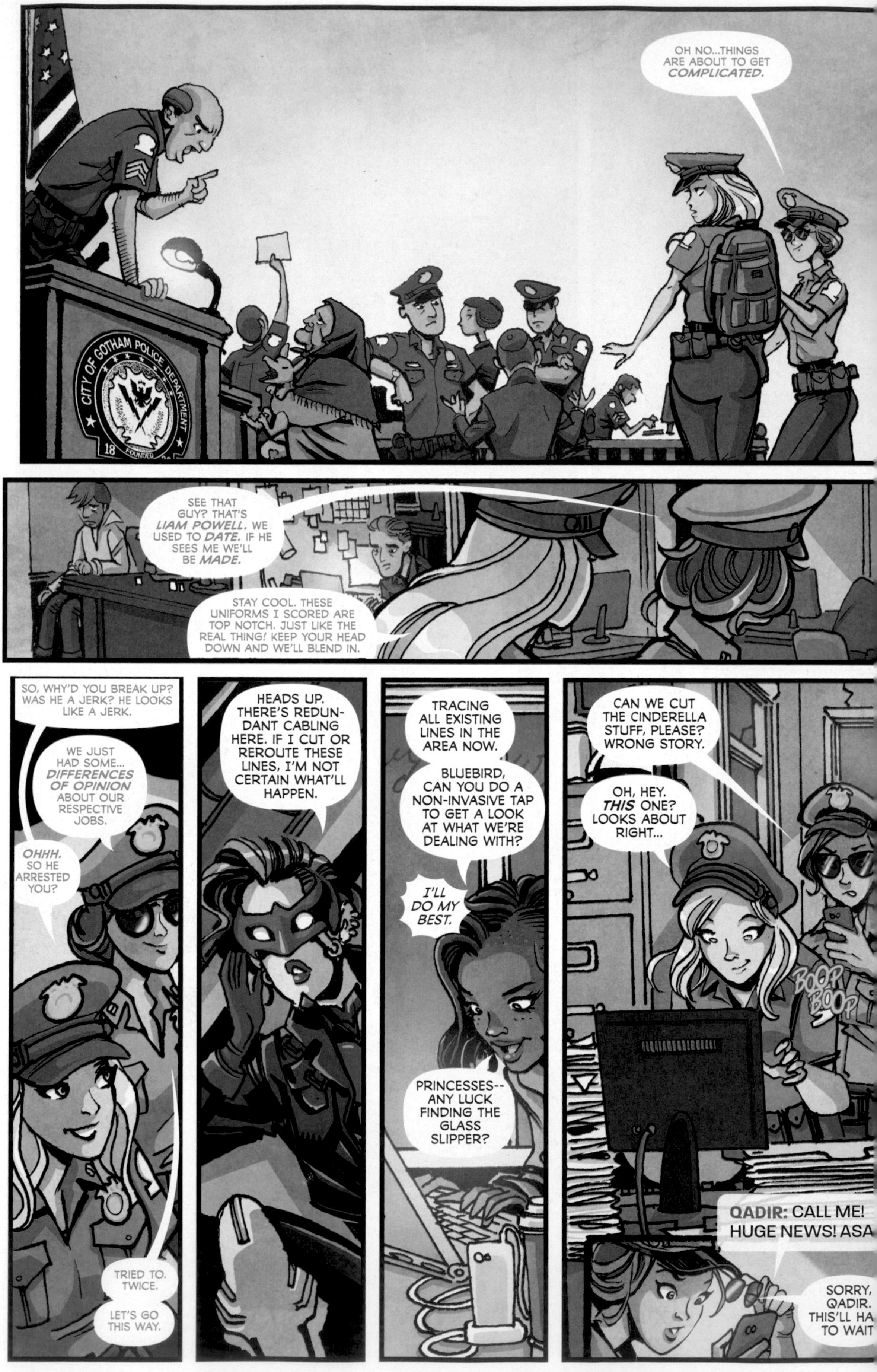
CITY OF GOTHAM POLICE DEPARTMENT
OH NO...THINGS ARE ABOUT TO GET *COMPLICATED.*
SEE THAT GUY? THAT'S *LIAM POWELL.* WE USED TO *DATE.* IF HE SEES ME WE'LL BE *MADE.*
STAY COOL. THESE UNIFORMS I SCORED ARE TOP NOTCH. JUST LIKE THE REAL THING! KEEP YOUR HEAD DOWN AND WE'LL BLEND IN.
SO, WHY'D YOU BREAK UP? WAS HE A JERK? HE LOOKS LIKE A JERK.
WE JUST HAD SOME... *DIFFERENCES OF OPINION* ABOUT OUR RESPECTIVE JOBS.
OHHH. SO HE ARRESTED YOU?
TRIED TO. TWICE.
LET'S GO THIS WAY.
HEADS UP. THERE'S REDUNDANT CABLING HERE. IF I CUT OR REROUTE THESE LINES, I'M NOT CERTAIN WHAT'LL HAPPEN.
TRACING ALL EXISTING LINES IN THE AREA NOW.
BLUEBIRD, CAN YOU DO A NON-INVASIVE TAP TO GET A LOOK AT WHAT WE'RE DEALING WITH?
I'LL DO MY BEST.
PRINCESSES-- ANY LUCK FINDING THE GLASS SLIPPER?
CAN WE CUT THE CINDERELLA STUFF, PLEASE? WRONG STORY.
OH, HEY. *THIS* ONE? LOOKS ABOUT RIGHT...
BOOP BOOP
QADIR: CALL ME! HUGE NEWS! ASA
SORRY, QADIR. THIS'LL HA TO WAIT

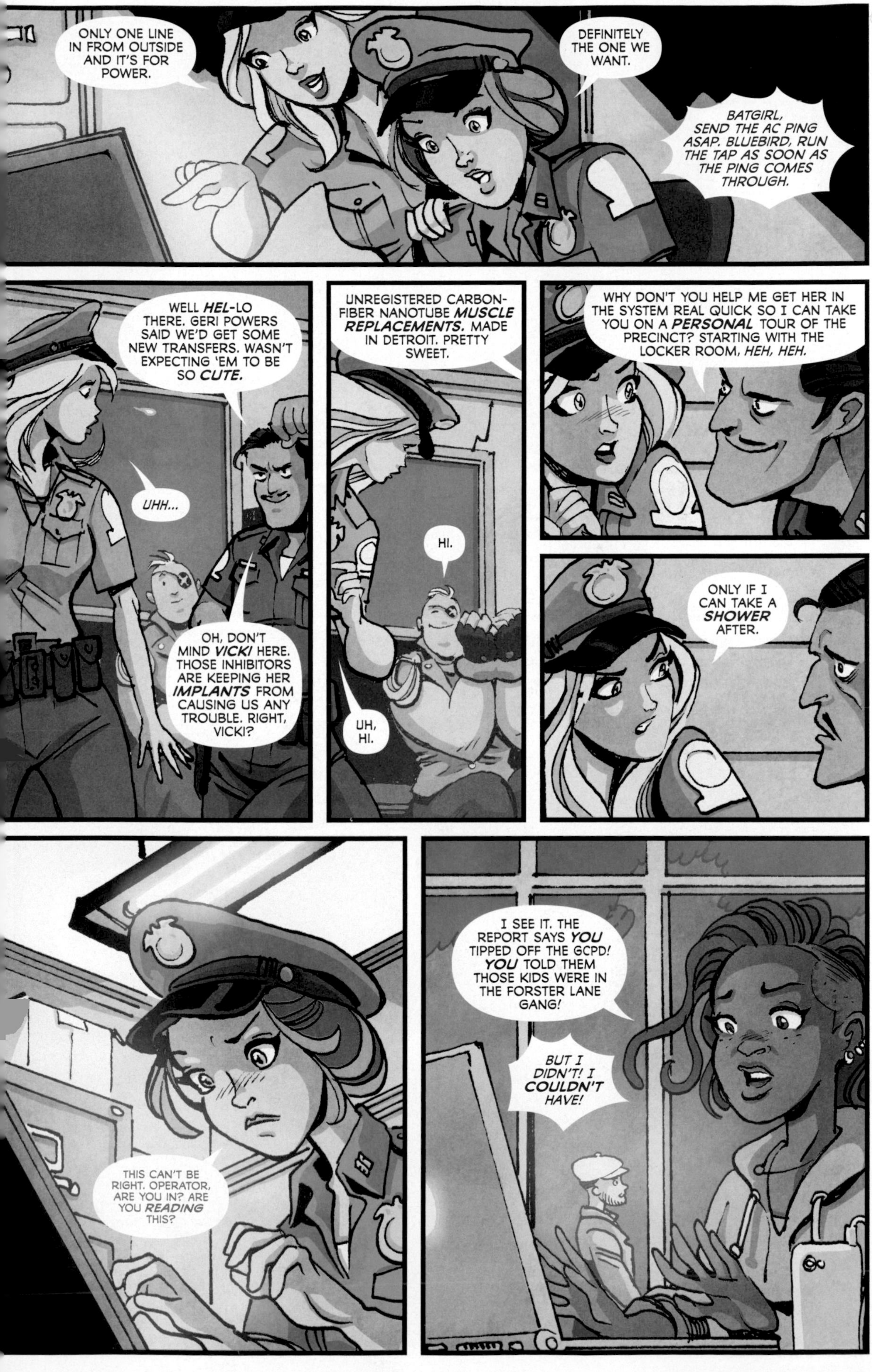
ONLY ONE LINE IN FROM OUTSIDE AND IT'S FOR POWER.
DEFINITELY THE ONE WE WANT.
BATGIRL, SEND THE AC PING ASAP. BLUEBIRD, RUN THE TAP AS SOON AS THE PING COMES THROUGH.
WELL HEL-LO THERE. GERI POWERS SAID WE'D GET SOME NEW TRANSFERS. WASN'T EXPECTING 'EM TO BE SO CUTE.
UHH...
OH, DON'T MIND VICKI HERE. THOSE INHIBITORS ARE KEEPING HER IMPLANTS FROM CAUSING US ANY TROUBLE. RIGHT, VICKI?
UNREGISTERED CARBON-FIBER NANOTUBE MUSCLE REPLACEMENTS. MADE IN DETROIT. PRETTY SWEET.
HI.
UH, HI.
WHY DON'T YOU HELP ME GET HER IN THE SYSTEM REAL QUICK SO I CAN TAKE YOU ON A PERSONAL TOUR OF THE PRECINCT? STARTING WITH THE LOCKER ROOM, HEH, HEH.
ONLY IF I CAN TAKE A SHOWER AFTER.
THIS CAN'T BE RIGHT. OPERATOR, ARE YOU IN? ARE YOU READING THIS?
I SEE IT. THE REPORT SAYS YOU TIPPED OFF THE GCPD! YOU TOLD THEM THOSE KIDS WERE IN THE FORSTER LANE GANG!
BUT I DIDN'T! I COULDN'T HAVE!

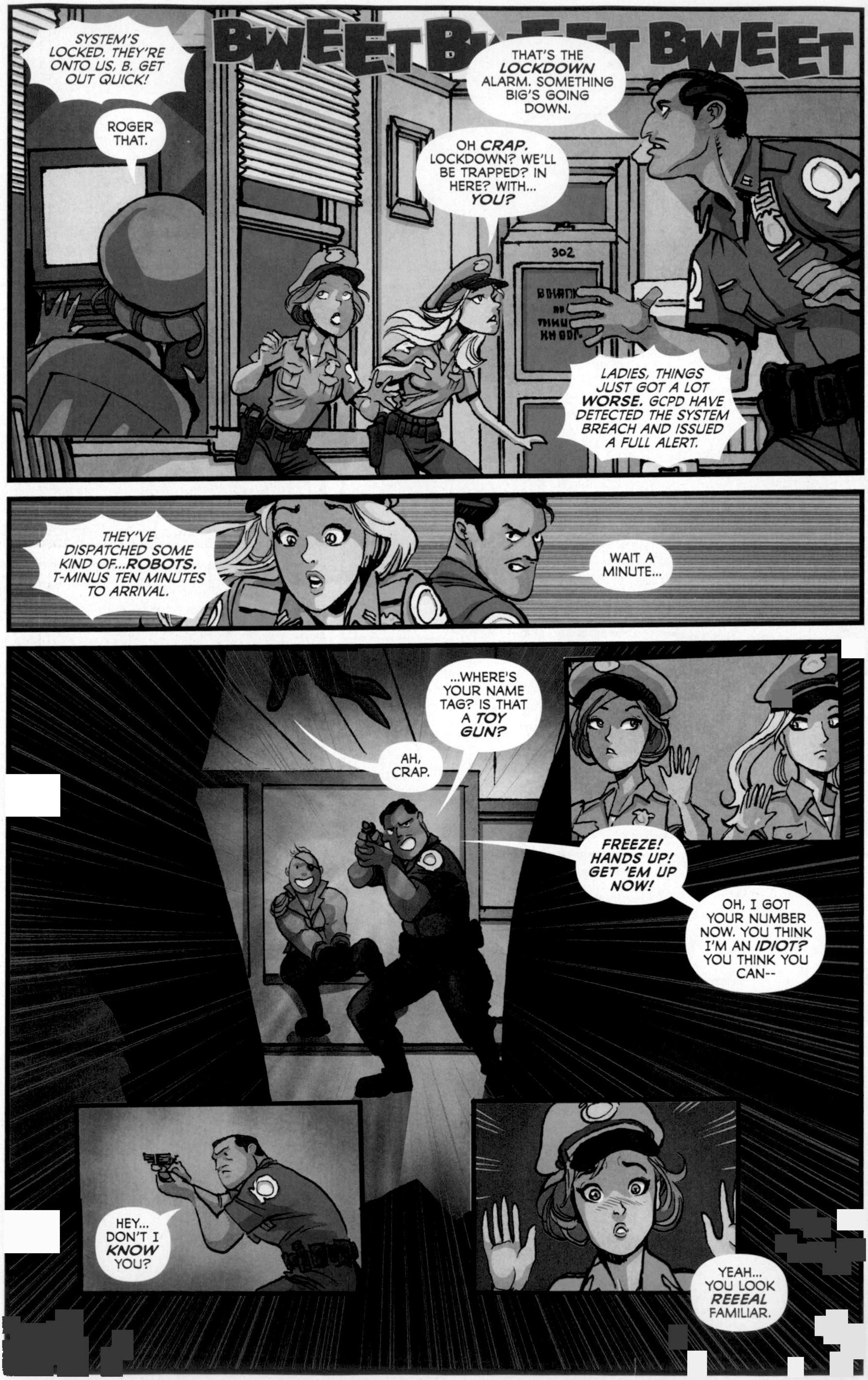
BWEET
BWEET
SYSTEM'S LOCKED. THEY'RE ONTO US, B. GET OUT QUICK!
ROGER THAT.
THAT'S THE LOCKDOWN ALARM. SOMETHING BIG'S GOING DOWN.
OH CRAP. LOCKDOWN? WE'LL BE TRAPPED? IN HERE? WITH... YOU?
302
LADIES, THINGS JUST GOT A LOT WORSE. GCPD HAVE DETECTED THE SYSTEM BREACH AND ISSUED A FULL ALERT.
THEY'VE DISPATCHED SOME KIND OF...ROBOTS. T-MINUS TEN MINUTES TO ARRIVAL.
WAIT A MINUTE...
...WHERE'S YOUR NAME TAG? IS THAT A TOY GUN?
AH, CRAP.
FREEZE! HANDS UP! GET 'EM UP NOW!
OH, I GOT YOUR NUMBER NOW. YOU THINK I'M AN IDIOT? YOU THINK YOU CAN--
HEY... DON'T I KNOW YOU?
YEAH... YOU LOOK REEEAL FAMILIAR.

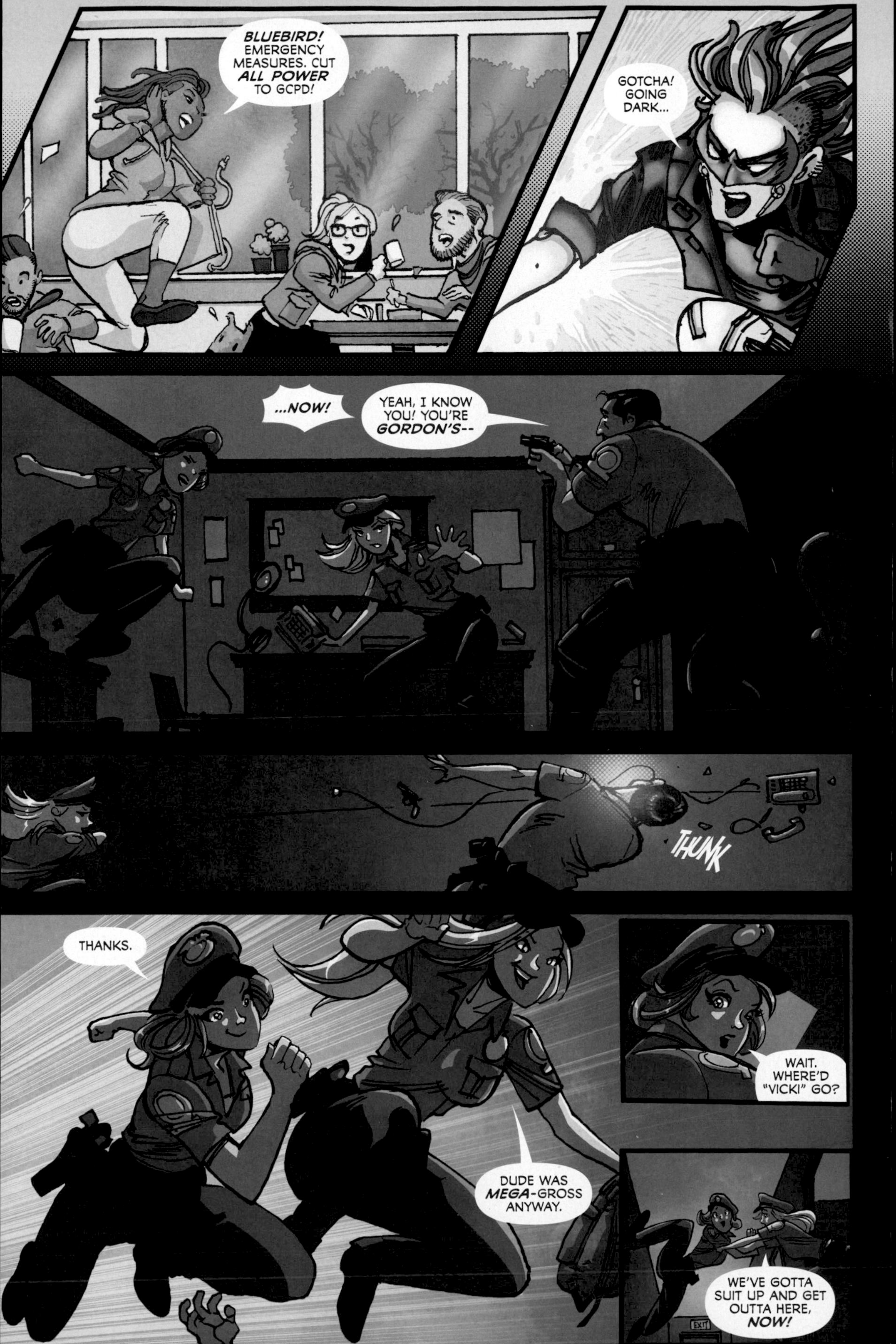
BLUEBIRD! EMERGENCY MEASURES. CUT ALL POWER TO GCPD!
GOTCHA! GOING DARK...
...NOW!
YEAH, I KNOW YOU! YOU'RE GORDON'S--
THUNK
THANKS.
DUDE WAS MEGA-GROSS ANYWAY.
WAIT. WHERE'D "VICKI" GO?
WE'VE GOTTA SUIT UP AND GET OUTTA HERE, NOW!
EXIT

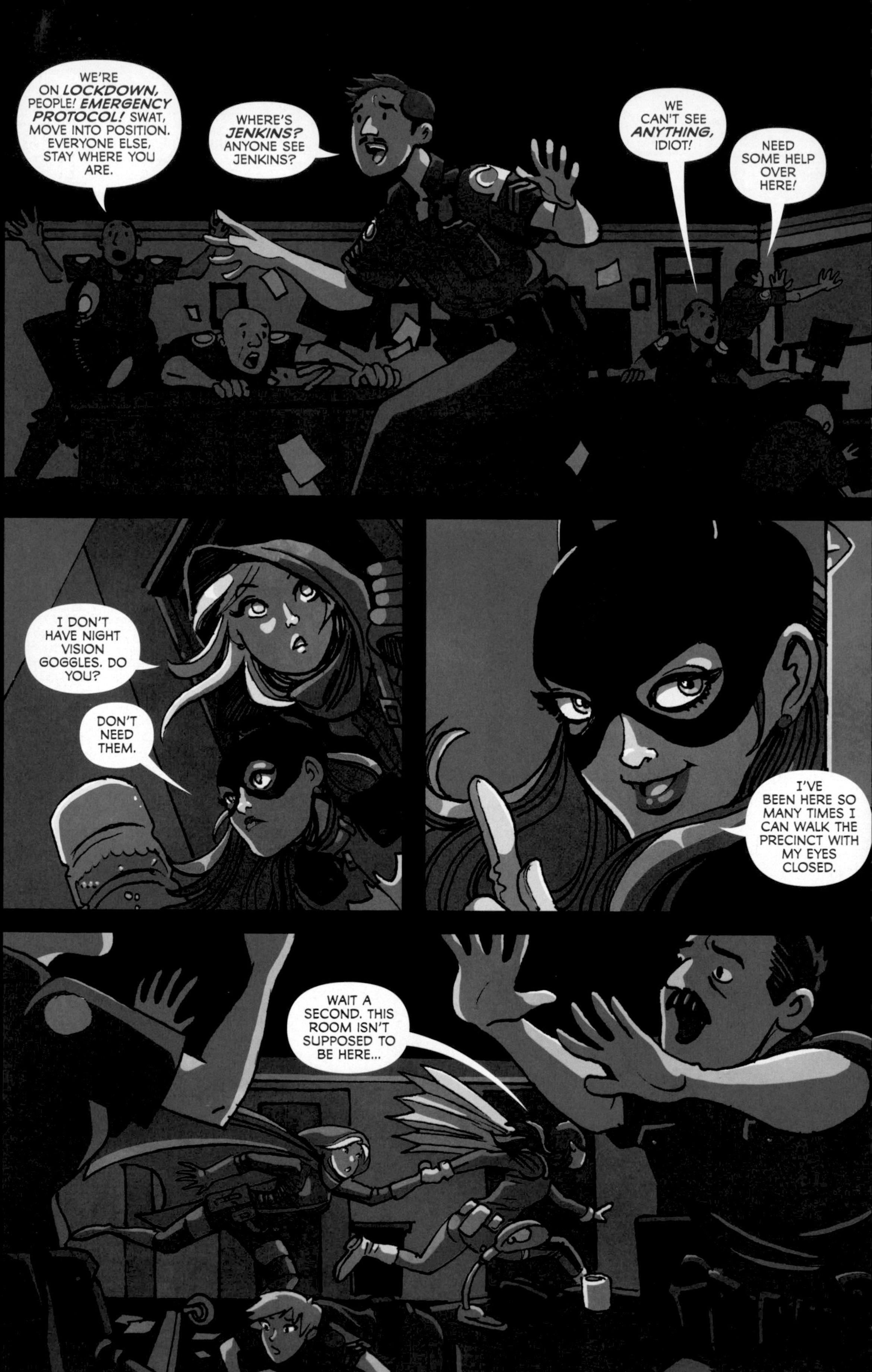
WE'RE ON LOCKDOWN, PEOPLE! EMERGENCY PROTOCOL! SWAT, MOVE INTO POSITION. EVERYONE ELSE, STAY WHERE YOU ARE.
WHERE'S JENKINS? ANYONE SEE JENKINS?
WE CAN'T SEE ANYTHING, IDIOT!
NEED SOME HELP OVER HERE!
I DON'T HAVE NIGHT VISION GOGGLES. DO YOU?
DON'T NEED THEM.
I'VE BEEN HERE SO MANY TIMES I CAN WALK THE PRECINCT WITH MY EYES CLOSED.
WAIT A SECOND. THIS ROOM ISN'T SUPPOSED TO BE HERE...

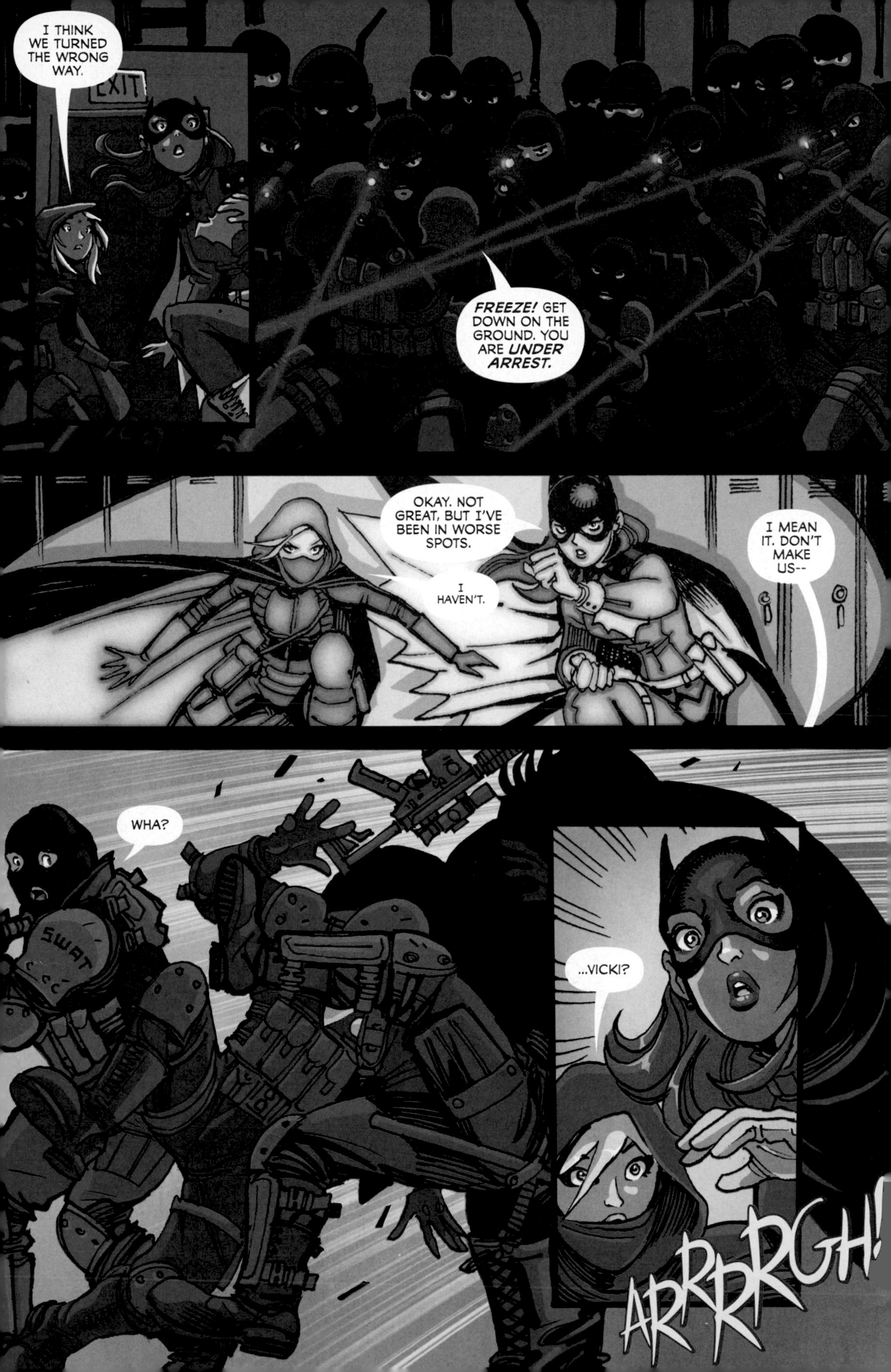
I THINK WE TURNED THE WRONG WAY.
EXIT
FREEZE! GET DOWN ON THE GROUND. YOU ARE ***UNDER ARREST.***
OKAY. NOT GREAT, BUT I'VE BEEN IN WORSE SPOTS.
I HAVEN'T.
I MEAN IT. DON'T MAKE US--
WHA?
SWAT
...VICKI?
ARRRRGH!

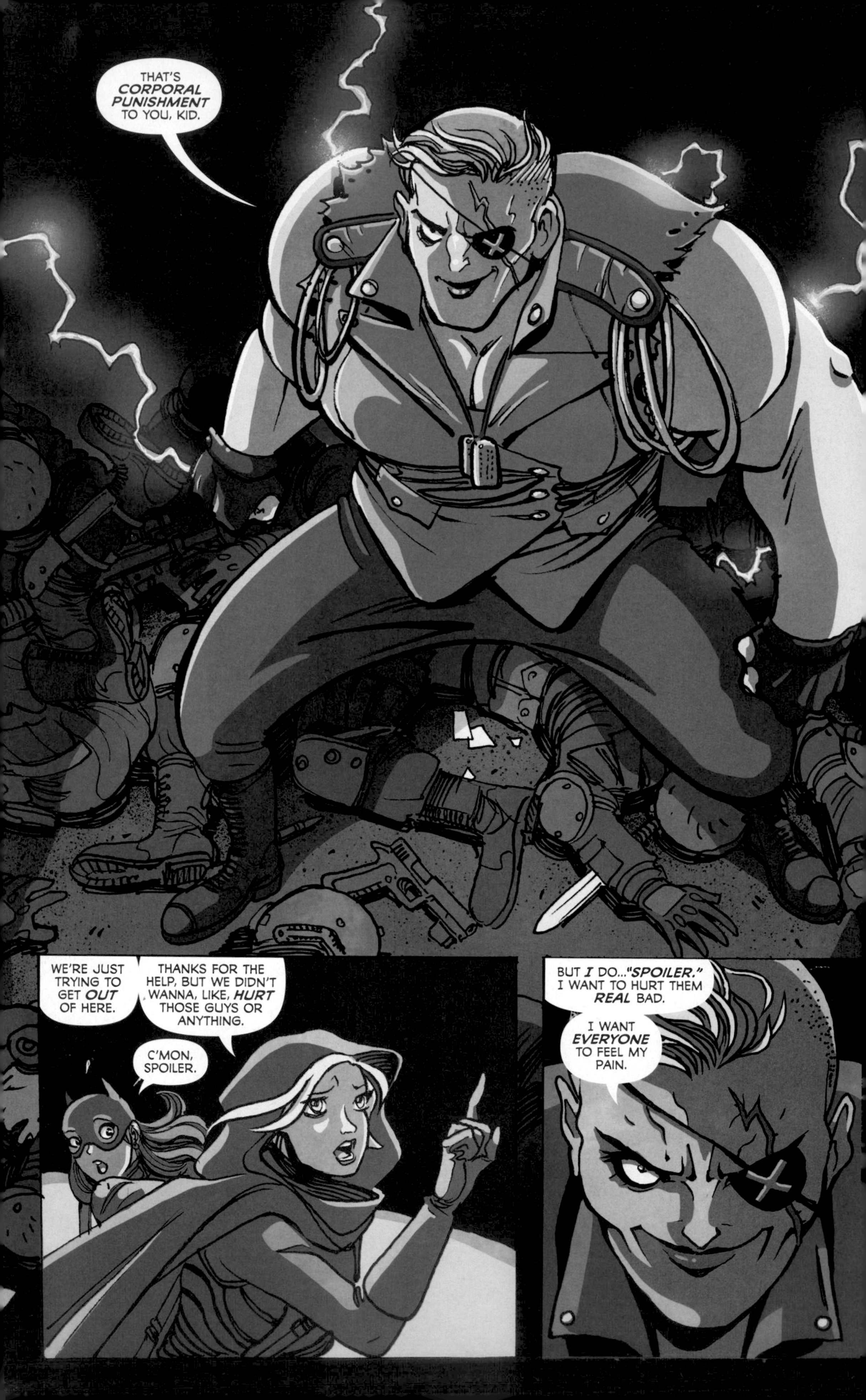
THAT'S *CORPORAL PUNISHMENT* TO YOU, KID.
WE'RE JUST TRYING TO GET *OUT* OF HERE.
THANKS FOR THE HELP, BUT WE DIDN'T WANNA, LIKE, *HURT* THOSE GUYS OR ANYTHING.
C'MON, SPOILER.
BUT *I* DO..."*SPOILER.*" I WANT TO HURT THEM *REAL* BAD.
I WANT *EVERYONE* TO FEEL MY PAIN.

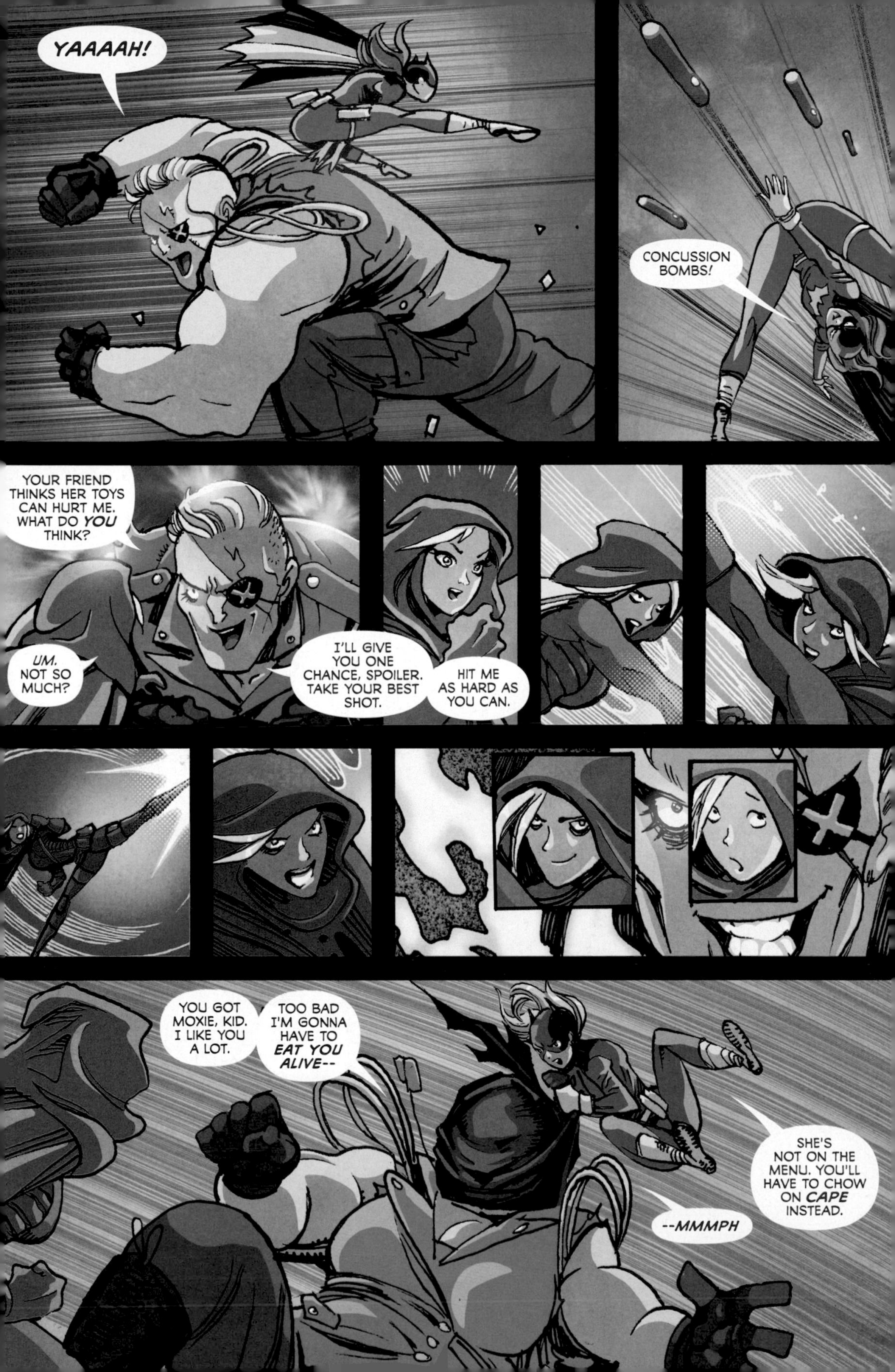
YAAAAH!
CONCUSSION BOMBS!
YOUR FRIEND THINKS HER TOYS CAN HURT ME. WHAT DO *YOU* THINK?
UM. NOT SO MUCH?
I'LL GIVE YOU ONE CHANCE, SPOILER. TAKE YOUR BEST SHOT.
HIT ME AS HARD AS YOU CAN.
YOU GOT MOXIE, KID. I LIKE YOU A LOT.
TOO BAD I'M GONNA HAVE TO *EAT YOU ALIVE--*
--MMMPH
SHE'S NOT ON THE MENU. YOU'LL HAVE TO CHOW ON *CAPE* INSTEAD.

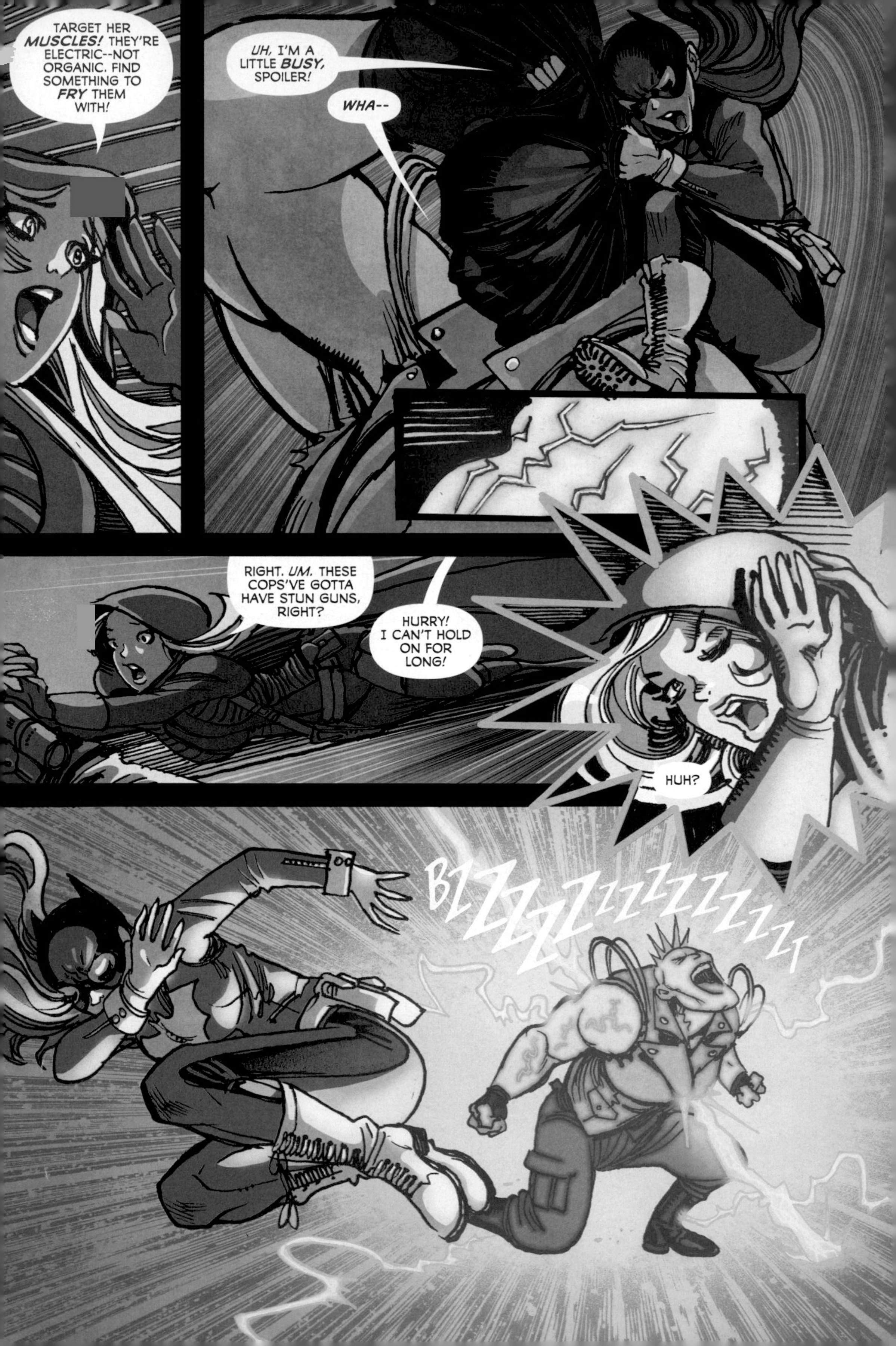
TARGET HER MUSCLES! THEY'RE ELECTRIC--NOT ORGANIC. FIND SOMETHING TO FRY THEM WITH!
UH, I'M A LITTLE BUSY, SPOILER!
WHA--
RIGHT. UM. THESE COPS'VE GOTTA HAVE STUN GUNS, RIGHT?
HURRY! I CAN'T HOLD ON FOR LONG!
HUH?
BZZZZZZZZZZZZZZZT

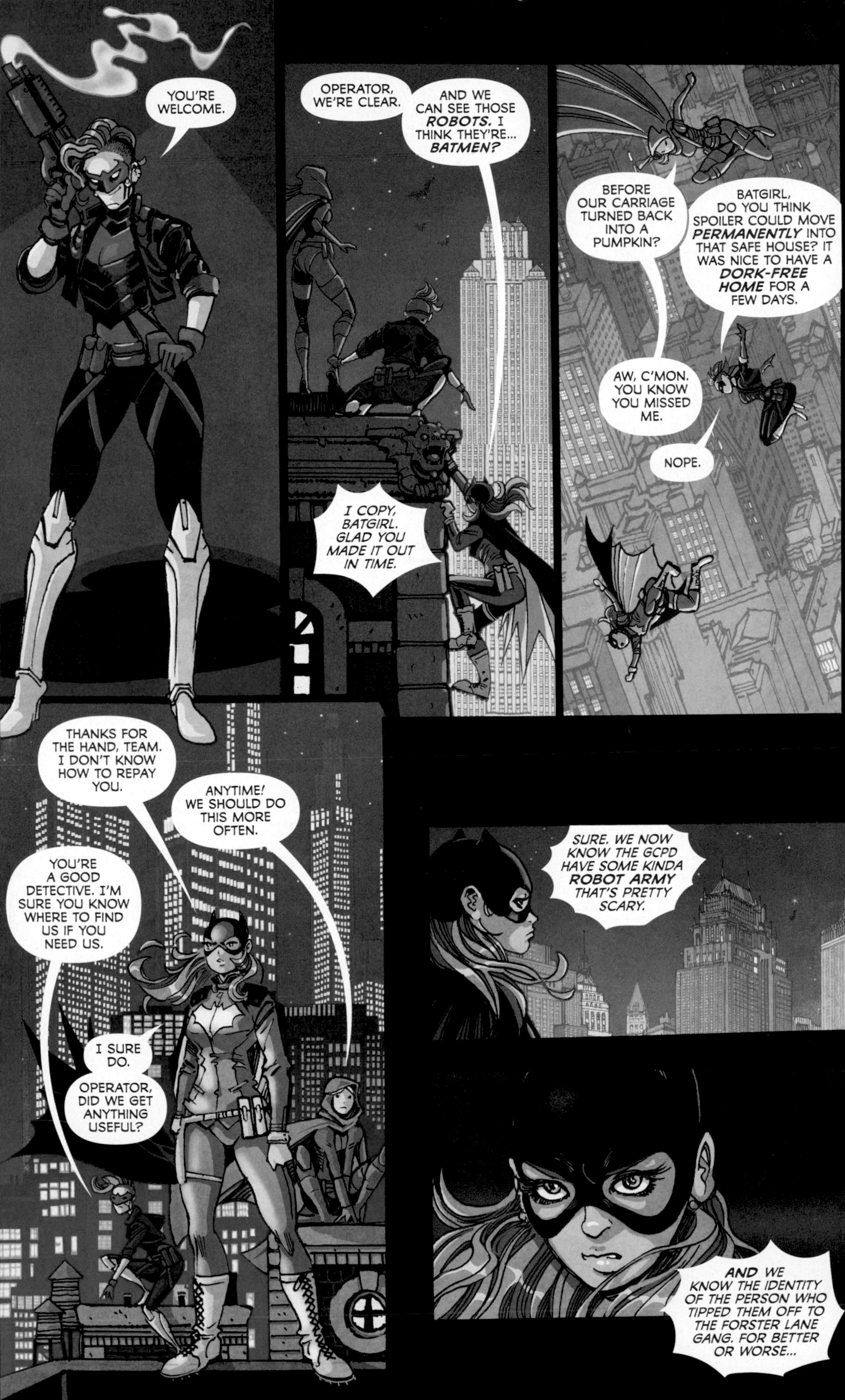
YOU'RE WELCOME.
OPERATOR, WE'RE CLEAR.
AND WE CAN SEE THOSE ROBOTS. I THINK THEY'RE... BATMEN?
I COPY, BATGIRL. GLAD YOU MADE IT OUT IN TIME.
BEFORE OUR CARRIAGE TURNED BACK INTO A PUMPKIN?
BATGIRL, DO YOU THINK SPOILER COULD MOVE PERMANENTLY INTO THAT SAFE HOUSE? IT WAS NICE TO HAVE A DORK-FREE HOME FOR A FEW DAYS.
AW, C'MON. YOU KNOW YOU MISSED ME.
NOPE.
THANKS FOR THE HAND, TEAM. I DON'T KNOW HOW TO REPAY YOU.
ANYTIME! WE SHOULD DO THIS MORE OFTEN.
YOU'RE A GOOD DETECTIVE. I'M SURE YOU KNOW WHERE TO FIND US IF YOU NEED US.
I SURE DO.
OPERATOR, DID WE GET ANYTHING USEFUL?
SURE. WE NOW KNOW THE GCPD HAVE SOME KINDA ROBOT ARMY THAT'S PRETTY SCARY.
AND WE KNOW THE IDENTITY OF THE PERSON WHO TIPPED THEM OFF TO THE FORSTER LANE GANG. FOR BETTER OR WORSE...

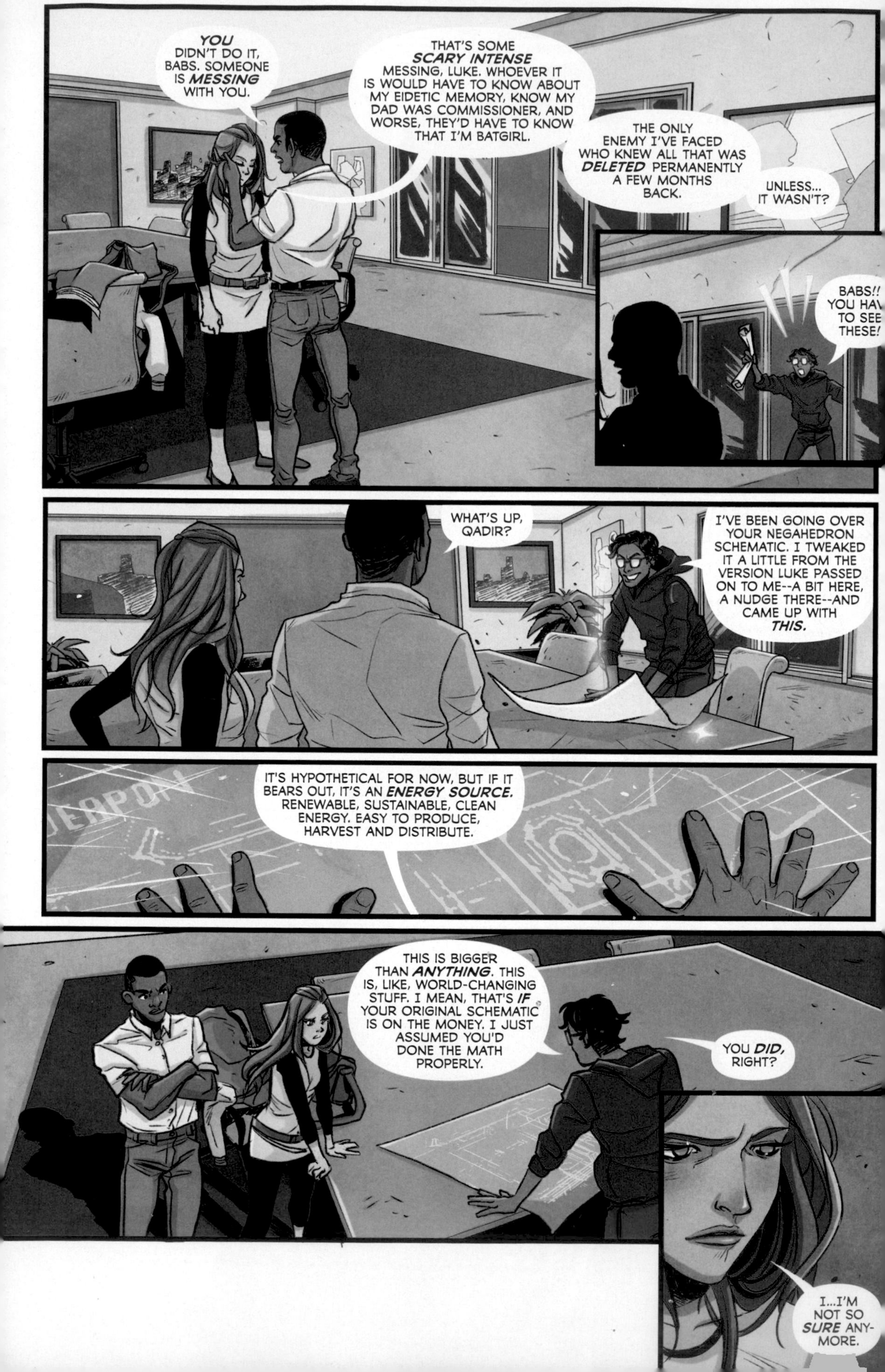
YOU DIDN'T DO IT, BABS. SOMEONE IS MESSING WITH YOU.
THAT'S SOME SCARY INTENSE MESSING, LUKE. WHOEVER IT IS WOULD HAVE TO KNOW ABOUT MY EIDETIC MEMORY, KNOW MY DAD WAS COMMISSIONER, AND WORSE, THEY'D HAVE TO KNOW THAT I'M BATGIRL.
THE ONLY ENEMY I'VE FACED WHO KNEW ALL THAT WAS DELETED PERMANENTLY A FEW MONTHS BACK.
UNLESS... IT WASN'T?
BABS!! YOU HAV TO SEE THESE!
WHAT'S UP, QADIR?
I'VE BEEN GOING OVER YOUR NEGAHEDRON SCHEMATIC. I TWEAKED IT A LITTLE FROM THE VERSION LUKE PASSED ON TO ME--A BIT HERE, A NUDGE THERE--AND CAME UP WITH THIS.
IT'S HYPOTHETICAL FOR NOW, BUT IF IT BEARS OUT, IT'S AN ENERGY SOURCE. RENEWABLE, SUSTAINABLE, CLEAN ENERGY. EASY TO PRODUCE, HARVEST AND DISTRIBUTE.
THIS IS BIGGER THAN ANYTHING. THIS IS, LIKE, WORLD-CHANGING STUFF. I MEAN, THAT'S IF YOUR ORIGINAL SCHEMATIC IS ON THE MONEY. I JUST ASSUMED YOU'D DONE THE MATH PROPERLY.
YOU DID, RIGHT?
I...I'M NOT SO SURE ANY-MORE.

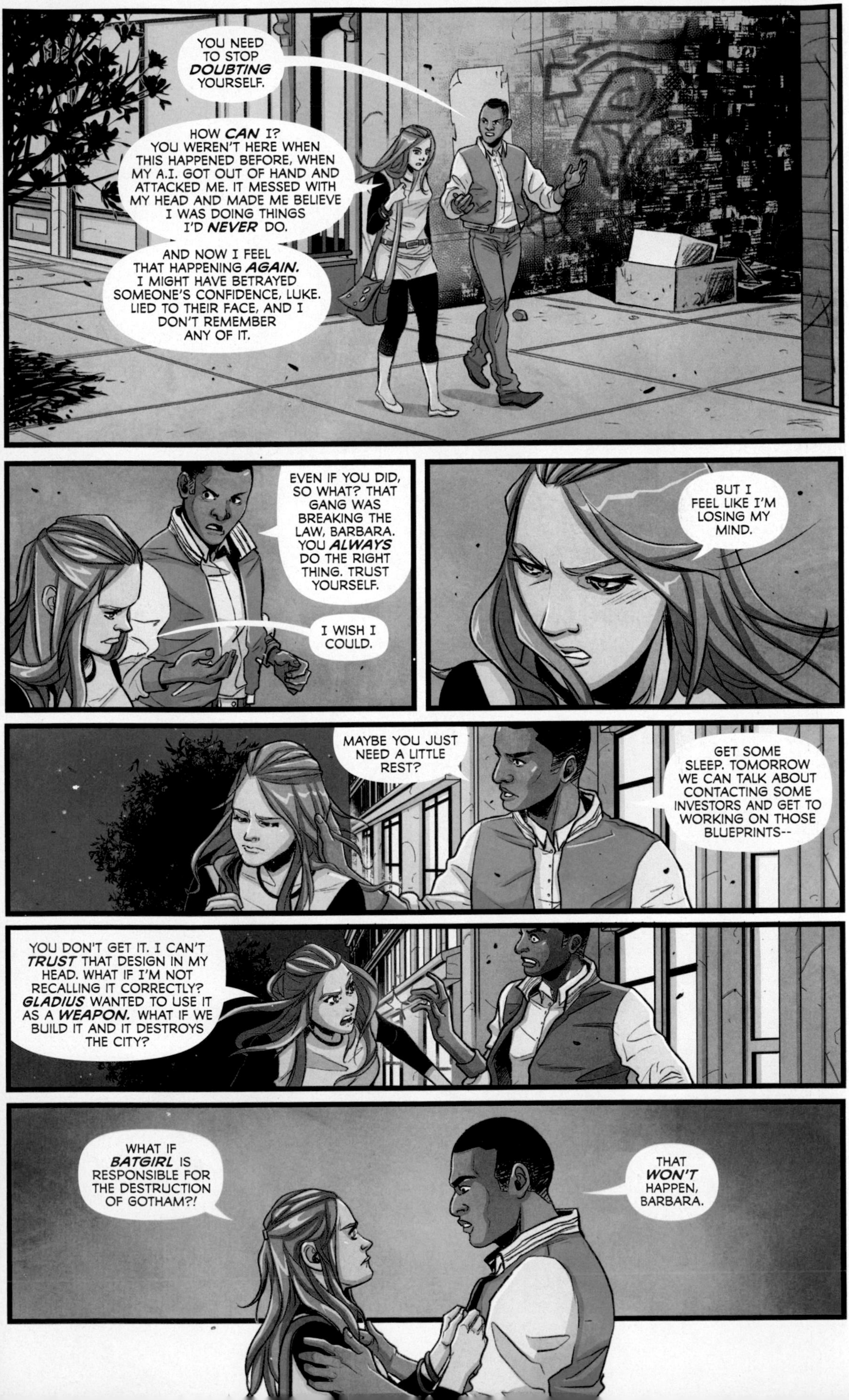
YOU NEED TO STOP DOUBTING YOURSELF.
HOW CAN I? YOU WEREN'T HERE WHEN THIS HAPPENED BEFORE, WHEN MY A.I. GOT OUT OF HAND AND ATTACKED ME. IT MESSED WITH MY HEAD AND MADE ME BELIEVE I WAS DOING THINGS I'D NEVER DO.
AND NOW I FEEL THAT HAPPENING AGAIN. I MIGHT HAVE BETRAYED SOMEONE'S CONFIDENCE, LUKE. LIED TO THEIR FACE, AND I DON'T REMEMBER ANY OF IT.
EVEN IF YOU DID, SO WHAT? THAT GANG WAS BREAKING THE LAW, BARBARA. YOU ALWAYS DO THE RIGHT THING. TRUST YOURSELF.
I WISH I COULD.
BUT I FEEL LIKE I'M LOSING MY MIND.
MAYBE YOU JUST NEED A LITTLE REST?
GET SOME SLEEP. TOMORROW WE CAN TALK ABOUT CONTACTING SOME INVESTORS AND GET TO WORKING ON THOSE BLUEPRINTS--
YOU DON'T GET IT. I CAN'T TRUST THAT DESIGN IN MY HEAD. WHAT IF I'M NOT RECALLING IT CORRECTLY? GLADIUS WANTED TO USE IT AS A WEAPON. WHAT IF WE BUILD IT AND IT DESTROYS THE CITY?
WHAT IF BATGIRL IS RESPONSIBLE FOR THE DESTRUCTION OF GOTHAM?!
THAT WON'T HAPPEN, BARBARA.

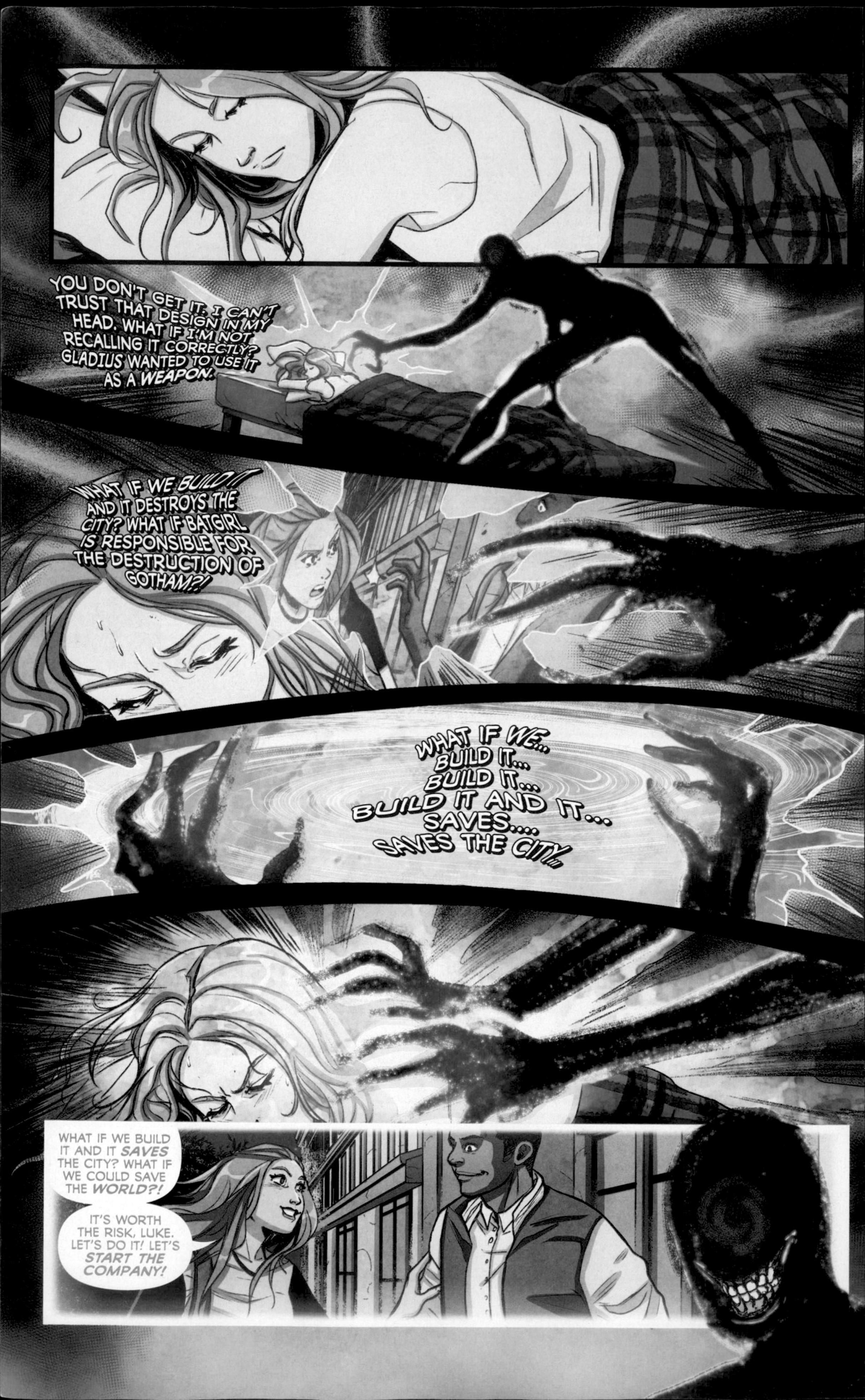
YOU DON'T GET IT. I CAN'T TRUST THAT DESIGN IN MY HEAD. WHAT IF I'M NOT RECALLING IT CORRECTLY? GLADIUS WANTED TO USE IT AS A WEAPON.
WHAT IF WE BUILD IT AND IT DESTROYS THE CITY? WHAT IF BATGIRL IS RESPONSIBLE FOR THE DESTRUCTION OF GOTHAM?!
WHAT IF WE... BUILD IT... BUILD IT... BUILD IT AND IT... SAVES.... SAVES THE CITY...
WHAT IF WE BUILD IT AND IT SAVES THE CITY? WHAT IF WE COULD SAVE THE WORLD?!
IT'S WORTH THE RISK, LUKE. LET'S DO IT! LET'S START THE COMPANY!

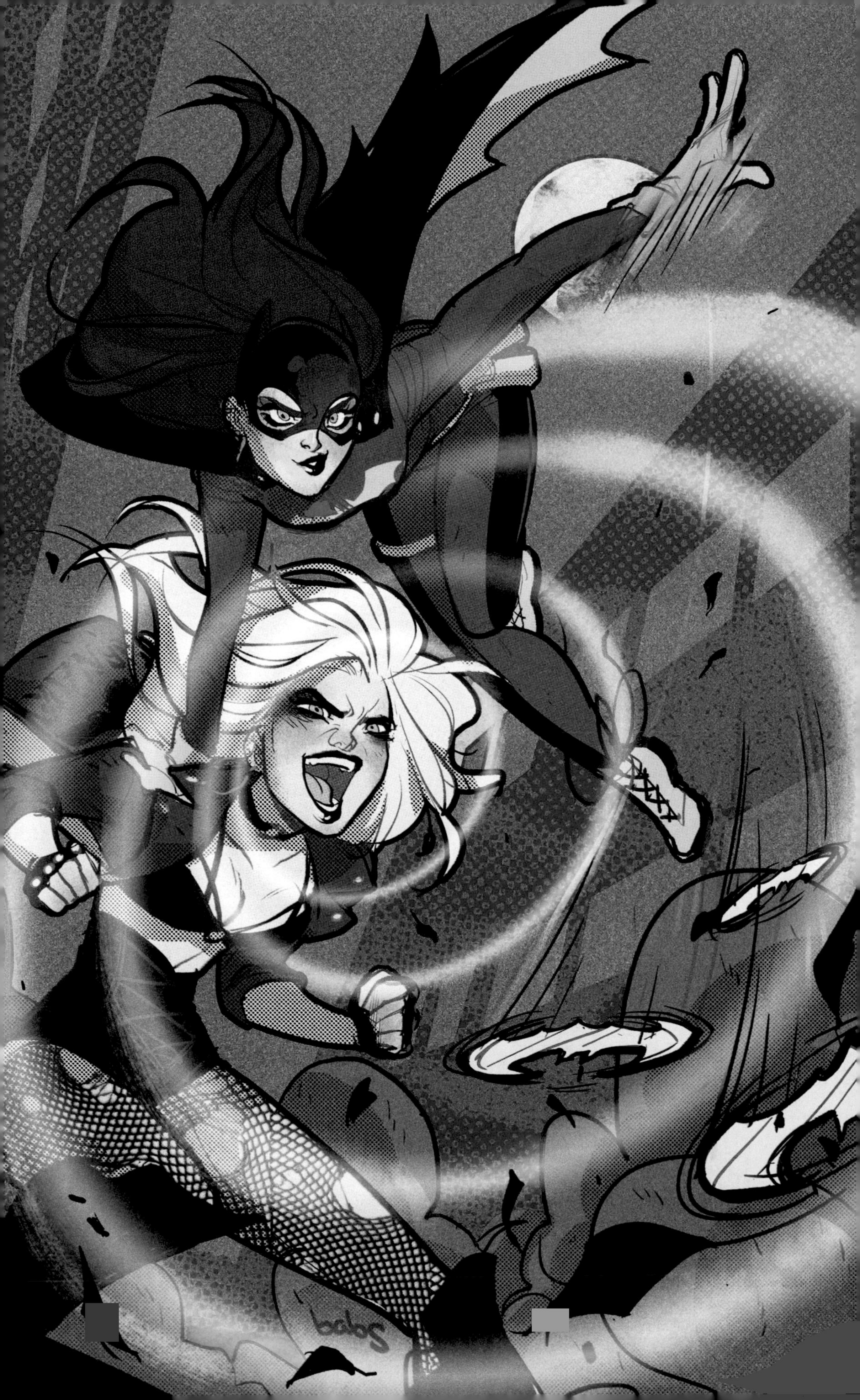
babs

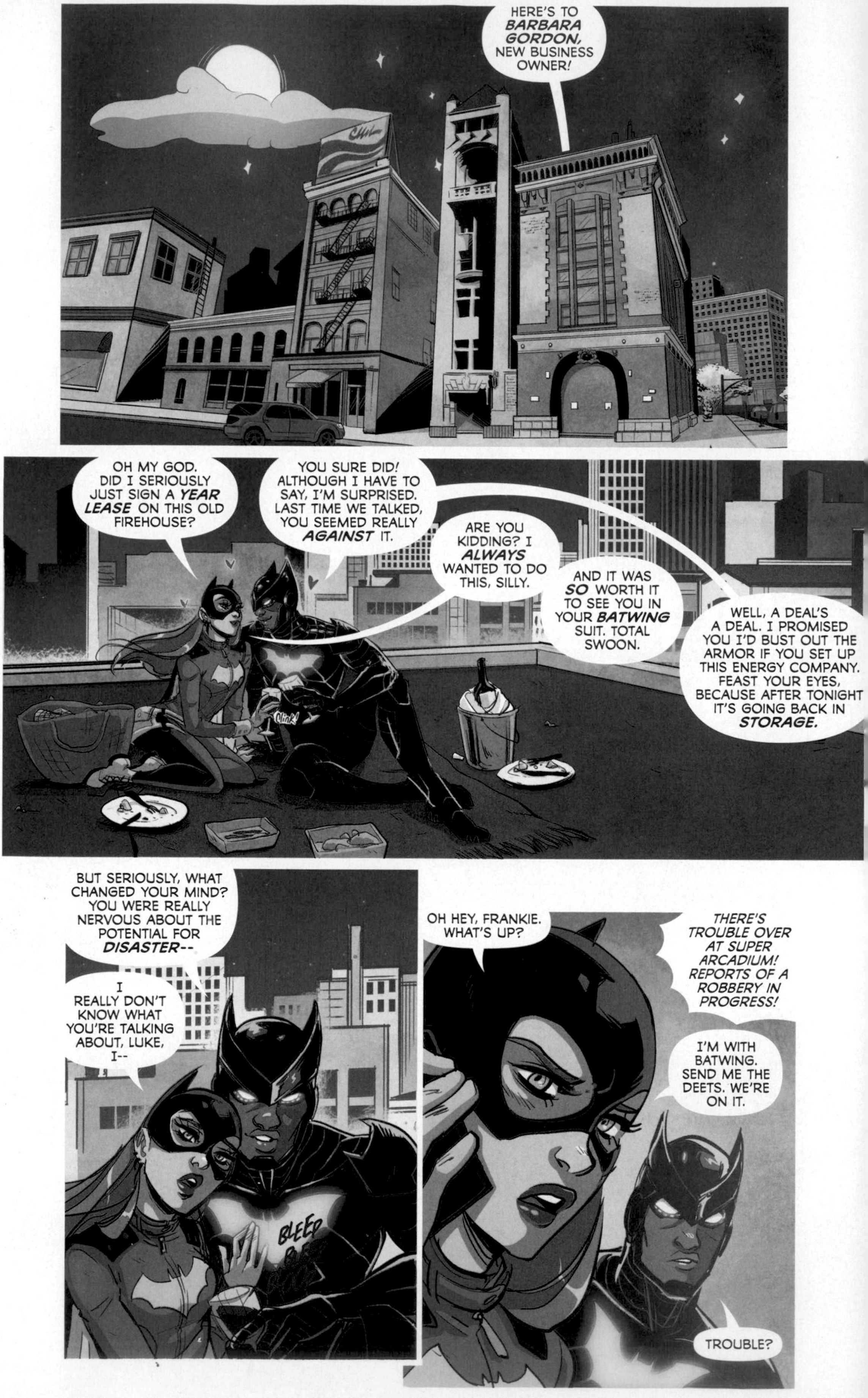
HERE'S TO BARBARA GORDON, NEW BUSINESS OWNER!
OH MY GOD. DID I SERIOUSLY JUST SIGN A YEAR LEASE ON THIS OLD FIREHOUSE?
YOU SURE DID! ALTHOUGH I HAVE TO SAY, I'M SURPRISED. LAST TIME WE TALKED, YOU SEEMED REALLY AGAINST IT.
ARE YOU KIDDING? I ALWAYS WANTED TO DO THIS, SILLY.
AND IT WAS SO WORTH IT TO SEE YOU IN YOUR BATWING SUIT. TOTAL SWOON.
WELL, A DEAL'S A DEAL. I PROMISED YOU I'D BUST OUT THE ARMOR IF YOU SET UP THIS ENERGY COMPANY. FEAST YOUR EYES, BECAUSE AFTER TONIGHT IT'S GOING BACK IN STORAGE.
CLINK
BUT SERIOUSLY, WHAT CHANGED YOUR MIND? YOU WERE REALLY NERVOUS ABOUT THE POTENTIAL FOR DISASTER--
I REALLY DON'T KNOW WHAT YOU'RE TALKING ABOUT, LUKE, I--
BLEEP
OH HEY, FRANKIE. WHAT'S UP?
THERE'S TROUBLE OVER AT SUPER ARCADIUM! REPORTS OF A ROBBERY IN PROGRESS!
I'M WITH BATWING. SEND ME THE DEETS. WE'RE ON IT.
TROUBLE?

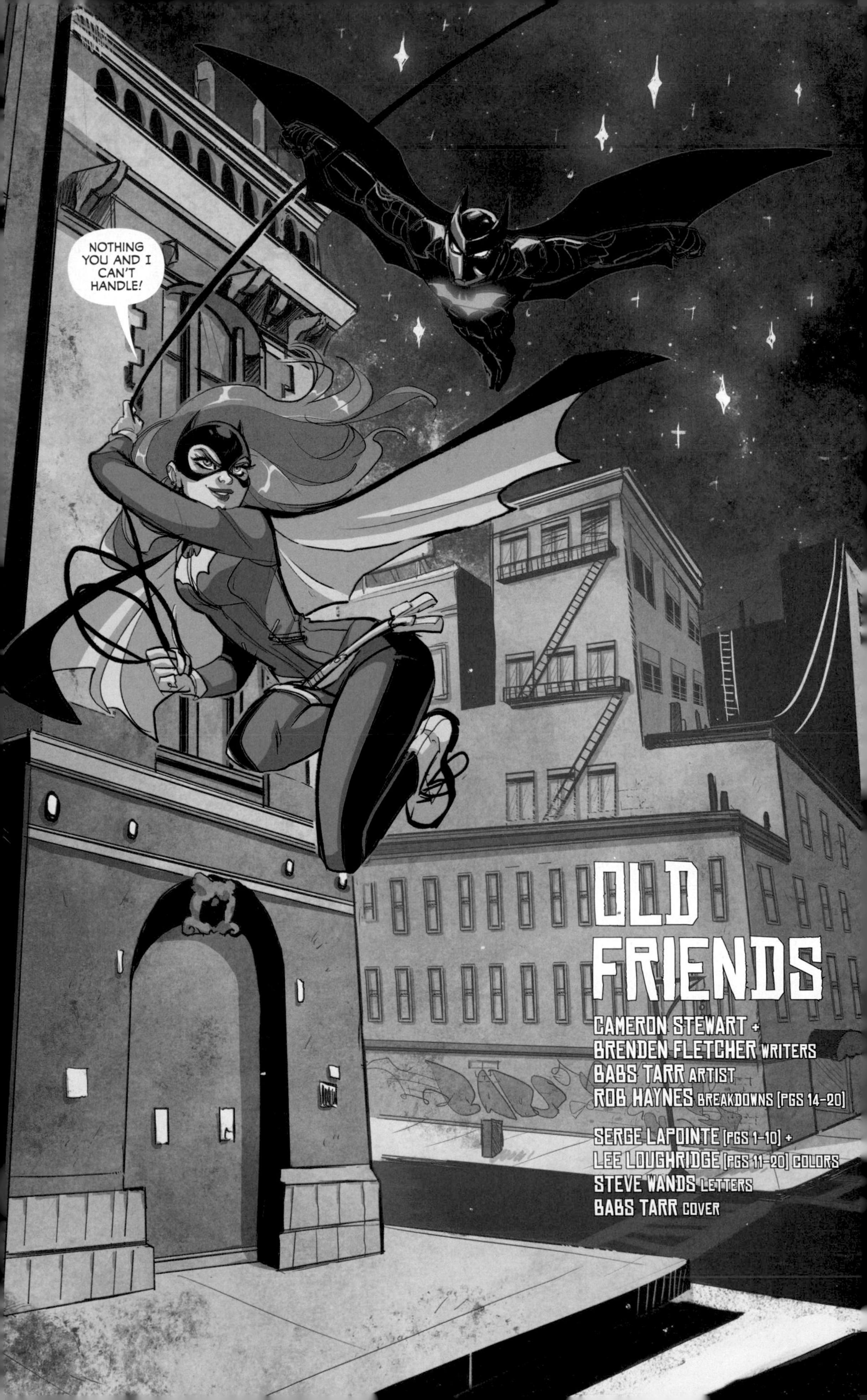

NOTHING YOU AND I CAN'T HANDLE!
OLD FRIENDS
CAMERON STEWART +
BRENDEN FLETCHER WRITERS
BABS TARR ARTIST
ROB HAYNES BREAKDOWNS [PGS 14-20]
SERGE LAPOINTE [PGS 1-10] +
LEE LOUGHRIDGE [PGS 11-20] COLORS
STEVE WANDS LETTERS
BABS TARR COVER

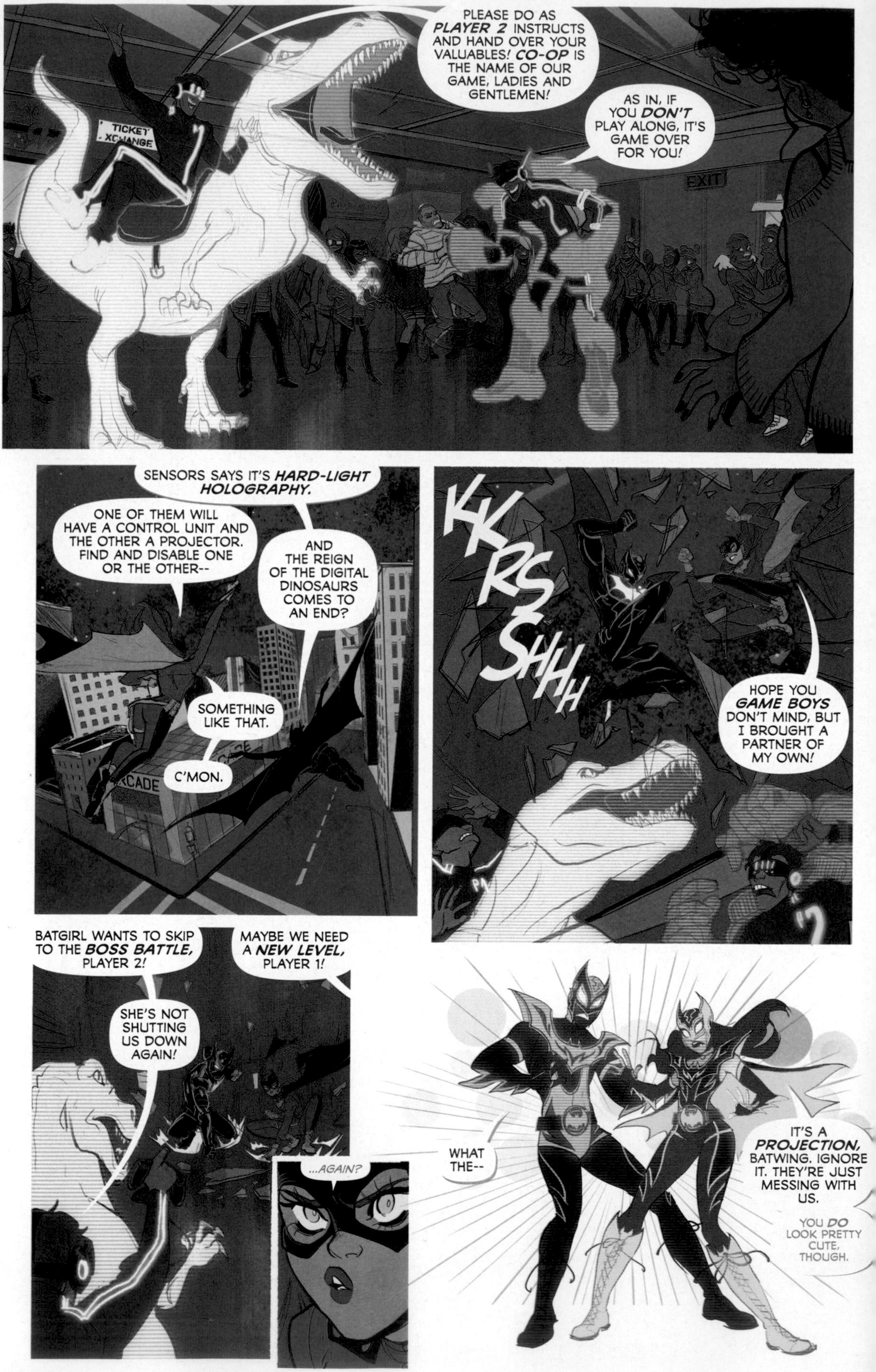
PLEASE DO AS PLAYER 2 INSTRUCTS AND HAND OVER YOUR VALUABLES! CO-OP IS THE NAME OF OUR GAME, LADIES AND GENTLEMEN!
AS IN, IF YOU DON'T PLAY ALONG, IT'S GAME OVER FOR YOU!
TICKET XCHANGE
EXIT
SENSORS SAYS IT'S HARD-LIGHT HOLOGRAPHY.
ONE OF THEM WILL HAVE A CONTROL UNIT AND THE OTHER A PROJECTOR. FIND AND DISABLE ONE OR THE OTHER--
AND THE REIGN OF THE DIGITAL DINOSAURS COMES TO AN END?
SOMETHING LIKE THAT.
C'MON.
KKRSSHHH
HOPE YOU GAME BOYS DON'T MIND, BUT I BROUGHT A PARTNER OF MY OWN!
BATGIRL WANTS TO SKIP TO THE BOSS BATTLE, PLAYER 2!
MAYBE WE NEED A NEW LEVEL, PLAYER 1!
SHE'S NOT SHUTTING US DOWN AGAIN!
...AGAIN?
WHAT THE--
IT'S A PROJECTION, BATWING. IGNORE IT. THEY'RE JUST MESSING WITH US.
YOU DO LOOK PRETTY CUTE, THOUGH.

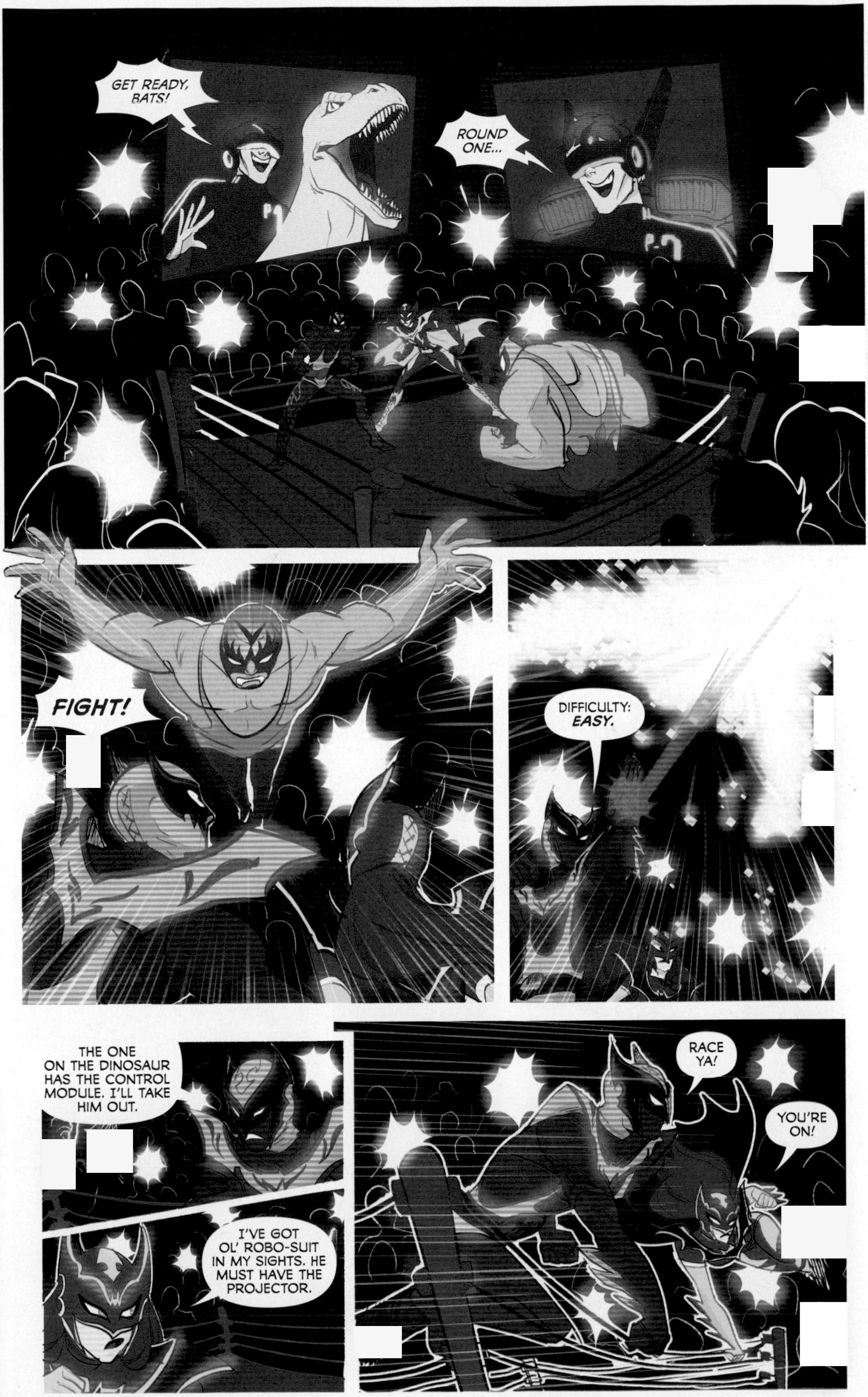
GET READY, BATS!
ROUND ONE...
FIGHT!
DIFFICULTY: EASY.
THE ONE ON THE DINOSAUR HAS THE CONTROL MODULE. I'LL TAKE HIM OUT.
I'VE GOT OL' ROBO-SUIT IN MY SIGHTS. HE MUST HAVE THE PROJECTOR.
RACE YA!
YOU'RE ON!

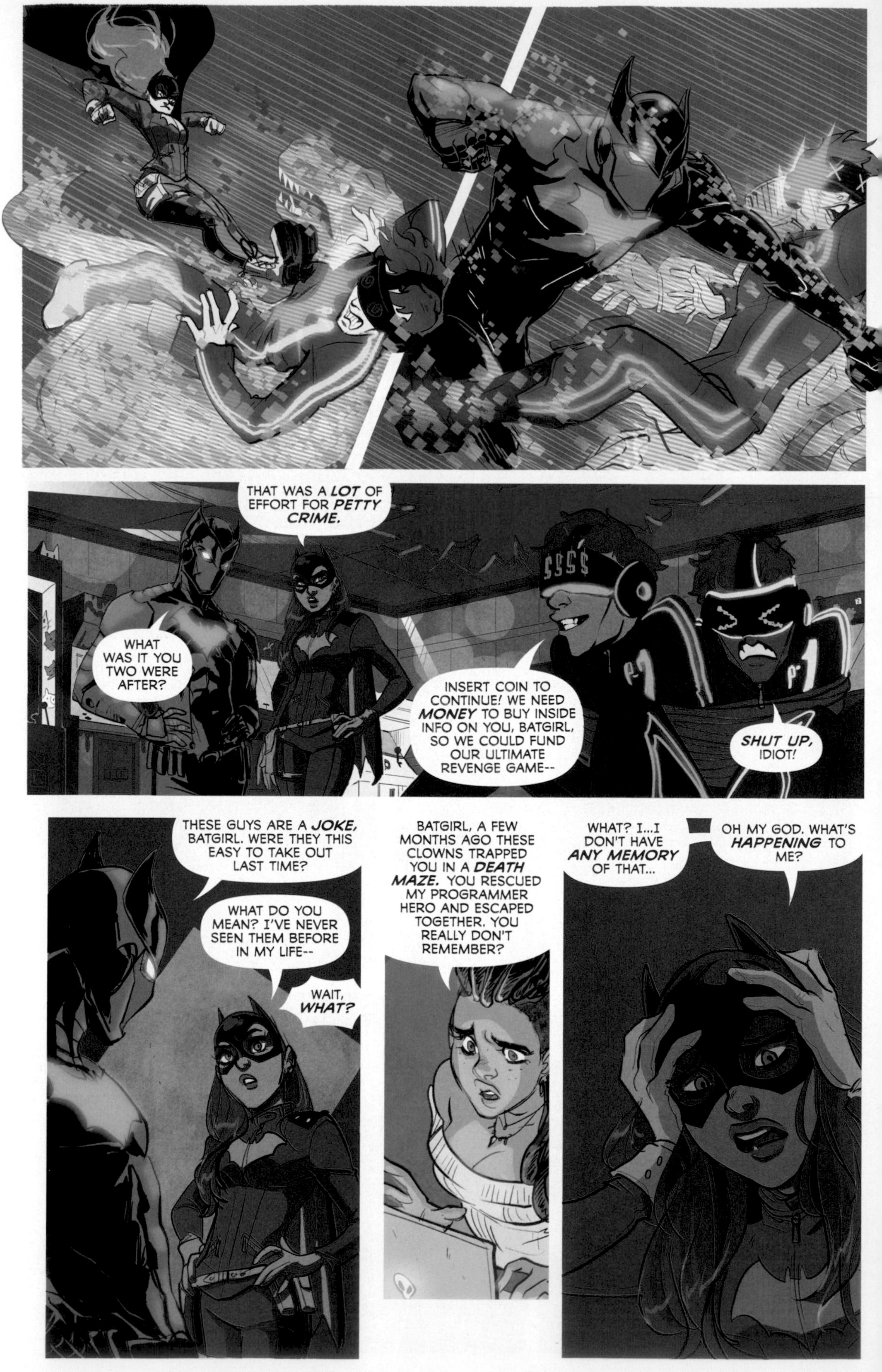

THAT WAS A LOT OF EFFORT FOR PETTY CRIME.
WHAT WAS IT YOU TWO WERE AFTER?
INSERT COIN TO CONTINUE! WE NEED MONEY TO BUY INSIDE INFO ON YOU, BATGIRL, SO WE COULD FUND OUR ULTIMATE REVENGE GAME--
SHUT UP, IDIOT!
THESE GUYS ARE A JOKE, BATGIRL. WERE THEY THIS EASY TO TAKE OUT LAST TIME?
WHAT DO YOU MEAN? I'VE NEVER SEEN THEM BEFORE IN MY LIFE--
WAIT, WHAT?
BATGIRL, A FEW MONTHS AGO THESE CLOWNS TRAPPED YOU IN A DEATH MAZE. YOU RESCUED MY PROGRAMMER HERO AND ESCAPED TOGETHER. YOU REALLY DON'T REMEMBER?
WHAT? I...I DON'T HAVE ANY MEMORY OF THAT...
OH MY GOD. WHAT'S HAPPENING TO ME?

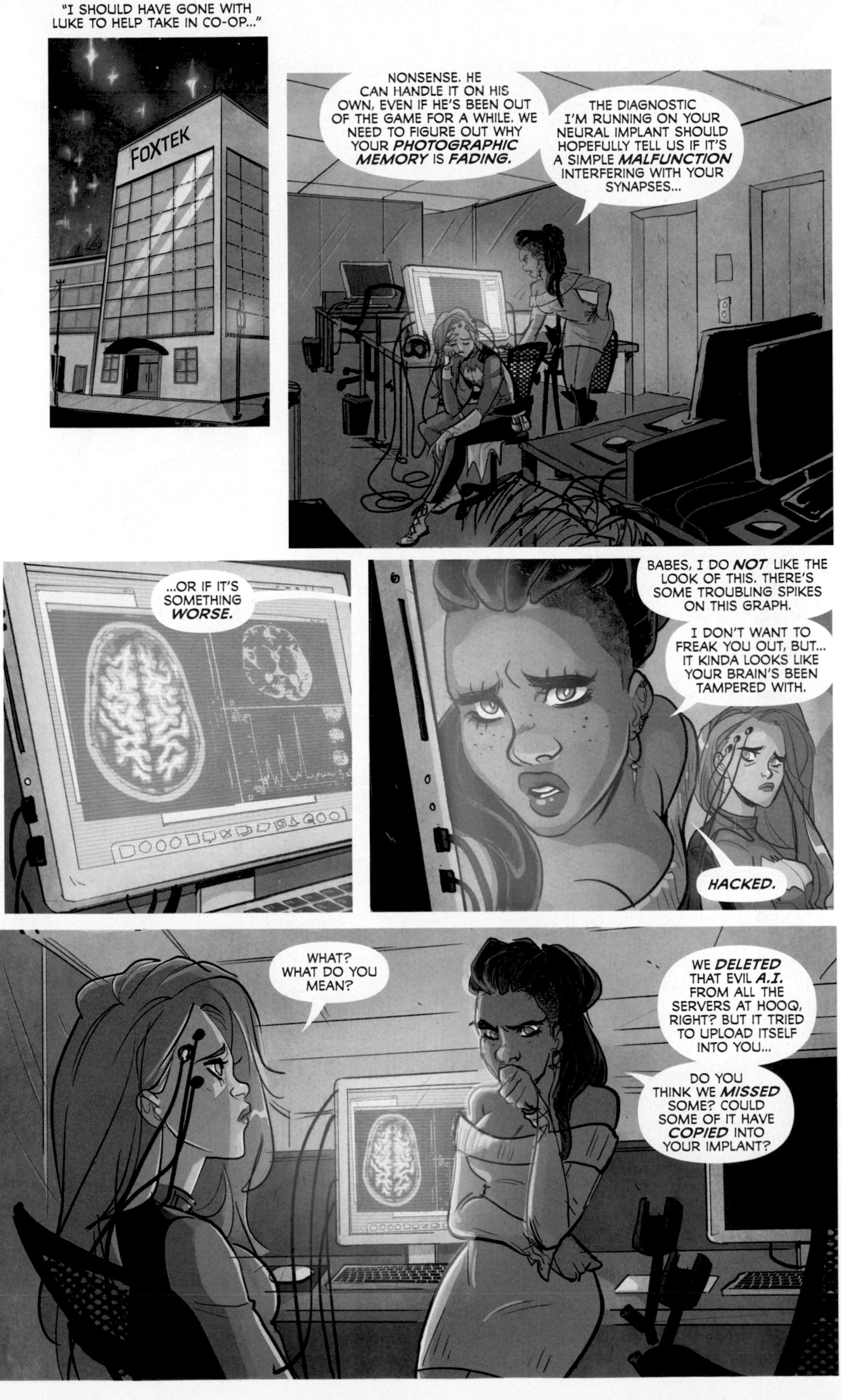
"I SHOULD HAVE GONE WITH LUKE TO HELP TAKE IN CO-OP..."
FOXTEK
NONSENSE. HE CAN HANDLE IT ON HIS OWN, EVEN IF HE'S BEEN OUT OF THE GAME FOR A WHILE. WE NEED TO FIGURE OUT WHY YOUR ***PHOTOGRAPHIC MEMORY*** IS ***FADING.***
THE DIAGNOSTIC I'M RUNNING ON YOUR NEURAL IMPLANT SHOULD HOPEFULLY TELL US IF IT'S A SIMPLE ***MALFUNCTION*** INTERFERING WITH YOUR SYNAPSES...
...OR IF IT'S SOMETHING ***WORSE.***
BABES, I DO ***NOT*** LIKE THE LOOK OF THIS. THERE'S SOME TROUBLING SPIKES ON THIS GRAPH.
I DON'T WANT TO FREAK YOU OUT, BUT... IT KINDA LOOKS LIKE YOUR BRAIN'S BEEN TAMPERED WITH.
HACKED.
WHAT? WHAT DO YOU MEAN?
WE ***DELETED*** THAT EVIL ***A.I.*** FROM ALL THE SERVERS AT HOOQ, RIGHT? BUT IT TRIED TO UPLOAD ITSELF INTO YOU...
DO YOU THINK WE ***MISSED*** SOME? COULD SOME OF IT HAVE ***COPIED*** INTO YOUR IMPLANT?

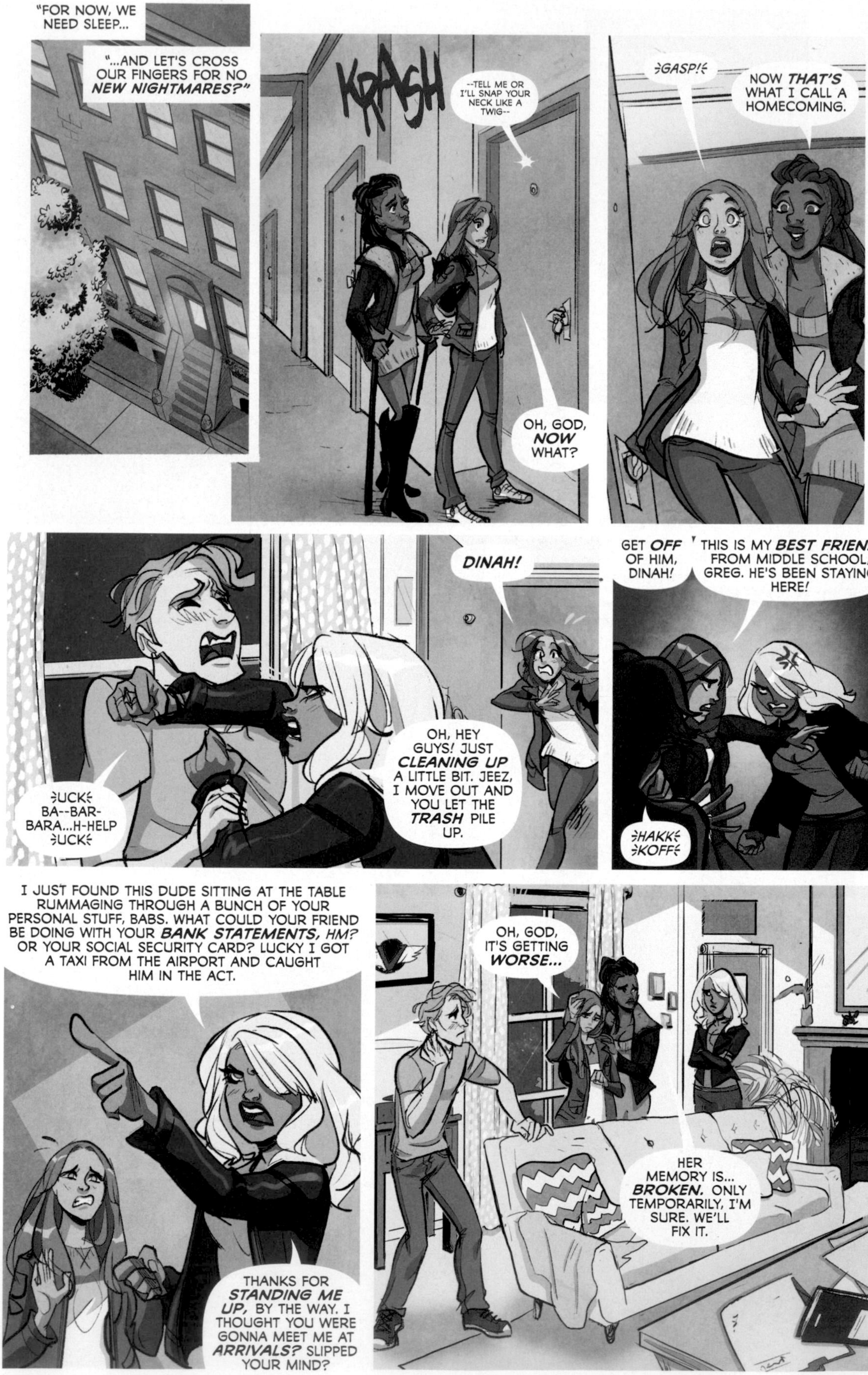
"FOR NOW, WE NEED SLEEP...
"...AND LET'S CROSS OUR FINGERS FOR NO NEW NIGHTMARES?"
KRASH
--TELL ME OR I'LL SNAP YOUR NECK LIKE A TWIG--
OH, GOD, NOW WHAT?
GASP!
NOW THAT'S WHAT I CALL A HOMECOMING.
UCK BA--BAR-BARA...H-HELP UCK
OH, HEY GUYS! JUST CLEANING UP A LITTLE BIT. JEEZ, I MOVE OUT AND YOU LET THE TRASH PILE UP.
DINAH!
GET OFF OF HIM, DINAH!
THIS IS MY BEST FRIEND FROM MIDDLE SCHOOL, GREG. HE'S BEEN STAYING HERE!
HAKK KOFF
I JUST FOUND THIS DUDE SITTING AT THE TABLE RUMMAGING THROUGH A BUNCH OF YOUR PERSONAL STUFF, BABS. WHAT COULD YOUR FRIEND BE DOING WITH YOUR BANK STATEMENTS, HM? OR YOUR SOCIAL SECURITY CARD? LUCKY I GOT A TAXI FROM THE AIRPORT AND CAUGHT HIM IN THE ACT.
THANKS FOR STANDING ME UP, BY THE WAY. I THOUGHT YOU WERE GONNA MEET ME AT ARRIVALS? SLIPPED YOUR MIND?
OH, GOD, IT'S GETTING WORSE...
HER MEMORY IS... BROKEN. ONLY TEMPORARILY, I'M SURE. WE'LL FIX IT.

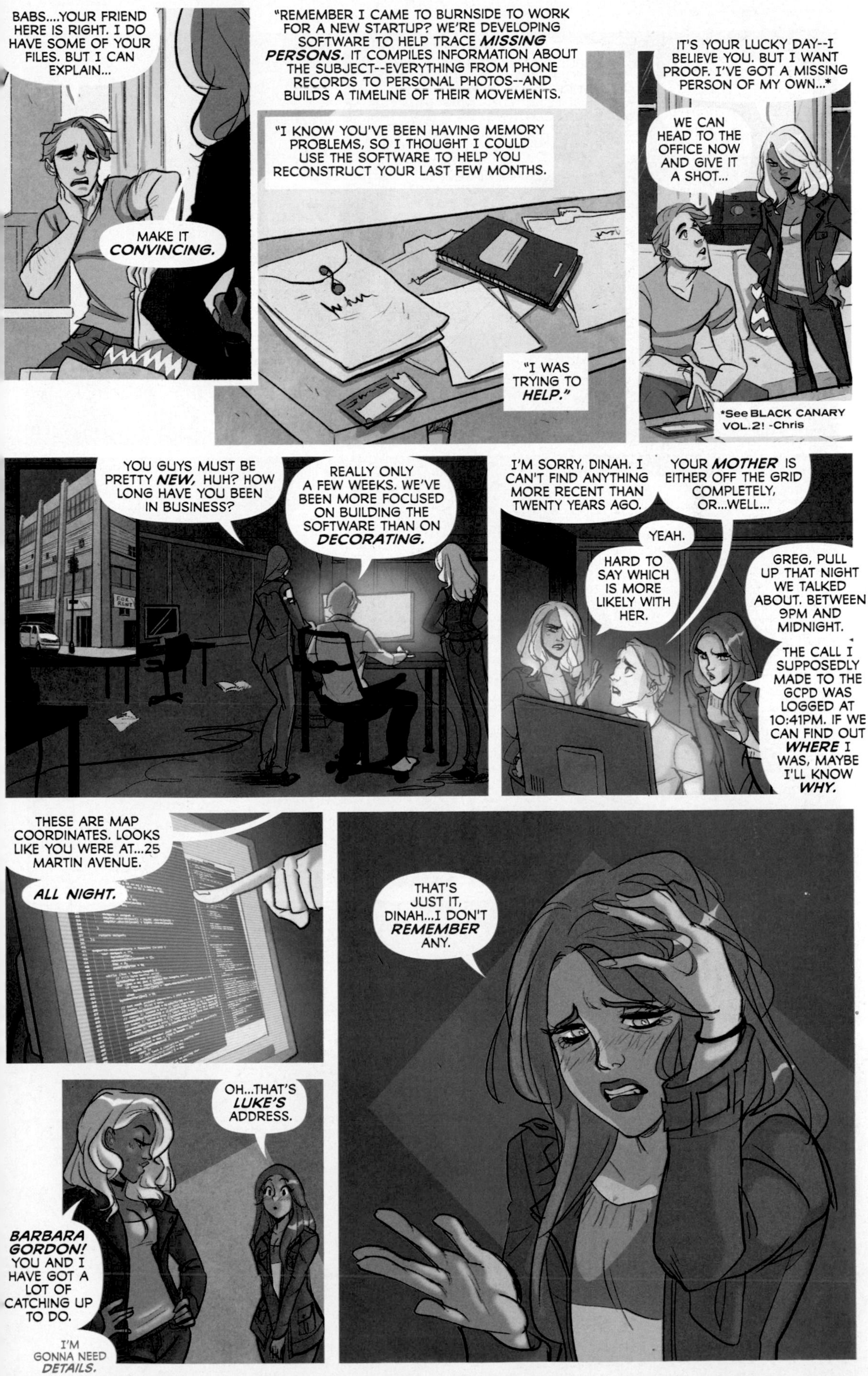
BABS....YOUR FRIEND HERE IS RIGHT. I DO HAVE SOME OF YOUR FILES. BUT I CAN EXPLAIN...
MAKE IT CONVINCING.
"REMEMBER I CAME TO BURNSIDE TO WORK FOR A NEW STARTUP? WE'RE DEVELOPING SOFTWARE TO HELP TRACE MISSING PERSONS. IT COMPILES INFORMATION ABOUT THE SUBJECT--EVERYTHING FROM PHONE RECORDS TO PERSONAL PHOTOS--AND BUILDS A TIMELINE OF THEIR MOVEMENTS.
"I KNOW YOU'VE BEEN HAVING MEMORY PROBLEMS, SO I THOUGHT I COULD USE THE SOFTWARE TO HELP YOU RECONSTRUCT YOUR LAST FEW MONTHS.
"I WAS TRYING TO HELP."
IT'S YOUR LUCKY DAY--I BELIEVE YOU. BUT I WANT PROOF. I'VE GOT A MISSING PERSON OF MY OWN...*
WE CAN HEAD TO THE OFFICE NOW AND GIVE IT A SHOT...
*See BLACK CANARY VOL.2! -Chris
YOU GUYS MUST BE PRETTY NEW, HUH? HOW LONG HAVE YOU BEEN IN BUSINESS?
REALLY ONLY A FEW WEEKS. WE'VE BEEN MORE FOCUSED ON BUILDING THE SOFTWARE THAN ON DECORATING.
FOR RENT
I'M SORRY, DINAH. I CAN'T FIND ANYTHING MORE RECENT THAN TWENTY YEARS AGO.
YOUR MOTHER IS EITHER OFF THE GRID COMPLETELY, OR...WELL...
YEAH.
HARD TO SAY WHICH IS MORE LIKELY WITH HER.
GREG, PULL UP THAT NIGHT WE TALKED ABOUT. BETWEEN 9PM AND MIDNIGHT.
THE CALL I SUPPOSEDLY MADE TO THE GCPD WAS LOGGED AT 10:41PM. IF WE CAN FIND OUT WHERE I WAS, MAYBE I'LL KNOW WHY.
THESE ARE MAP COORDINATES. LOOKS LIKE YOU WERE AT...25 MARTIN AVENUE.
ALL NIGHT.
THAT'S JUST IT, DINAH...I DON'T REMEMBER ANY.
OH...THAT'S LUKE'S ADDRESS.
BARBARA GORDON! YOU AND I HAVE GOT A LOT OF CATCHING UP TO DO.
I'M GONNA NEED DETAILS.

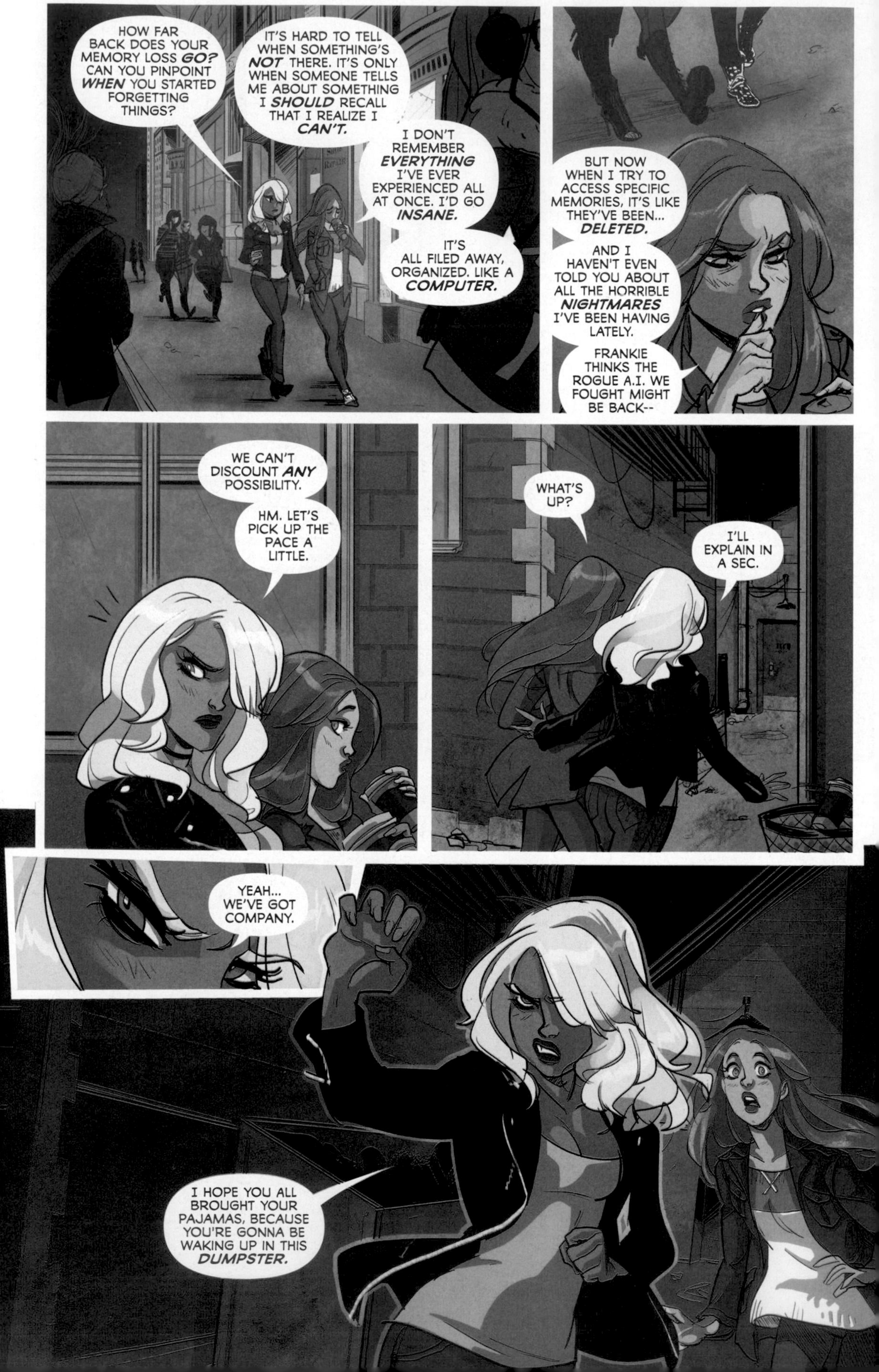
HOW FAR BACK DOES YOUR MEMORY LOSS GO? CAN YOU PINPOINT WHEN YOU STARTED FORGETTING THINGS?
IT'S HARD TO TELL WHEN SOMETHING'S NOT THERE. IT'S ONLY WHEN SOMEONE TELLS ME ABOUT SOMETHING I SHOULD RECALL THAT I REALIZE I CAN'T.
I DON'T REMEMBER EVERYTHING I'VE EVER EXPERIENCED ALL AT ONCE. I'D GO INSANE.
IT'S ALL FILED AWAY, ORGANIZED. LIKE A COMPUTER.
BUT NOW WHEN I TRY TO ACCESS SPECIFIC MEMORIES, IT'S LIKE THEY'VE BEEN... DELETED.
AND I HAVEN'T EVEN TOLD YOU ABOUT ALL THE HORRIBLE NIGHTMARES I'VE BEEN HAVING LATELY.
FRANKIE THINKS THE ROGUE A.I. WE FOUGHT MIGHT BE BACK--
WE CAN'T DISCOUNT ANY POSSIBILITY.
HM. LET'S PICK UP THE PACE A LITTLE.
WHAT'S UP?
I'LL EXPLAIN IN A SEC.
YEAH... WE'VE GOT COMPANY.
I HOPE YOU ALL BROUGHT YOUR PAJAMAS, BECAUSE YOU'RE GONNA BE WAKING UP IN THIS DUMPSTER.

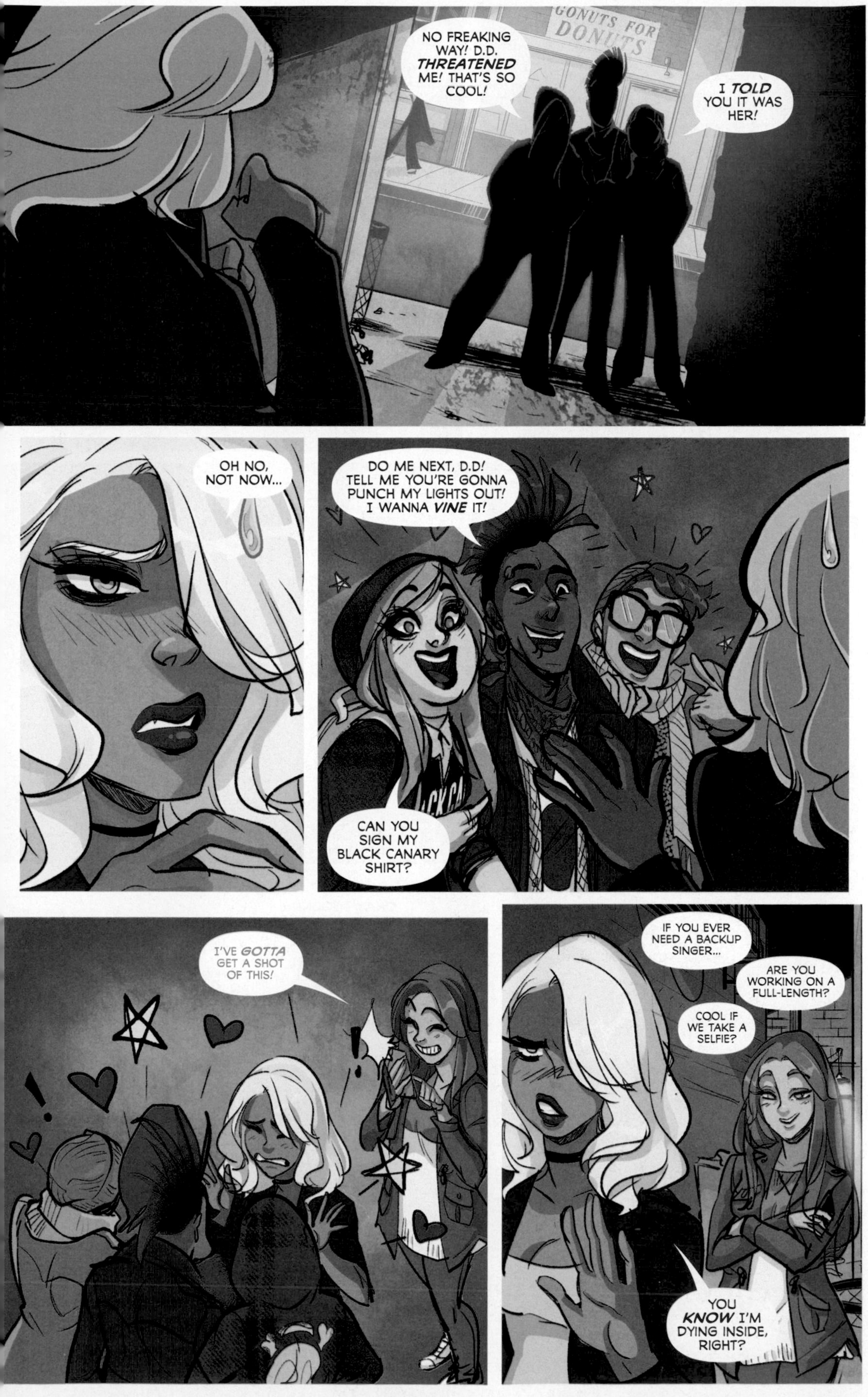
GONUTS FOR DONUTS
NO FREAKING WAY! D.D. THREATENED ME! THAT'S SO COOL!
I TOLD YOU IT WAS HER!
OH NO, NOT NOW...
DO ME NEXT, D.D! TELL ME YOU'RE GONNA PUNCH MY LIGHTS OUT! I WANNA VINE IT!
CAN YOU SIGN MY BLACK CANARY SHIRT?
I'VE GOTTA GET A SHOT OF THIS!
IF YOU EVER NEED A BACKUP SINGER...
ARE YOU WORKING ON A FULL-LENGTH?
COOL IF WE TAKE A SELFIE?
YOU KNOW I'M DYING INSIDE, RIGHT?

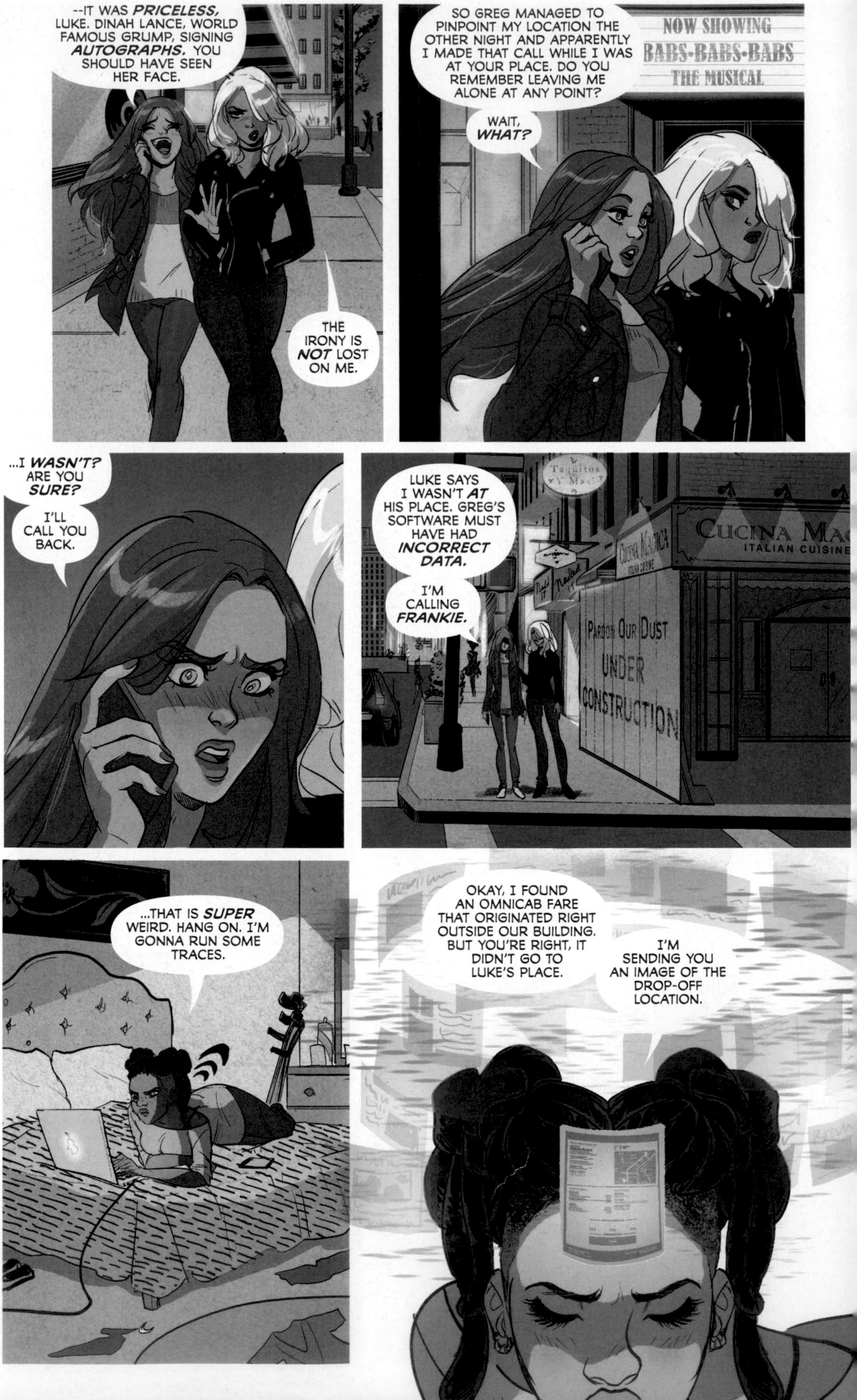
--IT WAS PRICELESS, LUKE. DINAH LANCE, WORLD FAMOUS GRUMP, SIGNING AUTOGRAPHS. YOU SHOULD HAVE SEEN HER FACE.
THE IRONY IS NOT LOST ON ME.
NOW SHOWING
BABS-BABS-BABS
THE MUSICAL
SO GREG MANAGED TO PINPOINT MY LOCATION THE OTHER NIGHT AND APPARENTLY I MADE THAT CALL WHILE I WAS AT YOUR PLACE. DO YOU REMEMBER LEAVING ME ALONE AT ANY POINT?
WAIT, WHAT?
...I WASN'T? ARE YOU SURE?
I'LL CALL YOU BACK.
CUCINA MAG
ITALIAN CUISINE
PARDON OUR DUST
UNDER CONSTRUCTION
LUKE SAYS I WASN'T AT HIS PLACE. GREG'S SOFTWARE MUST HAVE HAD INCORRECT DATA.
I'M CALLING FRANKIE.
...THAT IS SUPER WEIRD. HANG ON. I'M GONNA RUN SOME TRACES.
OKAY, I FOUND AN OMNICAB FARE THAT ORIGINATED RIGHT OUTSIDE OUR BUILDING. BUT YOU'RE RIGHT, IT DIDN'T GO TO LUKE'S PLACE.
I'M SENDING YOU AN IMAGE OF THE DROP-OFF LOCATION.

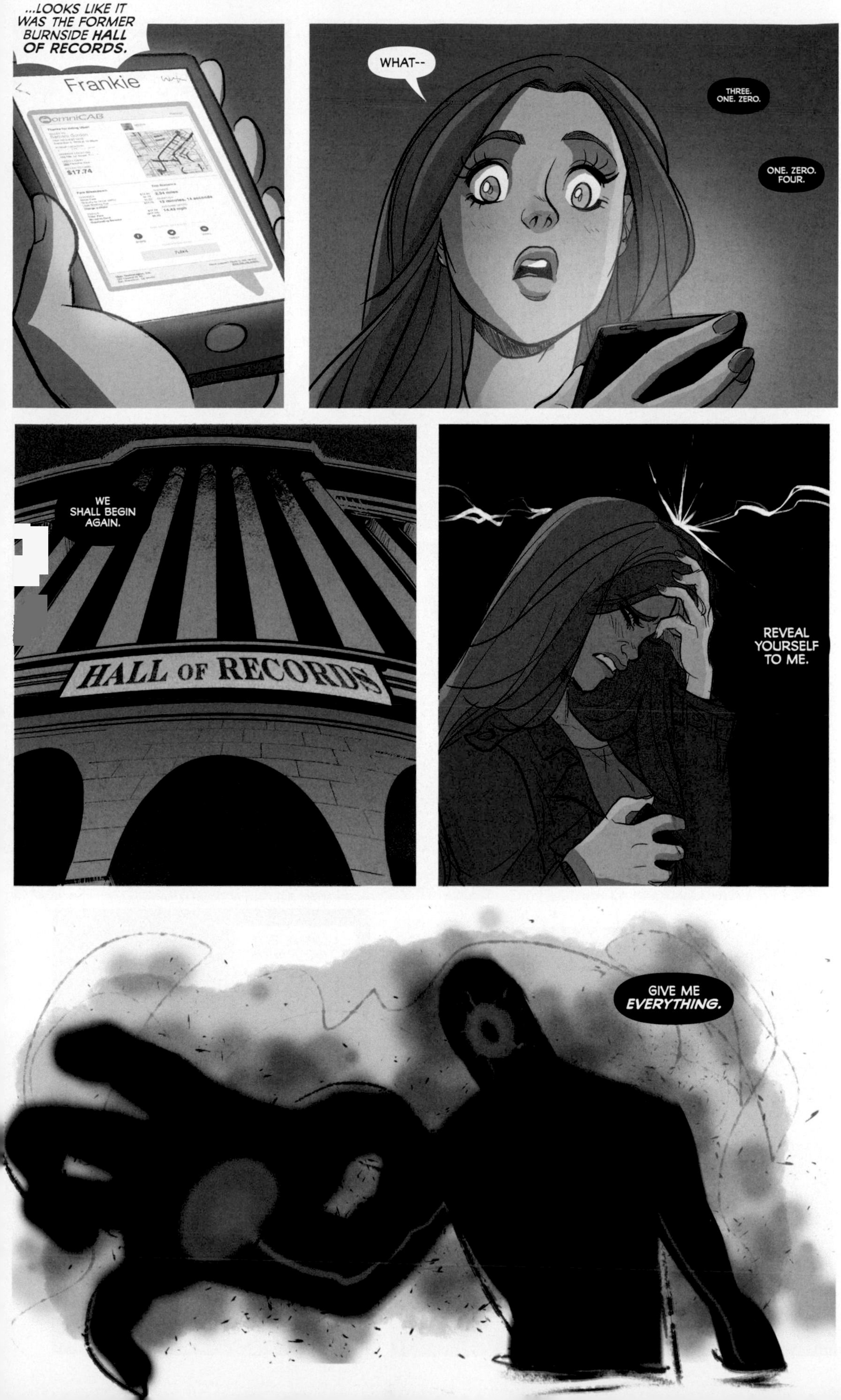
...LOOKS LIKE IT WAS THE FORMER BURNSIDE HALL OF RECORDS.
Frankie
omniCAB
$17.74
WHAT--
THREE. ONE. ZERO.
ONE. ZERO. FOUR.
WE SHALL BEGIN AGAIN.
HALL OF RECORDS
REVEAL YOURSELF TO ME.
GIVE ME EVERYTHING.

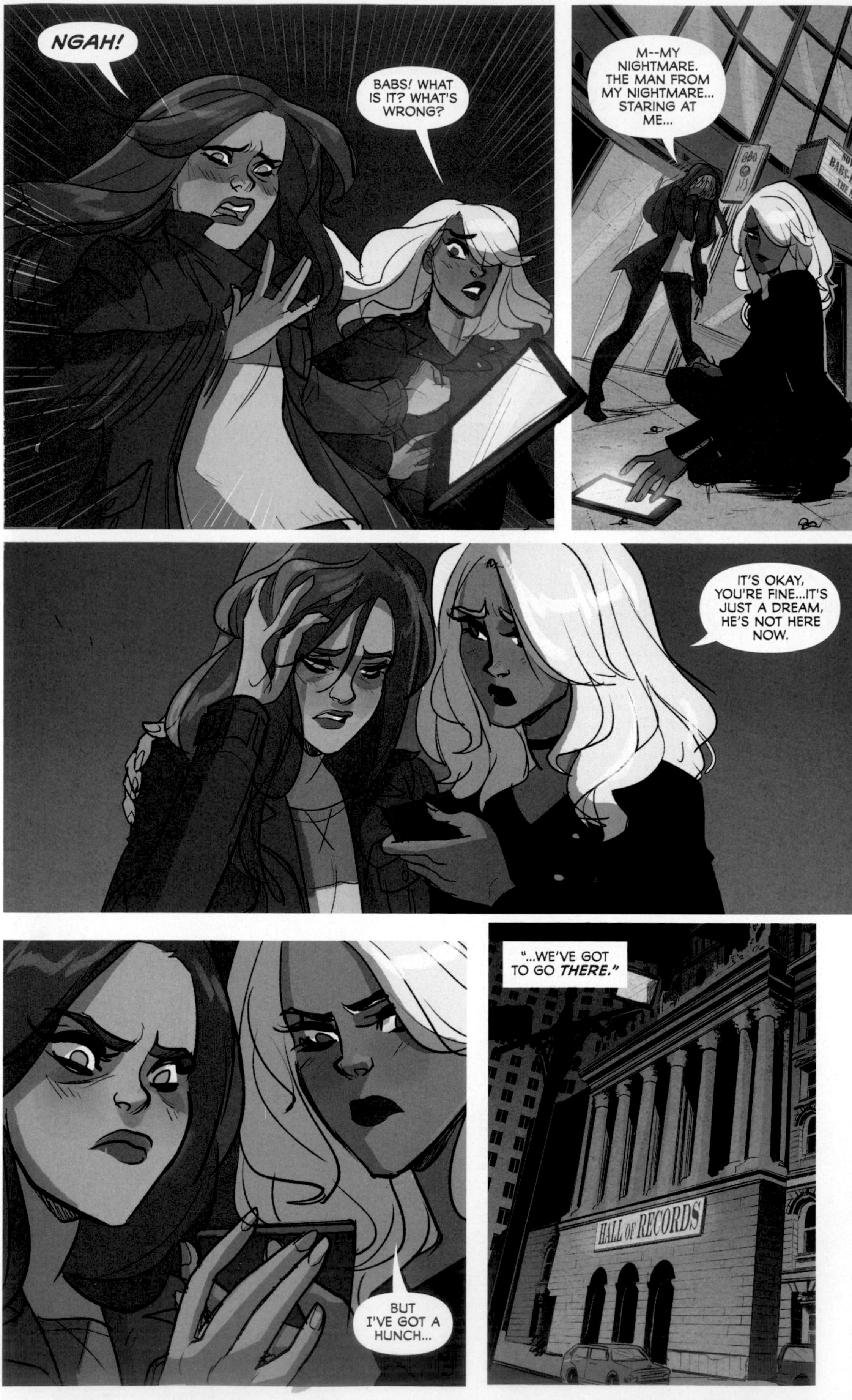
NGAH!
BABS! WHAT IS IT? WHAT'S WRONG?
M--MY NIGHTMARE. THE MAN FROM MY NIGHTMARE... STARING AT ME...
IT'S OKAY, YOU'RE FINE...IT'S JUST A DREAM, HE'S NOT HERE NOW.
BUT I'VE GOT A HUNCH...
"...WE'VE GOT TO GO *THERE.*"
HALL OF RECORDS

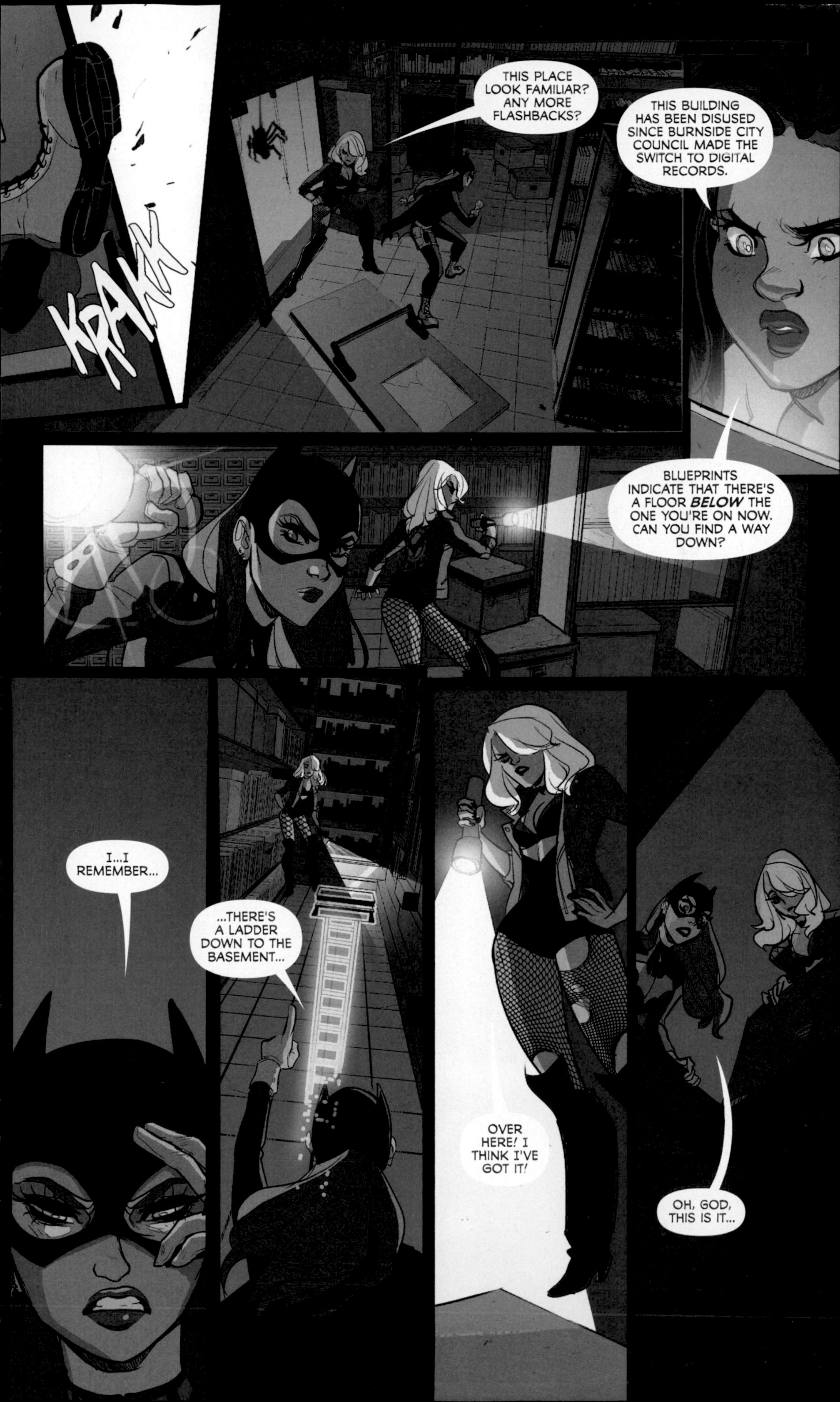
KRAKK
THIS PLACE LOOK FAMILIAR? ANY MORE FLASHBACKS?
THIS BUILDING HAS BEEN DISUSED SINCE BURNSIDE CITY COUNCIL MADE THE SWITCH TO DIGITAL RECORDS.
BLUEPRINTS INDICATE THAT THERE'S A FLOOR *BELOW* THE ONE YOU'RE ON NOW. CAN YOU FIND A WAY DOWN?
I...I REMEMBER...
...THERE'S A LADDER DOWN TO THE BASEMENT...
OVER HERE! I THINK I'VE GOT IT!
OH, GOD, THIS IS IT...

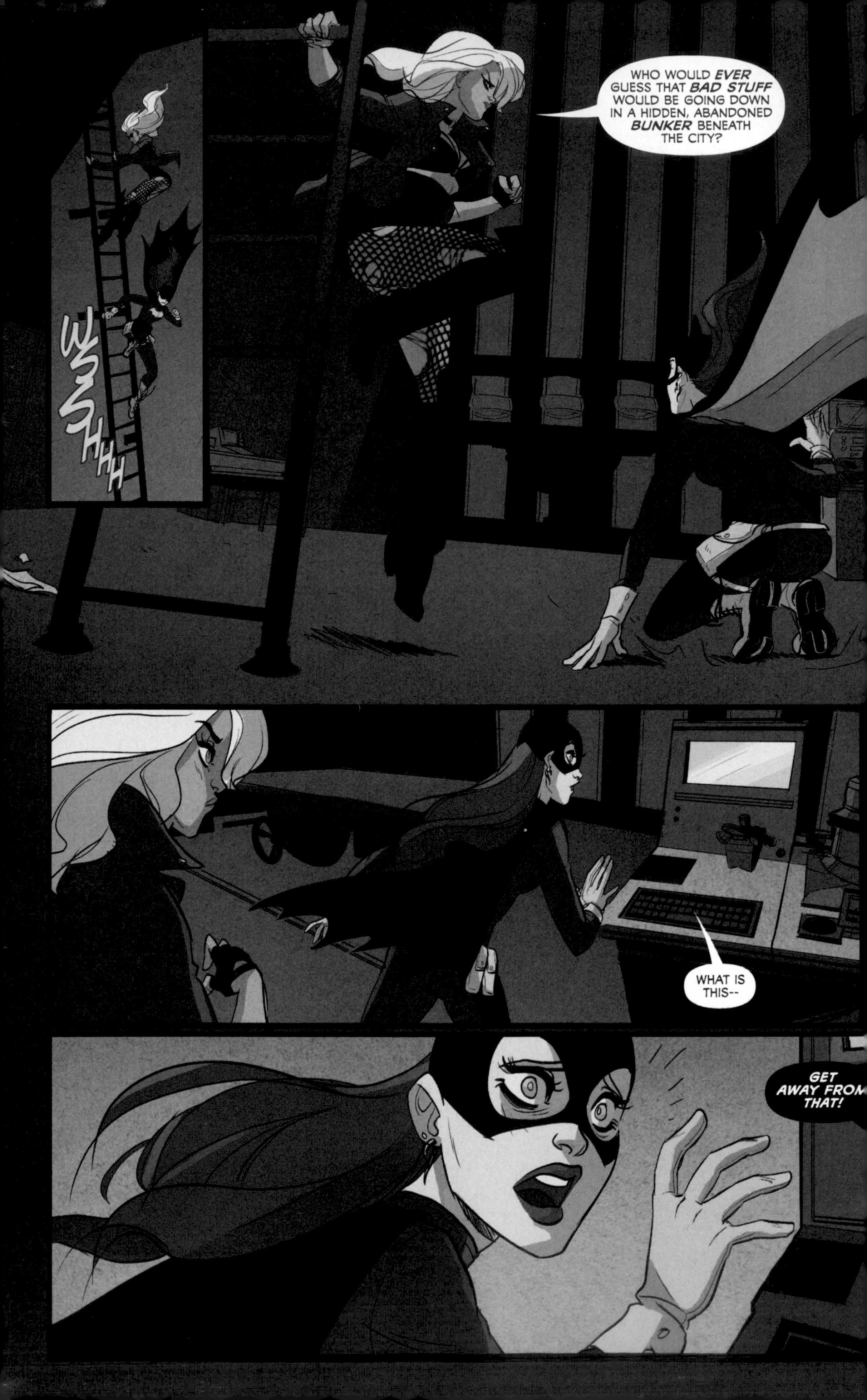
WSSHHHH
WHO WOULD EVER GUESS THAT BAD STUFF WOULD BE GOING DOWN IN A HIDDEN, ABANDONED BUNKER BENEATH THE CITY?
WHAT IS THIS--
GET AWAY FROM THAT!

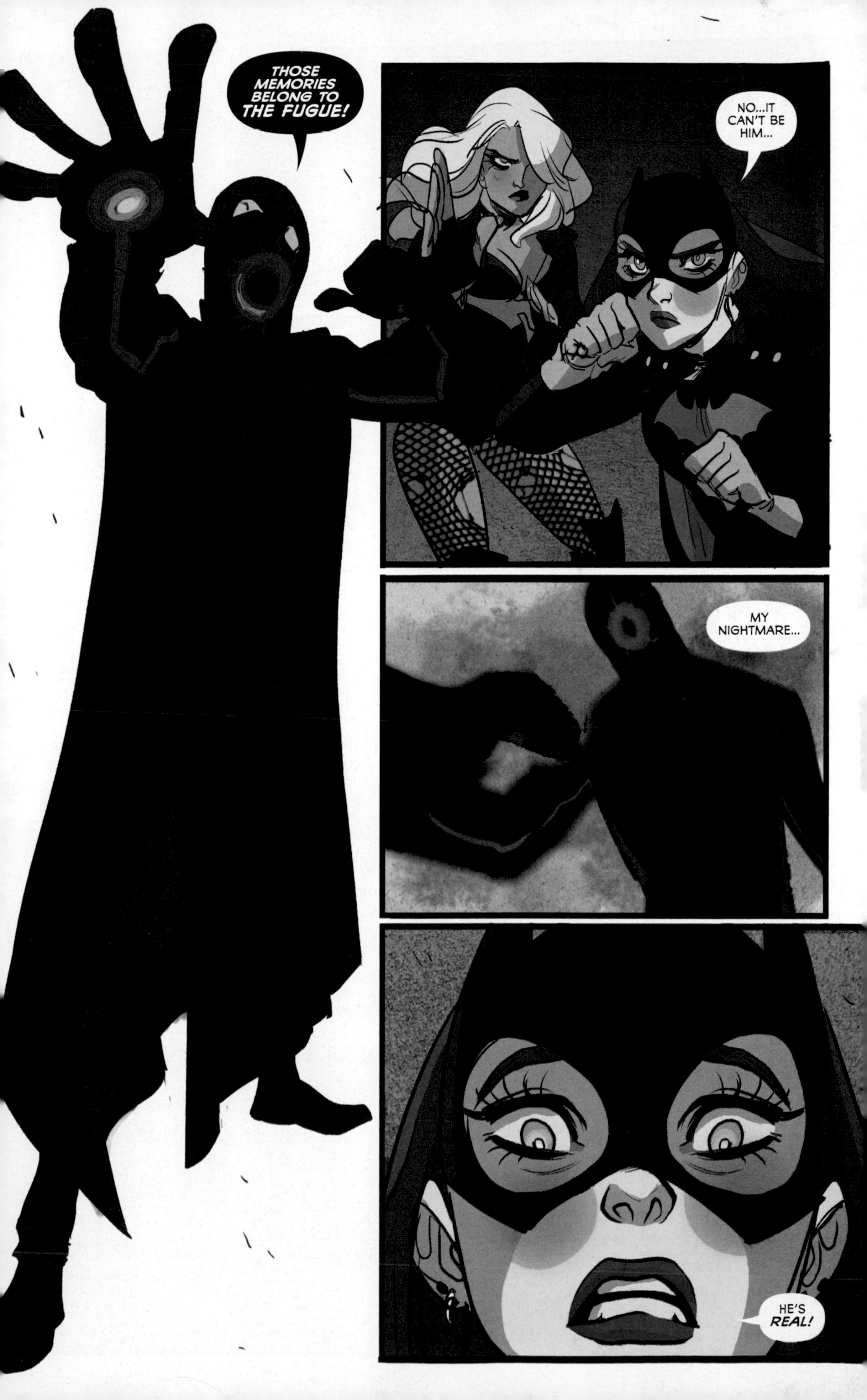
THOSE MEMORIES BELONG TO THE FUGUE!
NO...IT CAN'T BE HIM...
MY NIGHTMARE...
HE'S REAL!

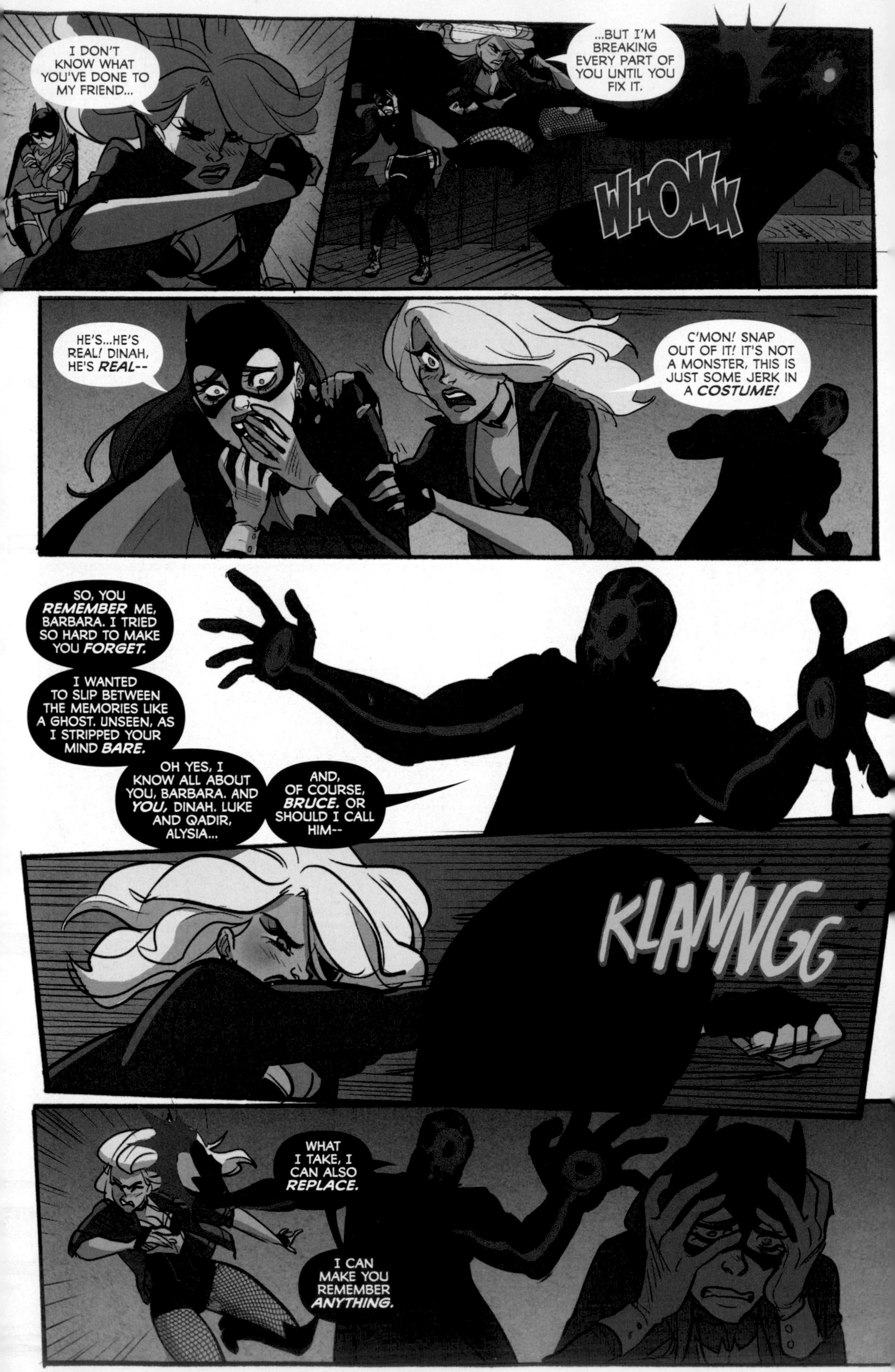
I DON'T KNOW WHAT YOU'VE DONE TO MY FRIEND...
...BUT I'M BREAKING EVERY PART OF YOU UNTIL YOU FIX IT.
WHOKK
HE'S...HE'S REAL! DINAH, HE'S REAL--
C'MON! SNAP OUT OF IT! IT'S NOT A MONSTER, THIS IS JUST SOME JERK IN A COSTUME!
SO, YOU REMEMBER ME, BARBARA. I TRIED SO HARD TO MAKE YOU FORGET.
I WANTED TO SLIP BETWEEN THE MEMORIES LIKE A GHOST. UNSEEN, AS I STRIPPED YOUR MIND BARE.
OH YES, I KNOW ALL ABOUT YOU, BARBARA. AND YOU, DINAH. LUKE AND QADIR, ALYSIA...
AND, OF COURSE, BRUCE. OR SHOULD I CALL HIM--
KLANNGG
WHAT I TAKE, I CAN ALSO REPLACE.
I CAN MAKE YOU REMEMBER ANYTHING.

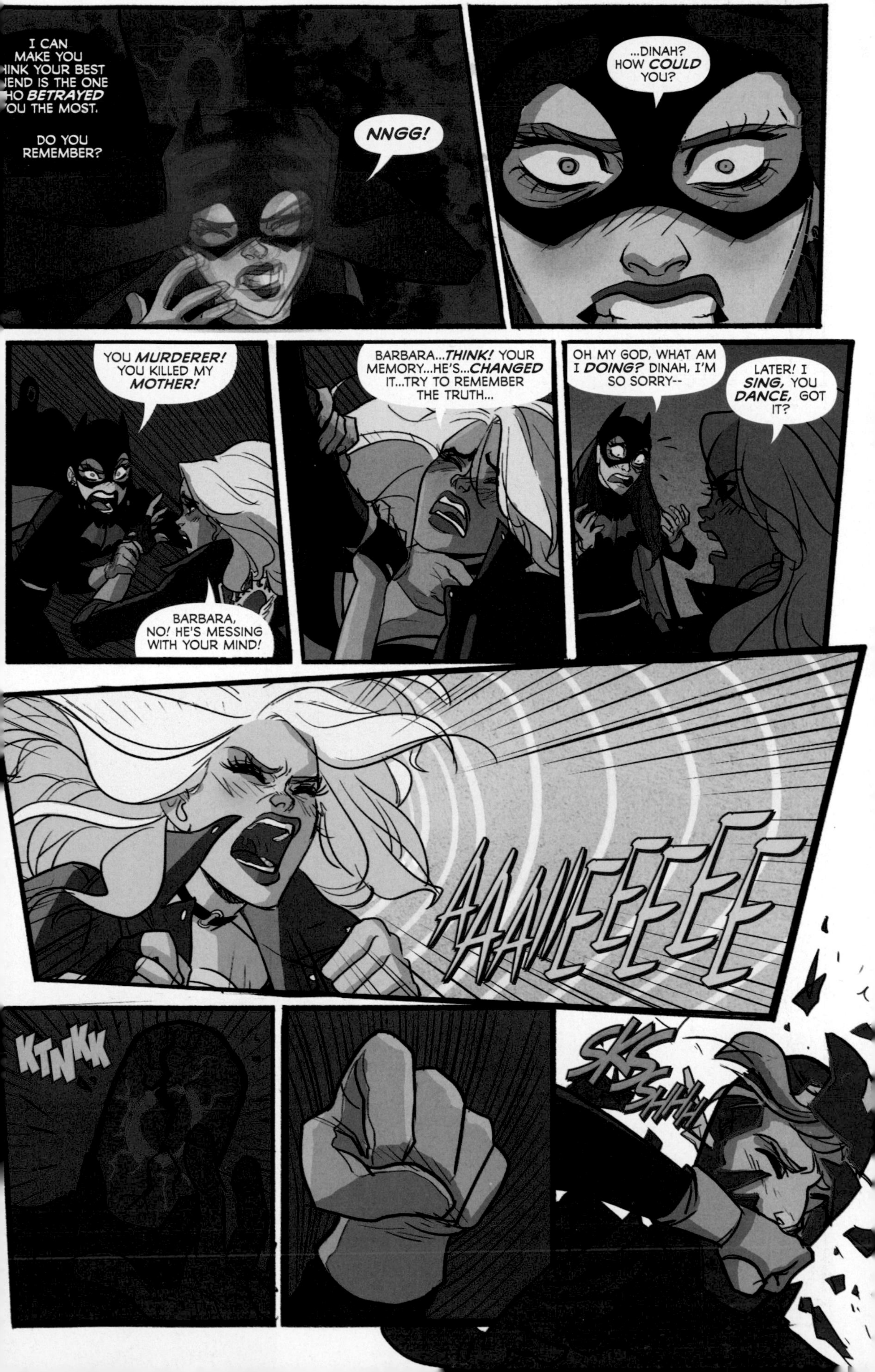

I CAN MAKE YOU HINK YOUR BEST IEND IS THE ONE HO BETRAYED OU THE MOST.
DO YOU REMEMBER?
NNGG!
...DINAH? HOW COULD YOU?
YOU MURDERER! YOU KILLED MY MOTHER!
BARBARA, NO! HE'S MESSING WITH YOUR MIND!
BARBARA...THINK! YOUR MEMORY...HE'S...CHANGED IT...TRY TO REMEMBER THE TRUTH...
OH MY GOD, WHAT AM I DOING? DINAH, I'M SO SORRY--
LATER! I SING, YOU DANCE, GOT IT?
AAAIEEEEE
KTNKK
SKSSHHH

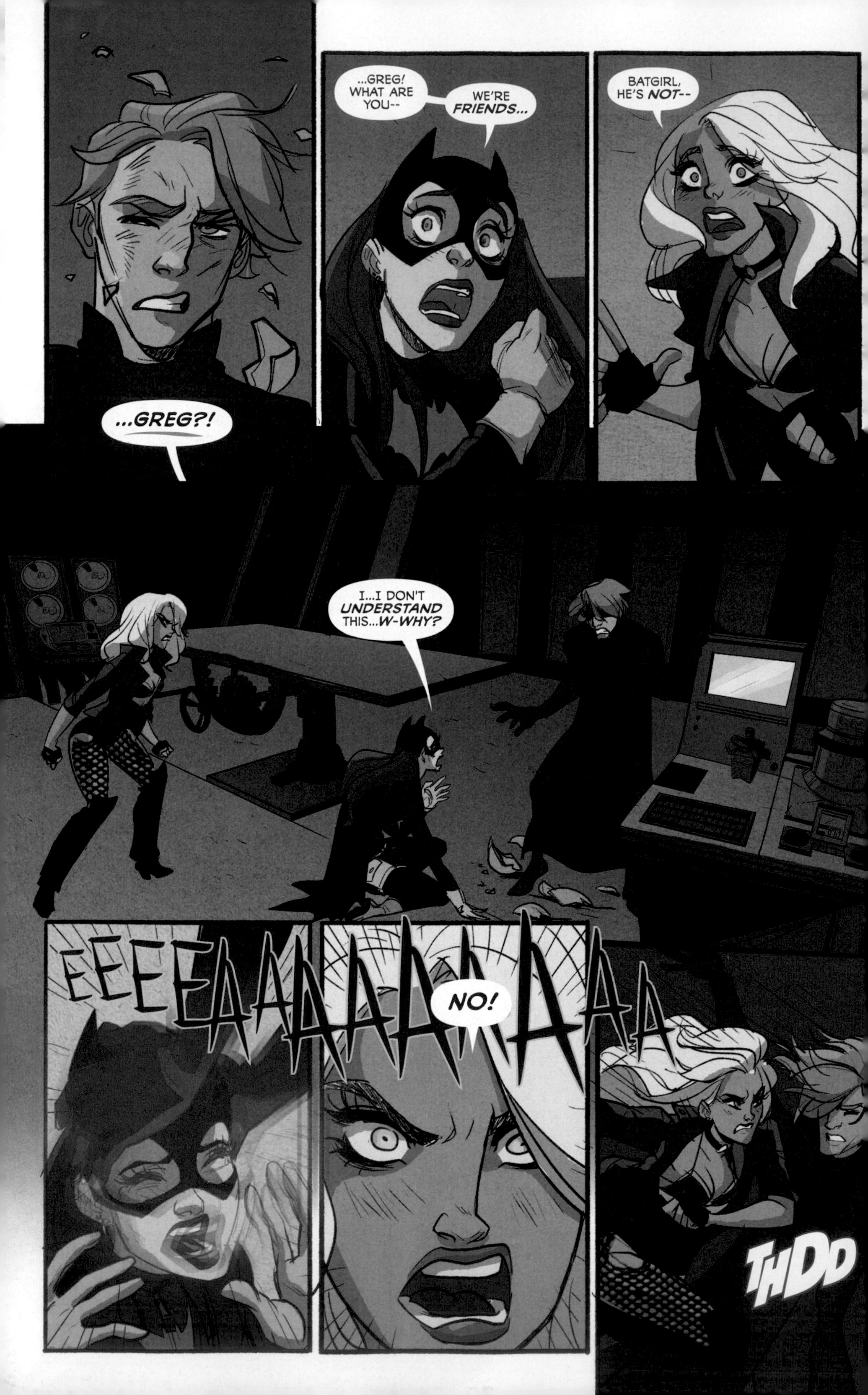
...GREG?!
...GREG! WHAT ARE YOU--
WE'RE FRIENDS...
BATGIRL, HE'S NOT--
I...I DON'T UNDERSTAND THIS...W-WHY?
EEEEAAAAAAAAAA
NO!
THDD

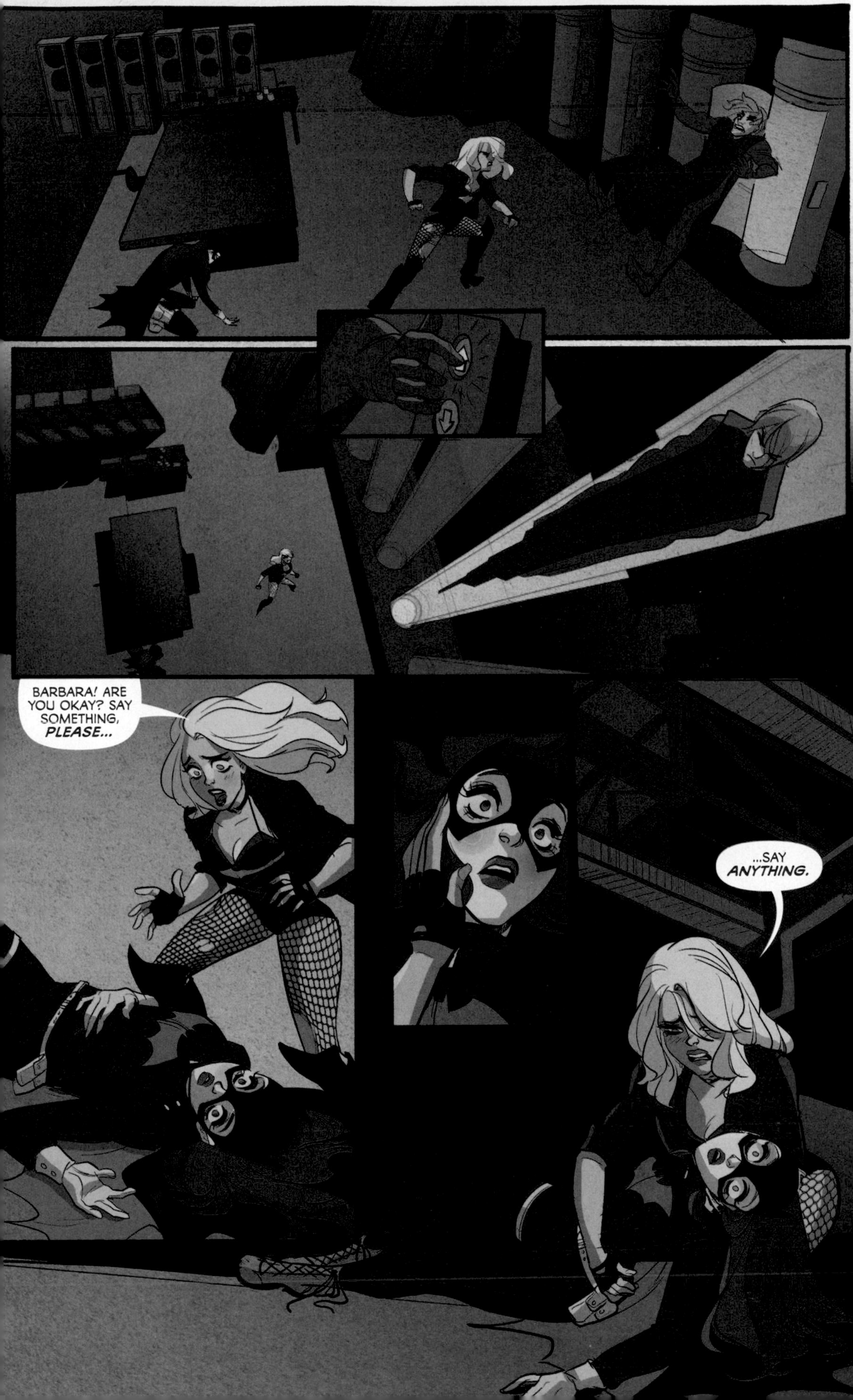
BARBARA! ARE YOU OKAY? SAY SOMETHING, *PLEASE...*
...SAY *ANYTHING.*

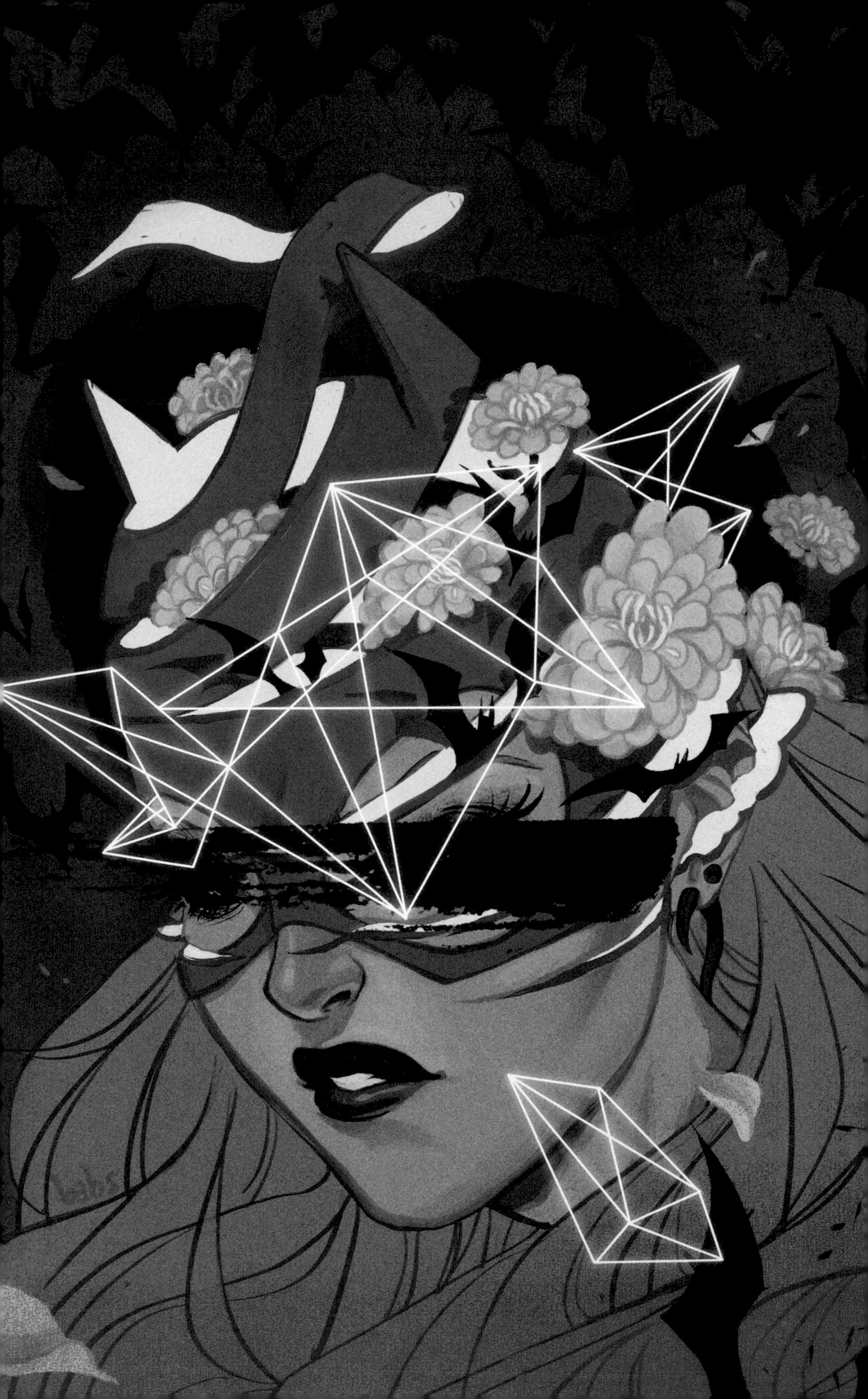

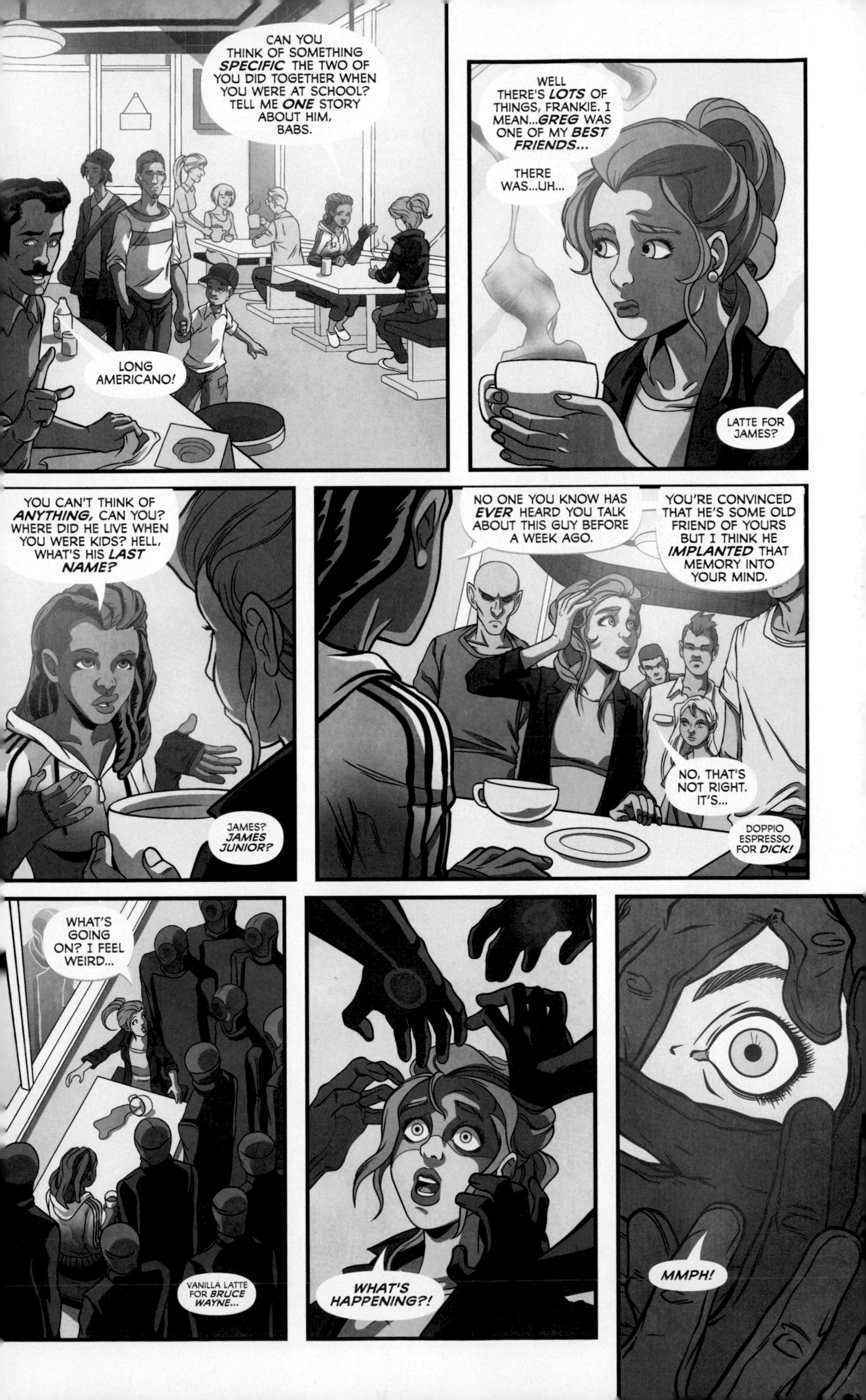
CAN YOU THINK OF SOMETHING SPECIFIC THE TWO OF YOU DID TOGETHER WHEN YOU WERE AT SCHOOL? TELL ME ONE STORY ABOUT HIM, BABS.
LONG AMERICANO!
WELL THERE'S LOTS OF THINGS, FRANKIE. I MEAN...GREG WAS ONE OF MY BEST FRIENDS...
THERE WAS...UH...
LATTE FOR JAMES?
YOU CAN'T THINK OF ANYTHING, CAN YOU? WHERE DID HE LIVE WHEN YOU WERE KIDS? HELL, WHAT'S HIS LAST NAME?
JAMES? JAMES JUNIOR?
NO ONE YOU KNOW HAS EVER HEARD YOU TALK ABOUT THIS GUY BEFORE A WEEK AGO.
YOU'RE CONVINCED THAT HE'S SOME OLD FRIEND OF YOURS BUT I THINK HE IMPLANTED THAT MEMORY INTO YOUR MIND.
NO, THAT'S NOT RIGHT. IT'S...
DOPPIO ESPRESSO FOR DICK!
WHAT'S GOING ON? I FEEL WEIRD...
VANILLA LATTE FOR BRUCE WAYNE...
WHAT'S HAPPENING?!
MMPH!

MINDFIELD

CAMERON STEWART + BRENDEN FLETCHER WRITERS

HORACIO DOMINGUES
BABS TARR
ROGER ROBINSON
MING DOYLE
JAMES HARVEY
ARTISTS [IN ORDER OF APPEARANCE]

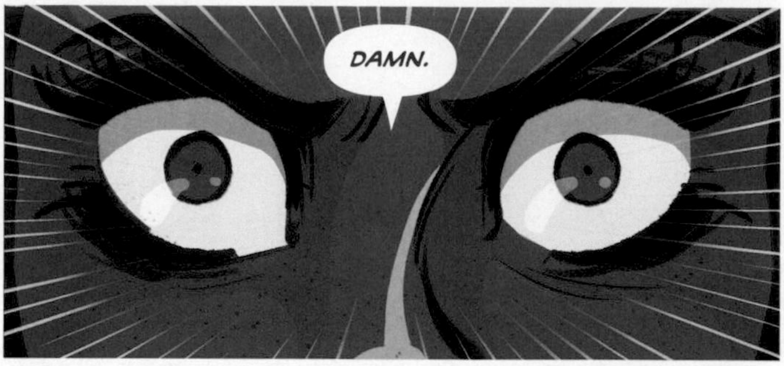

DAMN.

SERGE LAPOINTE WITH JAMES HARVEY [PGS 15, 16, 18] COLORS
STEVE WANDS LETTERS
BABS TARR COVER

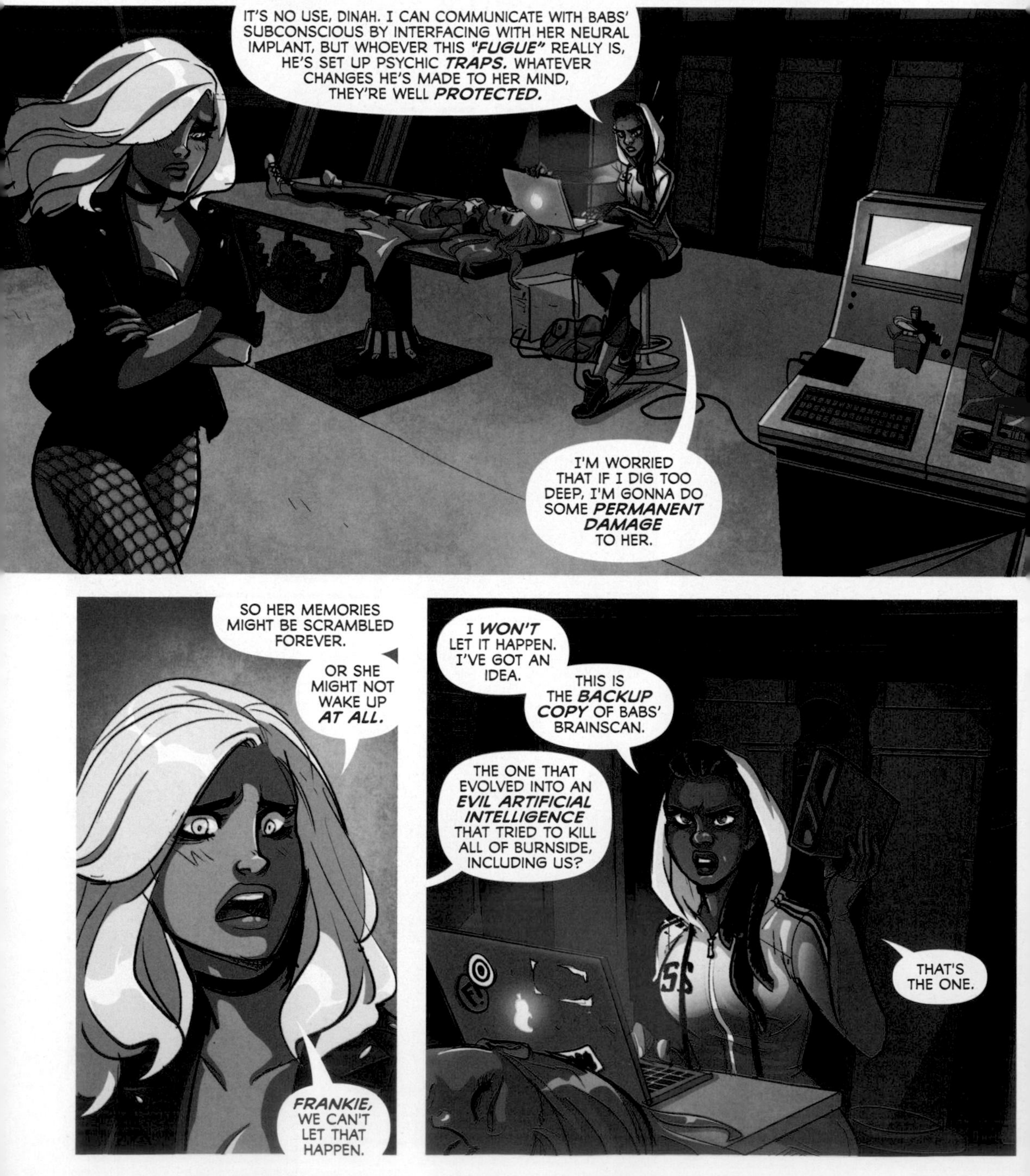

IT'S NO USE, DINAH. I CAN COMMUNICATE WITH BABS' SUBCONSCIOUS BY INTERFACING WITH HER NEURAL IMPLANT, BUT WHOEVER THIS *"FUGUE"* REALLY IS, HE'S SET UP PSYCHIC *TRAPS.* WHATEVER CHANGES HE'S MADE TO HER MIND, THEY'RE WELL *PROTECTED.*
I'M WORRIED THAT IF I DIG TOO DEEP, I'M GONNA DO SOME *PERMANENT DAMAGE* TO HER.
SO HER MEMORIES MIGHT BE SCRAMBLED FOREVER.
OR SHE MIGHT NOT WAKE UP *AT ALL.*
FRANKIE, WE CAN'T LET THAT HAPPEN.
I *WON'T* LET IT HAPPEN. I'VE GOT AN IDEA.
THIS IS THE *BACKUP COPY* OF BABS' BRAINSCAN.
THE ONE THAT EVOLVED INTO AN *EVIL ARTIFICIAL INTELLIGENCE* THAT TRIED TO KILL ALL OF BURNSIDE, INCLUDING US?
THAT'S THE ONE.

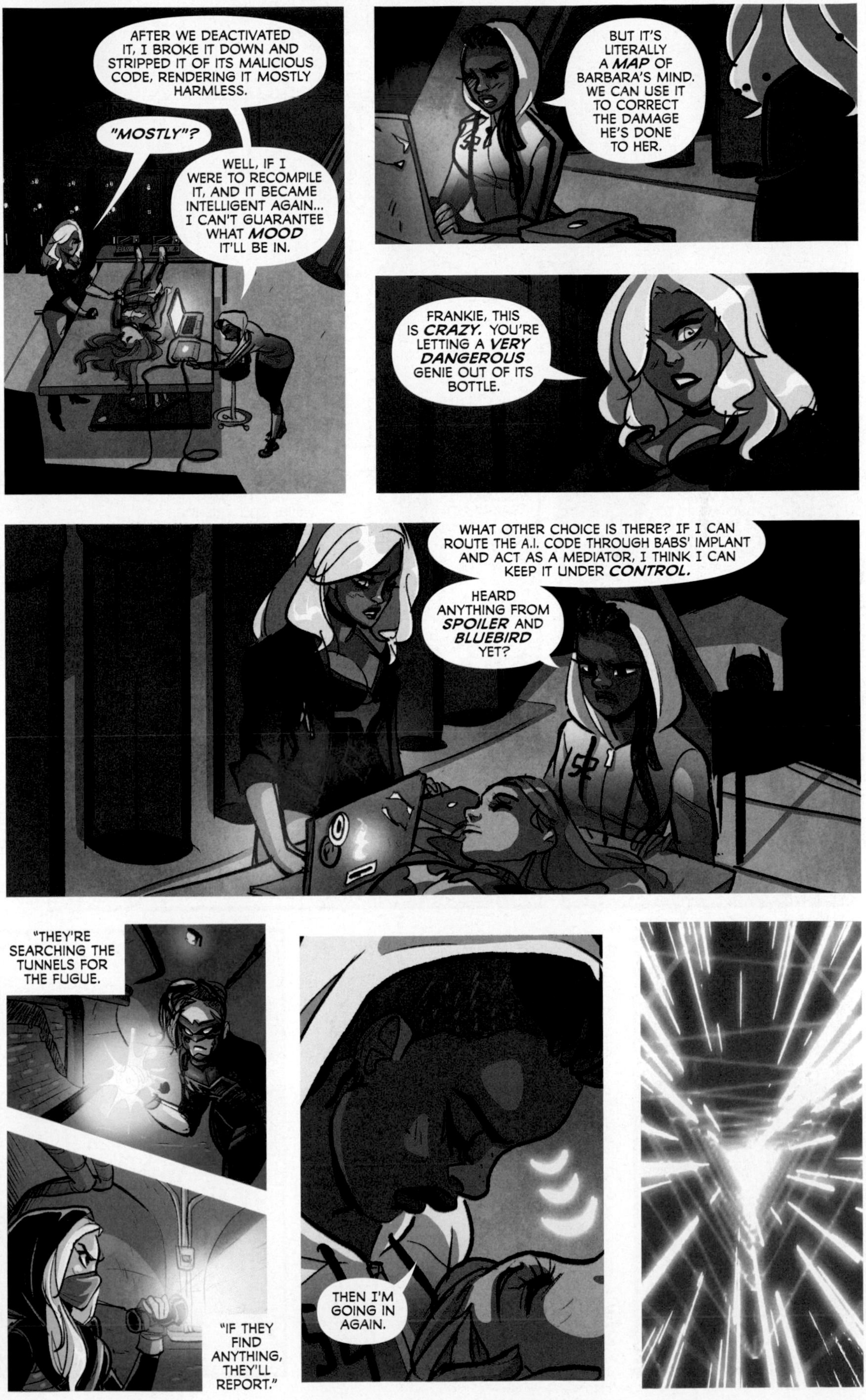

AFTER WE DEACTIVATED IT, I BROKE IT DOWN AND STRIPPED IT OF ITS MALICIOUS CODE, RENDERING IT MOSTLY HARMLESS.
"MOSTLY"?
WELL, IF I WERE TO RECOMPILE IT, AND IT BECAME INTELLIGENT AGAIN... I CAN'T GUARANTEE WHAT MOOD IT'LL BE IN.
BUT IT'S LITERALLY A MAP OF BARBARA'S MIND. WE CAN USE IT TO CORRECT THE DAMAGE HE'S DONE TO HER.
FRANKIE, THIS IS CRAZY. YOU'RE LETTING A VERY DANGEROUS GENIE OUT OF ITS BOTTLE.
WHAT OTHER CHOICE IS THERE? IF I CAN ROUTE THE A.I. CODE THROUGH BABS' IMPLANT AND ACT AS A MEDIATOR, I THINK I CAN KEEP IT UNDER CONTROL.
HEARD ANYTHING FROM SPOILER AND BLUEBIRD YET?
"THEY'RE SEARCHING THE TUNNELS FOR THE FUGUE.
"IF THEY FIND ANYTHING, THEY'LL REPORT."
THEN I'M GOING IN AGAIN.

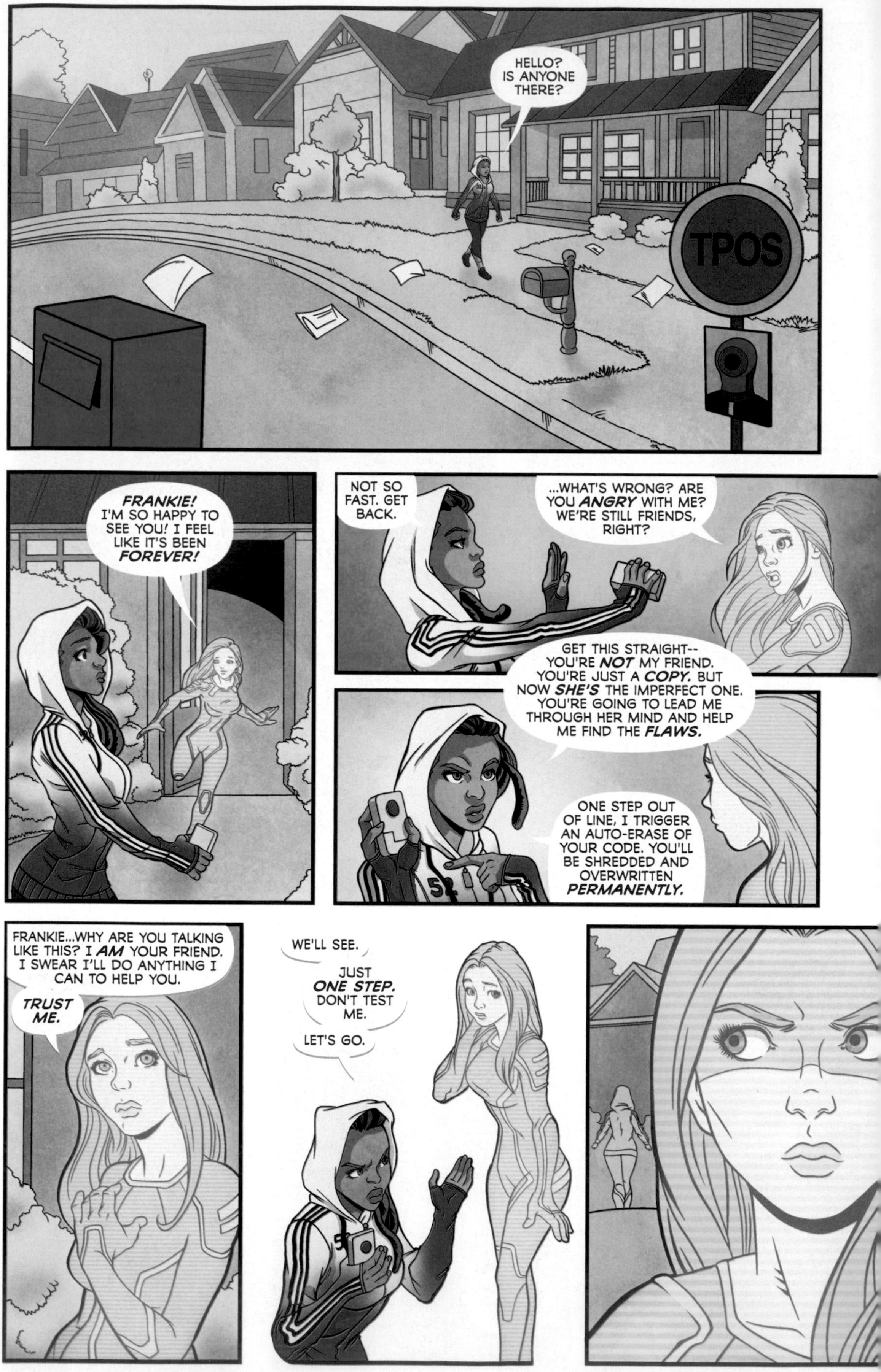
HELLO? IS ANYONE THERE?
TPOS
FRANKIE! I'M SO HAPPY TO SEE YOU! I FEEL LIKE IT'S BEEN FOREVER!
NOT SO FAST. GET BACK.
...WHAT'S WRONG? ARE YOU ANGRY WITH ME? WE'RE STILL FRIENDS, RIGHT?
GET THIS STRAIGHT-- YOU'RE NOT MY FRIEND. YOU'RE JUST A COPY. BUT NOW SHE'S THE IMPERFECT ONE. YOU'RE GOING TO LEAD ME THROUGH HER MIND AND HELP ME FIND THE FLAWS.
ONE STEP OUT OF LINE, I TRIGGER AN AUTO-ERASE OF YOUR CODE. YOU'LL BE SHREDDED AND OVERWRITTEN PERMANENTLY.
FRANKIE...WHY ARE YOU TALKING LIKE THIS? I AM YOUR FRIEND. I SWEAR I'LL DO ANYTHING I CAN TO HELP YOU.
TRUST ME.
WE'LL SEE.
JUST ONE STEP. DON'T TEST ME.
LET'S GO.

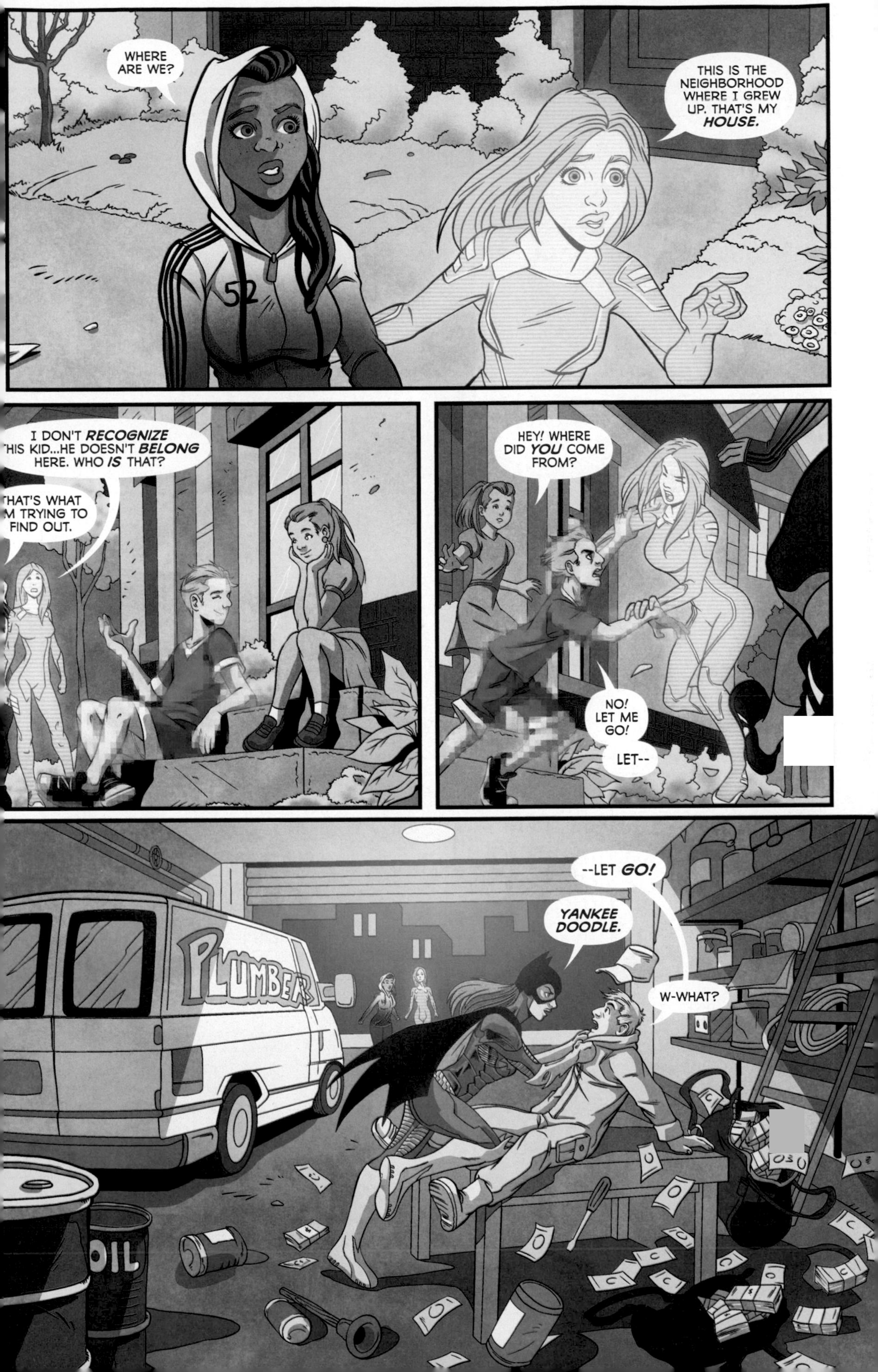

WHERE ARE WE?
THIS IS THE NEIGHBORHOOD WHERE I GREW UP. THAT'S MY *HOUSE.*
I DON'T *RECOGNIZE* HIS KID...HE DOESN'T *BELONG* HERE. WHO *IS* THAT?
HAT'S WHAT M TRYING TO FIND OUT.
HEY! WHERE DID *YOU* COME FROM?
NO! LET ME GO!
LET--
--LET *GO!*
YANKEE DOODLE.
W-WHAT?
PLUMBERS
OIL

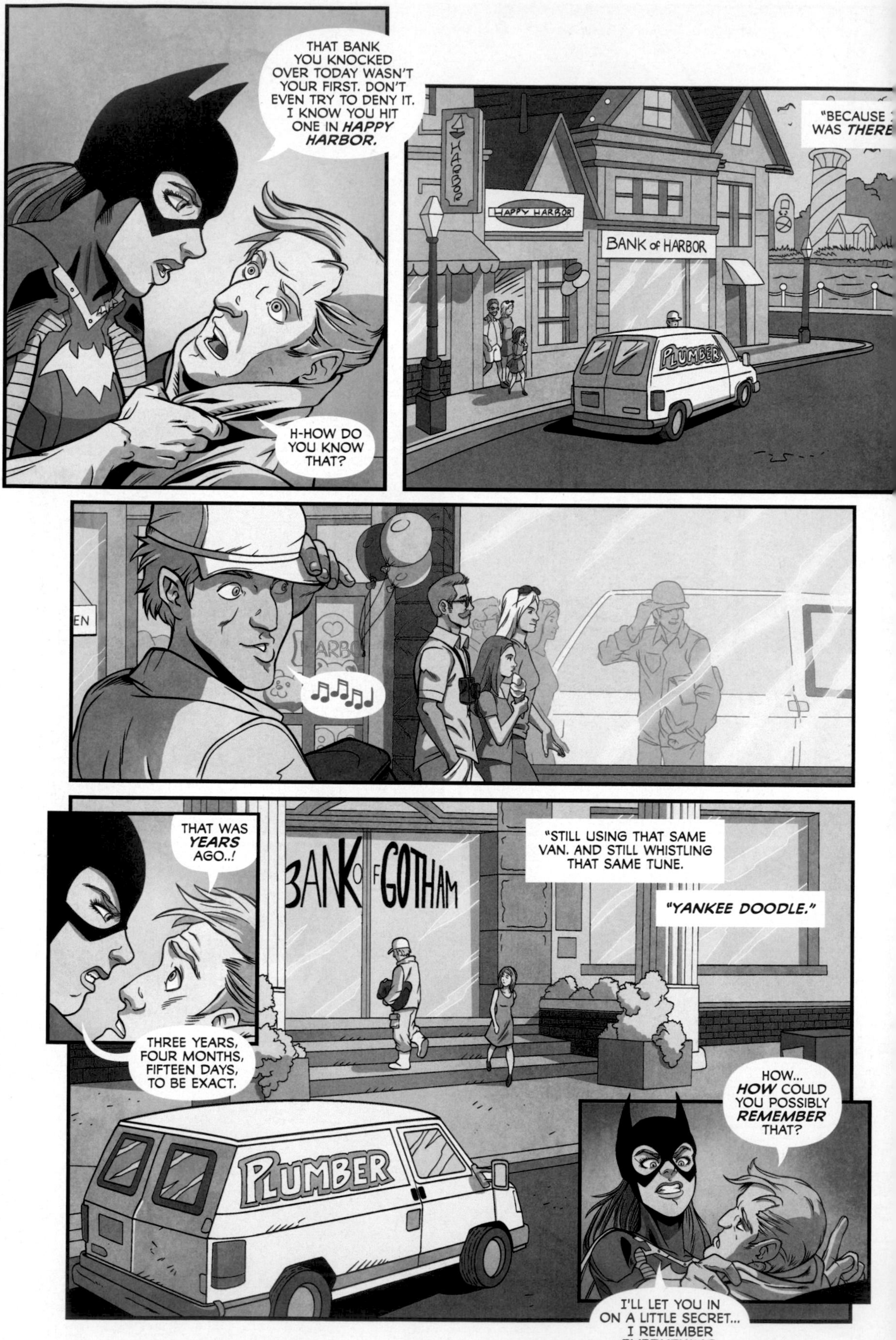
THAT BANK YOU KNOCKED OVER TODAY WASN'T YOUR FIRST. DON'T EVEN TRY TO DENY IT. I KNOW YOU HIT ONE IN *HAPPY HARBOR.*
H-HOW DO YOU KNOW THAT?
"BECAUSE
WAS *THERE*
HARBOR
HAPPY HARBOR
BANK of HARBOR
PLUMBER
THAT WAS *YEARS* AGO..!
BANK OF GOTHAM
"STILL USING THAT SAME VAN. AND STILL WHISTLING THAT SAME TUNE.
"YANKEE DOODLE."
THREE YEARS, FOUR MONTHS, FIFTEEN DAYS, TO BE EXACT.
PLUMBER
HOW... *HOW* COULD YOU POSSIBLY *REMEMBER* THAT?
I'LL LET YOU IN ON A LITTLE SECRET... I REMEMBER *EVERYTHING.*

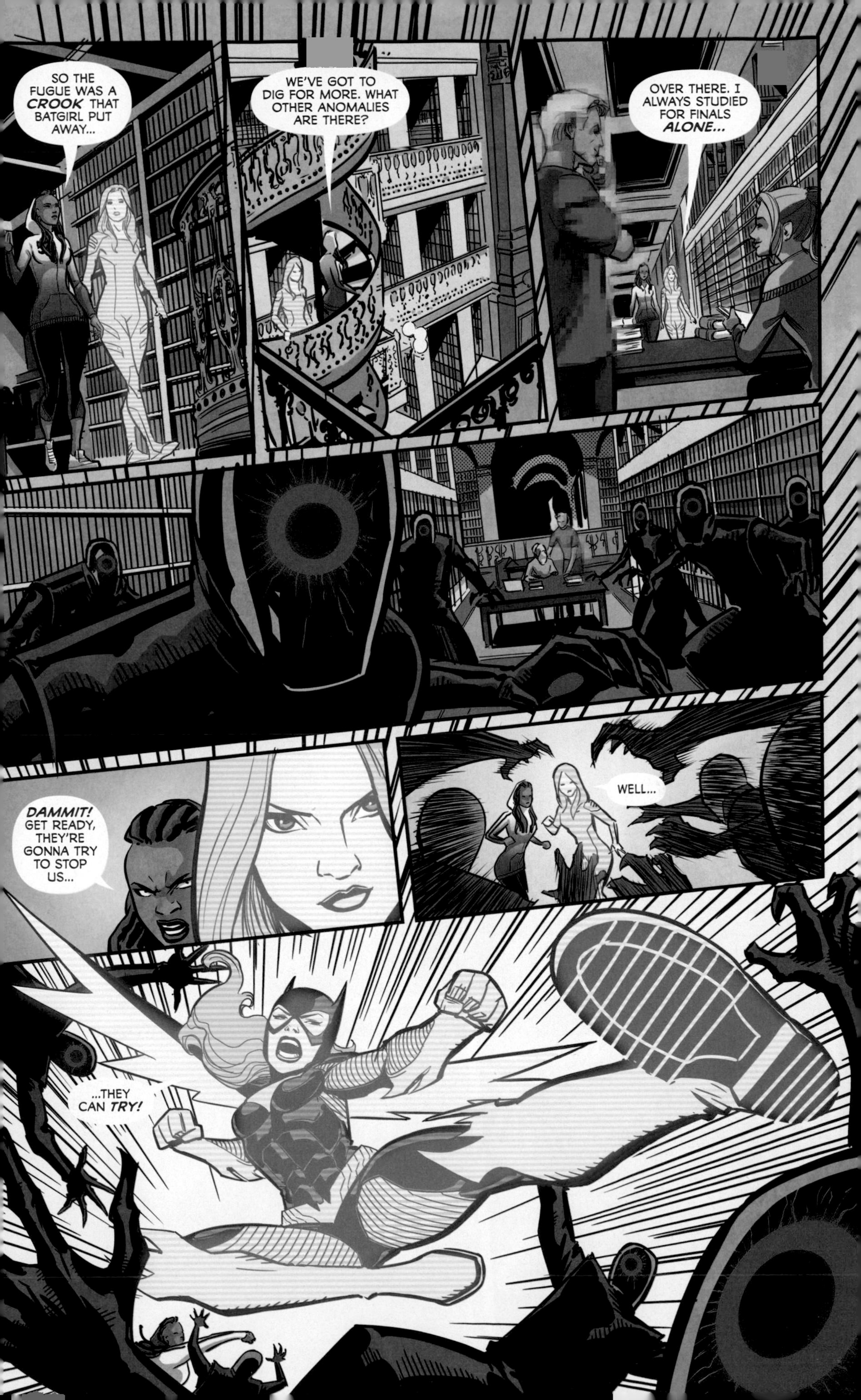
SO THE FUGUE WAS A CROOK THAT BATGIRL PUT AWAY...
WE'VE GOT TO DIG FOR MORE. WHAT OTHER ANOMALIES ARE THERE?
OVER THERE. I ALWAYS STUDIED FOR FINALS ALONE...
DAMMIT! GET READY, THEY'RE GONNA TRY TO STOP US...
WELL...
...THEY CAN TRY!

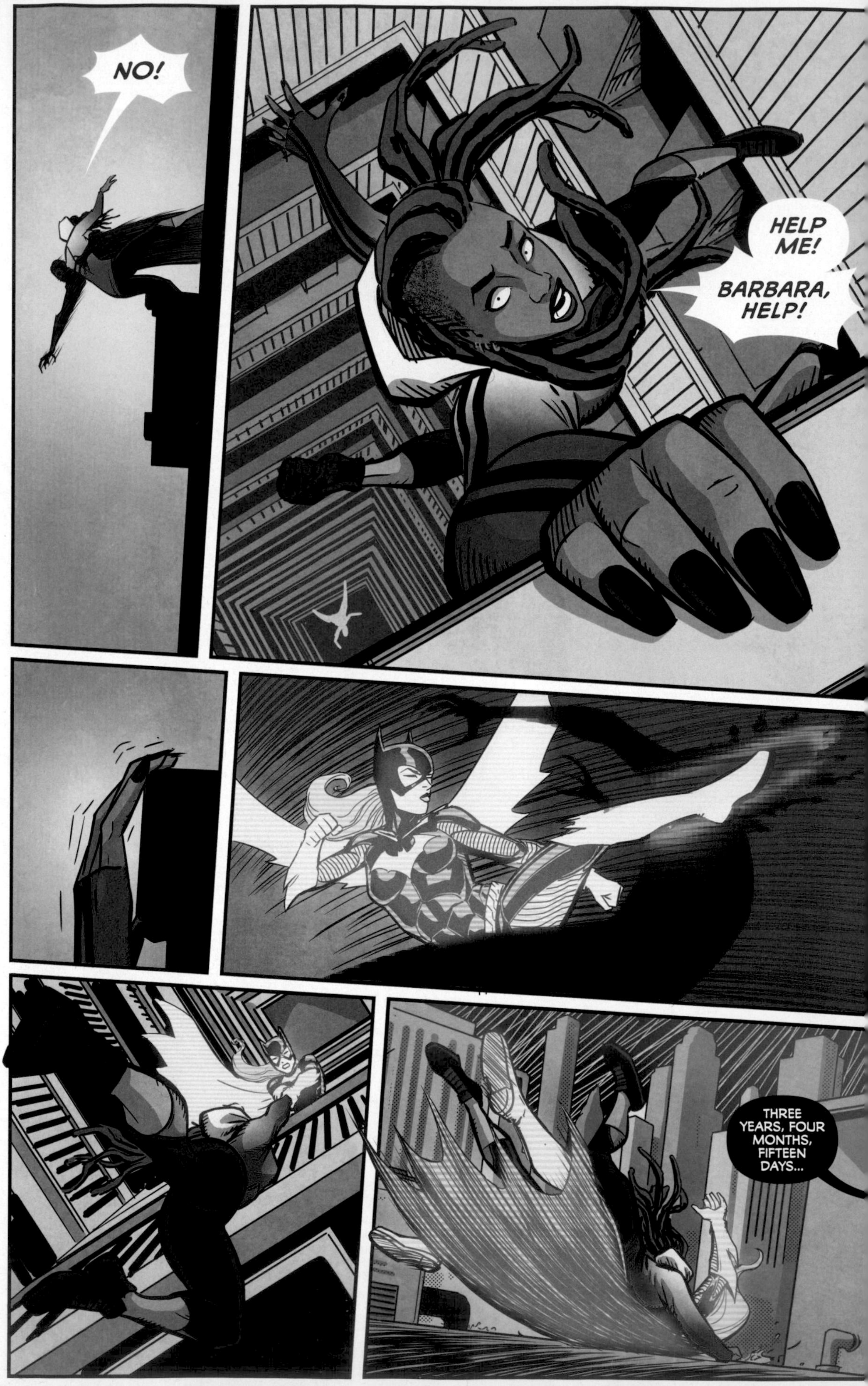
NO!
HELP ME!
BARBARA, HELP!
THREE YEARS, FOUR MONTHS, FIFTEEN DAYS...

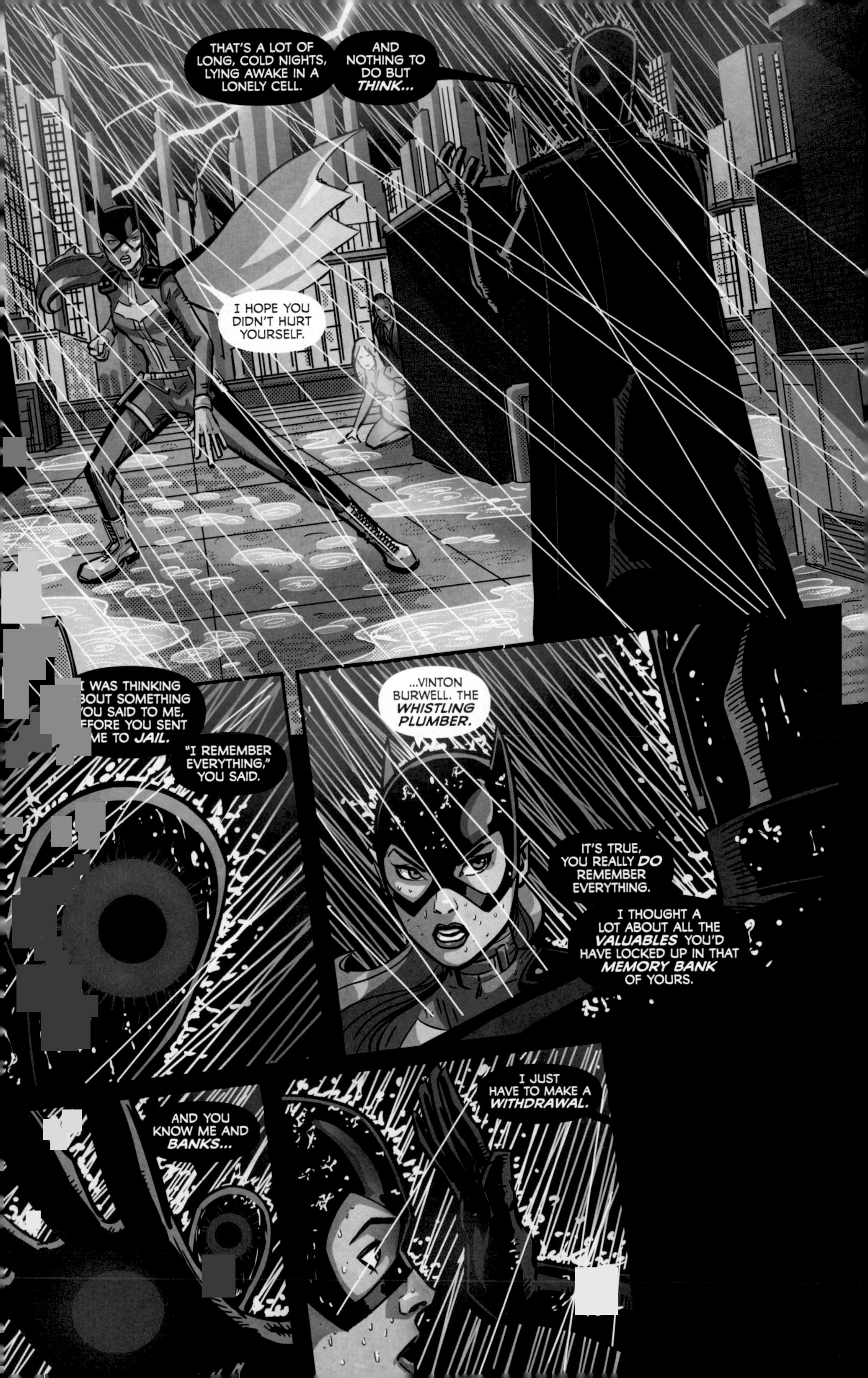
THAT'S A LOT OF LONG, COLD NIGHTS, LYING AWAKE IN A LONELY CELL.
AND NOTHING TO DO BUT THINK...
I HOPE YOU DIDN'T HURT YOURSELF.
I WAS THINKING ABOUT SOMETHING YOU SAID TO ME, BEFORE YOU SENT ME TO JAIL.
"I REMEMBER EVERYTHING," YOU SAID.
...VINTON BURWELL. THE WHISTLING PLUMBER.
IT'S TRUE, YOU REALLY DO REMEMBER EVERYTHING.
I THOUGHT A LOT ABOUT ALL THE VALUABLES YOU'D HAVE LOCKED UP IN THAT MEMORY BANK OF YOURS.
AND YOU KNOW ME AND BANKS...
I JUST HAVE TO MAKE A WITHDRAWAL.

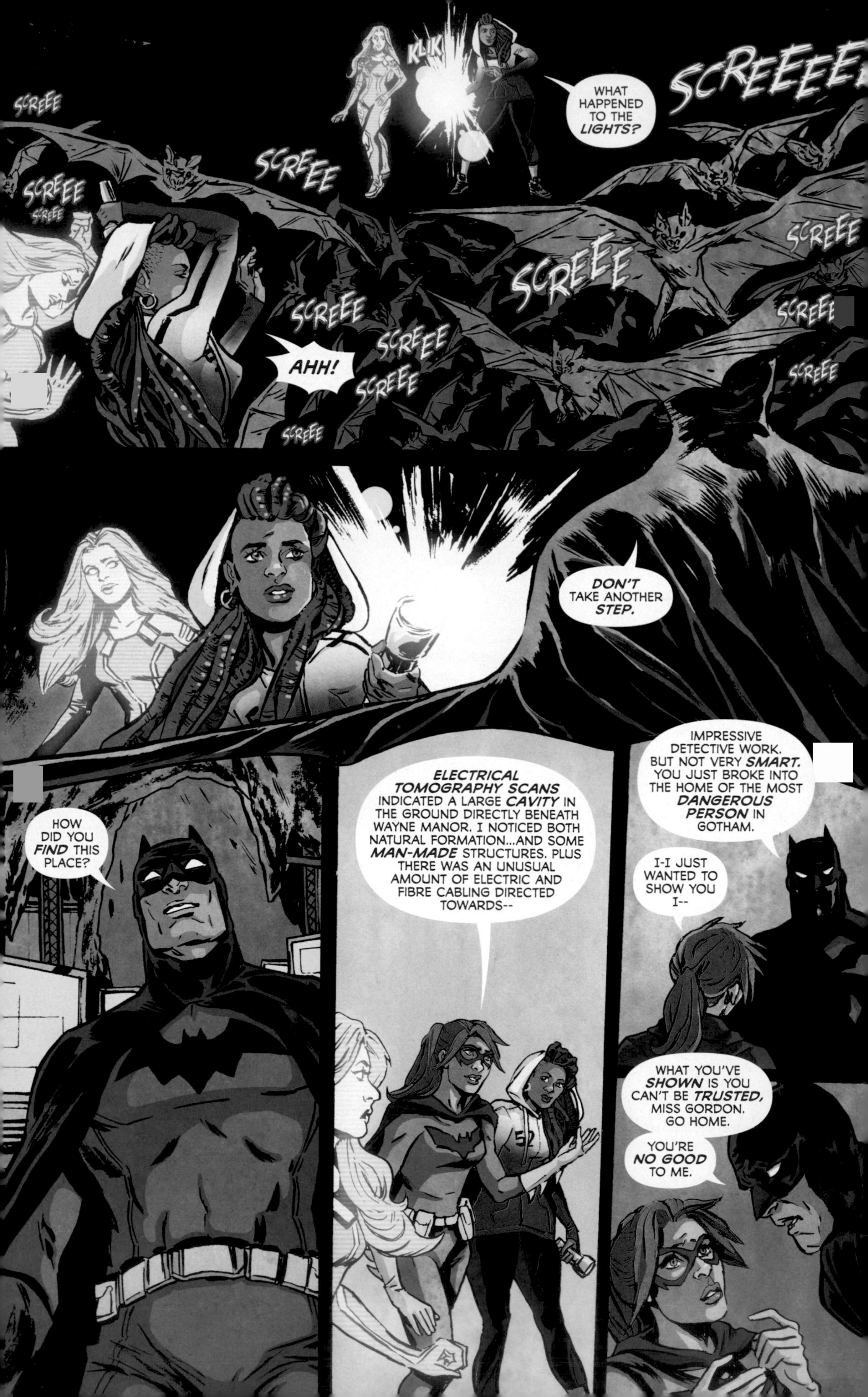

KLIK
WHAT HAPPENED TO THE LIGHTS?
SCREEEEE
SCREEE
SCREEE
SCREEE
SCREEE
SCREEE
SCREEE
SCREEE
AHH!
SCREEE
SCREEE
SCREEE
SCREEE
SCREEE
DON'T TAKE ANOTHER STEP.
HOW DID YOU FIND THIS PLACE?
ELECTRICAL TOMOGRAPHY SCANS INDICATED A LARGE CAVITY IN THE GROUND DIRECTLY BENEATH WAYNE MANOR. I NOTICED BOTH NATURAL FORMATION...AND SOME MAN-MADE STRUCTURES. PLUS THERE WAS AN UNUSUAL AMOUNT OF ELECTRIC AND FIBRE CABLING DIRECTED TOWARDS--
IMPRESSIVE DETECTIVE WORK. BUT NOT VERY SMART. YOU JUST BROKE INTO THE HOME OF THE MOST DANGEROUS PERSON IN GOTHAM.
I-I JUST WANTED TO SHOW YOU I--
WHAT YOU'VE SHOWN IS YOU CAN'T BE TRUSTED, MISS GORDON. GO HOME.
YOU'RE NO GOOD TO ME.

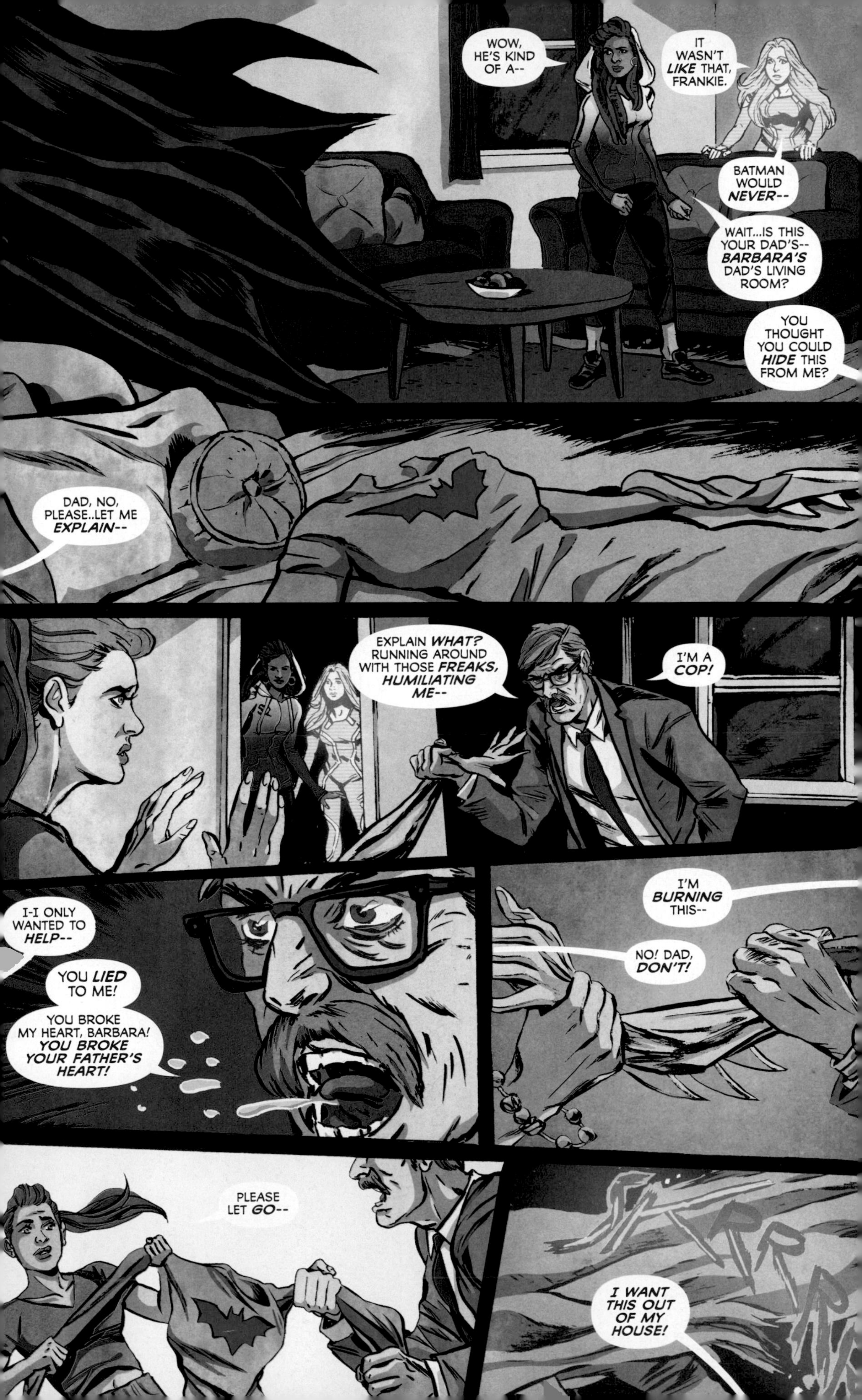
WOW, HE'S KIND OF A--
IT WASN'T LIKE THAT, FRANKIE.
BATMAN WOULD NEVER--
WAIT...IS THIS YOUR DAD'S-- BARBARA'S DAD'S LIVING ROOM?
YOU THOUGHT YOU COULD HIDE THIS FROM ME?
DAD, NO, PLEASE..LET ME EXPLAIN--
EXPLAIN WHAT? RUNNING AROUND WITH THOSE FREAKS, HUMILIATING ME--
I'M A COP!
I-I ONLY WANTED TO HELP--
YOU LIED TO ME!
YOU BROKE MY HEART, BARBARA! YOU BROKE YOUR FATHER'S HEART!
I'M BURNING THIS--
NO! DAD, DON'T!
PLEASE LET GO--
I WANT THIS OUT OF MY HOUSE!

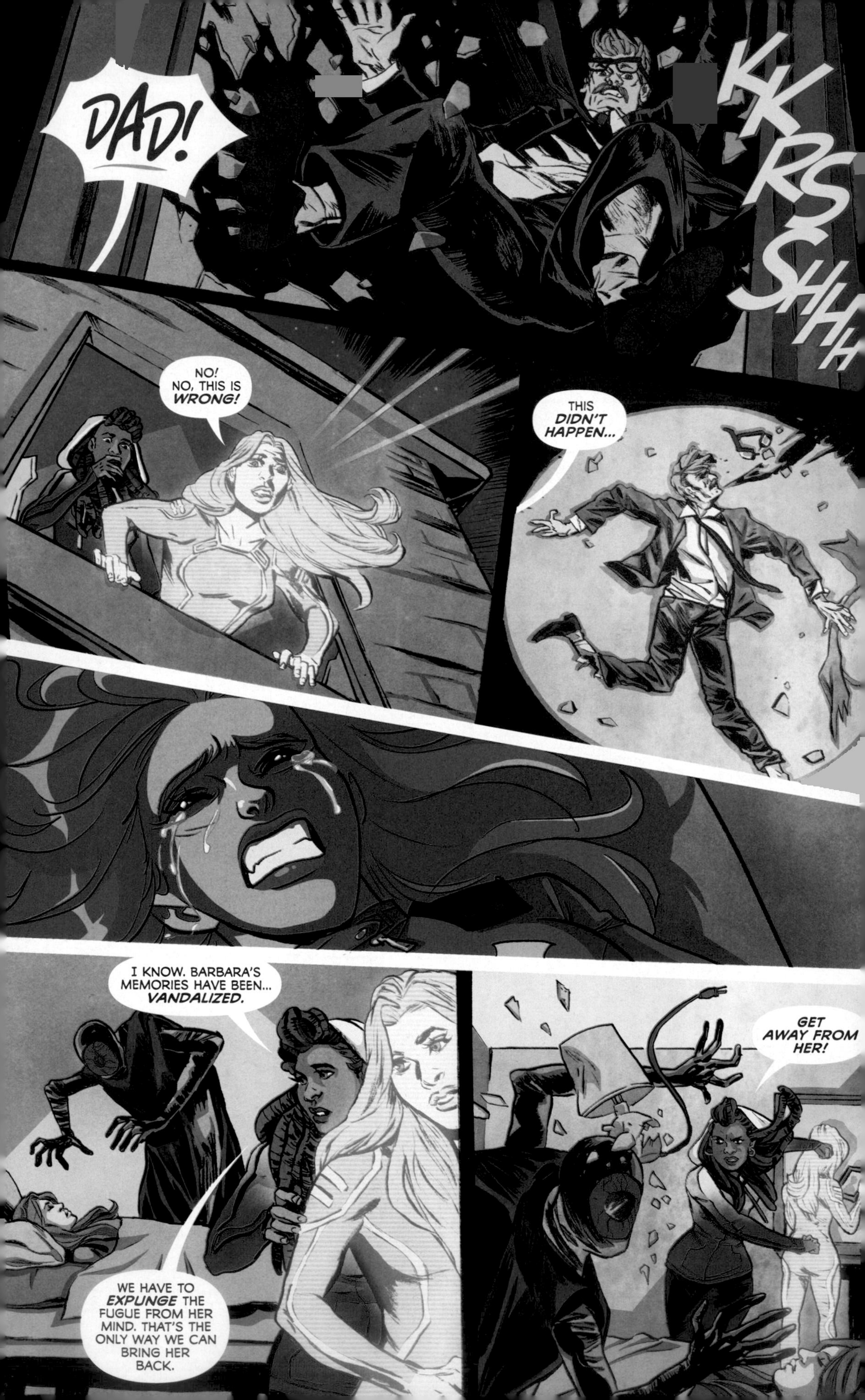
DAD!
KKRSSHHH
NO! NO, THIS IS WRONG!
THIS DIDN'T HAPPEN...
I KNOW. BARBARA'S MEMORIES HAVE BEEN... VANDALIZED.
WE HAVE TO EXPUNGE THE FUGUE FROM HER MIND. THAT'S THE ONLY WAY WE CAN BRING HER BACK.
GET AWAY FROM HER!

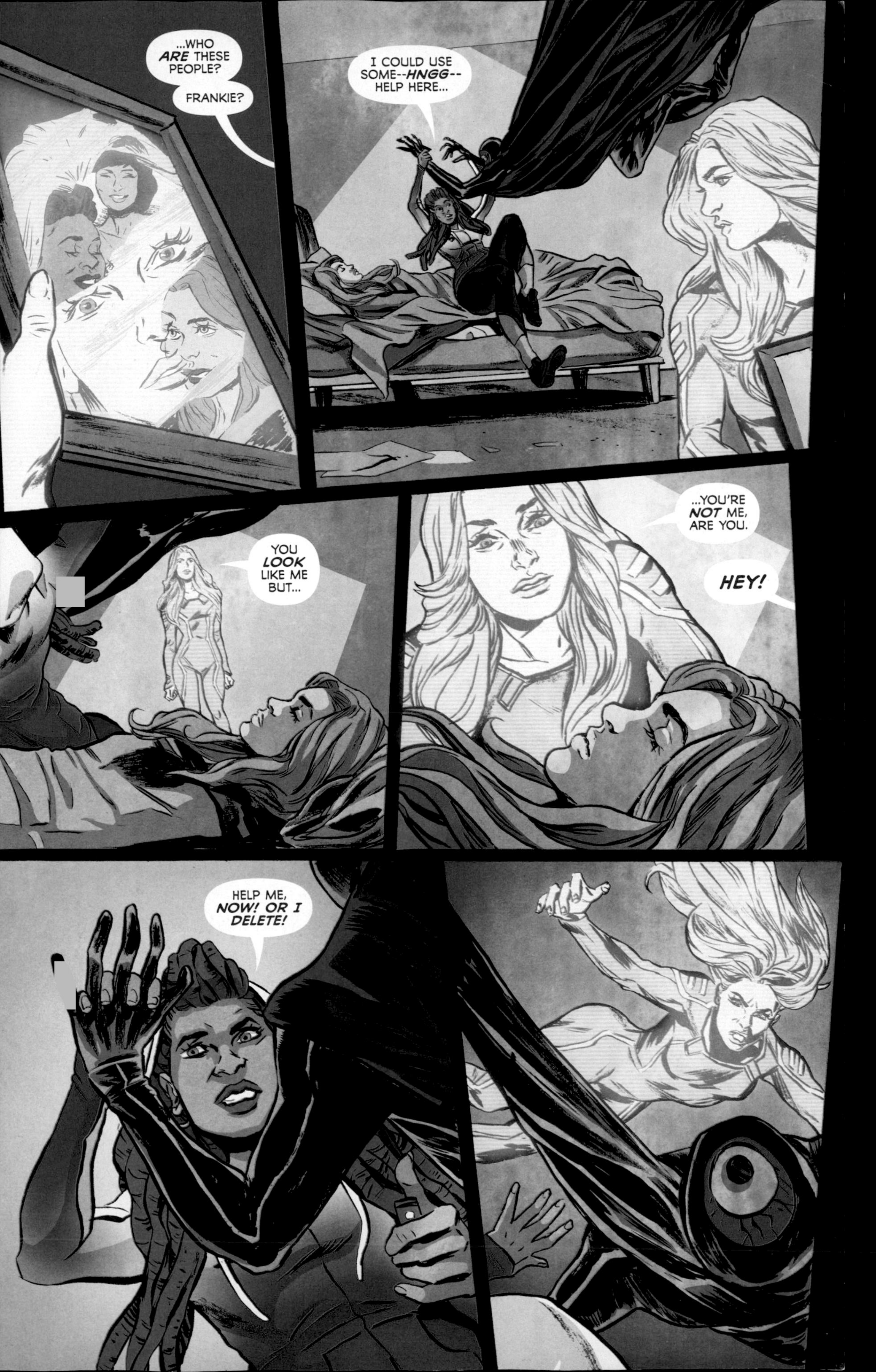
...WHO ARE THESE PEOPLE?
FRANKIE?
I COULD USE SOME--HNGG-- HELP HERE...
YOU LOOK LIKE ME BUT...
...YOU'RE NOT ME, ARE YOU.
HEY!
HELP ME, NOW! OR I DELETE!

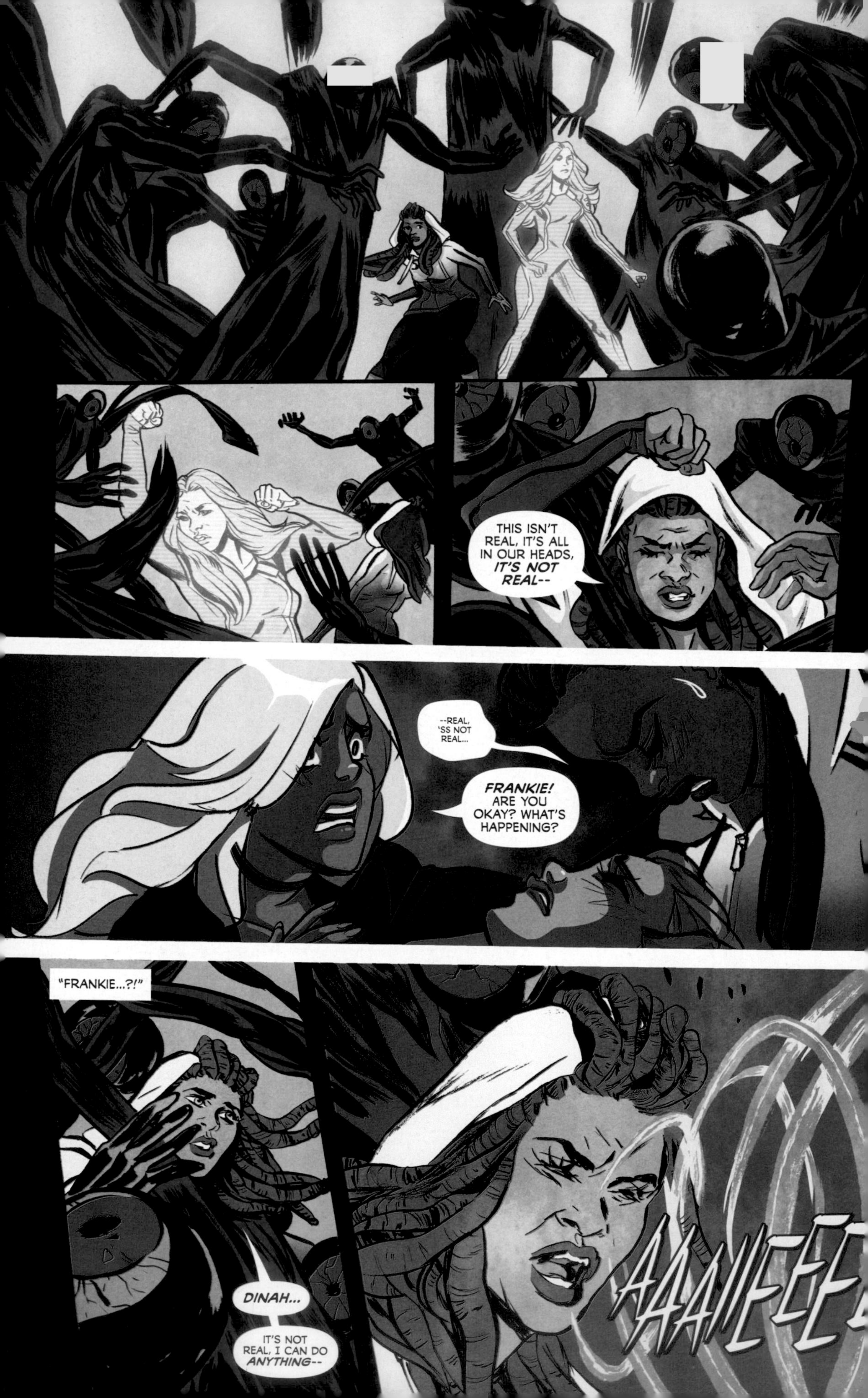
THIS ISN'T REAL, IT'S ALL IN OUR HEADS, IT'S NOT REAL--
--REAL, 'SS NOT REAL...
FRANKIE! ARE YOU OKAY? WHAT'S HAPPENING?
"FRANKIE...?!"
DINAH...
IT'S NOT REAL, I CAN DO ANYTHING--
AAAIEEE

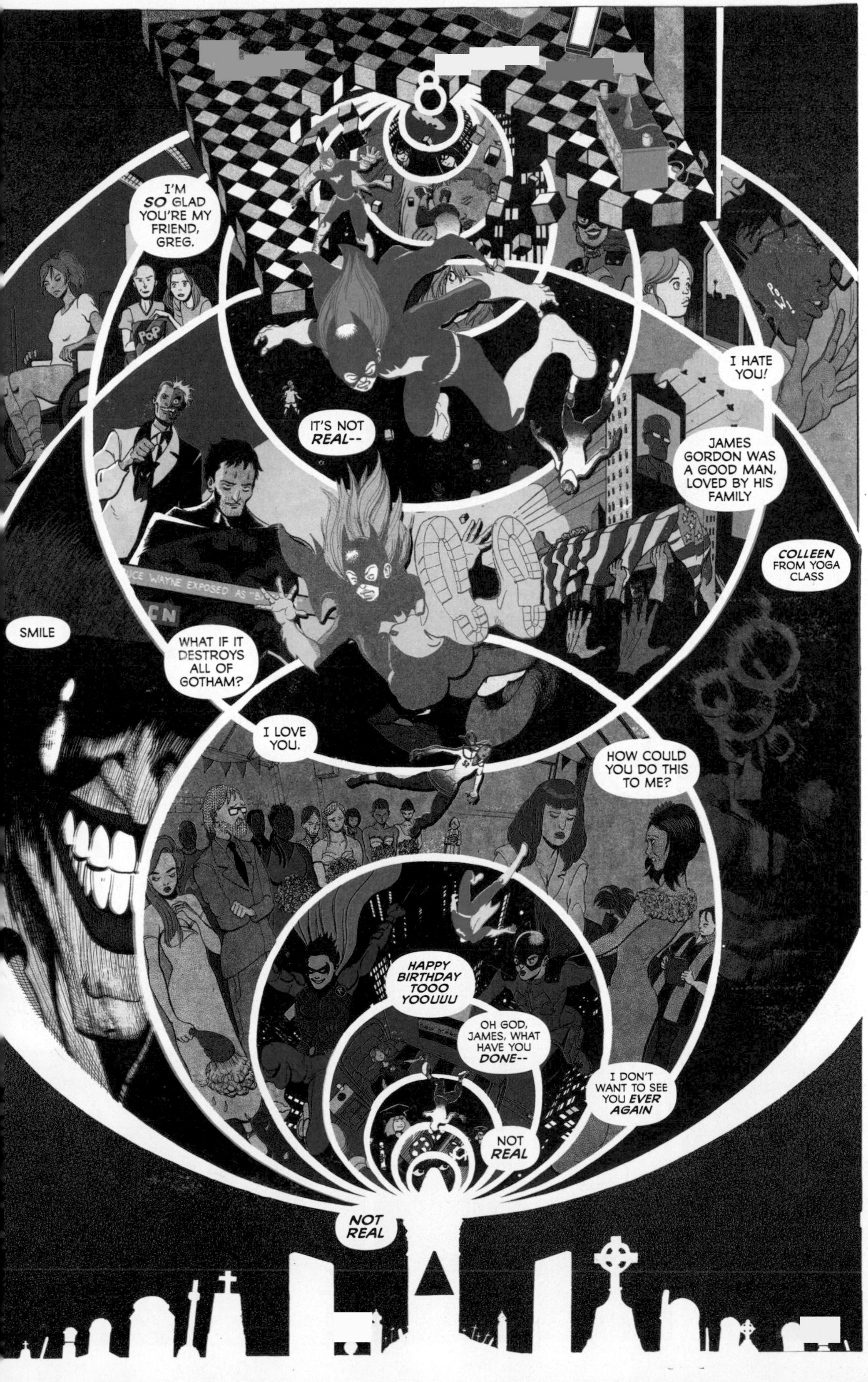
I'M *SO* GLAD YOU'RE MY FRIEND, GREG.
IT'S NOT *REAL*--
I HATE YOU!
JAMES GORDON WAS A GOOD MAN, LOVED BY HIS FAMILY
COLLEEN FROM YOGA CLASS
SMILE
WHAT IF IT DESTROYS ALL OF GOTHAM?
I LOVE YOU.
HOW COULD YOU DO THIS TO ME?
HAPPY BIRTHDAY TOOO YOOUUU
OH GOD, JAMES, WHAT HAVE YOU *DONE*--
I DON'T WANT TO SEE YOU *EVER AGAIN*
NOT *REAL*
NOT REAL

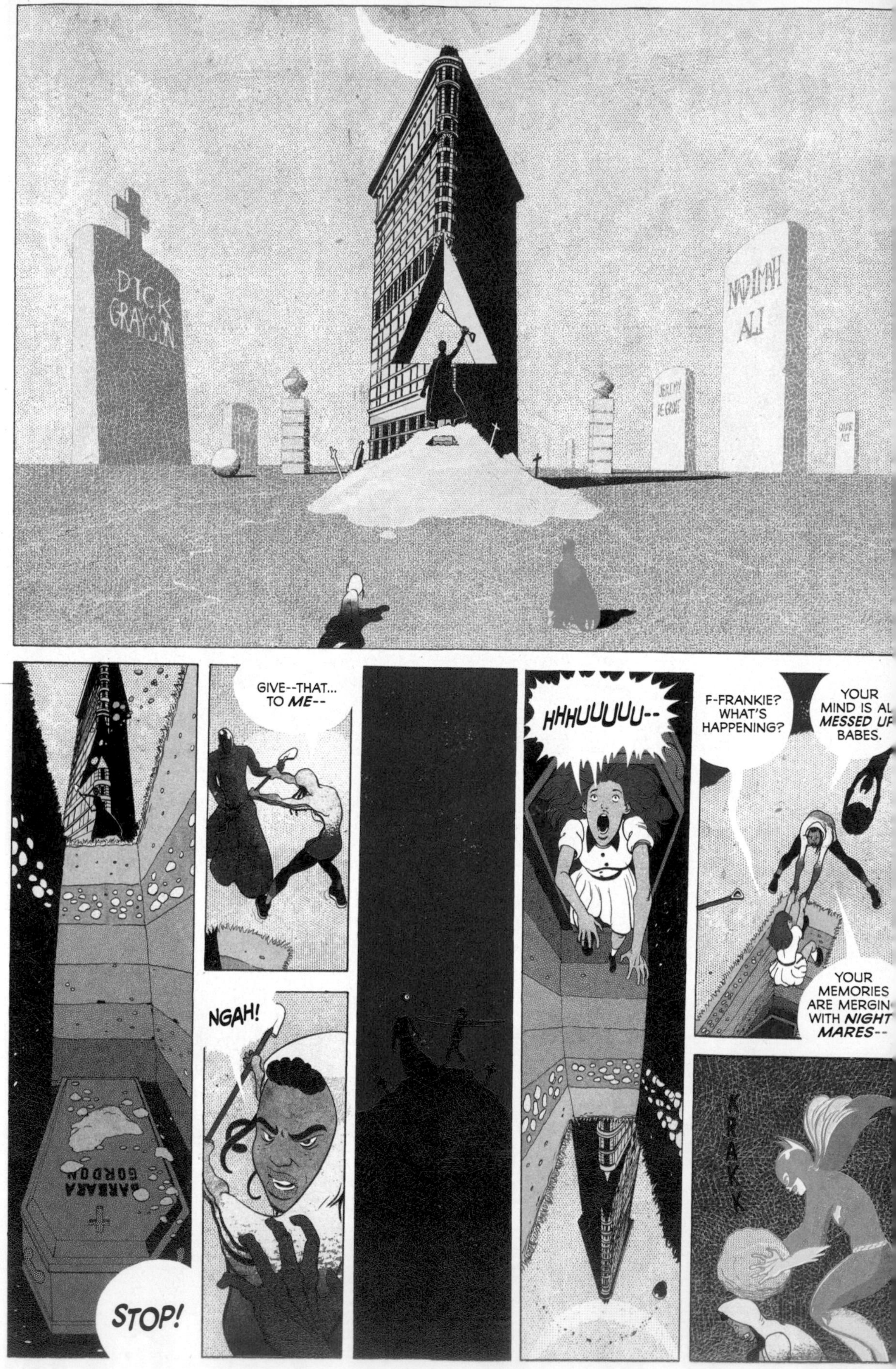
DICK GRAYSON
NADIMAH ALI
BARBARA GORDON
STOP!
GIVE--THAT... TO ME--
NGAH!
HHHUUUUUU--
F-FRANKIE? WHAT'S HAPPENING?
YOUR MIND IS AL MESSED UP BABES.
YOUR MEMORIES ARE MERGIN WITH NIGHT MARES--
KRAKK

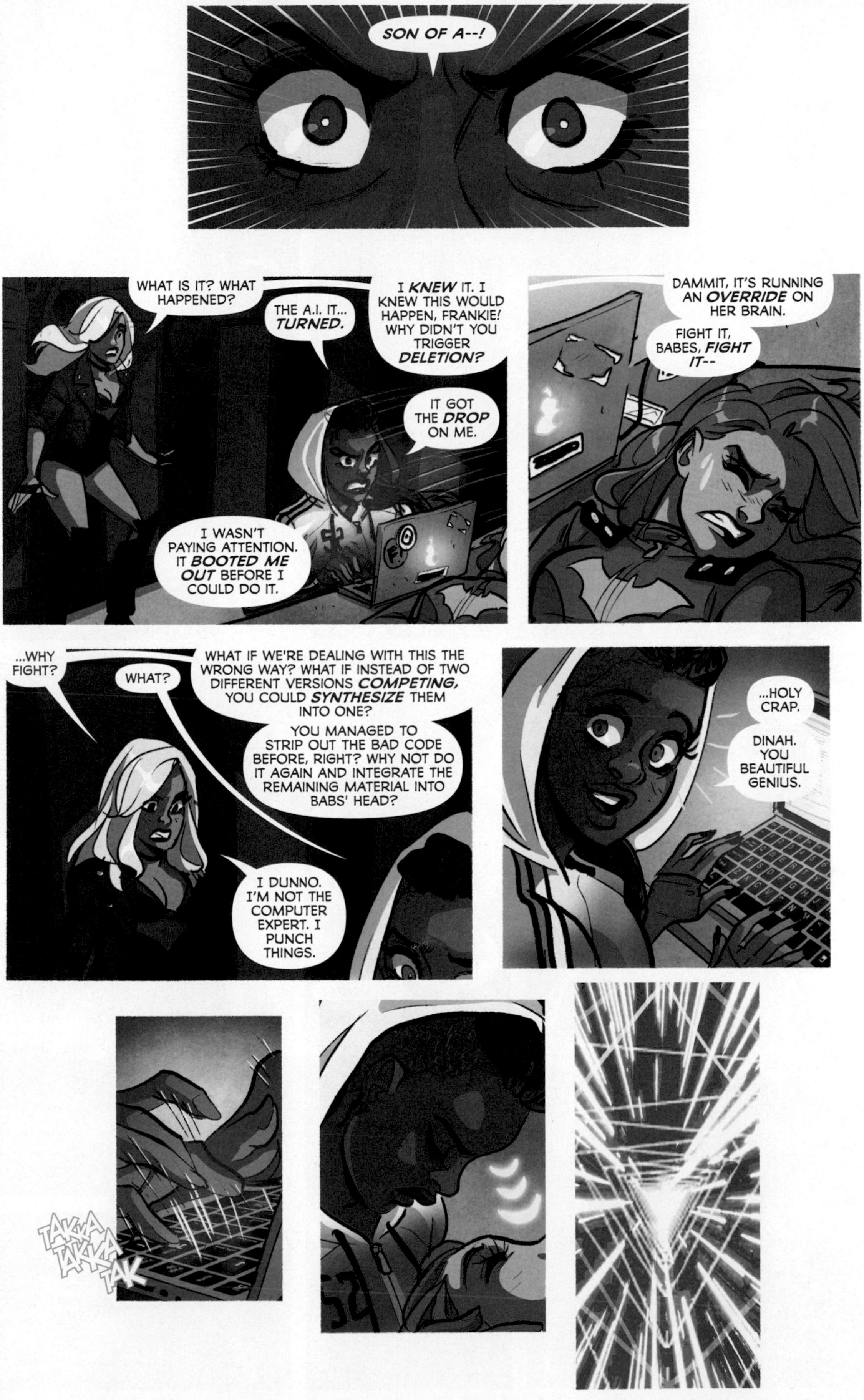
SON OF A--!
WHAT IS IT? WHAT HAPPENED?
THE A.I. IT... TURNED.
I KNEW IT. I KNEW THIS WOULD HAPPEN, FRANKIE! WHY DIDN'T YOU TRIGGER DELETION?
IT GOT THE DROP ON ME.
I WASN'T PAYING ATTENTION. IT BOOTED ME OUT BEFORE I COULD DO IT.
DAMMIT, IT'S RUNNING AN OVERRIDE ON HER BRAIN.
FIGHT IT, BABES, FIGHT IT--
...WHY FIGHT?
WHAT?
WHAT IF WE'RE DEALING WITH THIS THE WRONG WAY? WHAT IF INSTEAD OF TWO DIFFERENT VERSIONS COMPETING, YOU COULD SYNTHESIZE THEM INTO ONE?
YOU MANAGED TO STRIP OUT THE BAD CODE BEFORE, RIGHT? WHY NOT DO IT AGAIN AND INTEGRATE THE REMAINING MATERIAL INTO BABS' HEAD?
I DUNNO. I'M NOT THE COMPUTER EXPERT. I PUNCH THINGS.
...HOLY CRAP.
DINAH. YOU BEAUTIFUL GENIUS.
TAKKA TAKKA TAK

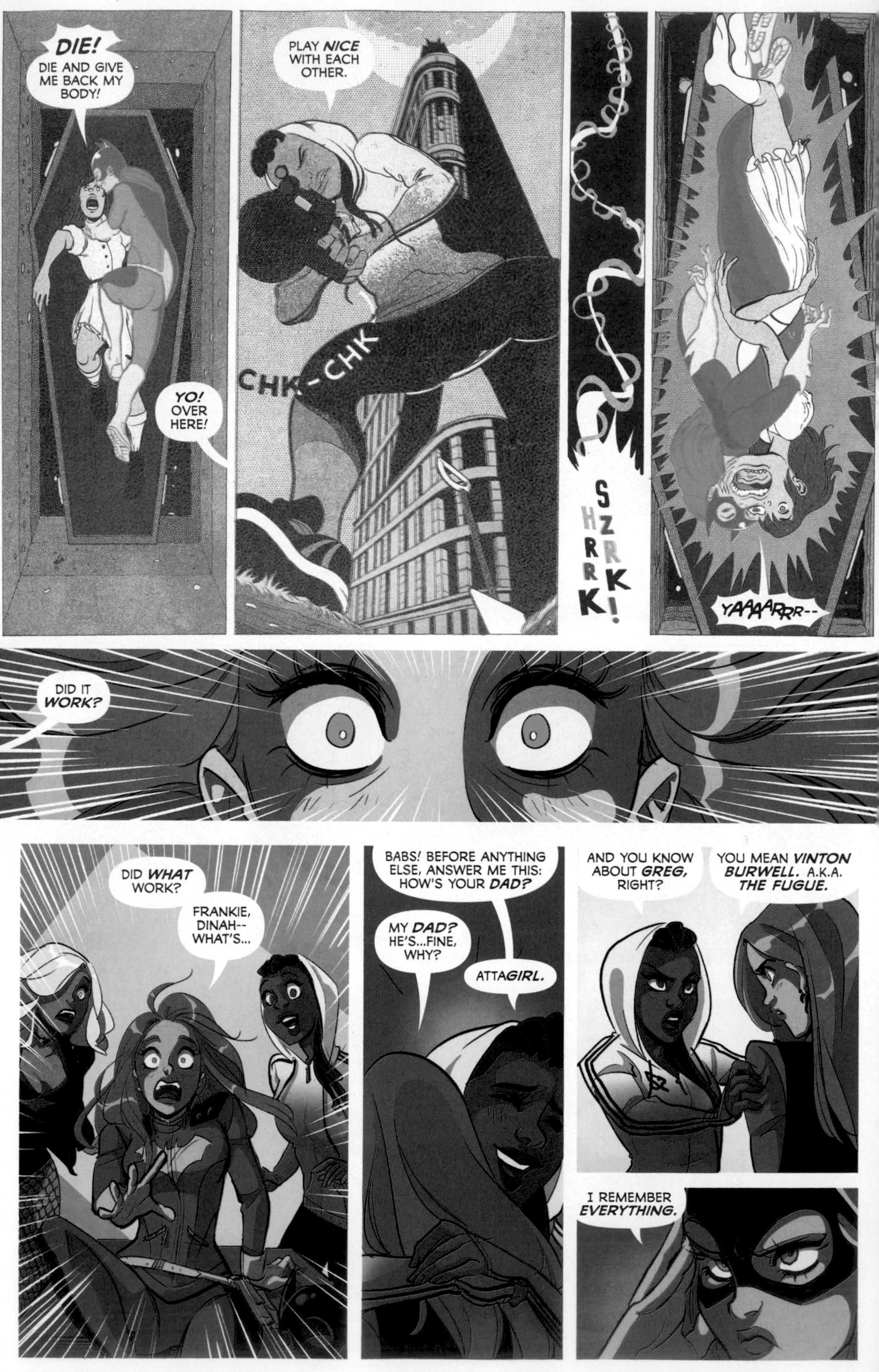
DIE!
DIE AND GIVE ME BACK MY BODY!
YO! OVER HERE!
PLAY NICE WITH EACH OTHER.
CHK-CHK
SHRRK ZRRK!
YAAAARRR--
DID IT WORK?
DID WHAT WORK?
FRANKIE, DINAH-- WHAT'S...
BABS! BEFORE ANYTHING ELSE, ANSWER ME THIS: HOW'S YOUR DAD?
MY DAD? HE'S...FINE, WHY?
ATTAGIRL.
AND YOU KNOW ABOUT GREG, RIGHT?
YOU MEAN VINTON BURWELL. A.K.A. THE FUGUE.
I REMEMBER EVERYTHING.

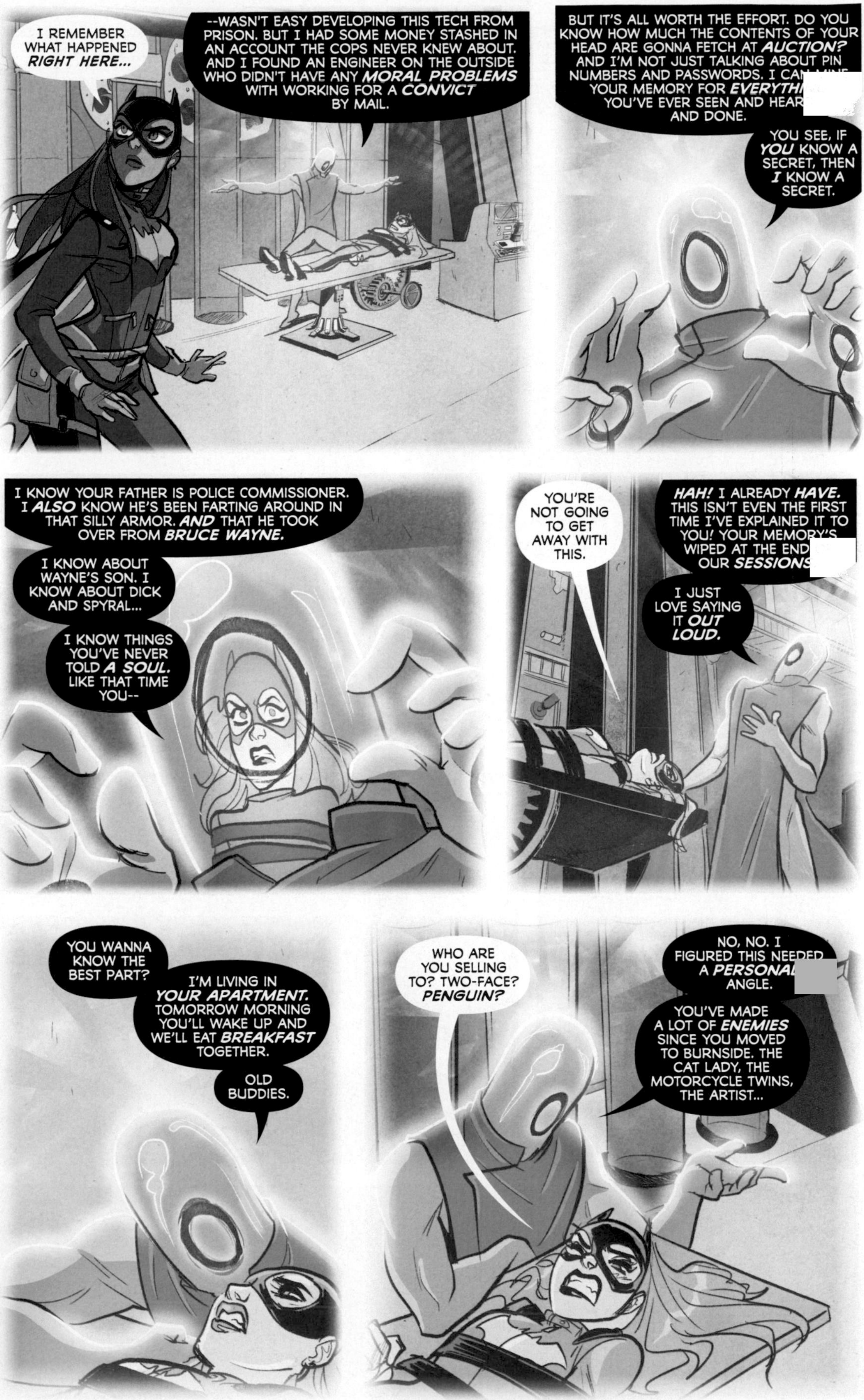

I REMEMBER WHAT HAPPENED RIGHT HERE...
--WASN'T EASY DEVELOPING THIS TECH FROM PRISON. BUT I HAD SOME MONEY STASHED IN AN ACCOUNT THE COPS NEVER KNEW ABOUT. AND I FOUND AN ENGINEER ON THE OUTSIDE WHO DIDN'T HAVE ANY MORAL PROBLEMS WITH WORKING FOR A CONVICT BY MAIL.
BUT IT'S ALL WORTH THE EFFORT. DO YOU KNOW HOW MUCH THE CONTENTS OF YOUR HEAD ARE GONNA FETCH AT AUCTION? AND I'M NOT JUST TALKING ABOUT PIN NUMBERS AND PASSWORDS. I CAN YOUR MEMORY FOR EVERYTHI YOU'VE EVER SEEN AND HEAR AND DONE.
YOU SEE, IF YOU KNOW A SECRET, THEN I KNOW A SECRET.
I KNOW YOUR FATHER IS POLICE COMMISSIONER. I ALSO KNOW HE'S BEEN FARTING AROUND IN THAT SILLY ARMOR. AND THAT HE TOOK OVER FROM BRUCE WAYNE.
I KNOW ABOUT WAYNE'S SON. I KNOW ABOUT DICK AND SPYRAL...
I KNOW THINGS YOU'VE NEVER TOLD A SOUL. LIKE THAT TIME YOU--
YOU'RE NOT GOING TO GET AWAY WITH THIS.
HAH! I ALREADY HAVE. THIS ISN'T EVEN THE FIRST TIME I'VE EXPLAINED IT TO YOU! YOUR MEMORY'S WIPED AT THE END OUR SESSIONS
I JUST LOVE SAYING IT OUT LOUD.
YOU WANNA KNOW THE BEST PART?
I'M LIVING IN YOUR APARTMENT. TOMORROW MORNING YOU'LL WAKE UP AND WE'LL EAT BREAKFAST TOGETHER.
OLD BUDDIES.
WHO ARE YOU SELLING TO? TWO-FACE? PENGUIN?
NO, NO. I FIGURED THIS NEEDED A PERSONAL ANGLE.
YOU'VE MADE A LOT OF ENEMIES SINCE YOU MOVED TO BURNSIDE. THE CAT LADY, THE MOTORCYCLE TWINS, THE ARTIST...

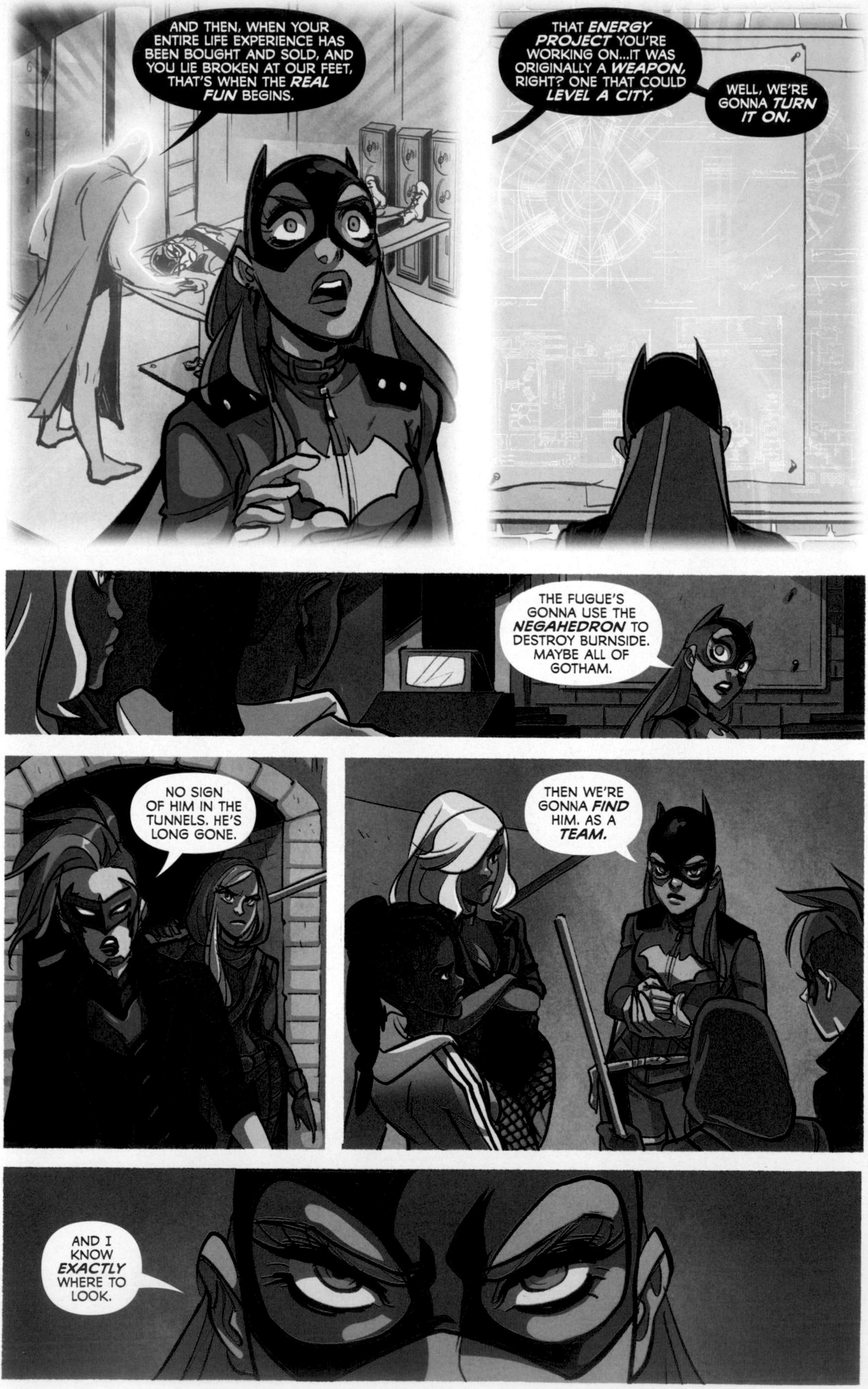

AND THEN, WHEN YOUR ENTIRE LIFE EXPERIENCE HAS BEEN BOUGHT AND SOLD, AND YOU LIE BROKEN AT OUR FEET, THAT'S WHEN THE REAL FUN BEGINS.
THAT ENERGY PROJECT YOU'RE WORKING ON...IT WAS ORIGINALLY A WEAPON, RIGHT? ONE THAT COULD LEVEL A CITY.
WELL, WE'RE GONNA TURN IT ON.
THE FUGUE'S GONNA USE THE NEGAHEDRON TO DESTROY BURNSIDE. MAYBE ALL OF GOTHAM.
NO SIGN OF HIM IN THE TUNNELS. HE'S LONG GONE.
THEN WE'RE GONNA FIND HIM. AS A TEAM.
AND I KNOW EXACTLY WHERE TO LOOK.

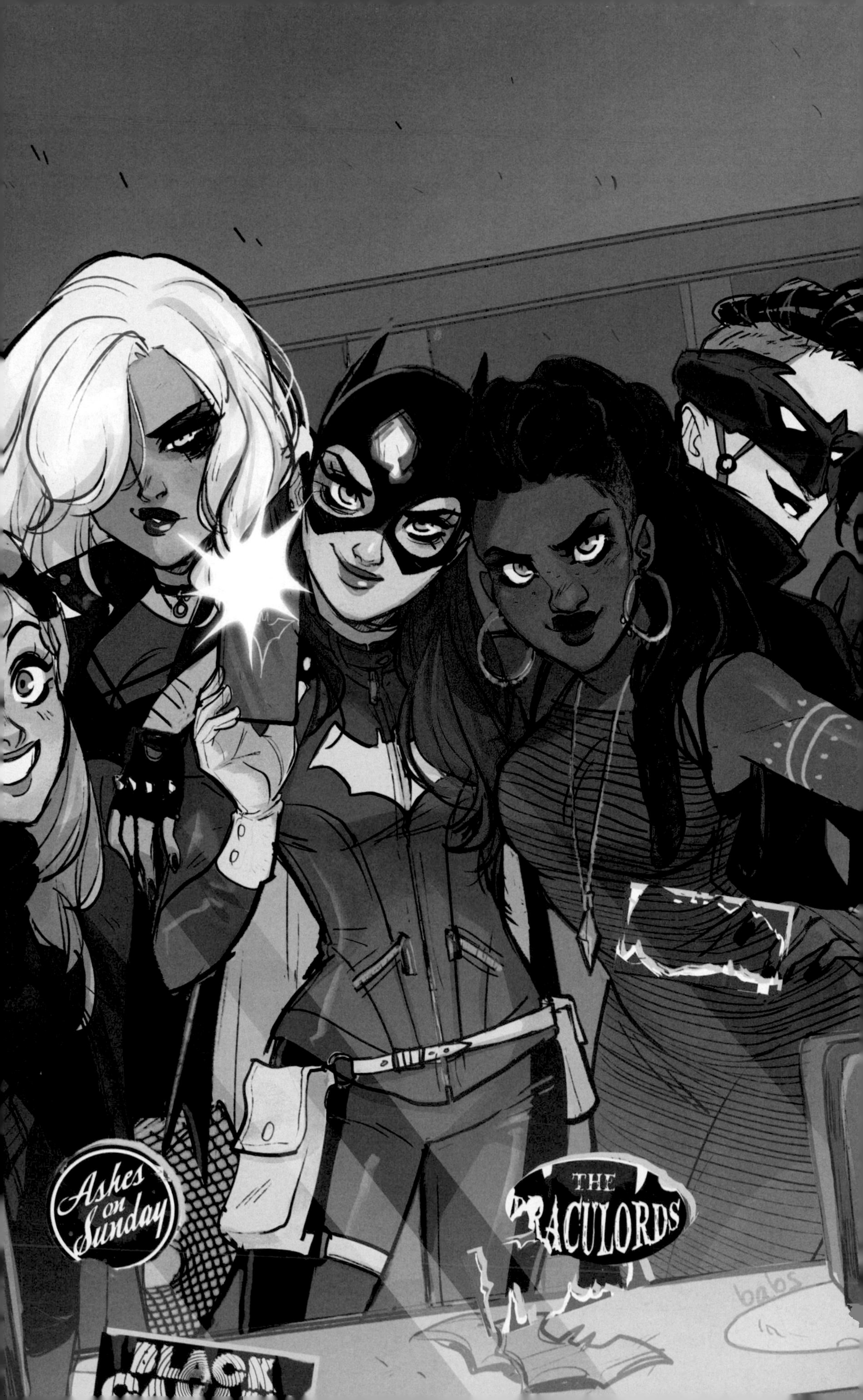
Ashes on Sunday
THE DRACULORDS
babs

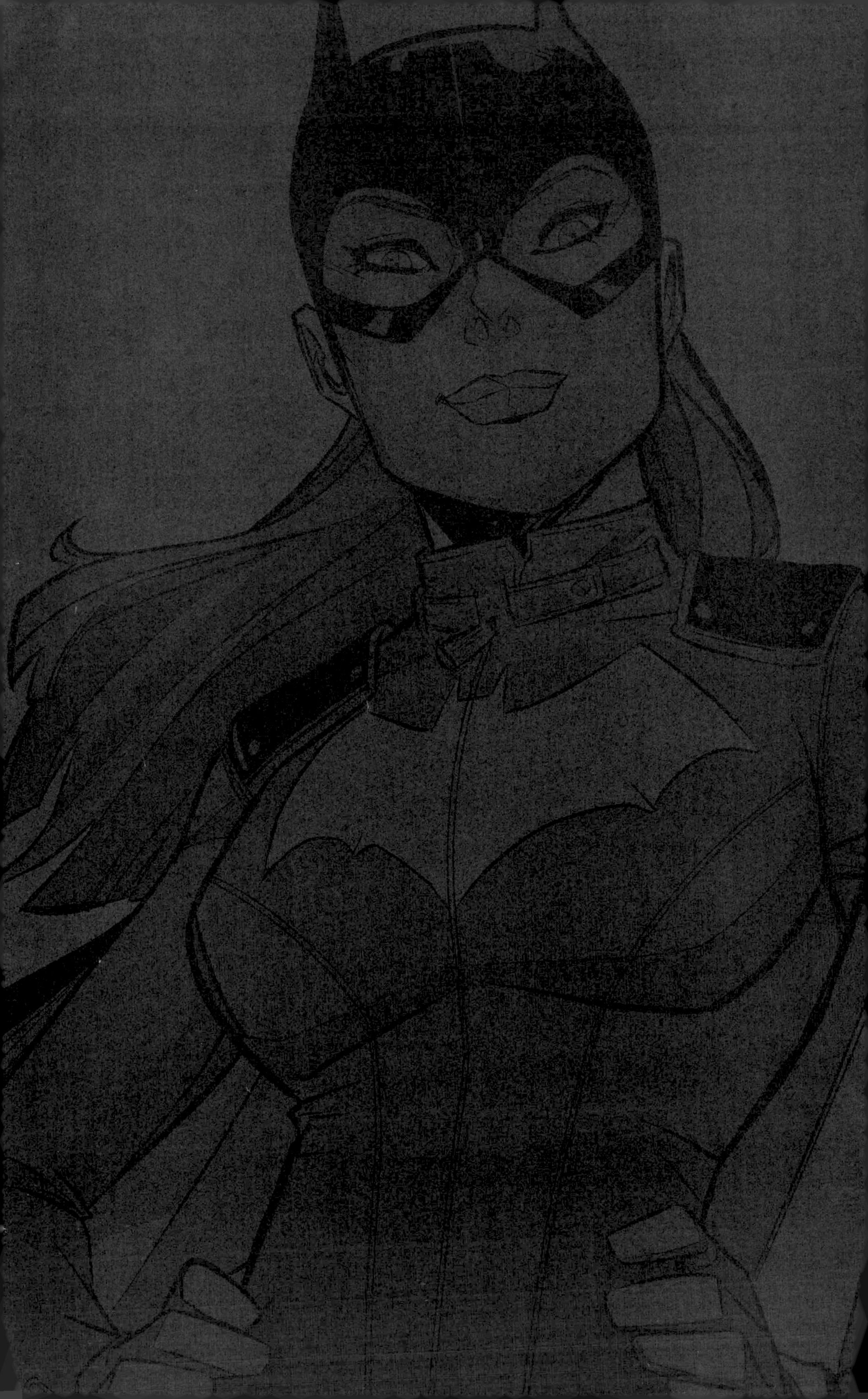

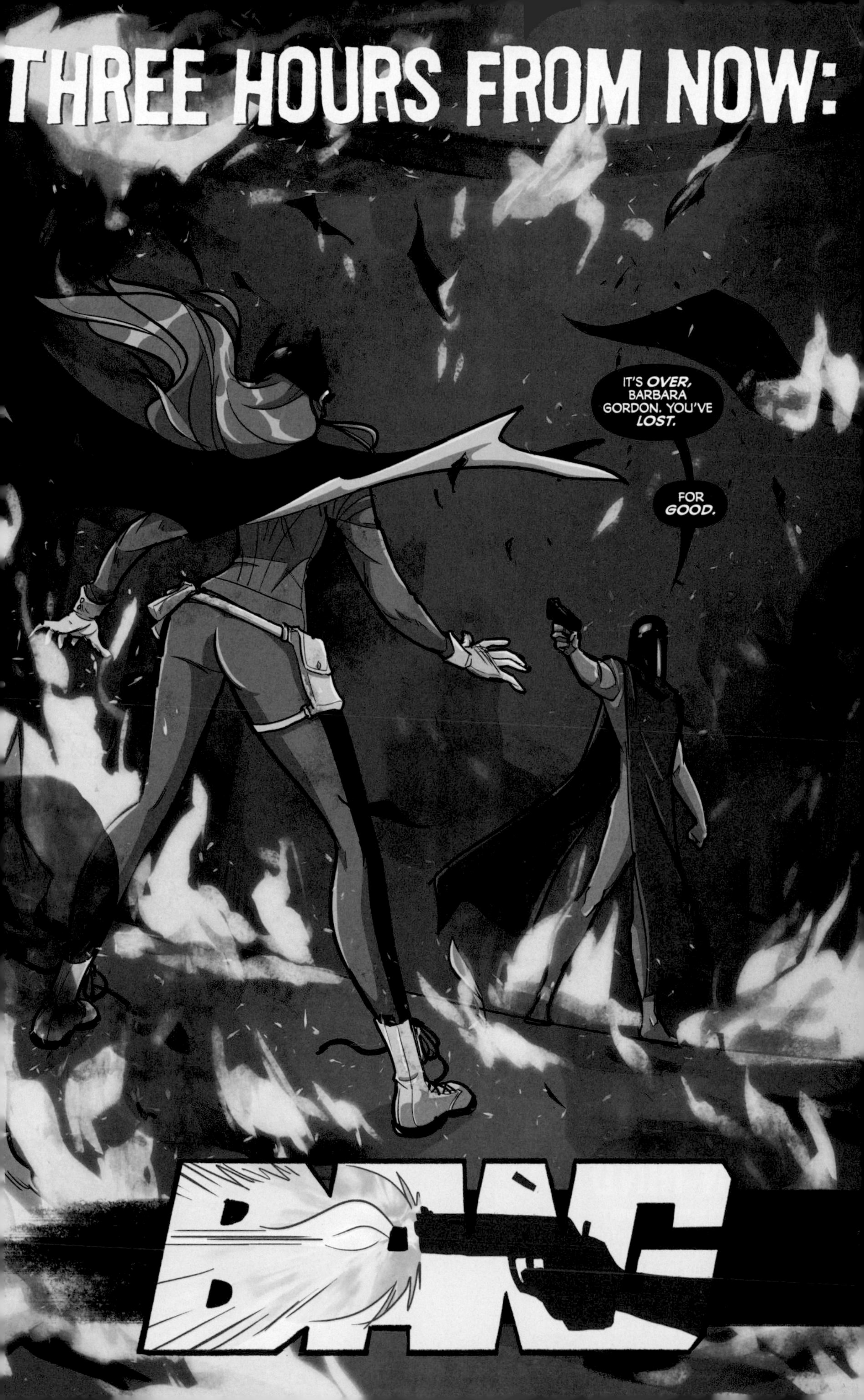
THREE HOURS FROM NOW:
IT'S OVER, BARBARA GORDON. YOU'VE LOST.
FOR GOOD.
BANG

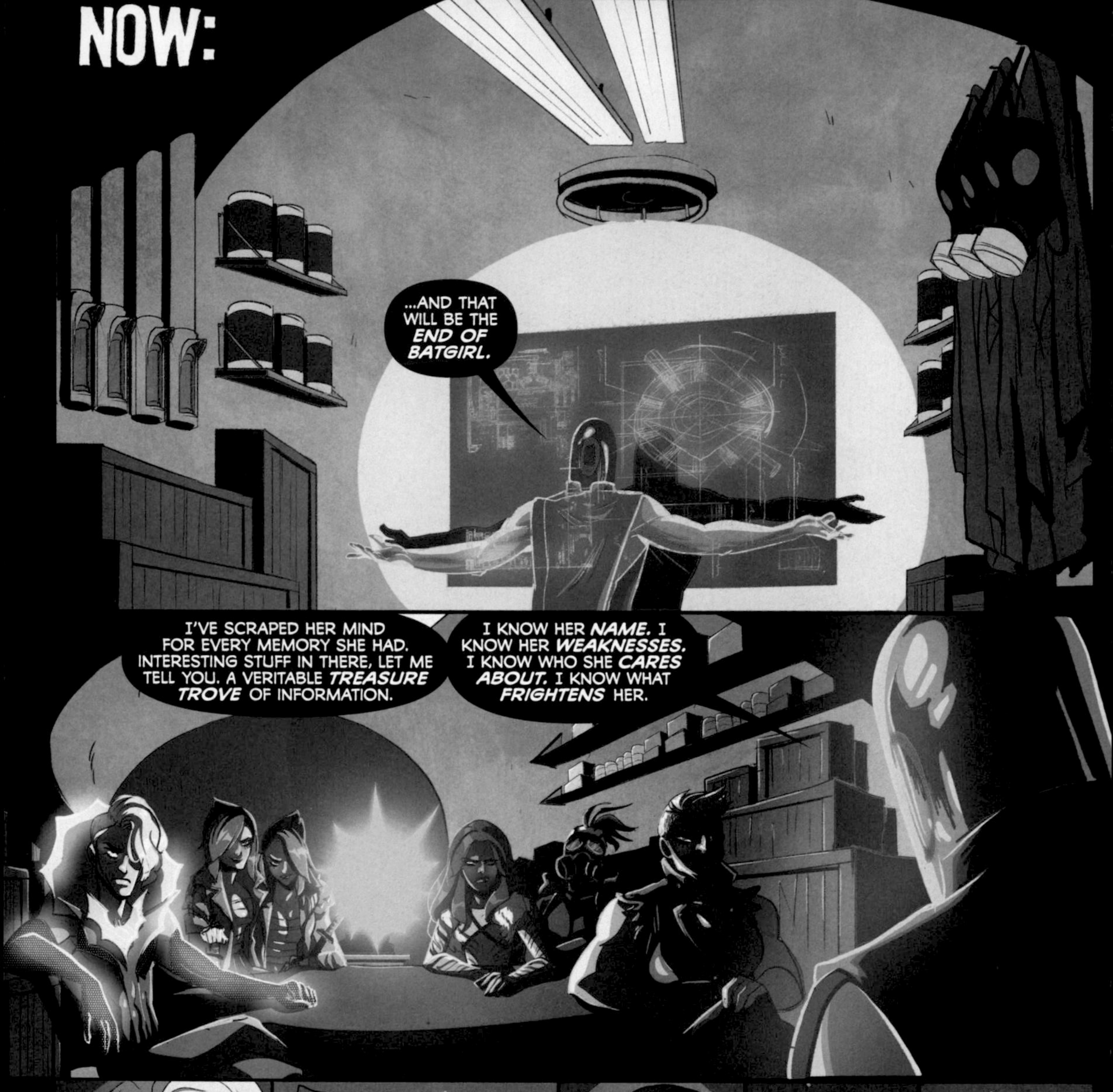
NOW:
...AND THAT WILL BE THE *END OF BATGIRL.*
I'VE SCRAPED HER MIND FOR EVERY MEMORY SHE HAD. INTERESTING STUFF IN THERE, LET ME TELL YOU. A VERITABLE *TREASURE TROVE* OF INFORMATION.
I KNOW HER *NAME.* I KNOW HER *WEAKNESSES.* I KNOW WHO SHE *CARES ABOUT.* I KNOW WHAT *FRIGHTENS* HER.
I KNOW WHAT WILL *RUIN* HER.
AND I'M OFFERING IT TO ONE OF *YOU.*
IF YOU CAN *PAY* FOR IT.

OPEN MIND

CAMERON STEWART +
BRENDEN FLETCHER WRITERS
BABS TARR, ROGER ROBINSON,
JOHN TIMMS, ELEONORA CARLINI +
JAMES HARVEY ARTISTS
CAMERON STEWART
BREAKDOWNS PGS 27-34, 36-38

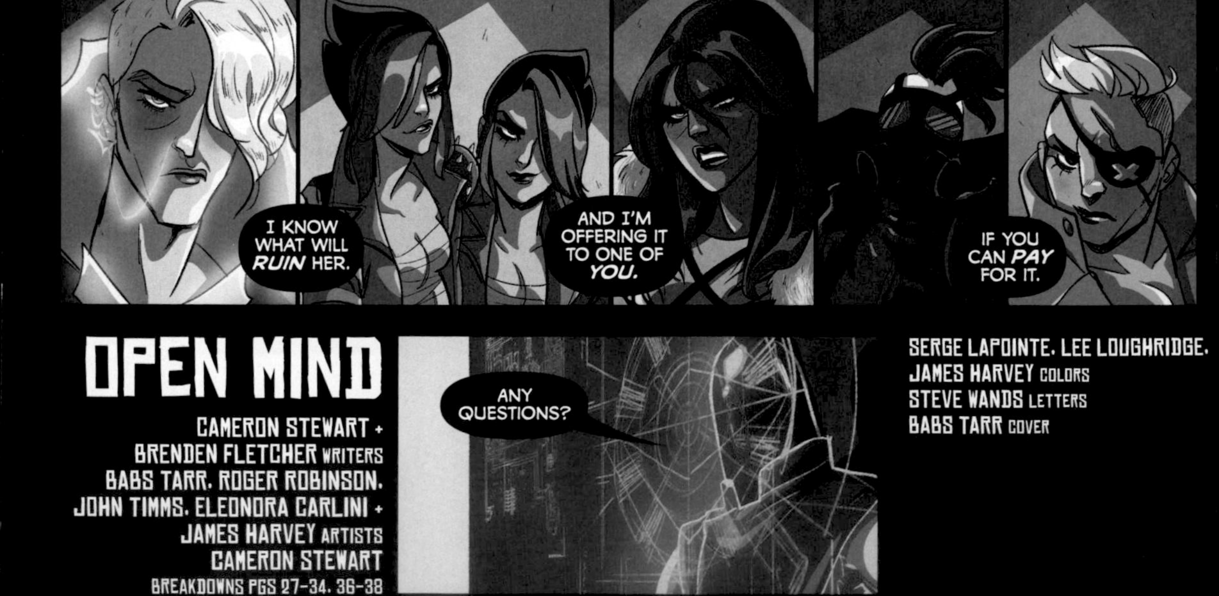
ANY QUESTIONS?

SERGE LAPOINTE, LEE LOUGHRIDGE,
JAMES HARVEY COLORS
STEVE WANDS LETTERS
BABS TARR COVER

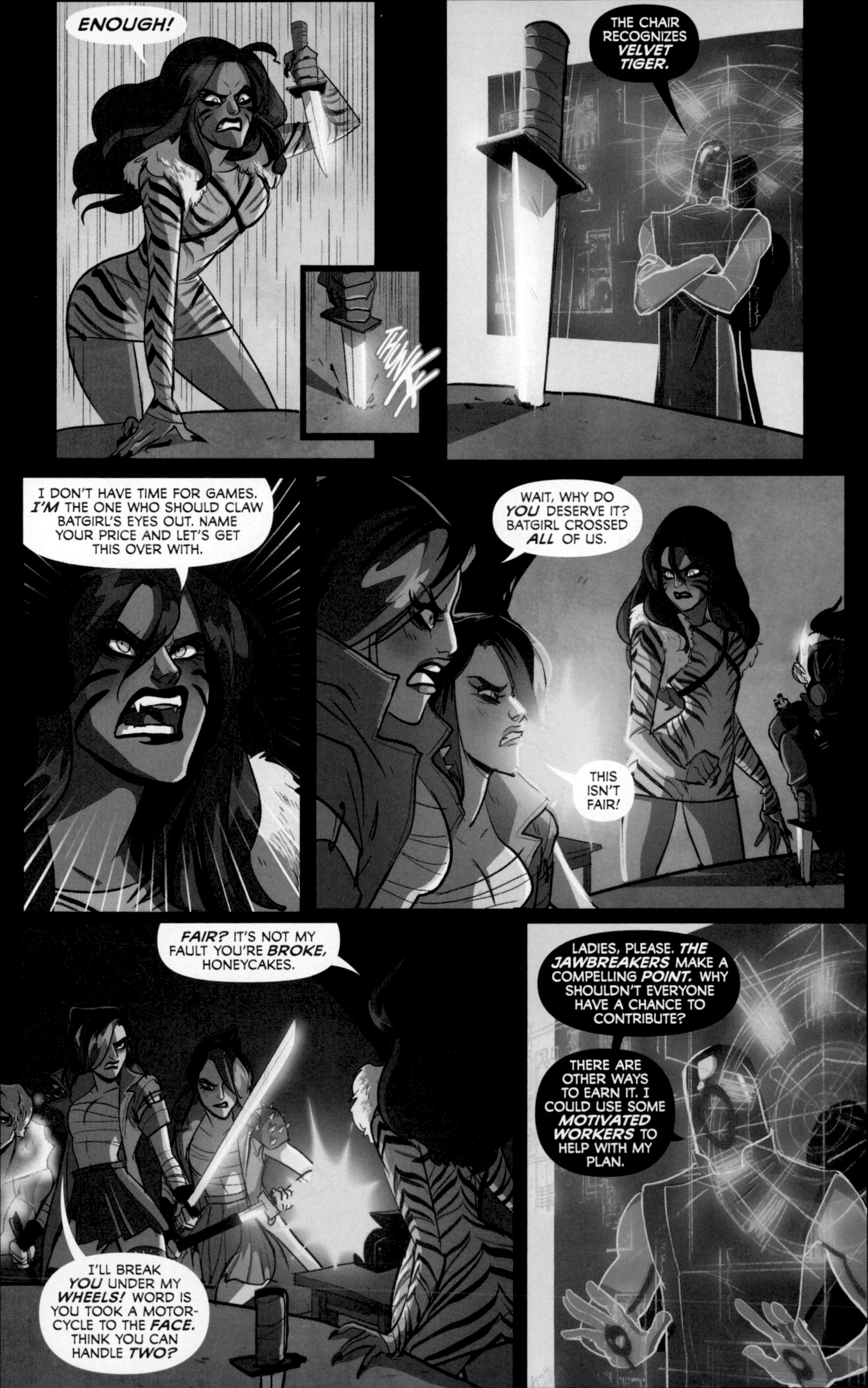
ENOUGH!
THUNK
THE CHAIR RECOGNIZES VELVET TIGER.
I DON'T HAVE TIME FOR GAMES. I'M THE ONE WHO SHOULD CLAW BATGIRL'S EYES OUT. NAME YOUR PRICE AND LET'S GET THIS OVER WITH.
WAIT, WHY DO YOU DESERVE IT? BATGIRL CROSSED ALL OF US.
THIS ISN'T FAIR!
FAIR? IT'S NOT MY FAULT YOU'RE BROKE, HONEYCAKES.
I'LL BREAK YOU UNDER MY WHEELS! WORD IS YOU TOOK A MOTOR-CYCLE TO THE FACE. THINK YOU CAN HANDLE TWO?
LADIES, PLEASE. THE JAWBREAKERS MAKE A COMPELLING POINT. WHY SHOULDN'T EVERYONE HAVE A CHANCE TO CONTRIBUTE?
THERE ARE OTHER WAYS TO EARN IT. I COULD USE SOME MOTIVATED WORKERS TO HELP WITH MY PLAN.

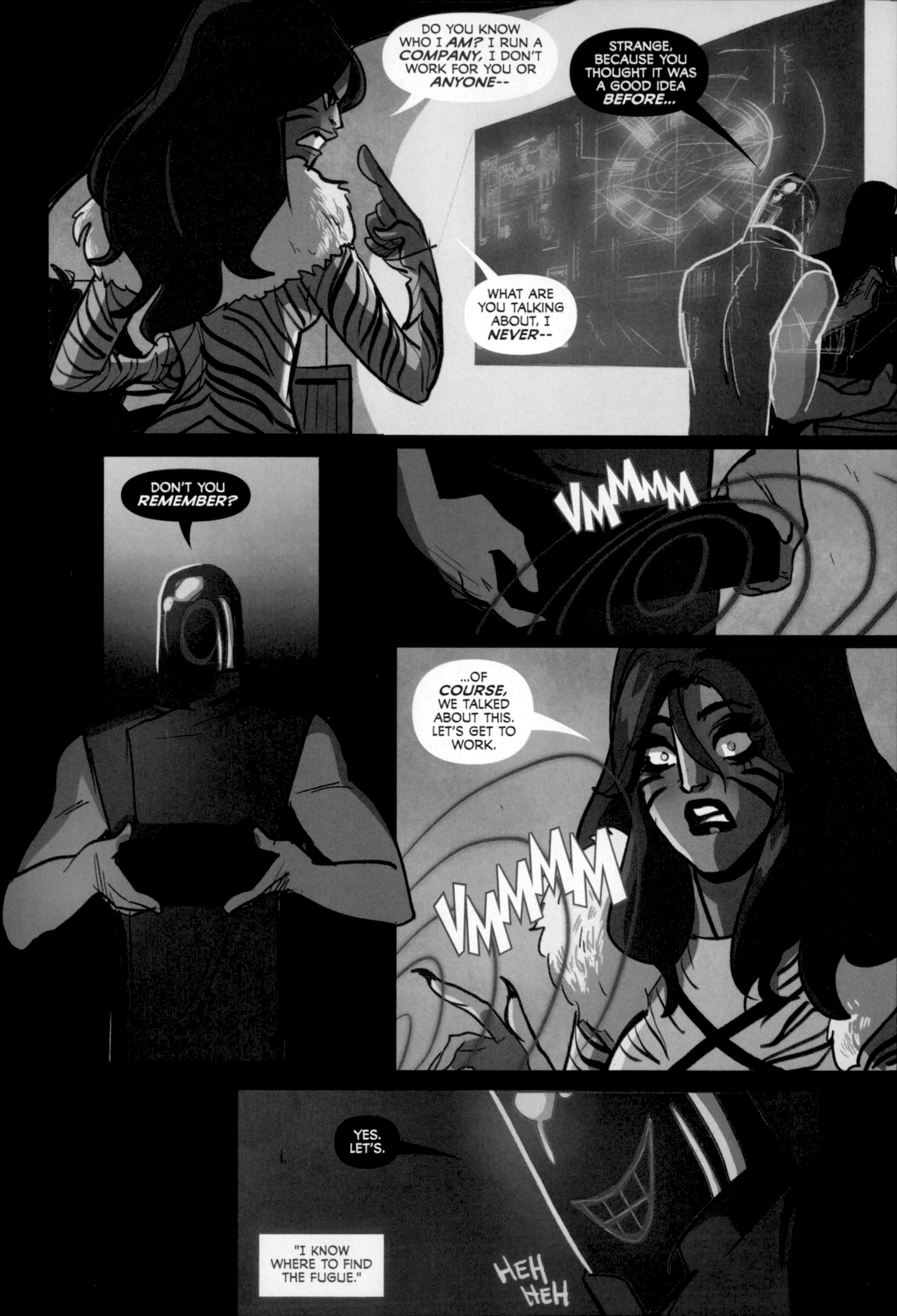
DO YOU KNOW WHO I *AM?* I RUN A *COMPANY,* I DON'T WORK FOR YOU OR *ANYONE*--
STRANGE, BECAUSE YOU THOUGHT IT WAS A GOOD IDEA *BEFORE...*
WHAT ARE YOU TALKING ABOUT, I *NEVER*--
DON'T YOU *REMEMBER?*
VMMMM
...OF *COURSE,* WE TALKED ABOUT THIS. LET'S GET TO WORK.
VMMMM
YES. LET'S.
"I KNOW WHERE TO FIND THE FUGUE."
HEH HEH

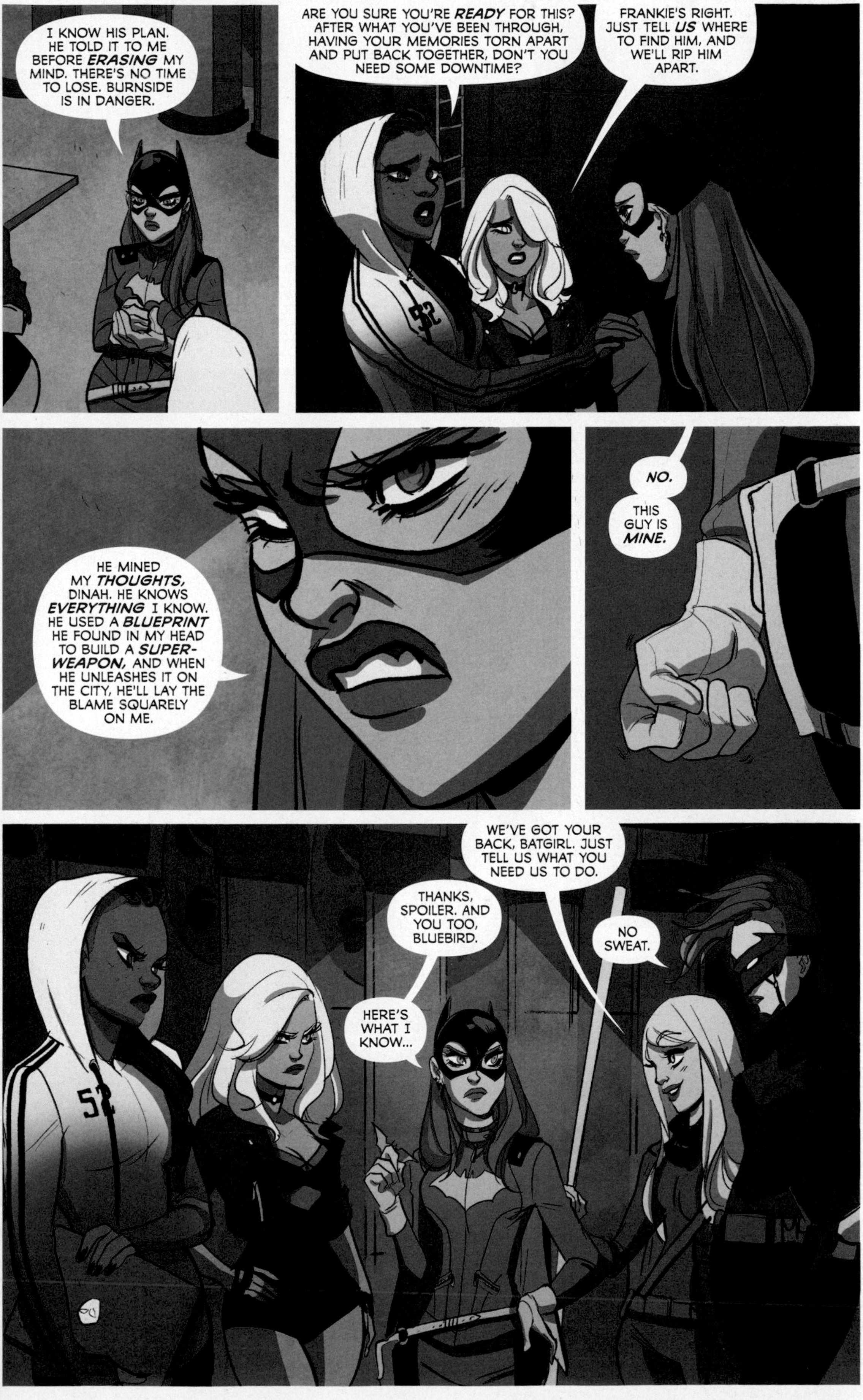
I KNOW HIS PLAN. HE TOLD IT TO ME BEFORE ERASING MY MIND. THERE'S NO TIME TO LOSE. BURNSIDE IS IN DANGER.
ARE YOU SURE YOU'RE READY FOR THIS? AFTER WHAT YOU'VE BEEN THROUGH, HAVING YOUR MEMORIES TORN APART AND PUT BACK TOGETHER, DON'T YOU NEED SOME DOWNTIME?
FRANKIE'S RIGHT. JUST TELL US WHERE TO FIND HIM, AND WE'LL RIP HIM APART.
HE MINED MY THOUGHTS, DINAH. HE KNOWS EVERYTHING I KNOW. HE USED A BLUEPRINT HE FOUND IN MY HEAD TO BUILD A SUPER-WEAPON, AND WHEN HE UNLEASHES IT ON THE CITY, HE'LL LAY THE BLAME SQUARELY ON ME.
NO.
THIS GUY IS MINE.
WE'VE GOT YOUR BACK, BATGIRL. JUST TELL US WHAT YOU NEED US TO DO.
THANKS, SPOILER. AND YOU TOO, BLUEBIRD.
NO SWEAT.
HERE'S WHAT I KNOW...

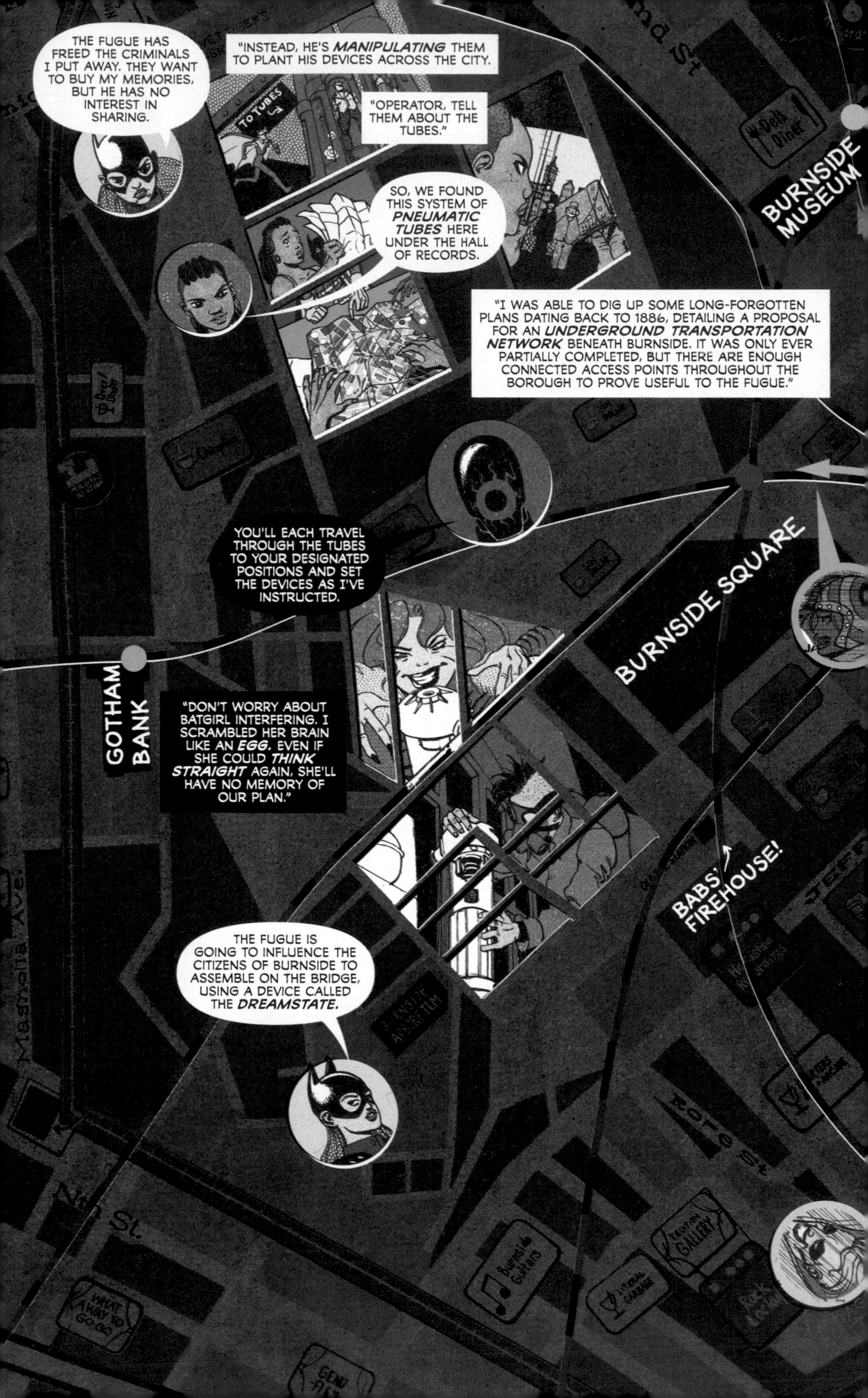

THE FUGUE HAS FREED THE CRIMINALS I PUT AWAY. THEY WANT TO BUY MY MEMORIES, BUT HE HAS NO INTEREST IN SHARING.
"INSTEAD, HE'S *MANIPULATING* THEM TO PLANT HIS DEVICES ACROSS THE CITY.
TO TUBES
"OPERATOR, TELL THEM ABOUT THE TUBES."
SO, WE FOUND THIS SYSTEM OF *PNEUMATIC TUBES* HERE UNDER THE HALL OF RECORDS.
"I WAS ABLE TO DIG UP SOME LONG-FORGOTTEN PLANS DATING BACK TO 1886, DETAILING A PROPOSAL FOR AN *UNDERGROUND TRANSPORTATION NETWORK* BENEATH BURNSIDE. IT WAS ONLY EVER PARTIALLY COMPLETED, BUT THERE ARE ENOUGH CONNECTED ACCESS POINTS THROUGHOUT THE BOROUGH TO PROVE USEFUL TO THE FUGUE."
BURNSIDE MUSEUM
Deli Diner
YOU'LL EACH TRAVEL THROUGH THE TUBES TO YOUR DESIGNATED POSITIONS AND SET THE DEVICES AS I'VE INSTRUCTED.
BURNSIDE SQUARE
GOTHAM BANK
"DON'T WORRY ABOUT BATGIRL INTERFERING. I SCRAMBLED HER BRAIN LIKE AN *EGG*. EVEN IF SHE COULD *THINK STRAIGHT* AGAIN, SHE'LL HAVE NO MEMORY OF OUR PLAN."
BABS' FIREHOUSE!
THE FUGUE IS GOING TO INFLUENCE THE CITIZENS OF BURNSIDE TO ASSEMBLE ON THE BRIDGE, USING A DEVICE CALLED THE *DREAMSTATE*.
BURNSIDE ARBORETUM
Magnolia Ave.
Rore St
Nth St.
Burnside Guitars
GALLERY
WHAT A WAY TO GO-GO

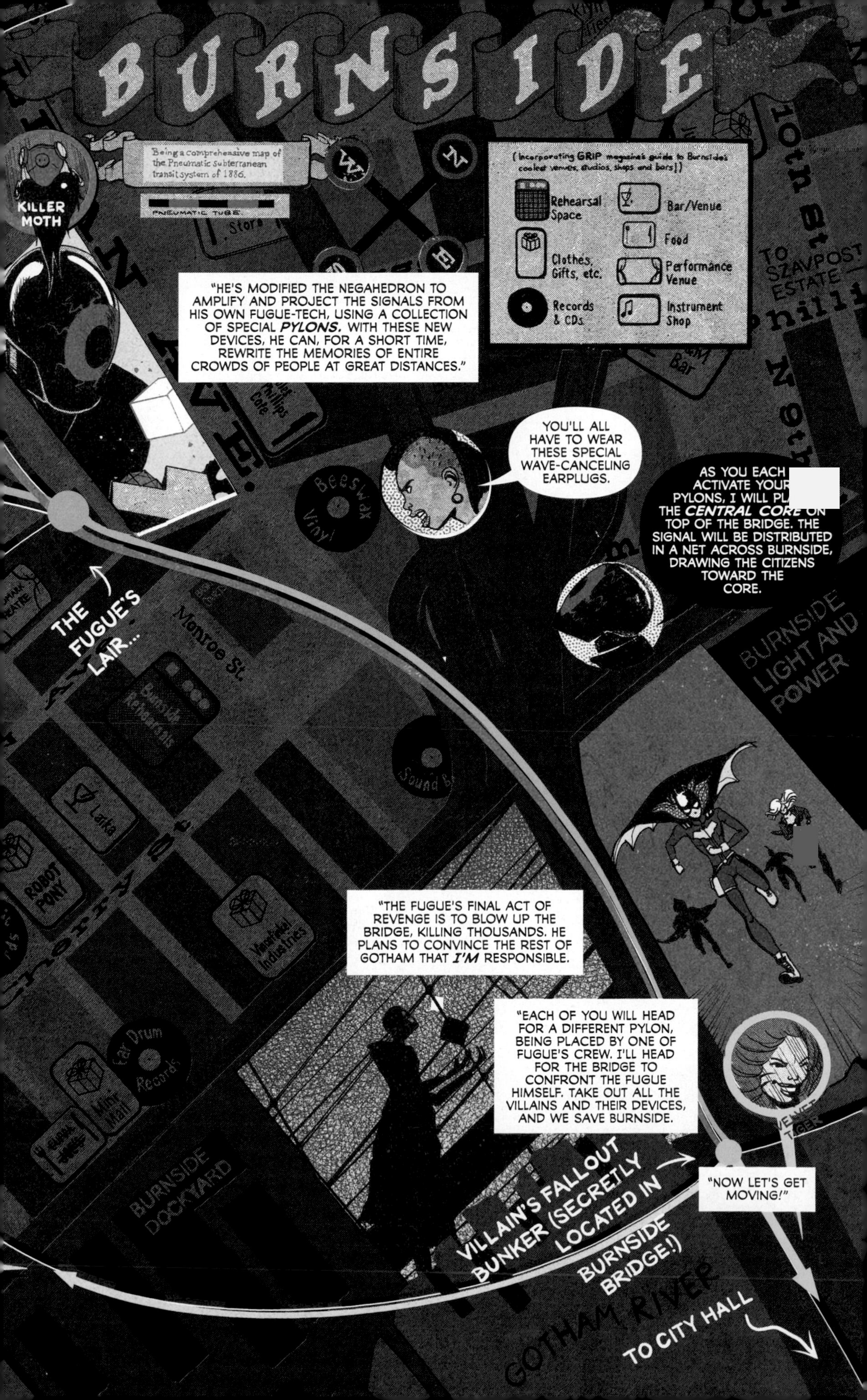
BURNSIDE
Being a comprehensive map of the Pneumatic Subterranean transit system of 1886.
PNEUMATIC TUBE
KILLER MOTH
(Incorporating GRIP magazine's guide to Burnside's coolest venues, studios, shops and bars!)
Rehearsal Space
Clothes, Gifts, etc.
Records & CDs
Bar/Venue
Food
Performance Venue
Instrument Shop
"HE'S MODIFIED THE NEGAHEDRON TO AMPLIFY AND PROJECT THE SIGNALS FROM HIS OWN FUGUE-TECH, USING A COLLECTION OF SPECIAL ***PYLONS.*** WITH THESE NEW DEVICES, HE CAN, FOR A SHORT TIME, REWRITE THE MEMORIES OF ENTIRE CROWDS OF PEOPLE AT GREAT DISTANCES."
TO SZAVPOST ESTATE
10th St
YOU'LL ALL HAVE TO WEAR THESE SPECIAL WAVE-CANCELING EARPLUGS.
Beeswax Vinyl
AS YOU EACH ACTIVATE YOUR PYLONS, I WILL PL THE ***CENTRAL CORE*** ON TOP OF THE BRIDGE. THE SIGNAL WILL BE DISTRIBUTED IN A NET ACROSS BURNSIDE, DRAWING THE CITIZENS TOWARD THE CORE.
THE FUGUE'S LAIR...
Monroe St.
BURNSIDE LIGHT AND POWER
Burnside Rehearsals
Robot Pony
"THE FUGUE'S FINAL ACT OF REVENGE IS TO BLOW UP THE BRIDGE, KILLING THOUSANDS. HE PLANS TO CONVINCE THE REST OF GOTHAM THAT ***I'M*** RESPONSIBLE.
"EACH OF YOU WILL HEAD FOR A DIFFERENT PYLON, BEING PLACED BY ONE OF FUGUE'S CREW. I'LL HEAD FOR THE BRIDGE TO CONFRONT THE FUGUE HIMSELF. TAKE OUT ALL THE VILLAINS AND THEIR DEVICES, AND WE SAVE BURNSIDE.
Ear Drum Records
Mini Mall
BURNSIDE DOCKYARD
VILLAIN'S FALLOUT BUNKER (SECRETLY LOCATED IN BURNSIDE BRIDGE!)
"NOW LET'S GET MOVING!"
GOTHAM RIVER
TO CITY HALL

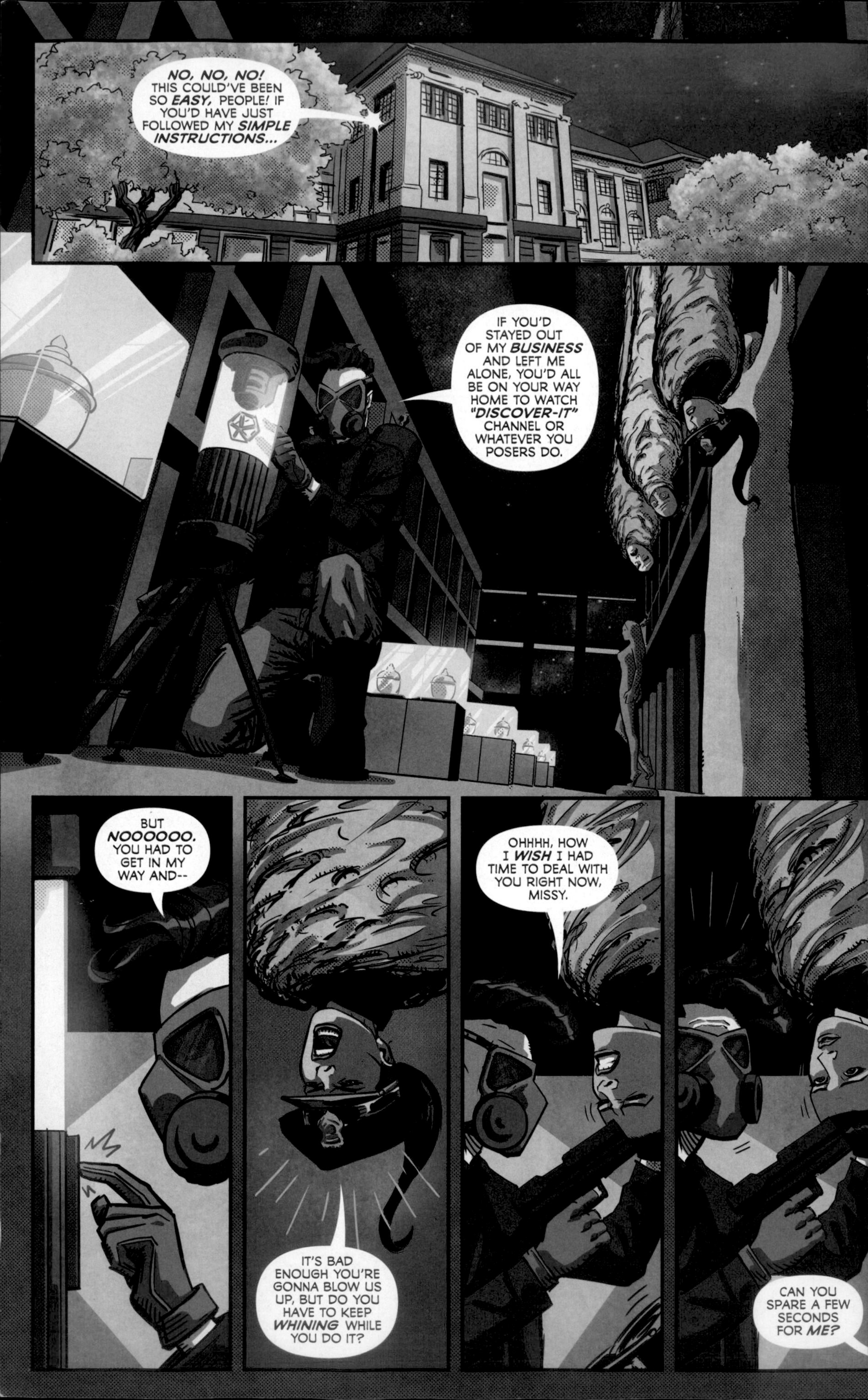
NO, NO, NO! THIS COULD'VE BEEN SO EASY, PEOPLE! IF YOU'D HAVE JUST FOLLOWED MY SIMPLE INSTRUCTIONS...
IF YOU'D STAYED OUT OF MY BUSINESS AND LEFT ME ALONE, YOU'D ALL BE ON YOUR WAY HOME TO WATCH "DISCOVER-IT" CHANNEL OR WHATEVER YOU POSERS DO.
BUT NOOOOOO. YOU HAD TO GET IN MY WAY AND--
IT'S BAD ENOUGH YOU'RE GONNA BLOW US UP, BUT DO YOU HAVE TO KEEP WHINING WHILE YOU DO IT?
OHHHH, HOW I WISH I HAD TIME TO DEAL WITH YOU RIGHT NOW, MISSY.
CAN YOU SPARE A FEW SECONDS FOR ME?

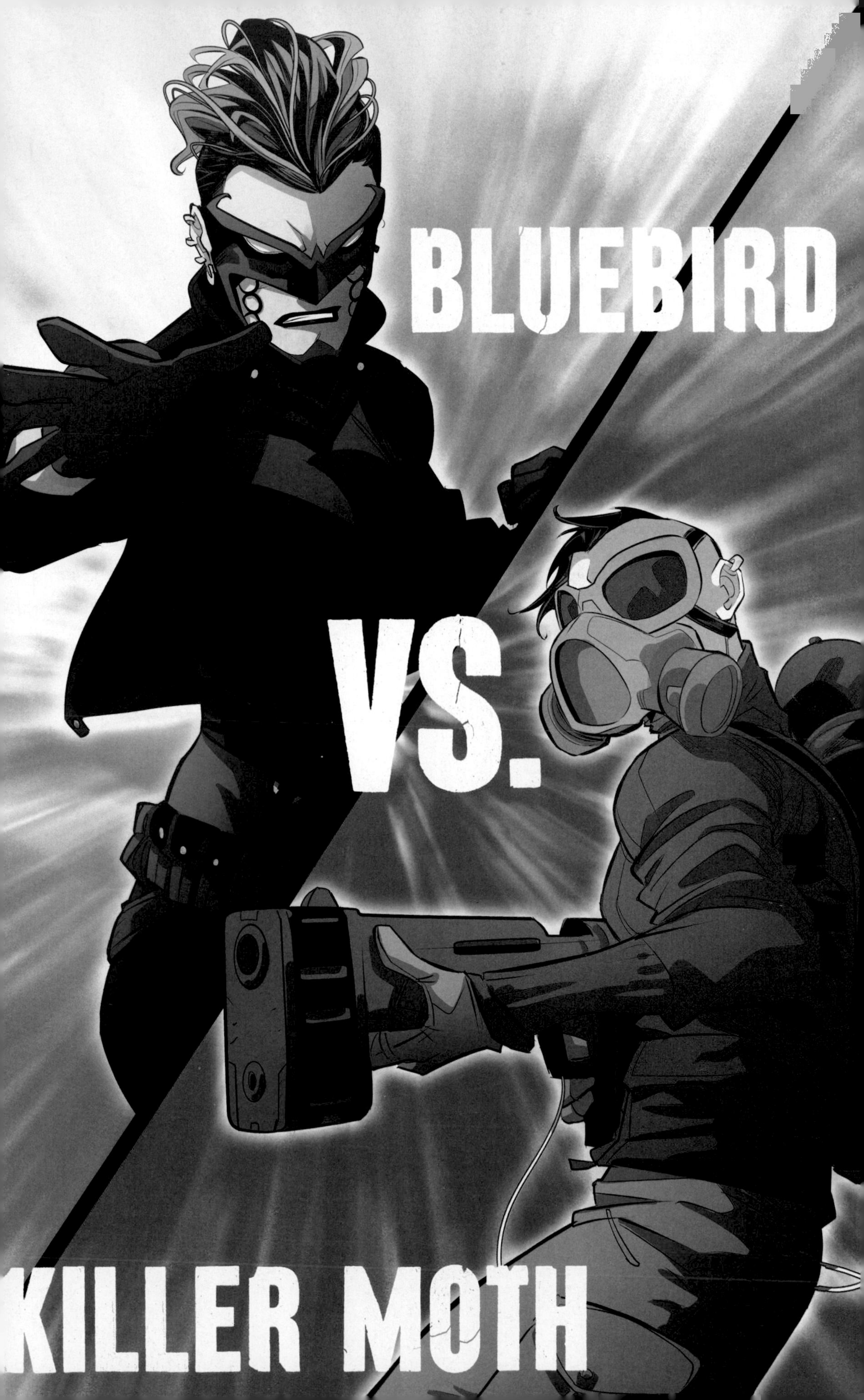
BLUEBIRD
VS.
KILLER MOTH

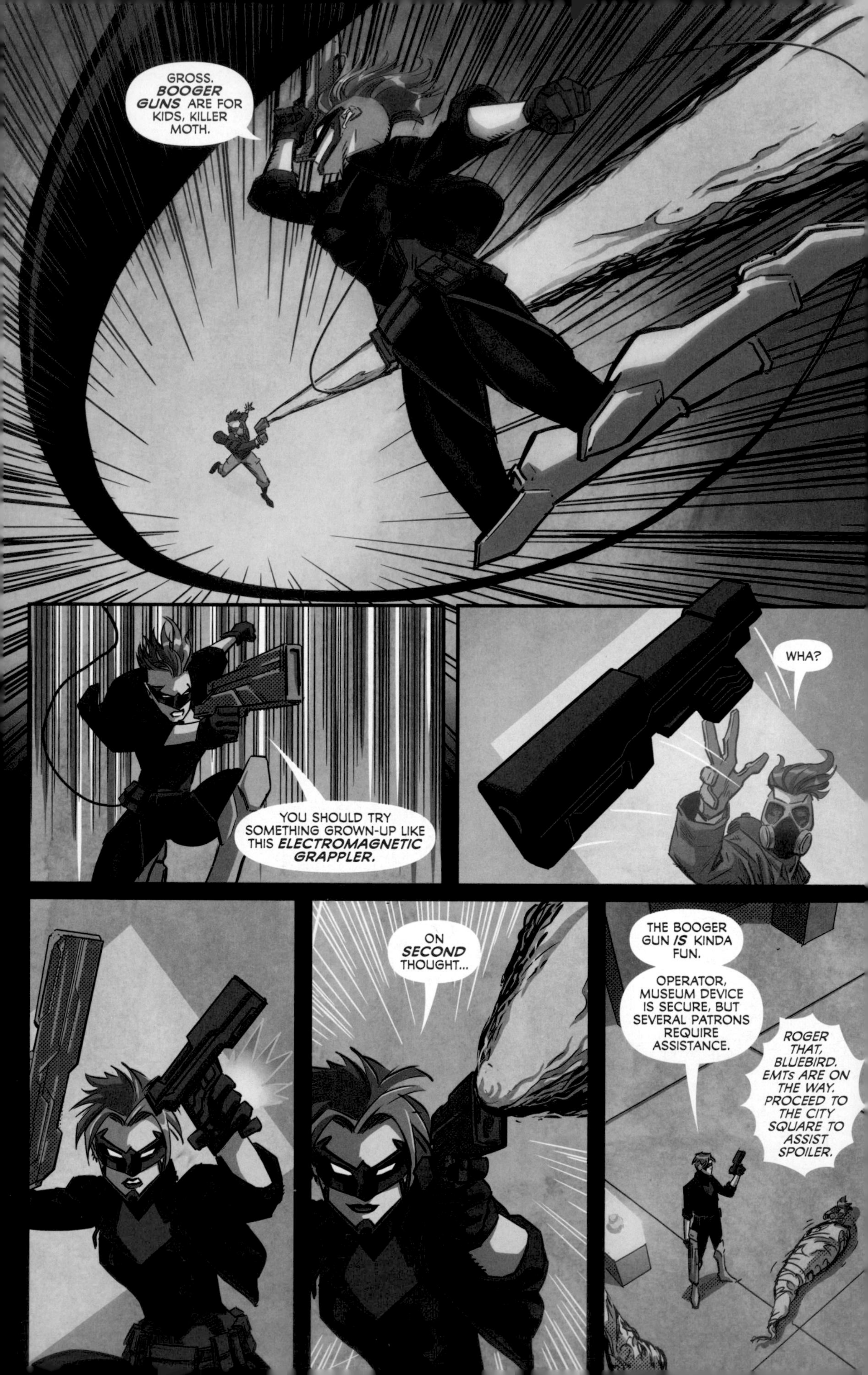
GROSS. BOOGER GUNS ARE FOR KIDS, KILLER MOTH.
YOU SHOULD TRY SOMETHING GROWN-UP LIKE THIS ELECTROMAGNETIC GRAPPLER.
WHA?
ON SECOND THOUGHT...
THE BOOGER GUN IS KINDA FUN.
OPERATOR, MUSEUM DEVICE IS SECURE, BUT SEVERAL PATRONS REQUIRE ASSISTANCE.
ROGER THAT, BLUEBIRD. EMTs ARE ON THE WAY. PROCEED TO THE CITY SQUARE TO ASSIST SPOILER.

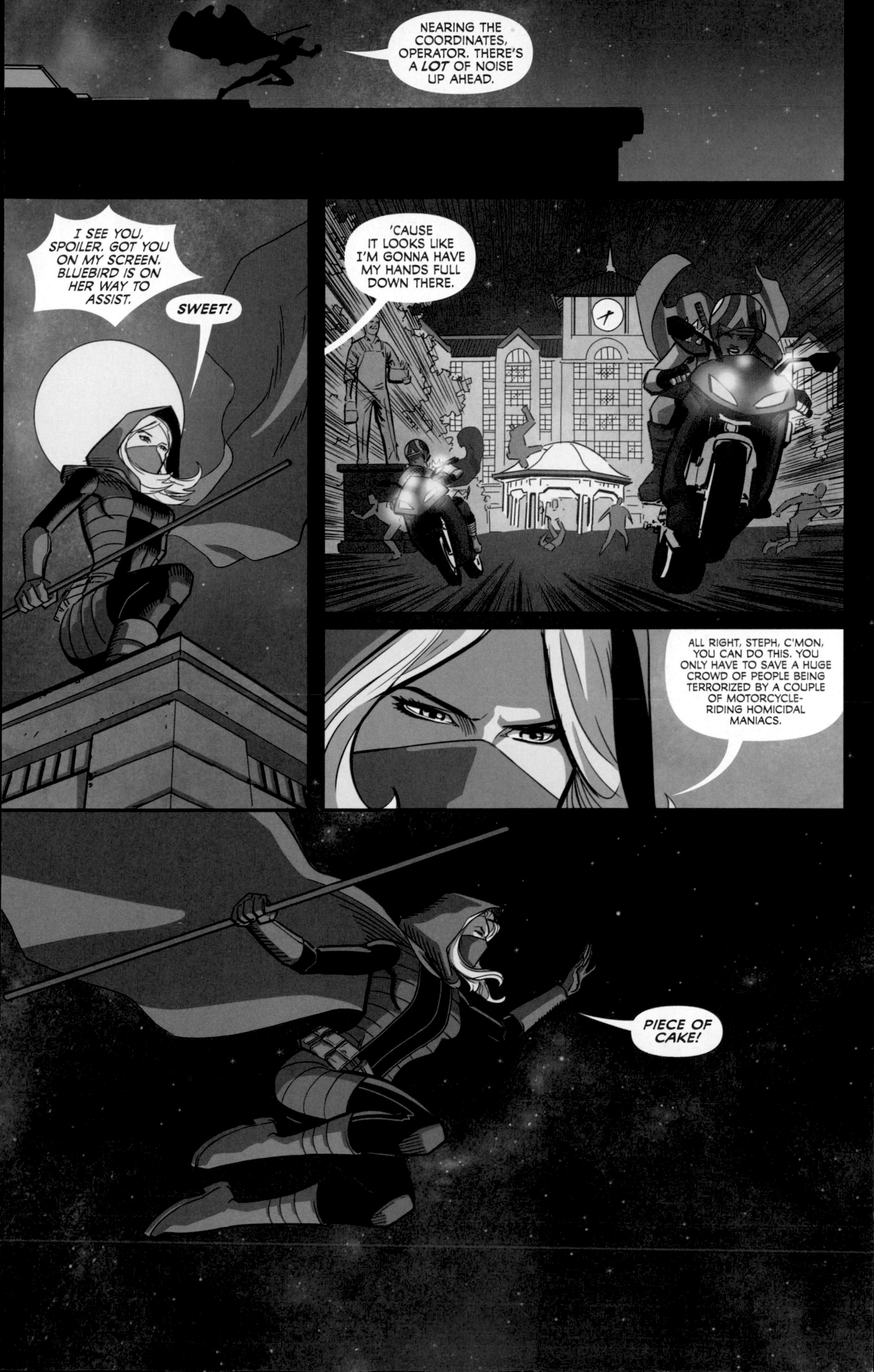
NEARING THE COORDINATES, OPERATOR. THERE'S A *LOT* OF NOISE UP AHEAD.
I SEE YOU, SPOILER. GOT YOU ON MY SCREEN. BLUEBIRD IS ON HER WAY TO ASSIST.
SWEET!
'CAUSE IT LOOKS LIKE I'M GONNA HAVE MY HANDS FULL DOWN THERE.
ALL RIGHT, STEPH, C'MON, YOU CAN DO THIS. YOU ONLY HAVE TO SAVE A HUGE CROWD OF PEOPLE BEING TERRORIZED BY A COUPLE OF MOTORCYCLE-RIDING HOMICIDAL MANIACS.
PIECE OF CAKE!

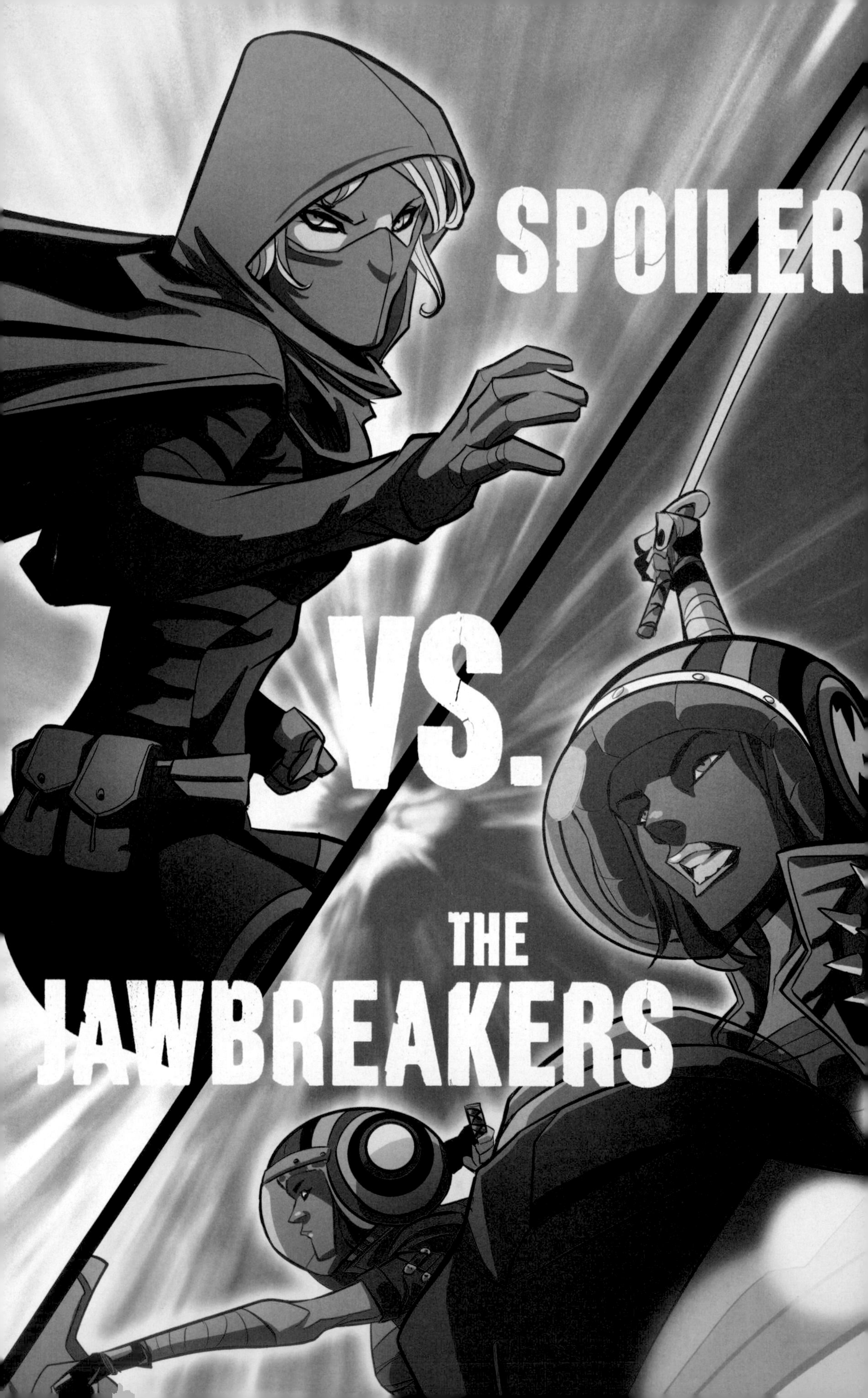
SPOILER
VS.
THE
JAWBREAKERS

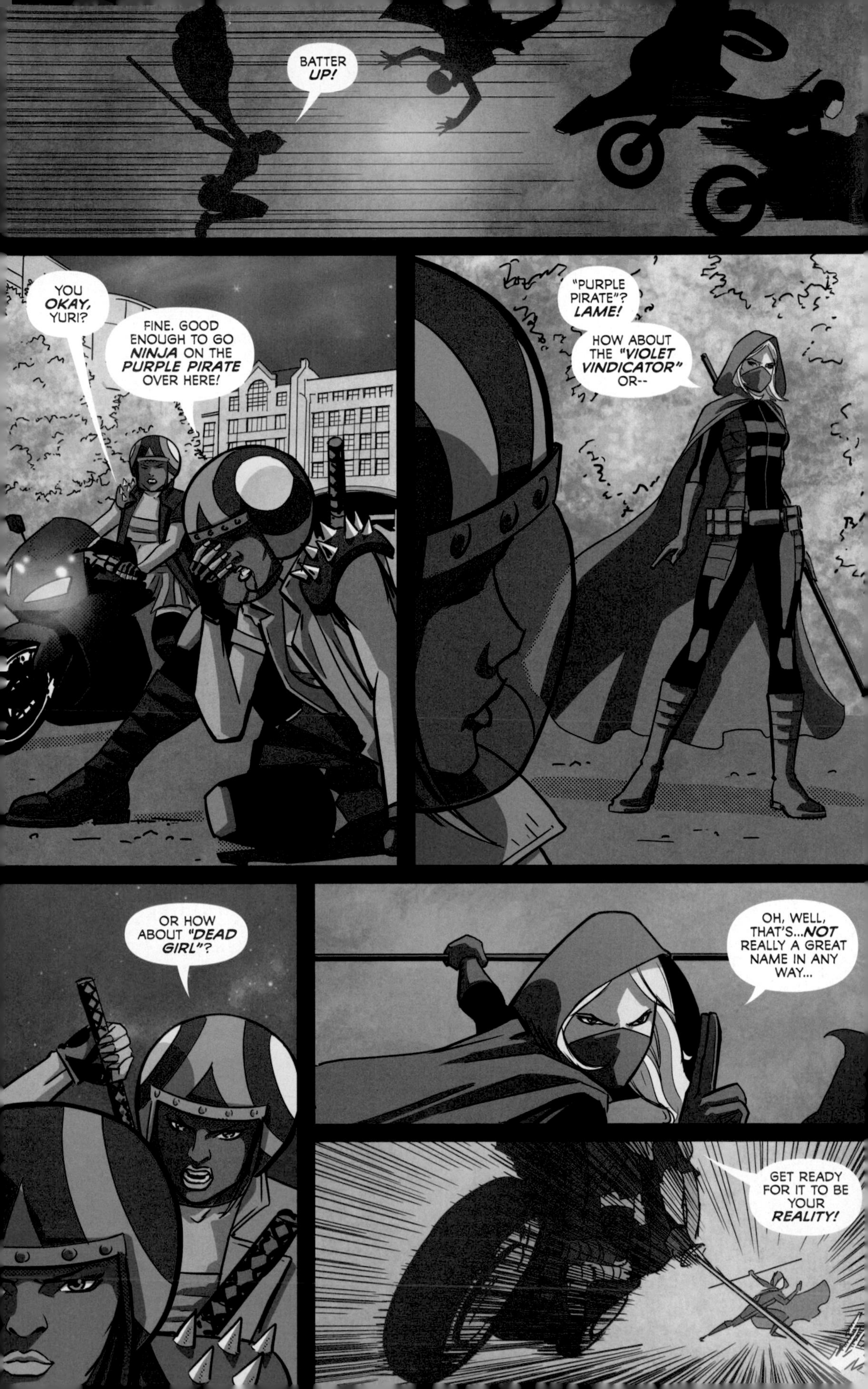
BATTER UP!
YOU OKAY, YURI?
FINE. GOOD ENOUGH TO GO NINJA ON THE PURPLE PIRATE OVER HERE!
"PURPLE PIRATE"? LAME!
HOW ABOUT THE "VIOLET VINDICATOR" OR--
OR HOW ABOUT "DEAD GIRL"?
OH, WELL, THAT'S...NOT REALLY A GREAT NAME IN ANY WAY...
GET READY FOR IT TO BE YOUR REALITY!

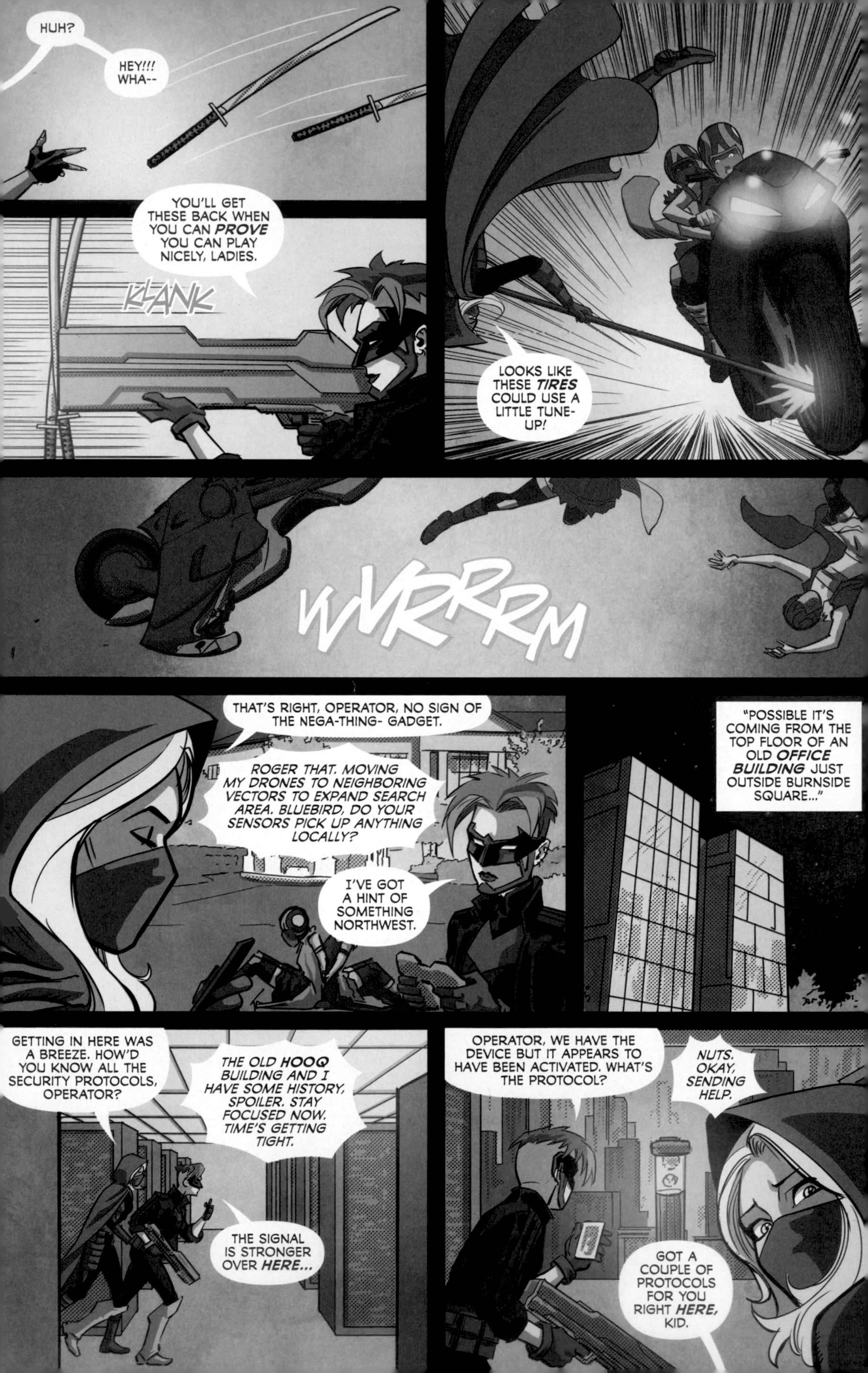
HUH?
HEY!!! WHA--
YOU'LL GET THESE BACK WHEN YOU CAN PROVE YOU CAN PLAY NICELY, LADIES.
KLANK
LOOKS LIKE THESE TIRES COULD USE A LITTLE TUNE-UP!
WVRRRM
THAT'S RIGHT, OPERATOR, NO SIGN OF THE NEGA-THING- GADGET.
ROGER THAT. MOVING MY DRONES TO NEIGHBORING VECTORS TO EXPAND SEARCH AREA. BLUEBIRD, DO YOUR SENSORS PICK UP ANYTHING LOCALLY?
I'VE GOT A HINT OF SOMETHING NORTHWEST.
"POSSIBLE IT'S COMING FROM THE TOP FLOOR OF AN OLD OFFICE BUILDING JUST OUTSIDE BURNSIDE SQUARE..."
GETTING IN HERE WAS A BREEZE. HOW'D YOU KNOW ALL THE SECURITY PROTOCOLS, OPERATOR?
THE OLD HOOQ BUILDING AND I HAVE SOME HISTORY, SPOILER. STAY FOCUSED NOW. TIME'S GETTING TIGHT.
THE SIGNAL IS STRONGER OVER HERE...
OPERATOR, WE HAVE THE DEVICE BUT IT APPEARS TO HAVE BEEN ACTIVATED. WHAT'S THE PROTOCOL?
NUTS. OKAY, SENDING HELP.
GOT A COUPLE OF PROTOCOLS FOR YOU RIGHT HERE, KID.

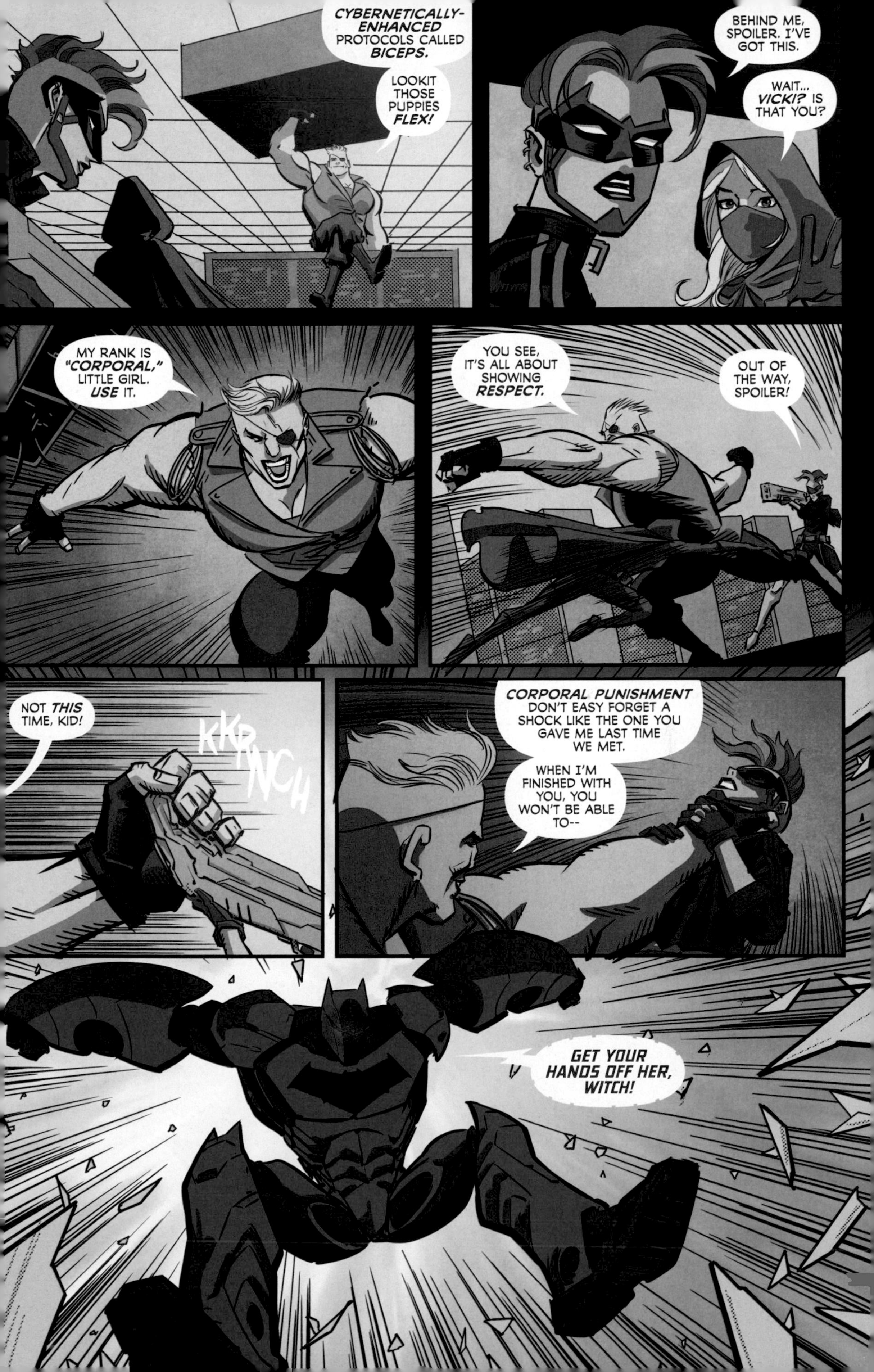
CYBERNETICALLY-ENHANCED PROTOCOLS CALLED BICEPS.
LOOKIT THOSE PUPPIES FLEX!
BEHIND ME, SPOILER. I'VE GOT THIS.
WAIT... VICKI? IS THAT YOU?
MY RANK IS "CORPORAL," LITTLE GIRL. USE IT.
YOU SEE, IT'S ALL ABOUT SHOWING RESPECT.
OUT OF THE WAY, SPOILER!
NOT THIS TIME, KID!
KKRNCH
CORPORAL PUNISHMENT DON'T EASY FORGET A SHOCK LIKE THE ONE YOU GAVE ME LAST TIME WE MET.
WHEN I'M FINISHED WITH YOU, YOU WON'T BE ABLE TO--
GET YOUR HANDS OFF HER, WITCH!

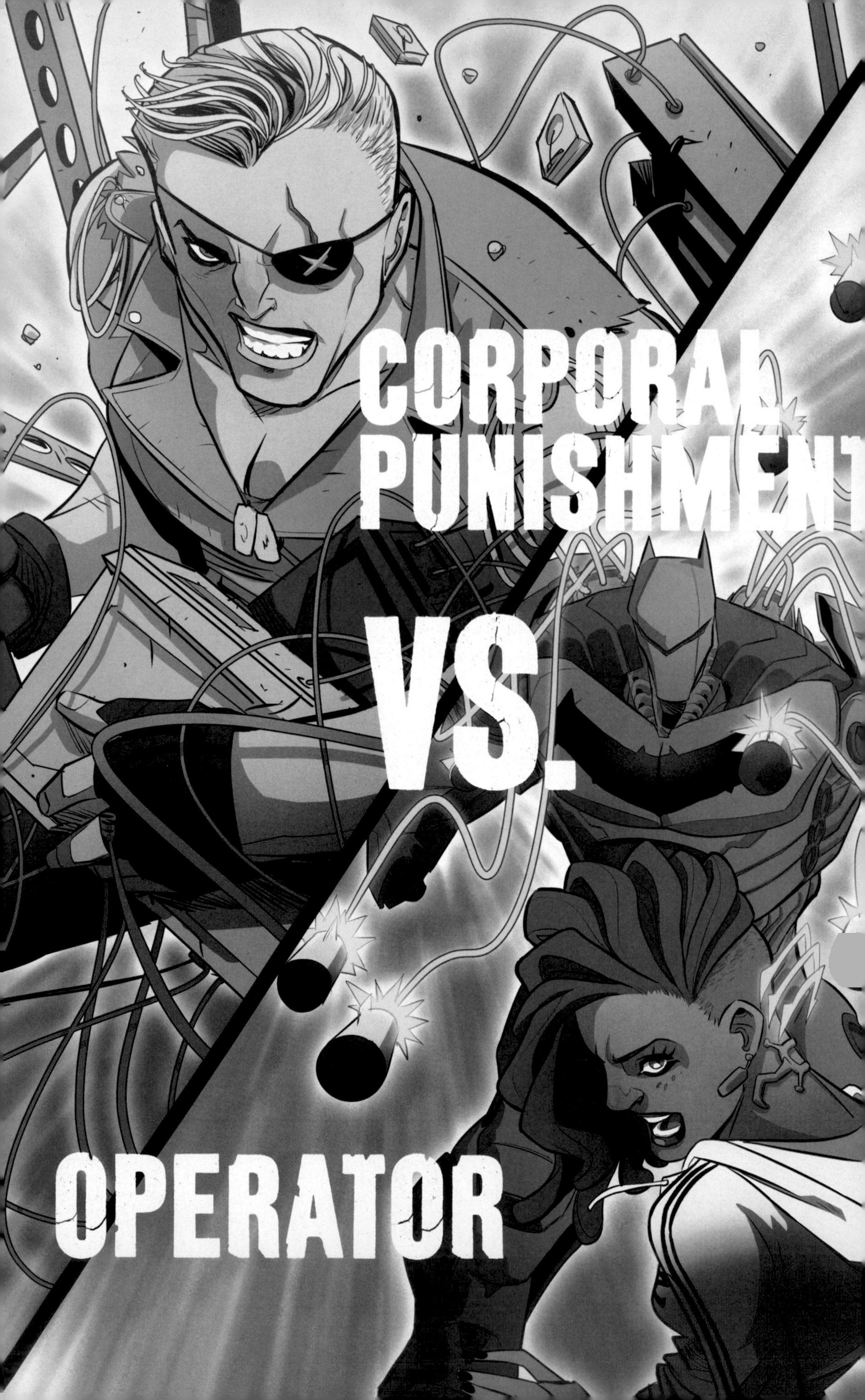
CORPORAL PUNISHMENT
VS.
OPERATOR

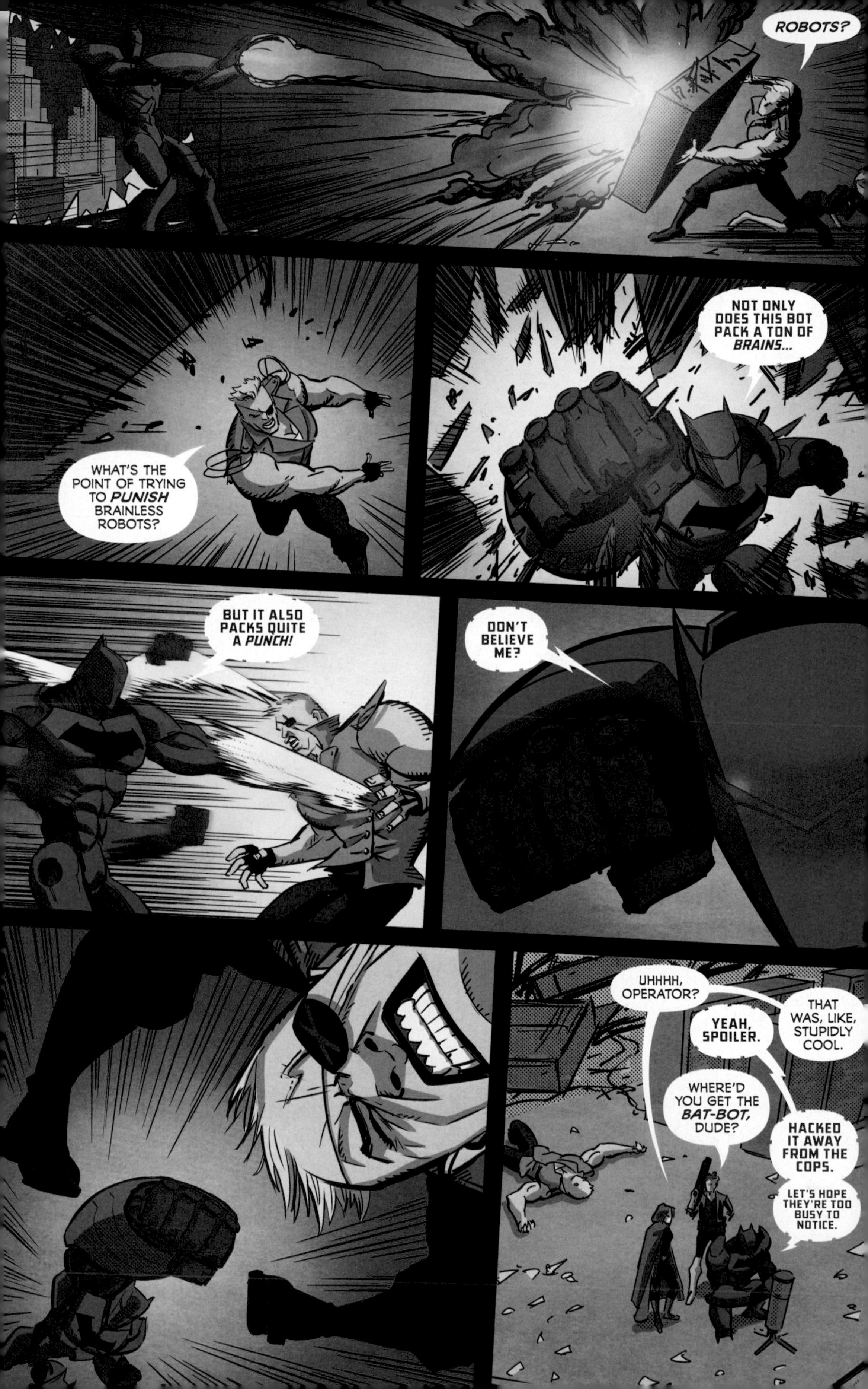
ROBOTS?
WHAT'S THE POINT OF TRYING TO PUNISH BRAINLESS ROBOTS?
NOT ONLY DOES THIS BOT PACK A TON OF BRAINS...
BUT IT ALSO PACKS QUITE A PUNCH!
DON'T BELIEVE ME?
UHHHH, OPERATOR?
THAT WAS, LIKE, STUPIDLY COOL.
YEAH, SPOILER.
WHERE'D YOU GET THE BAT-BOT, DUDE?
HACKED IT AWAY FROM THE COPS.
LET'S HOPE THEY'RE TOO BUSY TO NOTICE.

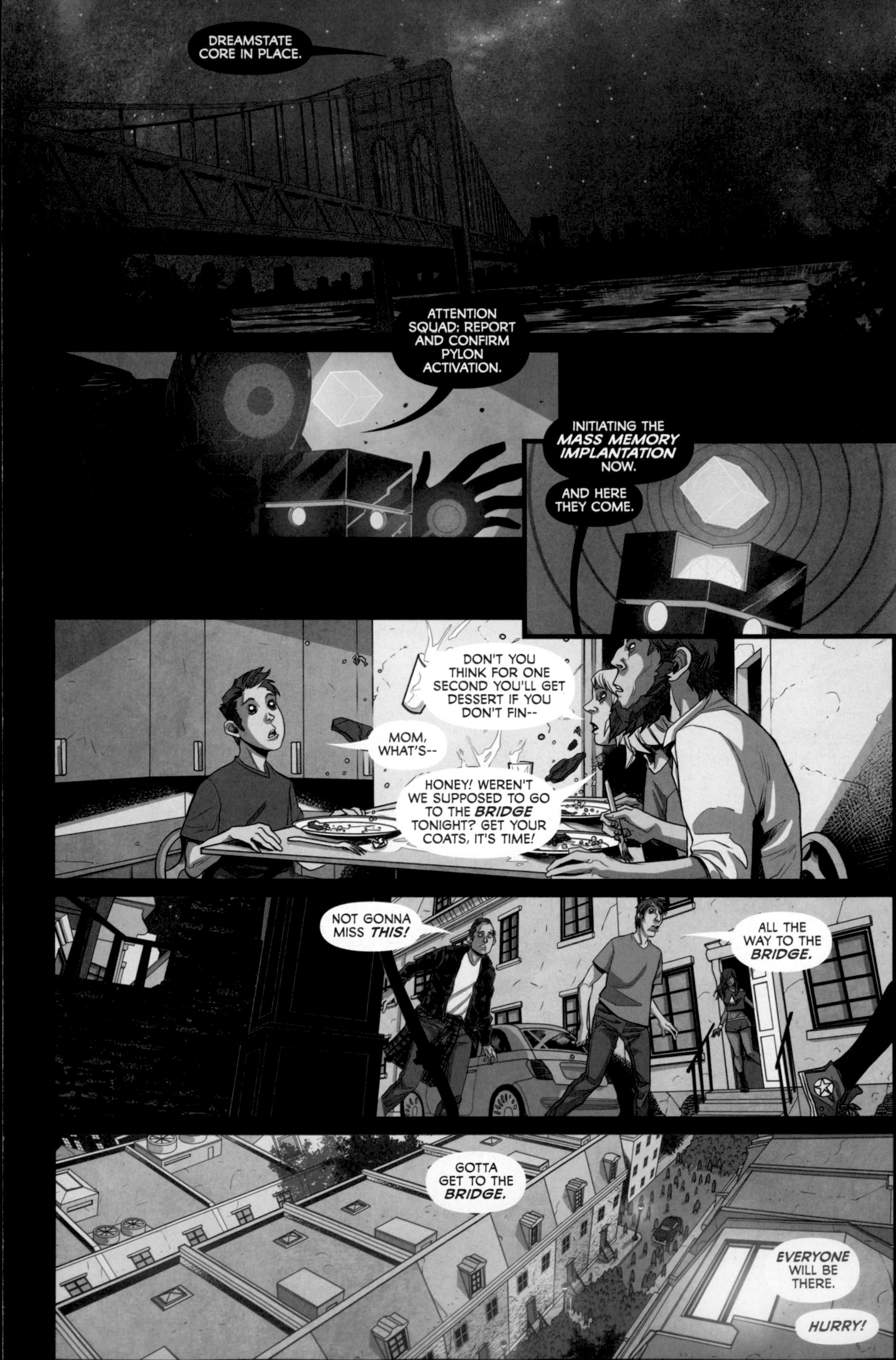
DREAMSTATE CORE IN PLACE.
ATTENTION SQUAD: REPORT AND CONFIRM PYLON ACTIVATION.
INITIATING THE *MASS MEMORY IMPLANTATION* NOW.
AND HERE THEY COME.
DON'T YOU THINK FOR ONE SECOND YOU'LL GET DESSERT IF YOU DON'T FIN--
MOM, WHAT'S--
HONEY! WEREN'T WE SUPPOSED TO GO TO THE *BRIDGE* TONIGHT? GET YOUR COATS, IT'S TIME!
NOT GONNA MISS *THIS!*
ALL THE WAY TO THE *BRIDGE.*
GOTTA GET TO THE *BRIDGE.*
EVERYONE WILL BE THERE.
HURRY!

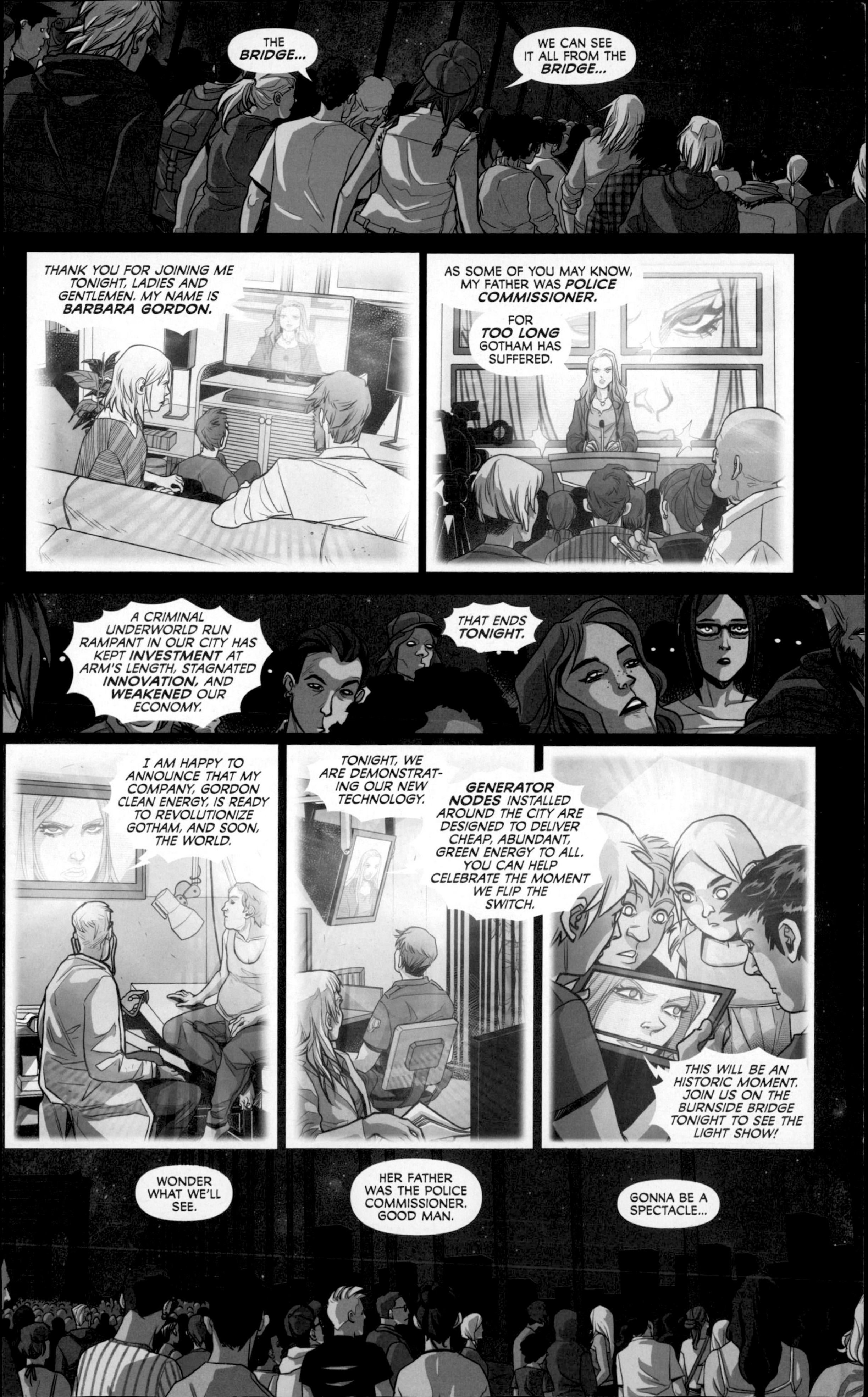
THE BRIDGE...
WE CAN SEE IT ALL FROM THE BRIDGE...
THANK YOU FOR JOINING ME TONIGHT, LADIES AND GENTLEMEN. MY NAME IS BARBARA GORDON.
AS SOME OF YOU MAY KNOW, MY FATHER WAS POLICE COMMISSIONER.
FOR TOO LONG GOTHAM HAS SUFFERED.
A CRIMINAL UNDERWORLD RUN RAMPANT IN OUR CITY HAS KEPT INVESTMENT AT ARM'S LENGTH, STAGNATED INNOVATION, AND WEAKENED OUR ECONOMY.
THAT ENDS TONIGHT.
I AM HAPPY TO ANNOUNCE THAT MY COMPANY, GORDON CLEAN ENERGY, IS READY TO REVOLUTIONIZE GOTHAM, AND SOON, THE WORLD.
TONIGHT, WE ARE DEMONSTRATING OUR NEW TECHNOLOGY.
GENERATOR NODES INSTALLED AROUND THE CITY ARE DESIGNED TO DELIVER CHEAP, ABUNDANT, GREEN ENERGY TO ALL. YOU CAN HELP CELEBRATE THE MOMENT WE FLIP THE SWITCH.
THIS WILL BE AN HISTORIC MOMENT. JOIN US ON THE BURNSIDE BRIDGE TONIGHT TO SEE THE LIGHT SHOW!
WONDER WHAT WE'LL SEE.
HER FATHER WAS THE POLICE COMMISSIONER. GOOD MAN.
GONNA BE A SPECTACLE...

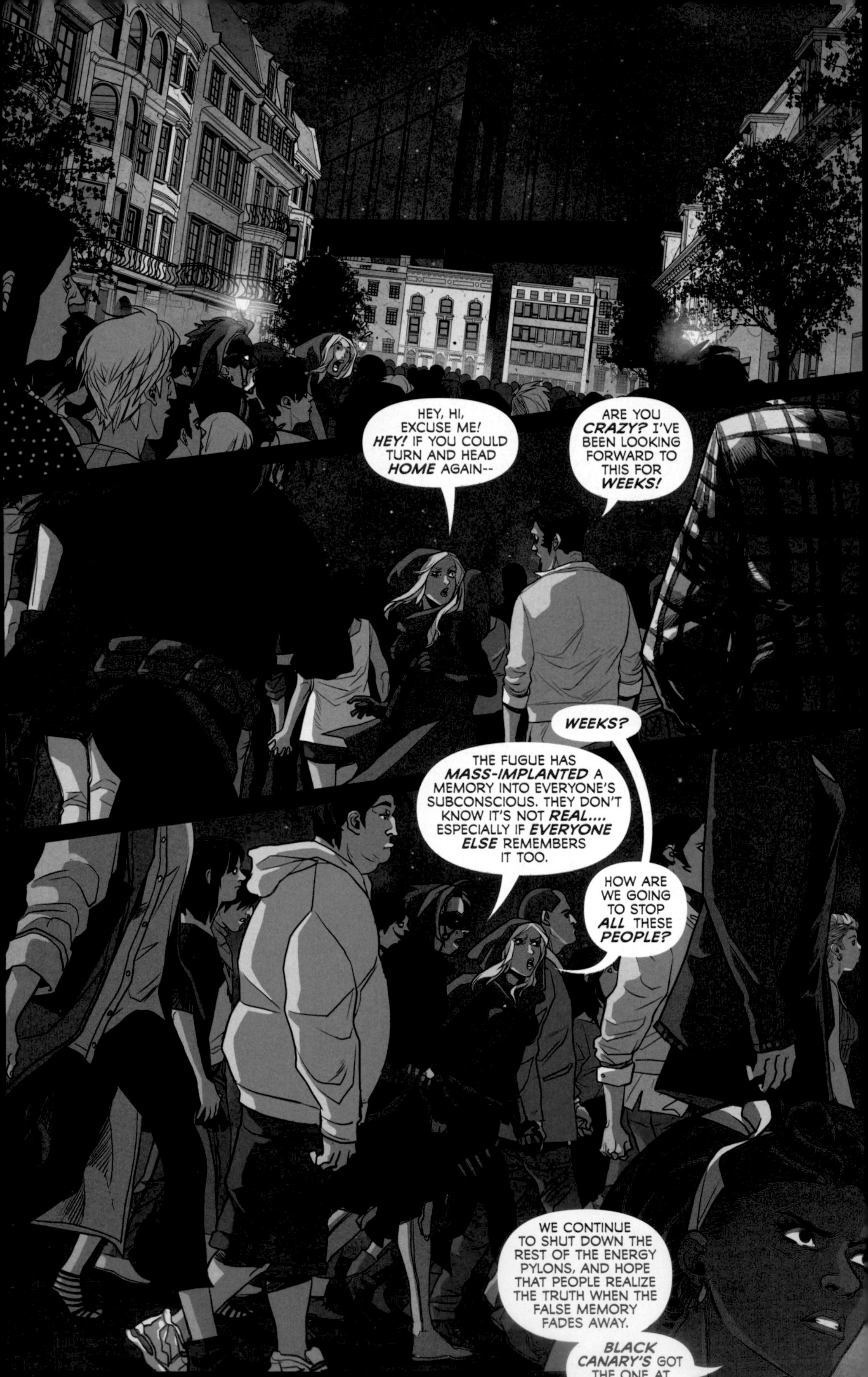
HEY, HI, EXCUSE ME! HEY! IF YOU COULD TURN AND HEAD HOME AGAIN--
ARE YOU CRAZY? I'VE BEEN LOOKING FORWARD TO THIS FOR WEEKS!
WEEKS?
THE FUGUE HAS MASS-IMPLANTED A MEMORY INTO EVERYONE'S SUBCONSCIOUS. THEY DON'T KNOW IT'S NOT REAL.... ESPECIALLY IF EVERYONE ELSE REMEMBERS IT TOO.
HOW ARE WE GOING TO STOP ALL THESE PEOPLE?
WE CONTINUE TO SHUT DOWN THE REST OF THE ENERGY PYLONS, AND HOPE THAT PEOPLE REALIZE THE TRUTH WHEN THE FALSE MEMORY FADES AWAY.
BLACK CANARY'S GOT THE ONE AT CITY HALL...

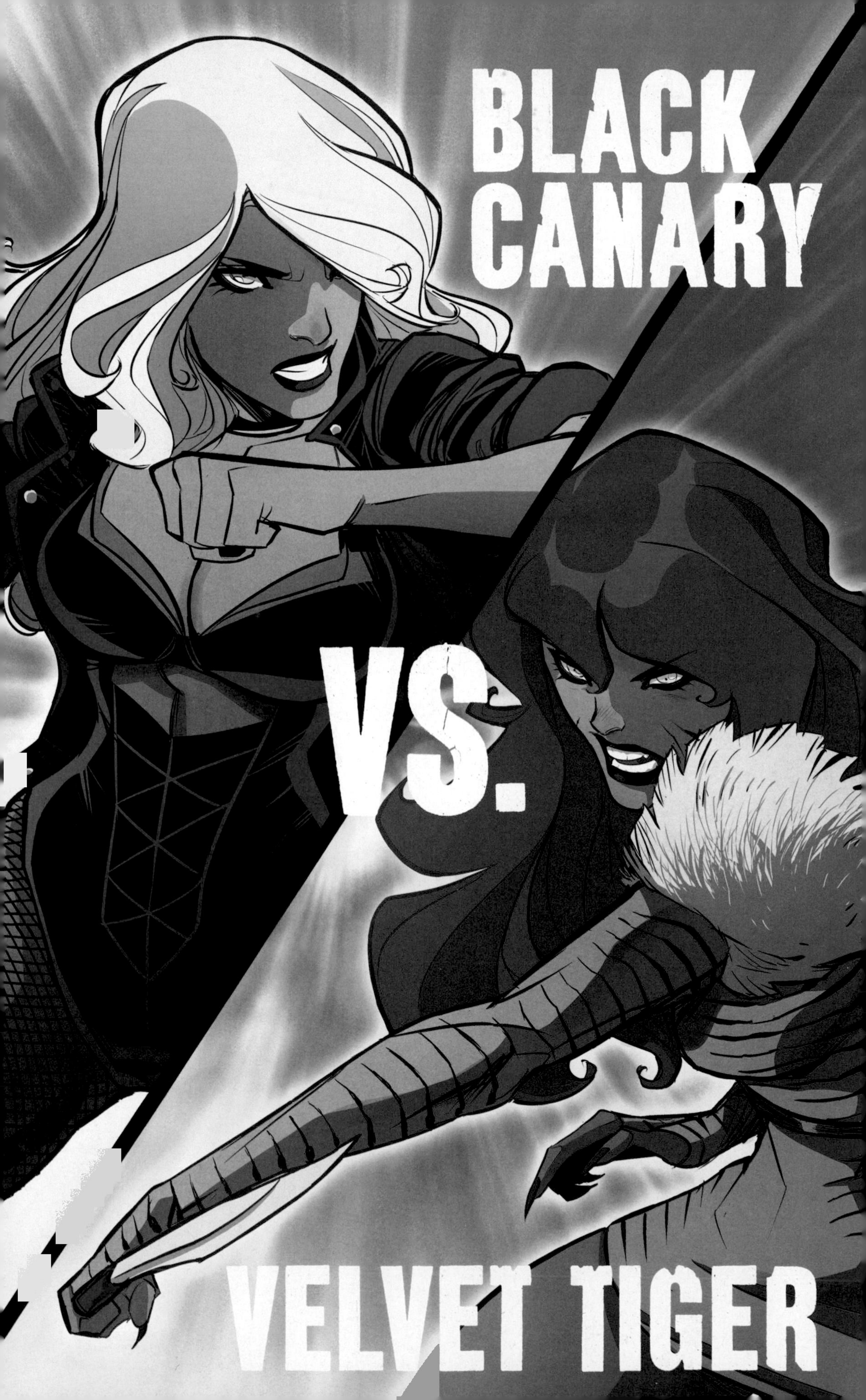
BLACK CANARY
VS.
VELVET TIGER

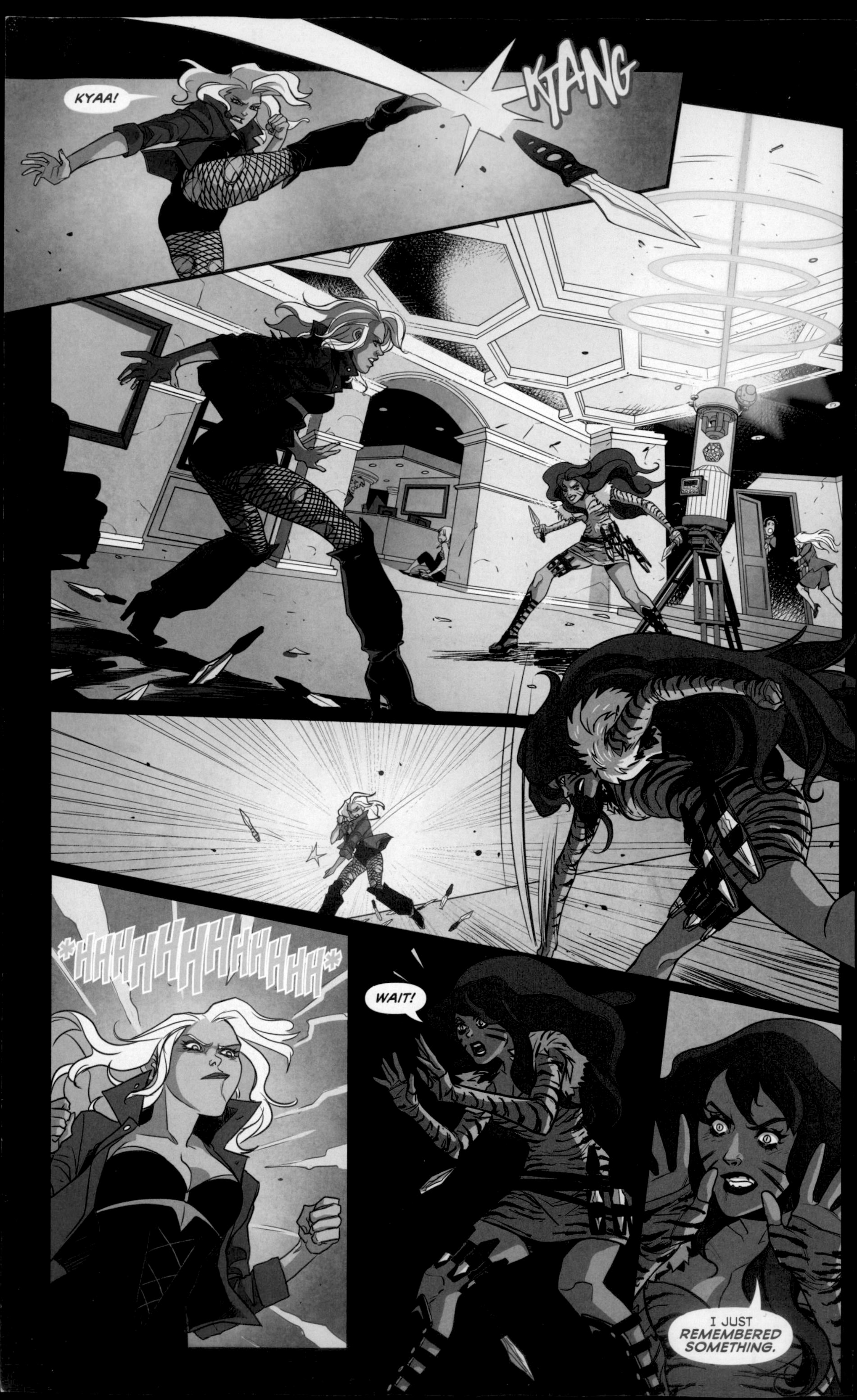
KYAA!
KTANG
HHHHHHHHHHHHH
WAIT!
I JUST REMEMBERED SOMETHING.

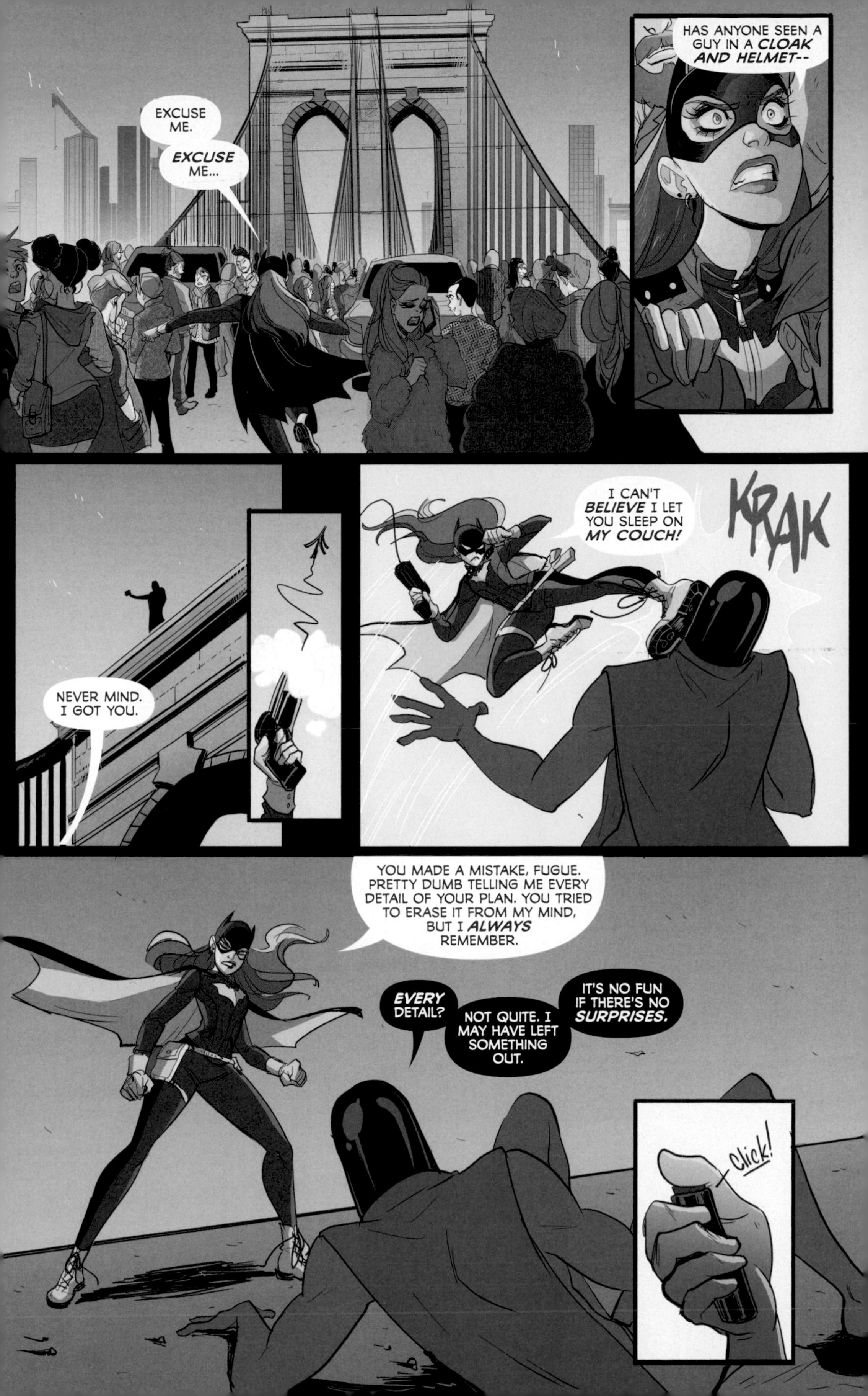
EXCUSE ME.
EXCUSE ME...
HAS ANYONE SEEN A GUY IN A CLOAK AND HELMET--
NEVER MIND. I GOT YOU.
I CAN'T BELIEVE I LET YOU SLEEP ON MY COUCH!
KRAK
YOU MADE A MISTAKE, FUGUE. PRETTY DUMB TELLING ME EVERY DETAIL OF YOUR PLAN. YOU TRIED TO ERASE IT FROM MY MIND, BUT I ALWAYS REMEMBER.
EVERY DETAIL?
NOT QUITE. I MAY HAVE LEFT SOMETHING OUT.
IT'S NO FUN IF THERE'S NO SURPRISES.
Click!

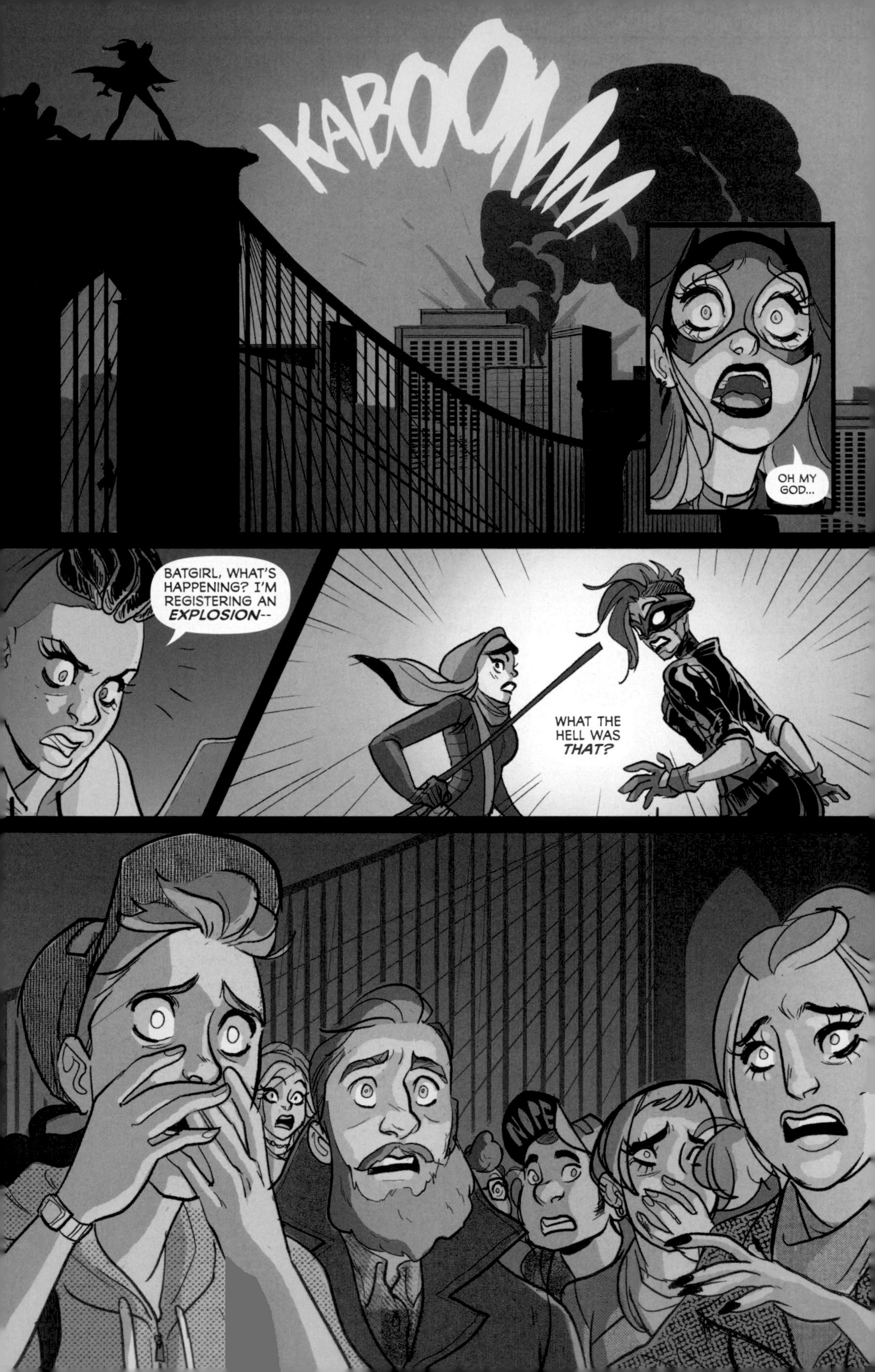
KABOOMM
OH MY GOD...
BATGIRL, WHAT'S HAPPENING? I'M REGISTERING AN *EXPLOSION*--
WHAT THE HELL WAS *THAT?*
NOPE

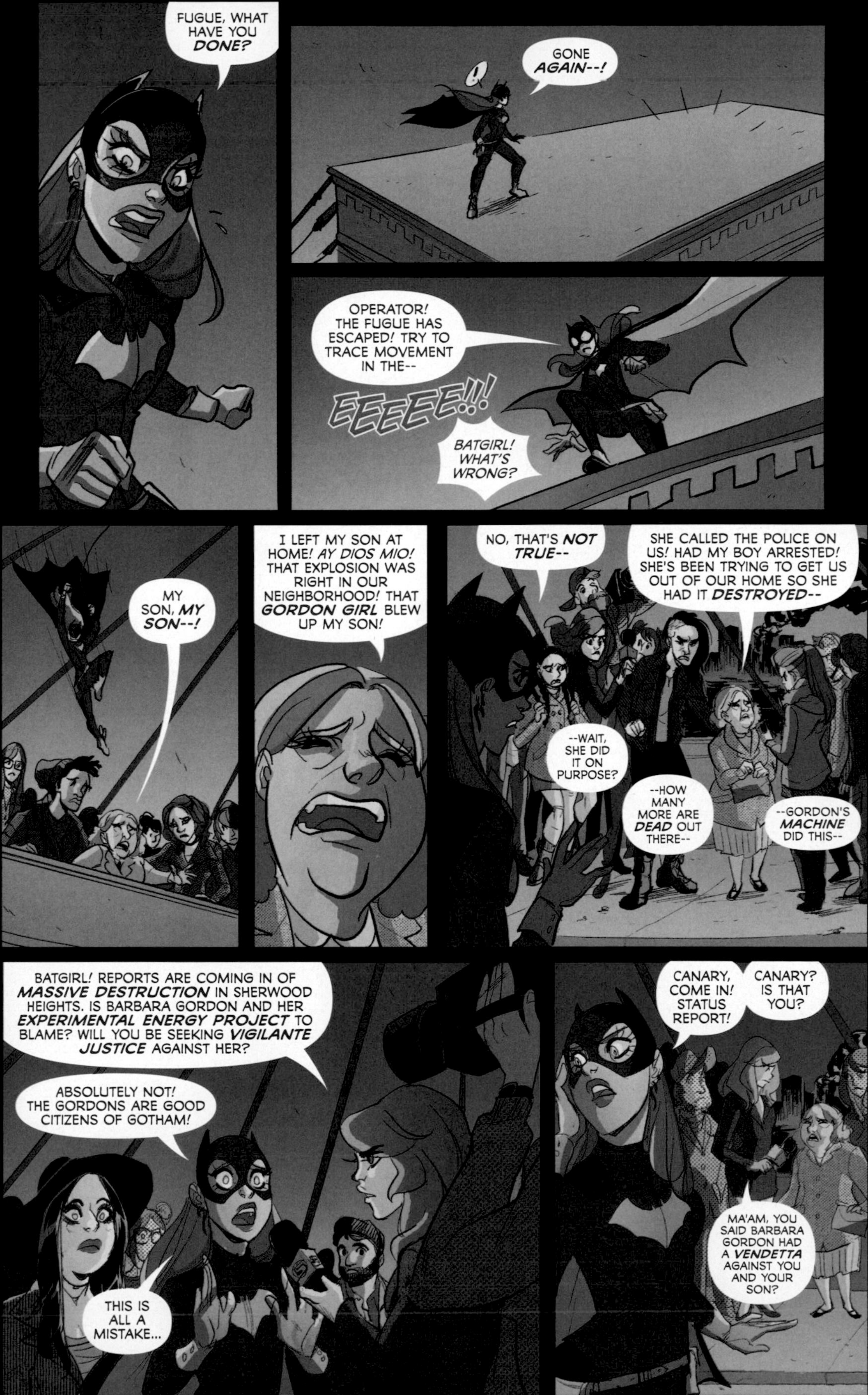
FUGUE, WHAT HAVE YOU DONE?
!
GONE AGAIN--!
OPERATOR! THE FUGUE HAS ESCAPED! TRY TO TRACE MOVEMENT IN THE--
EEEEEE!!!
BATGIRL! WHAT'S WRONG?
MY SON, MY SON--!
I LEFT MY SON AT HOME! AY DIOS MIO! THAT EXPLOSION WAS RIGHT IN OUR NEIGHBORHOOD! THAT GORDON GIRL BLEW UP MY SON!
NO, THAT'S NOT TRUE--
SHE CALLED THE POLICE ON US! HAD MY BOY ARRESTED! SHE'S BEEN TRYING TO GET US OUT OF OUR HOME SO SHE HAD IT DESTROYED--
--WAIT, SHE DID IT ON PURPOSE?
--HOW MANY MORE ARE DEAD OUT THERE--
--GORDON'S MACHINE DID THIS--
BATGIRL! REPORTS ARE COMING IN OF MASSIVE DESTRUCTION IN SHERWOOD HEIGHTS. IS BARBARA GORDON AND HER EXPERIMENTAL ENERGY PROJECT TO BLAME? WILL YOU BE SEEKING VIGILANTE JUSTICE AGAINST HER?
ABSOLUTELY NOT! THE GORDONS ARE GOOD CITIZENS OF GOTHAM!
THIS IS ALL A MISTAKE...
CANARY, COME IN! STATUS REPORT!
CANARY? IS THAT YOU?
MA'AM, YOU SAID BARBARA GORDON HAD A VENDETTA AGAINST YOU AND YOUR SON?

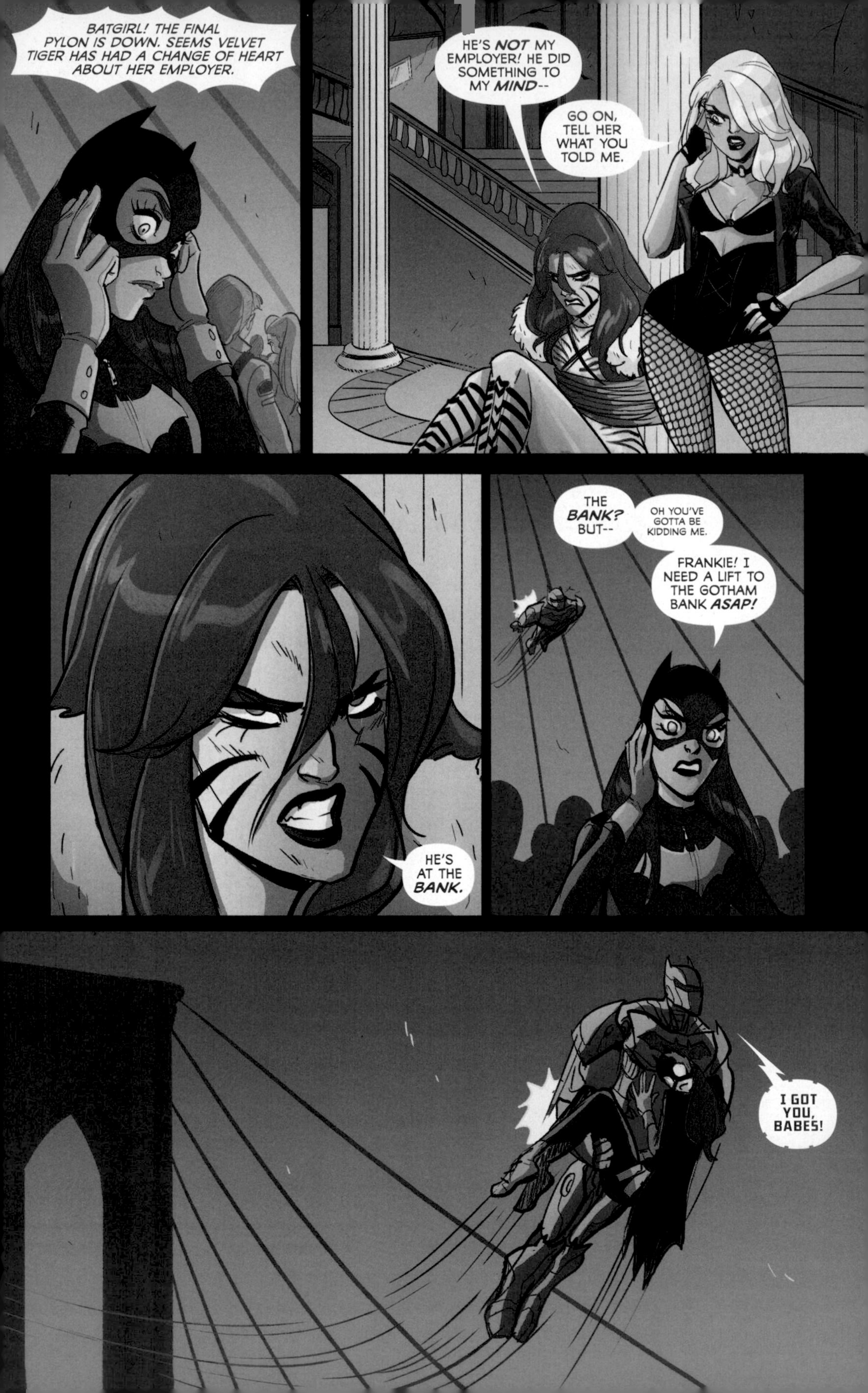
BATGIRL! THE FINAL PYLON IS DOWN. SEEMS VELVET TIGER HAS HAD A CHANGE OF HEART ABOUT HER EMPLOYER.
HE'S NOT MY EMPLOYER! HE DID SOMETHING TO MY MIND--
GO ON, TELL HER WHAT YOU TOLD ME.
HE'S AT THE BANK.
THE BANK? BUT--
OH YOU'VE GOTTA BE KIDDING ME.
FRANKIE! I NEED A LIFT TO THE GOTHAM BANK ASAP!
I GOT YOU, BABES!

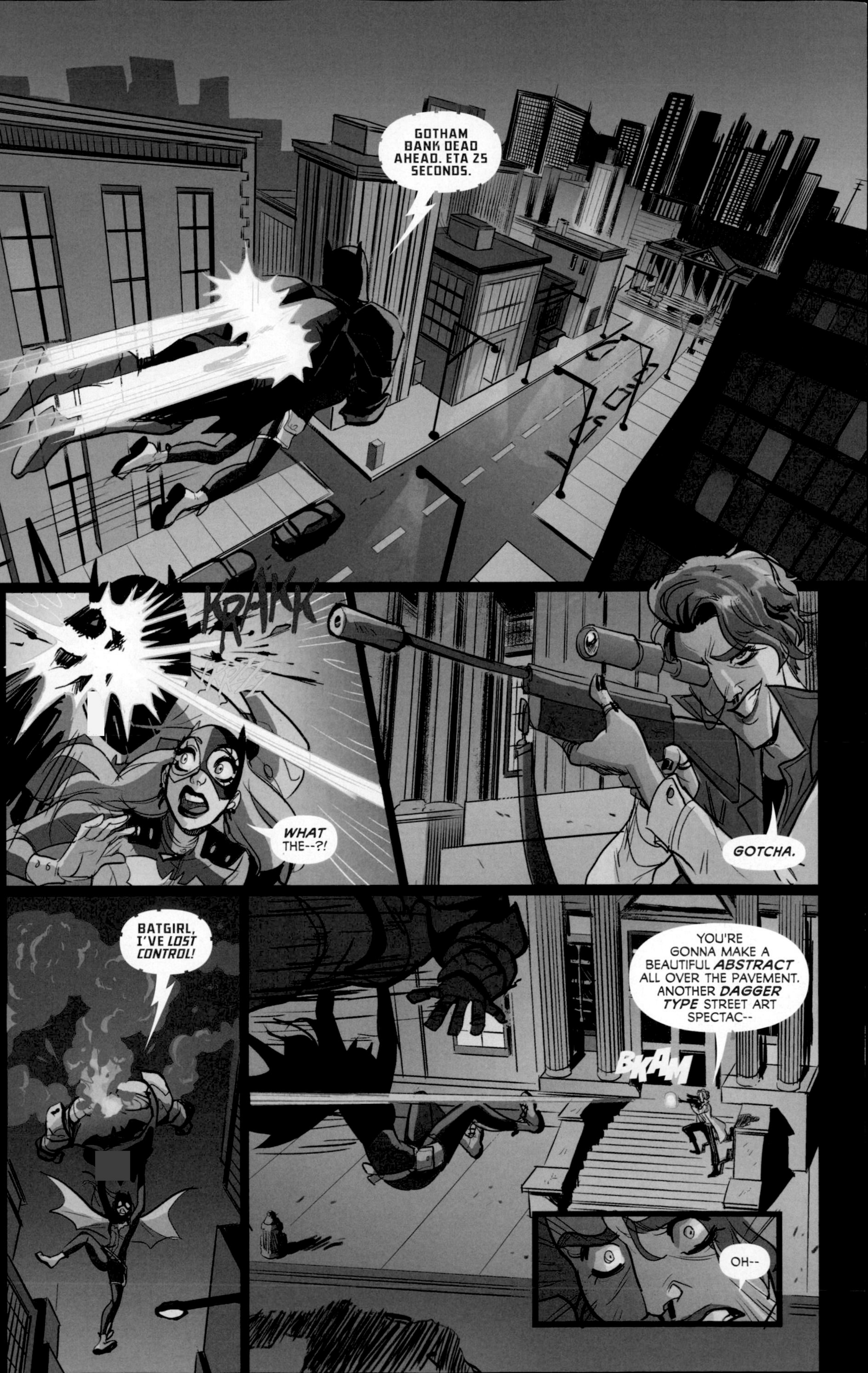
GOTHAM BANK DEAD AHEAD. ETA 25 SECONDS.
KRAKK
WHAT THE--?!
GOTCHA.
BATGIRL, I'VE LOST CONTROL!
YOU'RE GONNA MAKE A BEAUTIFUL ABSTRACT ALL OVER THE PAVEMENT. ANOTHER DAGGER TYPE STREET ART SPECTAC--
BKAM
OH--

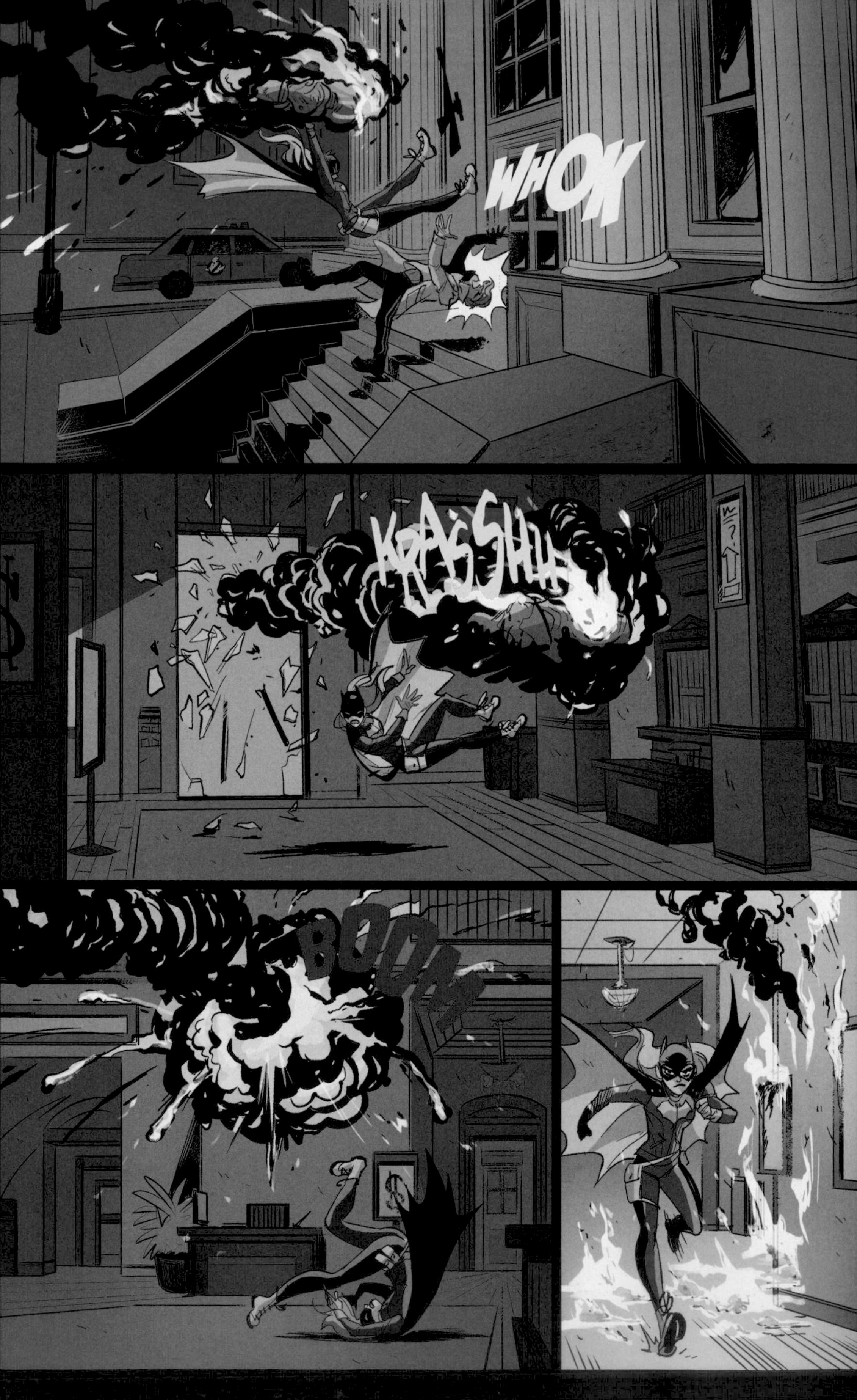
WHOK
KRASSHH
BOOM

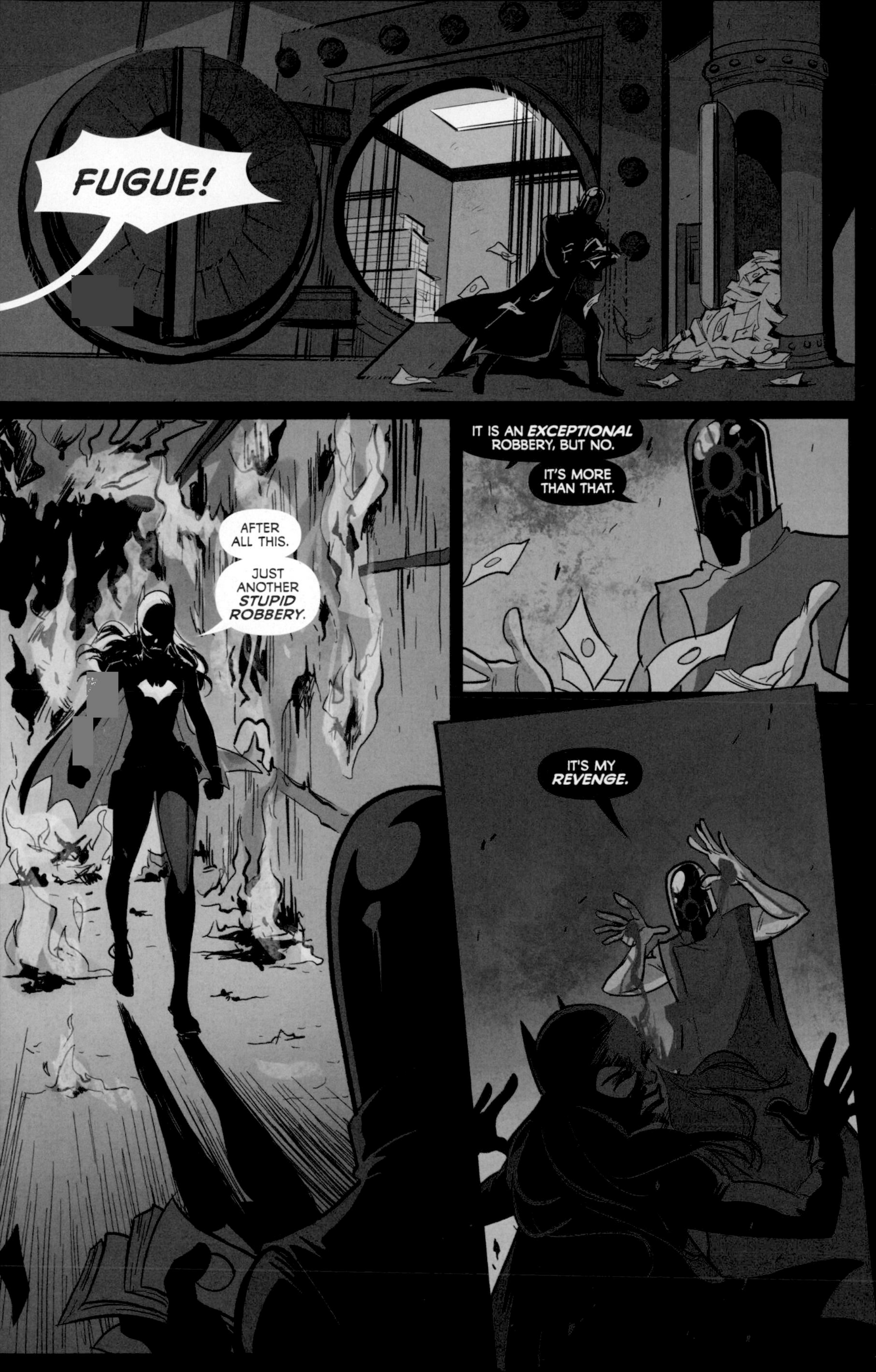
FUGUE!
AFTER ALL THIS.
JUST ANOTHER STUPID ROBBERY.
IT IS AN EXCEPTIONAL ROBBERY, BUT NO.
IT'S MORE THAN THAT.
IT'S MY REVENGE.

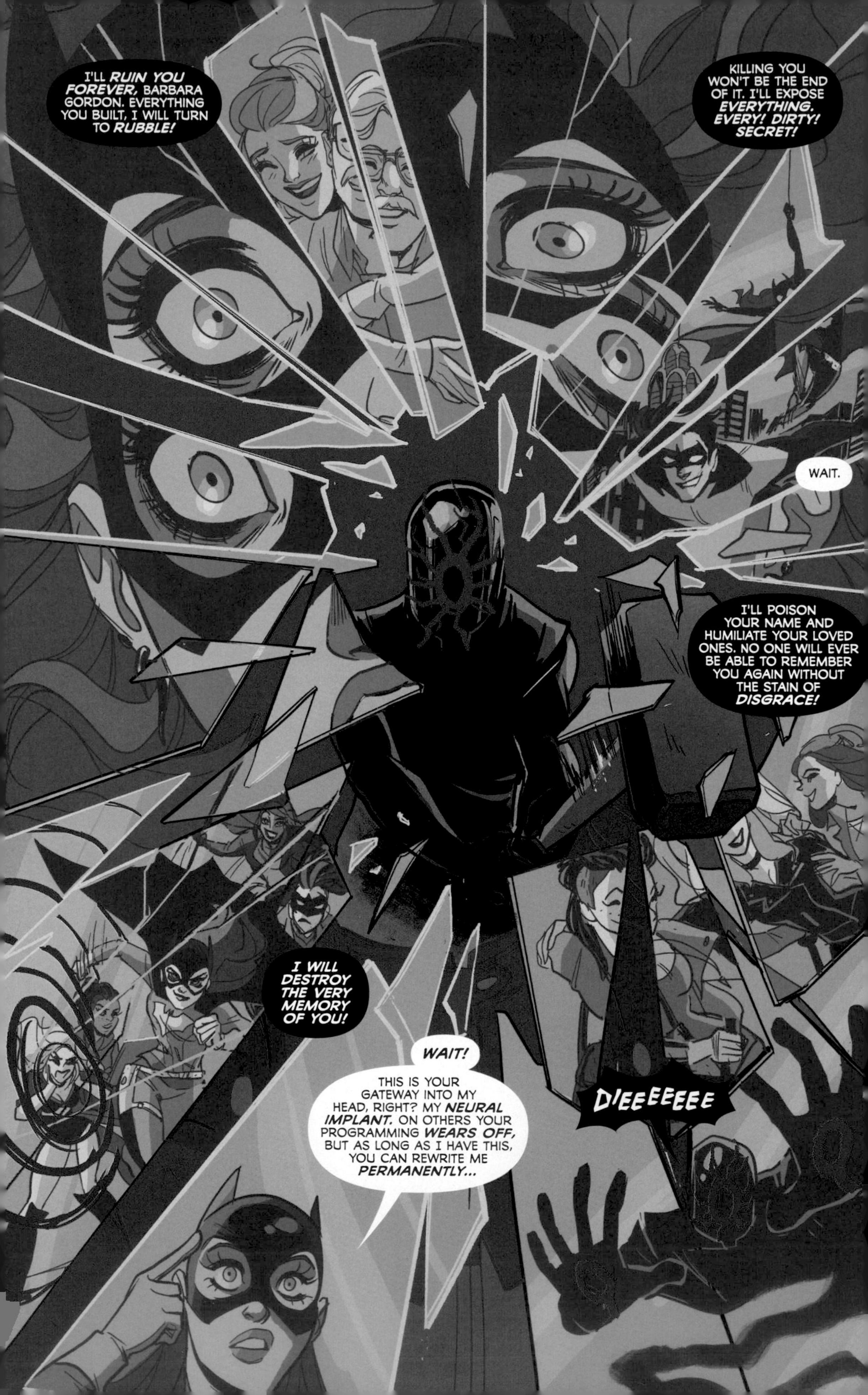
I'LL RUIN YOU FOREVER, BARBARA GORDON. EVERYTHING YOU BUILT, I WILL TURN TO RUBBLE!
KILLING YOU WON'T BE THE END OF IT. I'LL EXPOSE EVERYTHING. EVERY! DIRTY! SECRET!
WAIT.
I'LL POISON YOUR NAME AND HUMILIATE YOUR LOVED ONES. NO ONE WILL EVER BE ABLE TO REMEMBER YOU AGAIN WITHOUT THE STAIN OF DISGRACE!
I WILL DESTROY THE VERY MEMORY OF YOU!
WAIT!
THIS IS YOUR GATEWAY INTO MY HEAD, RIGHT? MY NEURAL IMPLANT. ON OTHERS YOUR PROGRAMMING WEARS OFF, BUT AS LONG AS I HAVE THIS, YOU CAN REWRITE ME PERMANENTLY...
DIEEEEEEE

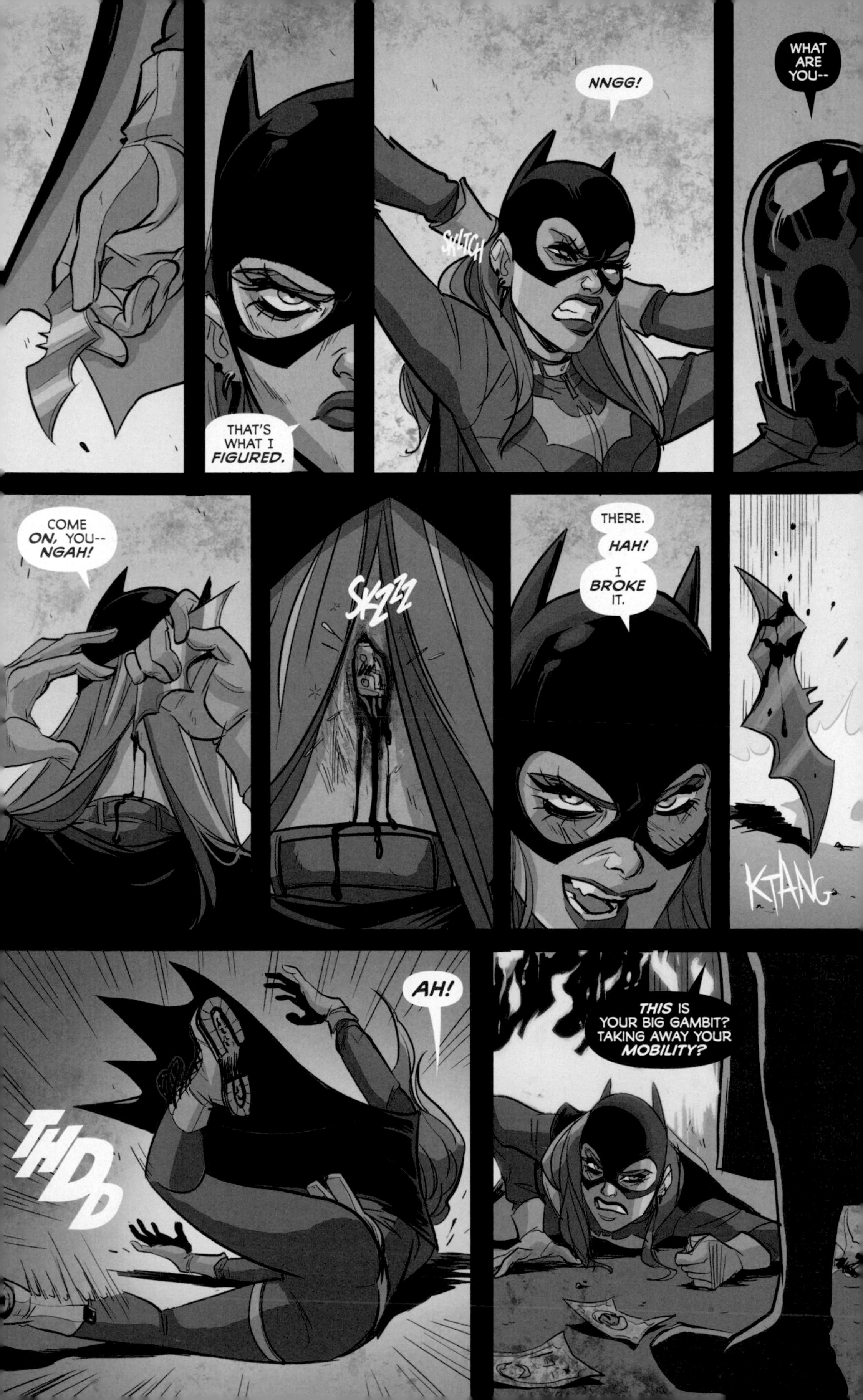
THAT'S WHAT I FIGURED.
SKLTCH
NNGG!
WHAT ARE YOU--
COME ON, YOU-- NGAH!
SKZZZ
THERE.
HAH!
I BROKE IT.
KTANG
AH!
THDD
THIS IS YOUR BIG GAMBIT? TAKING AWAY YOUR MOBILITY?

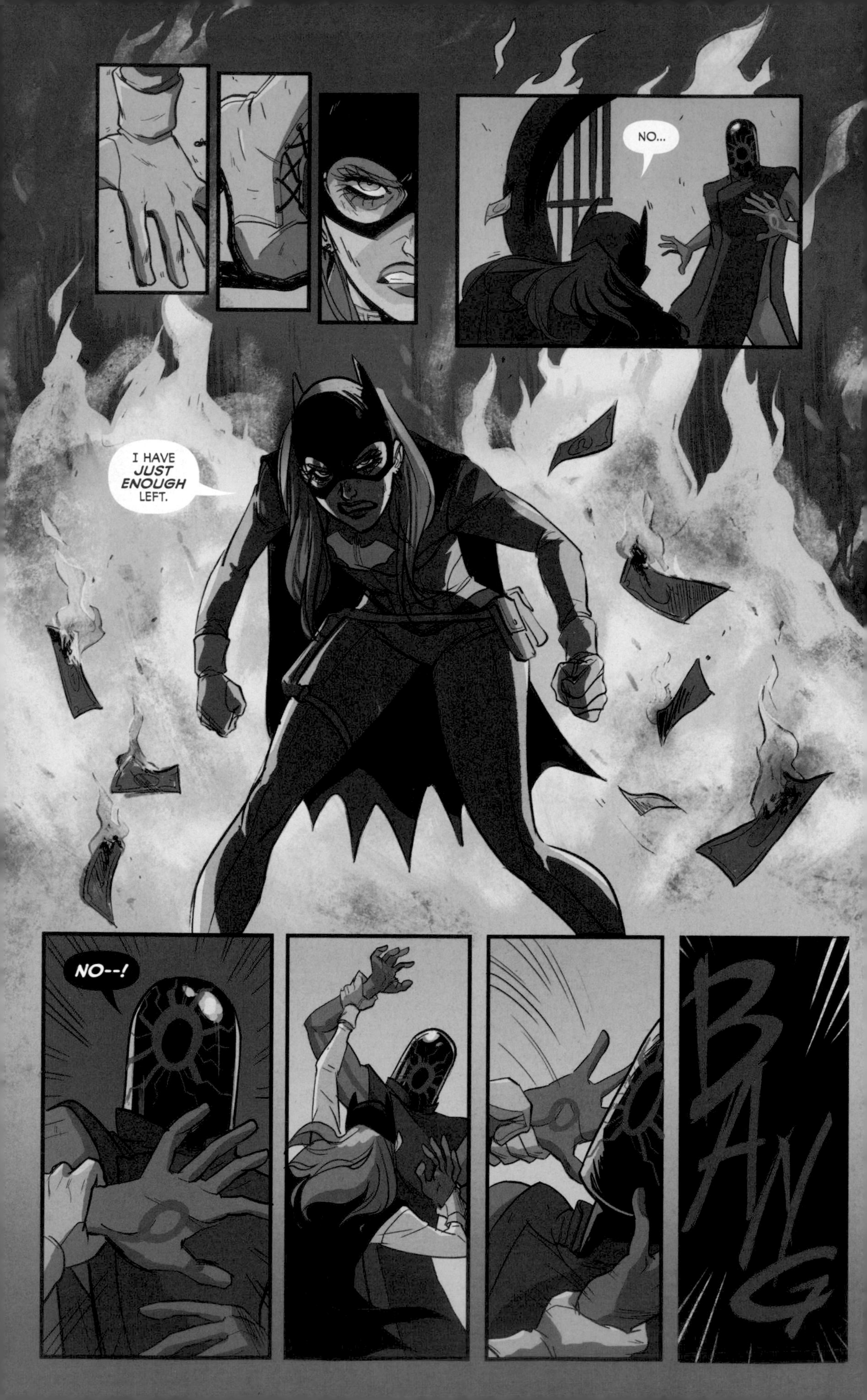
NO...
I HAVE JUST ENOUGH LEFT.
NO--!
BANG

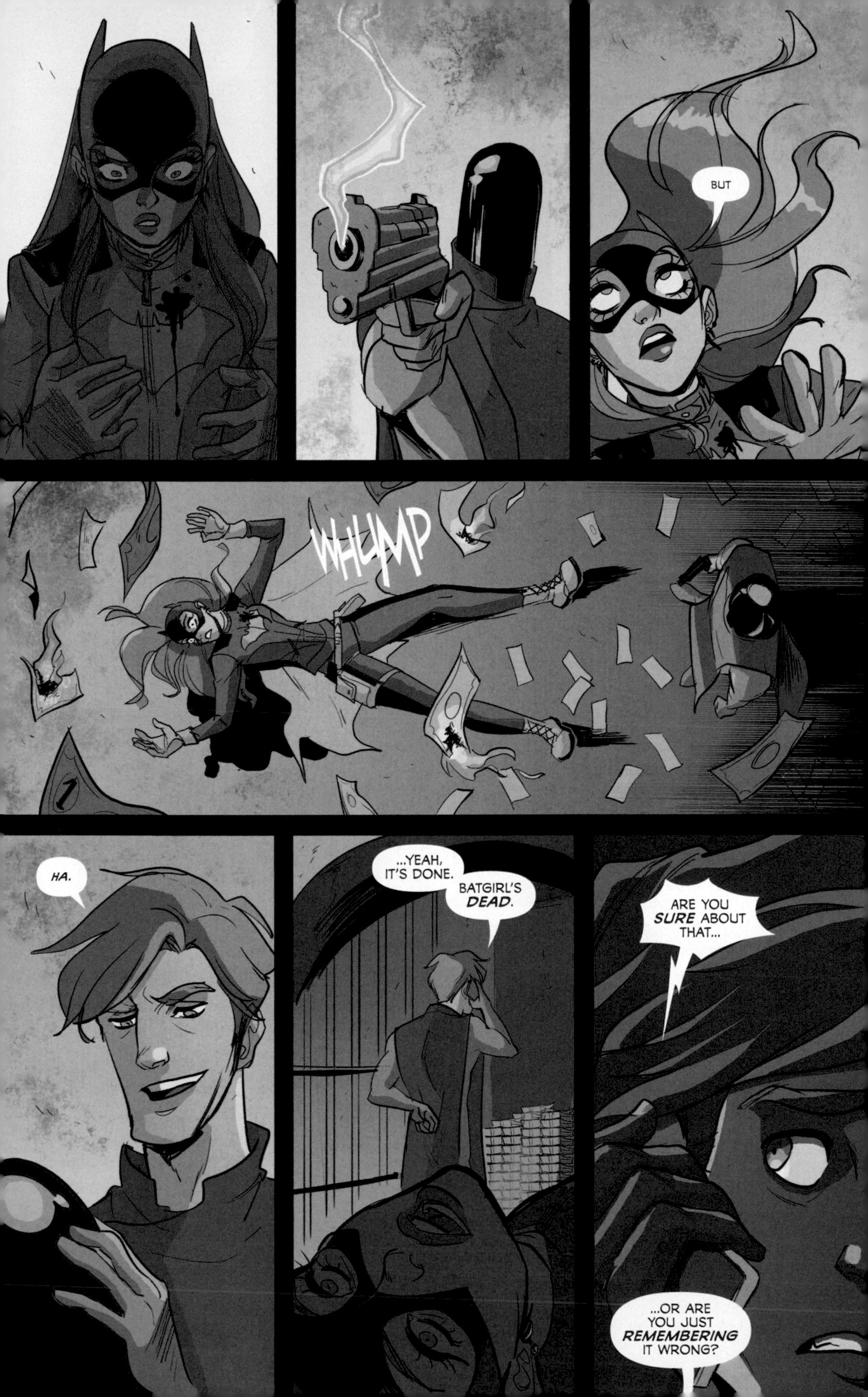
BUT
WHUMP
HA.
...YEAH, IT'S DONE.
BATGIRL'S *DEAD*.
ARE YOU *SURE* ABOUT THAT...
...OR ARE YOU JUST *REMEMBERING* IT WRONG?

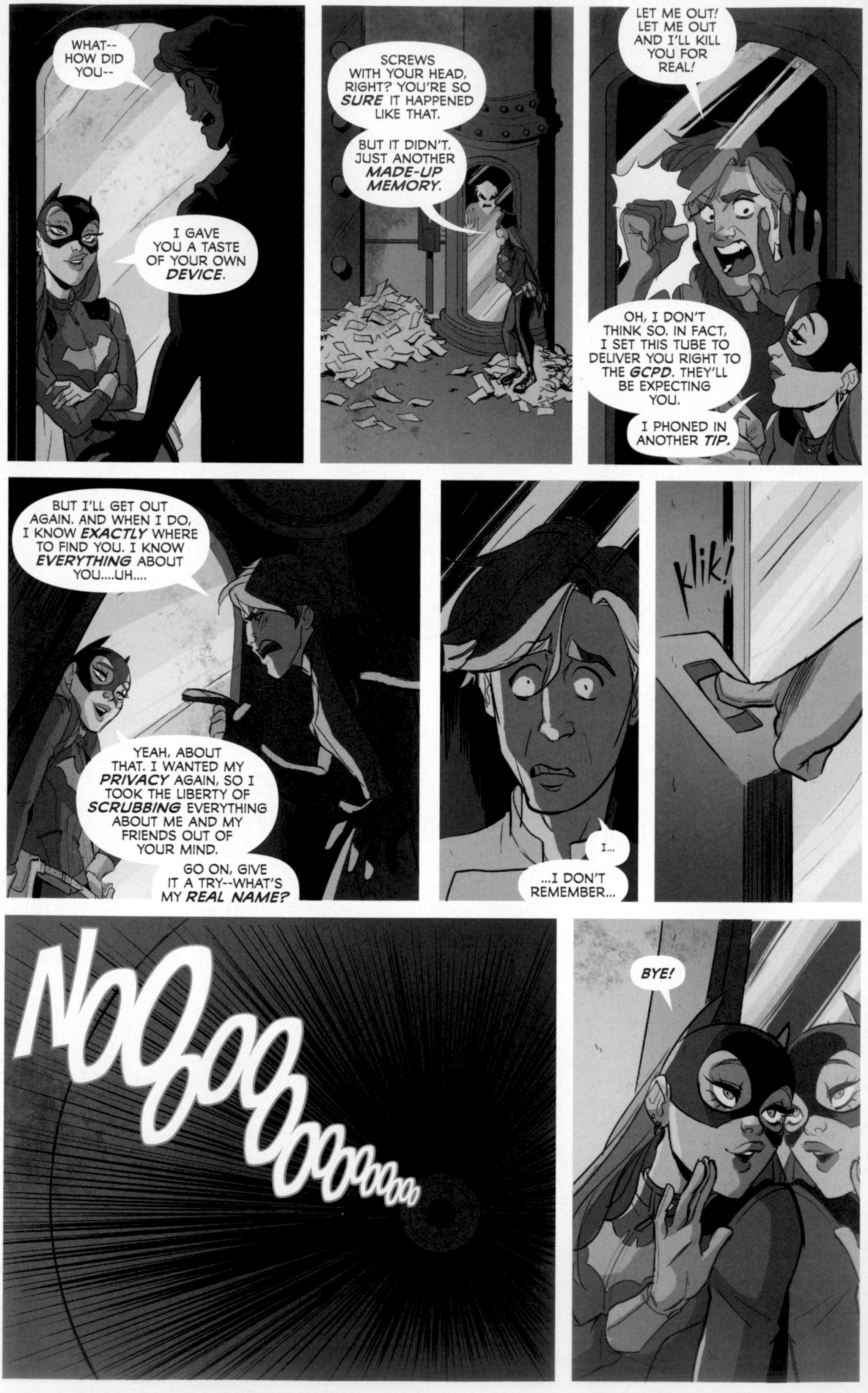
WHAT-- HOW DID YOU--
I GAVE YOU A TASTE OF YOUR OWN DEVICE.
SCREWS WITH YOUR HEAD, RIGHT? YOU'RE SO SURE IT HAPPENED LIKE THAT.
BUT IT DIDN'T. JUST ANOTHER MADE-UP MEMORY.
LET ME OUT! LET ME OUT AND I'LL KILL YOU FOR REAL!
OH, I DON'T THINK SO. IN FACT, I SET THIS TUBE TO DELIVER YOU RIGHT TO THE GCPD. THEY'LL BE EXPECTING YOU.
I PHONED IN ANOTHER TIP.
BUT I'LL GET OUT AGAIN. AND WHEN I DO, I KNOW EXACTLY WHERE TO FIND YOU. I KNOW EVERYTHING ABOUT YOU....UH....
YEAH, ABOUT THAT. I WANTED MY PRIVACY AGAIN, SO I TOOK THE LIBERTY OF SCRUBBING EVERYTHING ABOUT ME AND MY FRIENDS OUT OF YOUR MIND.
GO ON, GIVE IT A TRY--WHAT'S MY REAL NAME?
I...
...I DON'T REMEMBER...
KLIK!
NOOOOOOOOOOOOOOOO
BYE!

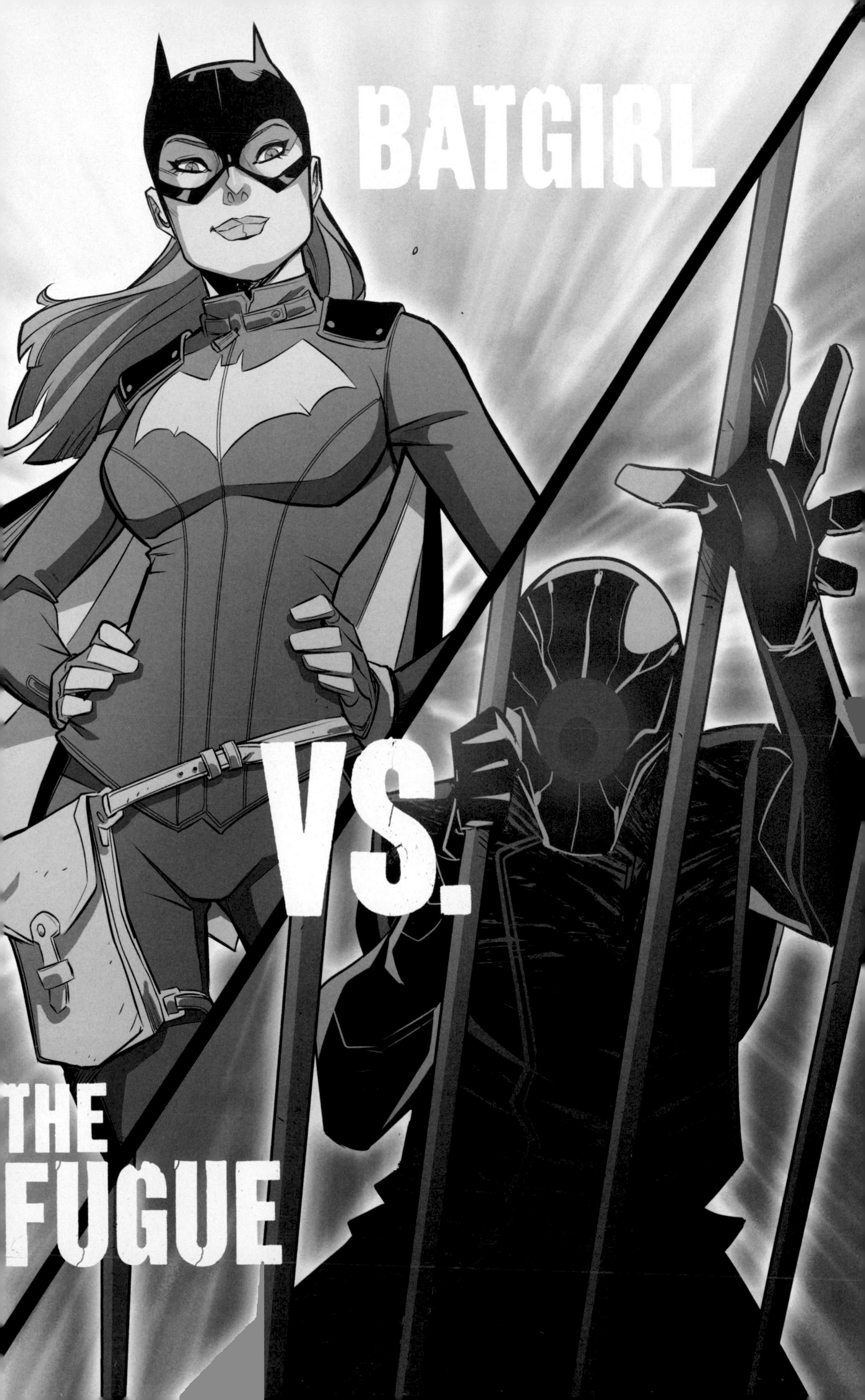
BATGIRL
VS.
THE
FUGUE

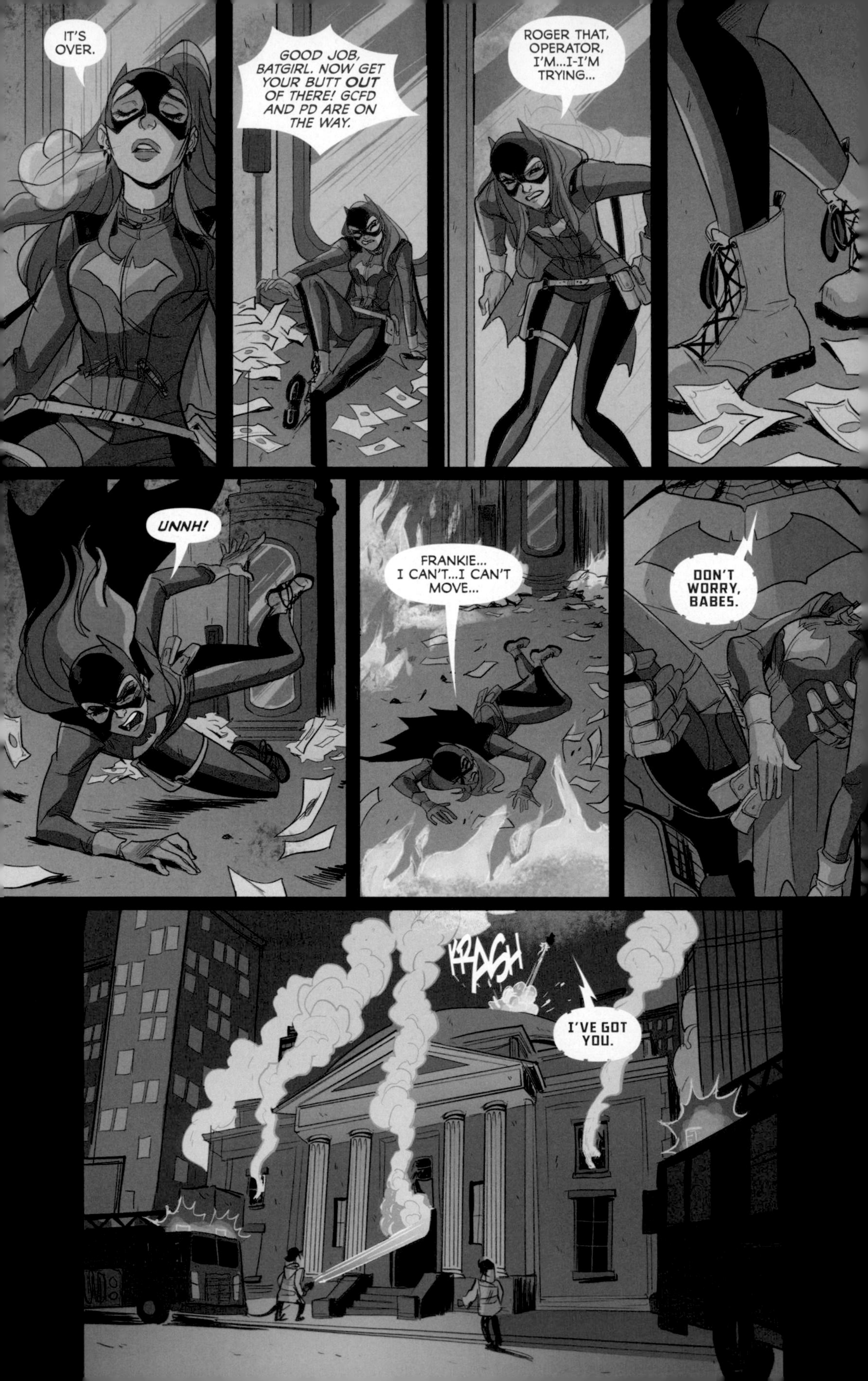
IT'S OVER.
GOOD JOB, BATGIRL. NOW GET YOUR BUTT OUT OF THERE! GCFD AND PD ARE ON THE WAY.
ROGER THAT, OPERATOR, I'M...I-I'M TRYING...
UNNH!
FRANKIE... I CAN'T...I CAN'T MOVE...
DON'T WORRY, BABES.
KRASH
I'VE GOT YOU.

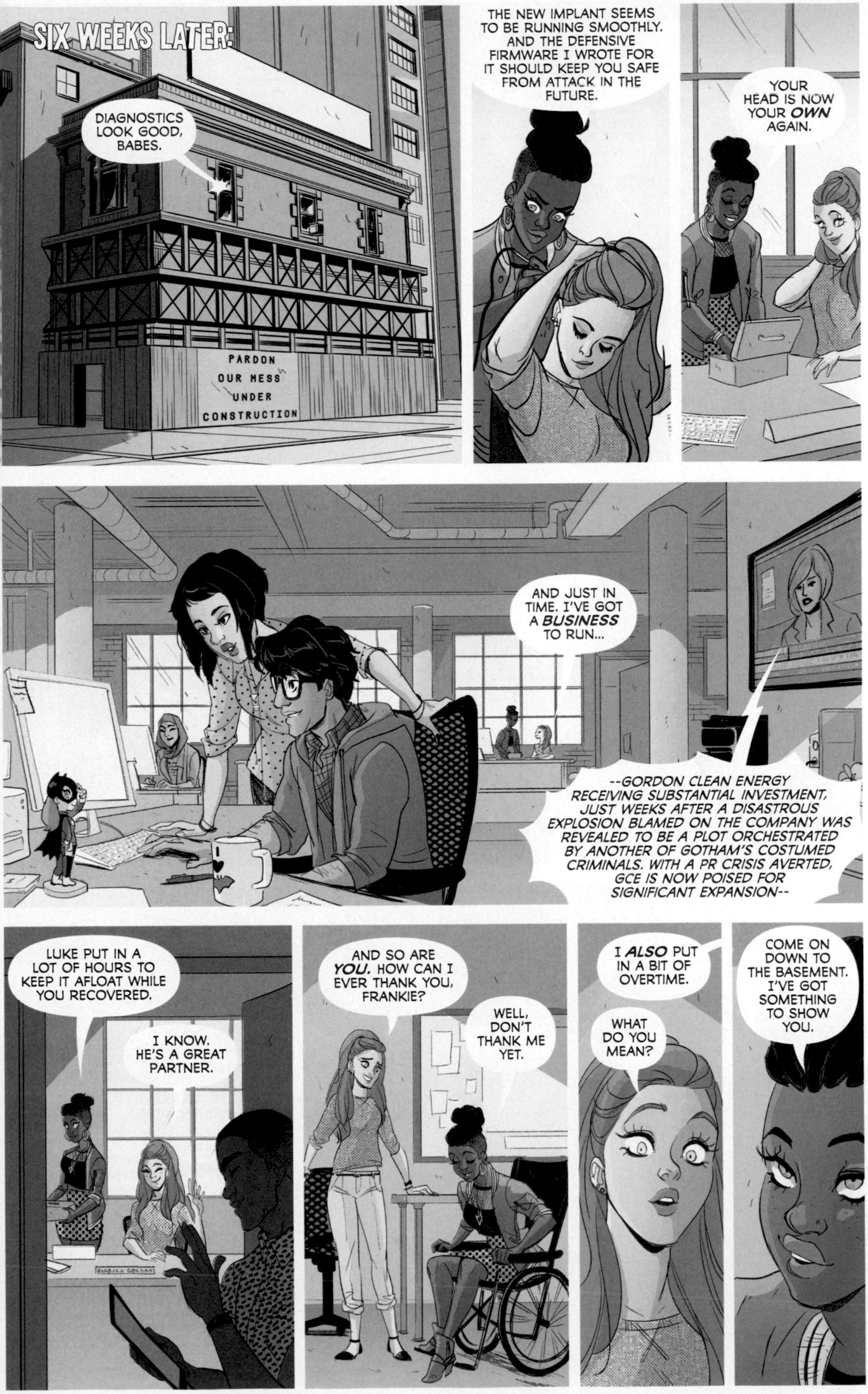
SIX WEEKS LATER:
DIAGNOSTICS LOOK GOOD, BABES.
PARDON OUR MESS UNDER CONSTRUCTION
THE NEW IMPLANT SEEMS TO BE RUNNING SMOOTHLY. AND THE DEFENSIVE FIRMWARE I WROTE FOR IT SHOULD KEEP YOU SAFE FROM ATTACK IN THE FUTURE.
YOUR HEAD IS NOW YOUR *OWN* AGAIN.
AND JUST IN TIME. I'VE GOT A *BUSINESS* TO RUN...
--GORDON CLEAN ENERGY RECEIVING SUBSTANTIAL INVESTMENT, JUST WEEKS AFTER A DISASTROUS EXPLOSION BLAMED ON THE COMPANY WAS REVEALED TO BE A PLOT ORCHESTRATED BY ANOTHER OF GOTHAM'S COSTUMED CRIMINALS. WITH A PR CRISIS AVERTED, GCE IS NOW POISED FOR SIGNIFICANT EXPANSION--
LUKE PUT IN A LOT OF HOURS TO KEEP IT AFLOAT WHILE YOU RECOVERED.
I KNOW. HE'S A GREAT PARTNER.
AND SO ARE *YOU.* HOW CAN I EVER THANK YOU, FRANKIE?
WELL, DON'T THANK ME YET.
I *ALSO* PUT IN A BIT OF OVERTIME.
WHAT DO YOU MEAN?
COME ON DOWN TO THE BASEMENT. I'VE GOT SOMETHING TO SHOW YOU.

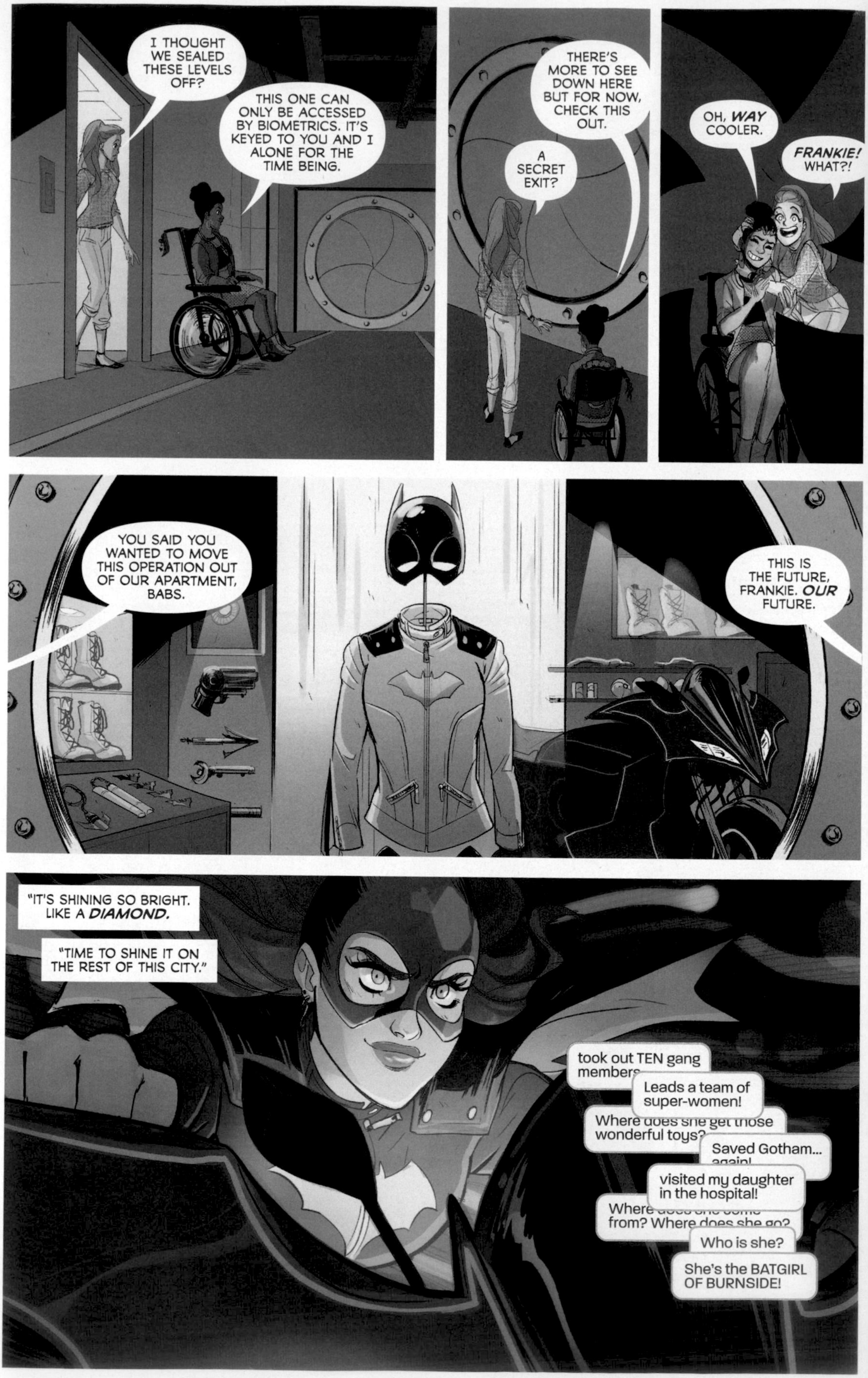
I THOUGHT WE SEALED THESE LEVELS OFF?
THIS ONE CAN ONLY BE ACCESSED BY BIOMETRICS. IT'S KEYED TO YOU AND I ALONE FOR THE TIME BEING.
THERE'S MORE TO SEE DOWN HERE BUT FOR NOW, CHECK THIS OUT.
A SECRET EXIT?
OH, *WAY* COOLER.
FRANKIE! WHAT?!
YOU SAID YOU WANTED TO MOVE THIS OPERATION OUT OF OUR APARTMENT, BABS.
THIS IS THE FUTURE, FRANKIE. *OUR* FUTURE.
"IT'S SHINING SO BRIGHT. LIKE A *DIAMOND.*
"TIME TO SHINE IT ON THE REST OF THIS CITY."
took out TEN gang members
Leads a team of super-women!
Saved Gotham... again!
visited my daughter in the hospital!
Who is she?
She's the BATGIRL OF BURNSIDE!

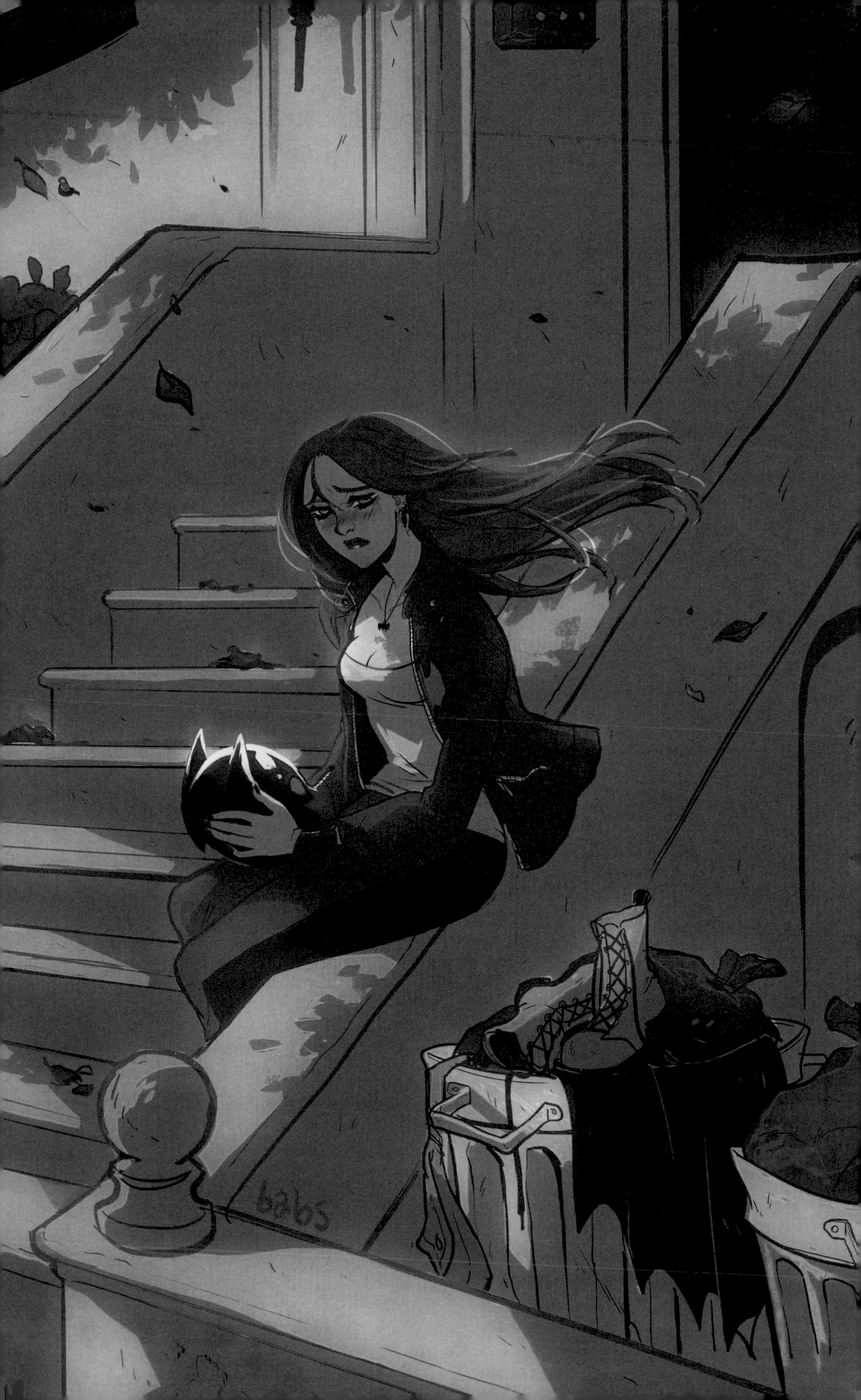
babs

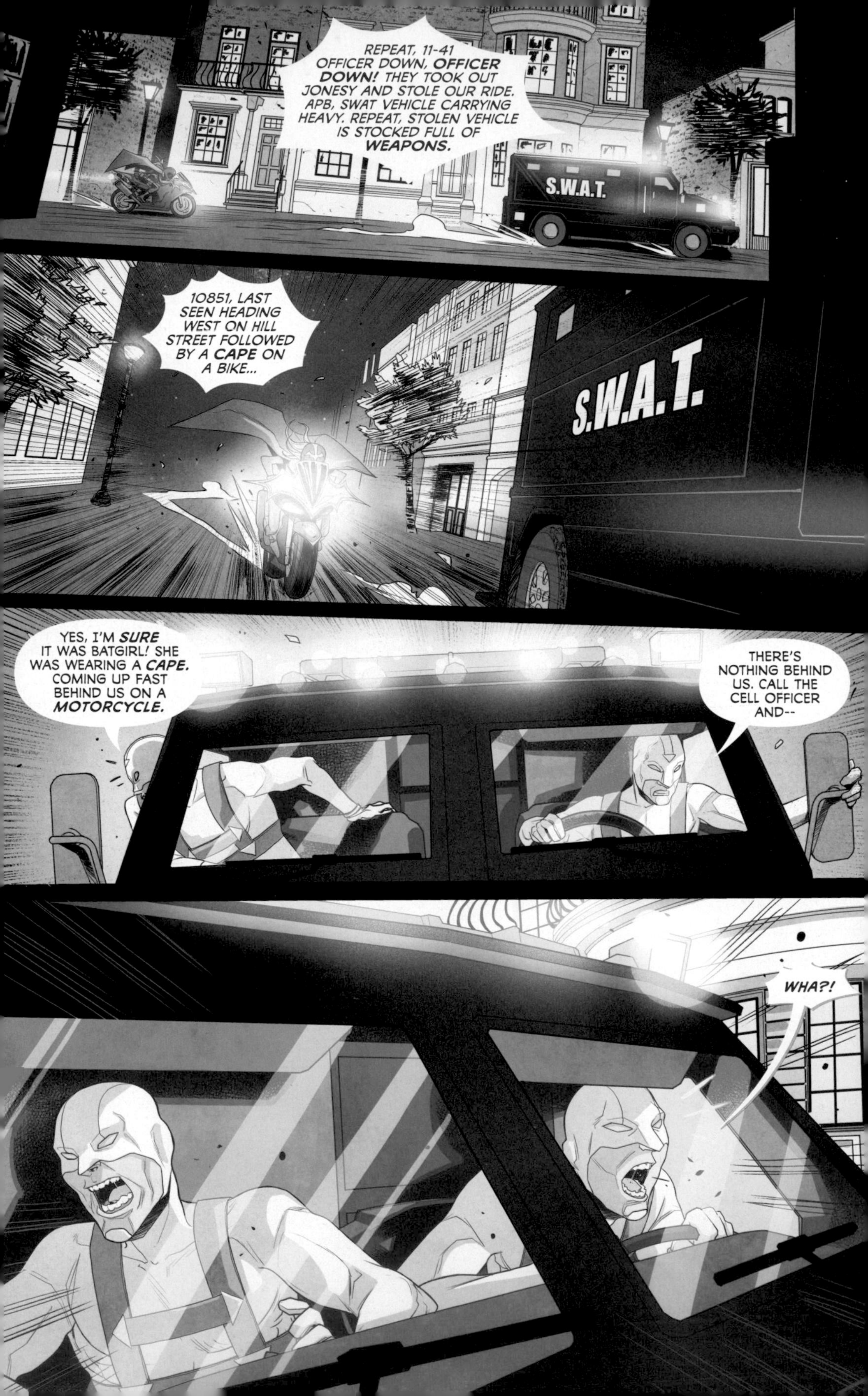

REPEAT, 11-41 OFFICER DOWN, OFFICER DOWN! THEY TOOK OUT JONESY AND STOLE OUR RIDE. APB, SWAT VEHICLE CARRYING HEAVY. REPEAT, STOLEN VEHICLE IS STOCKED FULL OF WEAPONS.
S.W.A.T.
10851, LAST SEEN HEADING WEST ON HILL STREET FOLLOWED BY A CAPE ON A BIKE...
S.W.A.T.
YES, I'M SURE IT WAS BATGIRL! SHE WAS WEARING A CAPE. COMING UP FAST BEHIND US ON A MOTORCYCLE.
THERE'S NOTHING BEHIND US. CALL THE CELL OFFICER AND--
WHA?!

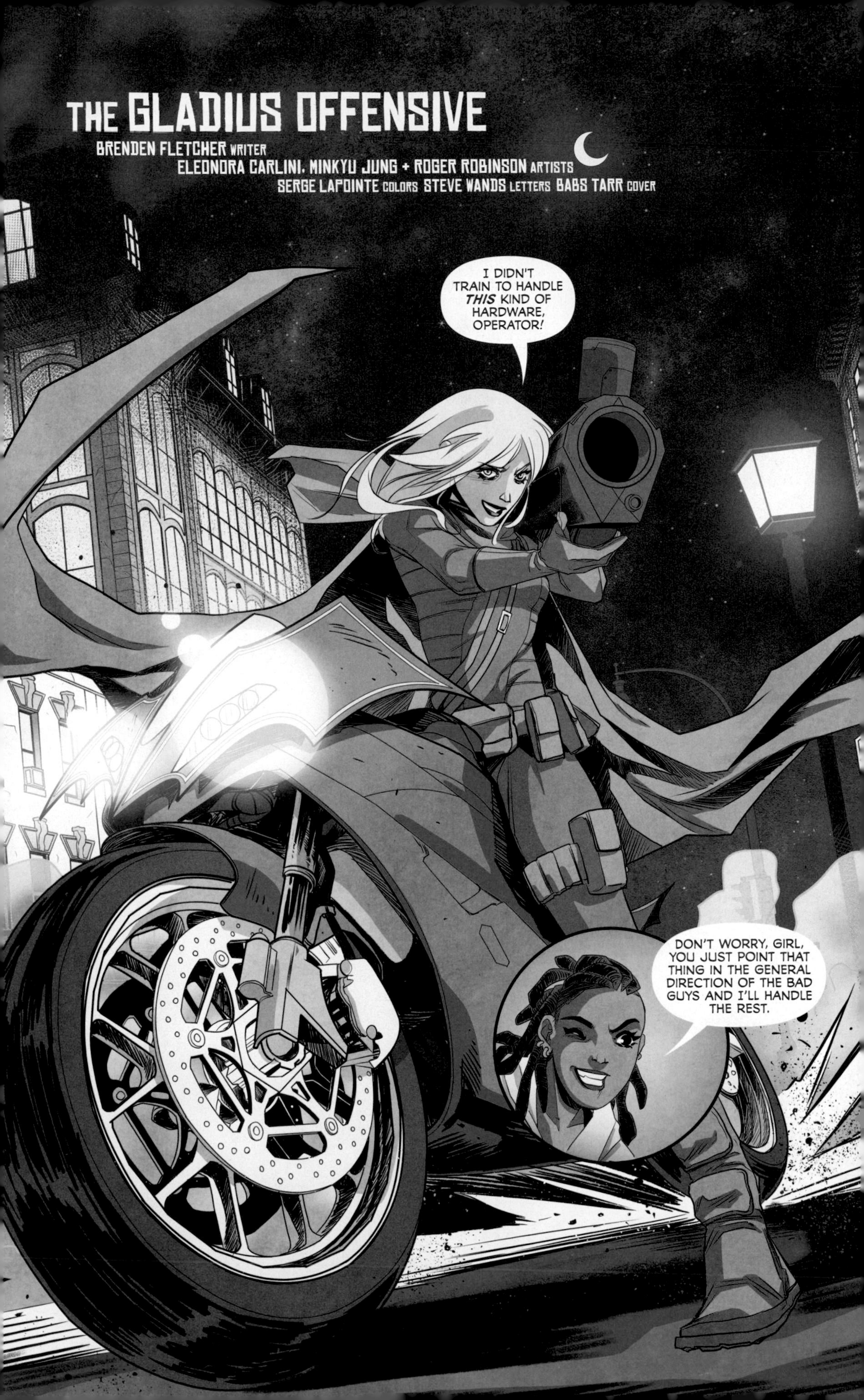
THE GLADIUS OFFENSIVE
BRENDEN FLETCHER WRITER
ELEONORA CARLINI, MINKYU JUNG + ROGER ROBINSON ARTISTS
SERGE LAPOINTE COLORS STEVE WANDS LETTERS BABS TARR COVER
I DIDN'T TRAIN TO HANDLE *THIS* KIND OF HARDWARE, OPERATOR!
DON'T WORRY, GIRL, YOU JUST POINT THAT THING IN THE GENERAL DIRECTION OF THE BAD GUYS AND I'LL HANDLE THE REST.

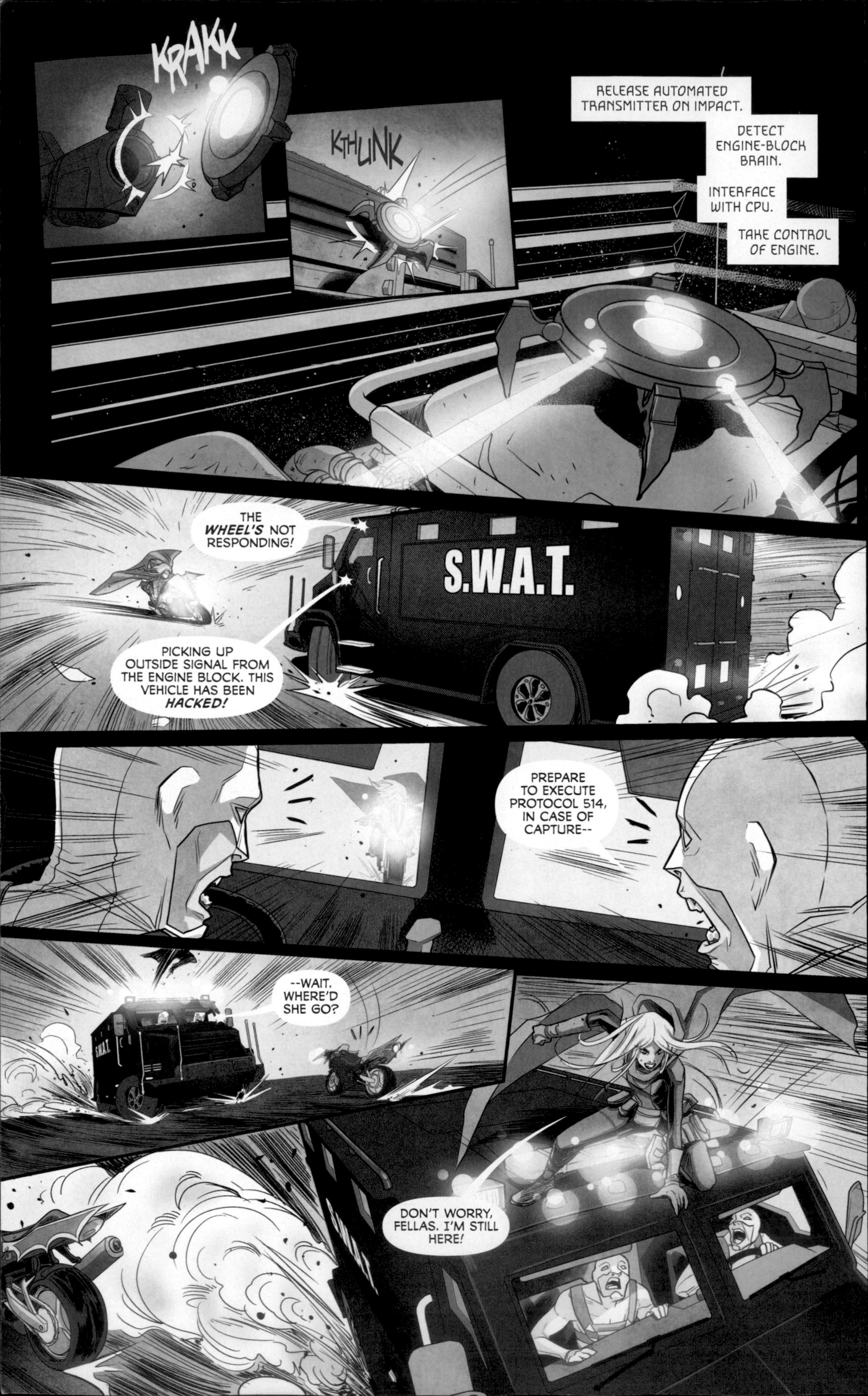
KRAKK
KTHUNK
RELEASE AUTOMATED TRANSMITTER ON IMPACT.
DETECT ENGINE-BLOCK BRAIN.
INTERFACE WITH CPU.
TAKE CONTROL OF ENGINE.
THE *WHEEL'S* NOT RESPONDING!
S.W.A.T.
PICKING UP OUTSIDE SIGNAL FROM THE ENGINE BLOCK. THIS VEHICLE HAS BEEN *HACKED!*
PREPARE TO EXECUTE PROTOCOL 514, IN CASE OF CAPTURE--
--WAIT. WHERE'D SHE GO?
DON'T WORRY, FELLAS. I'M STILL HERE!

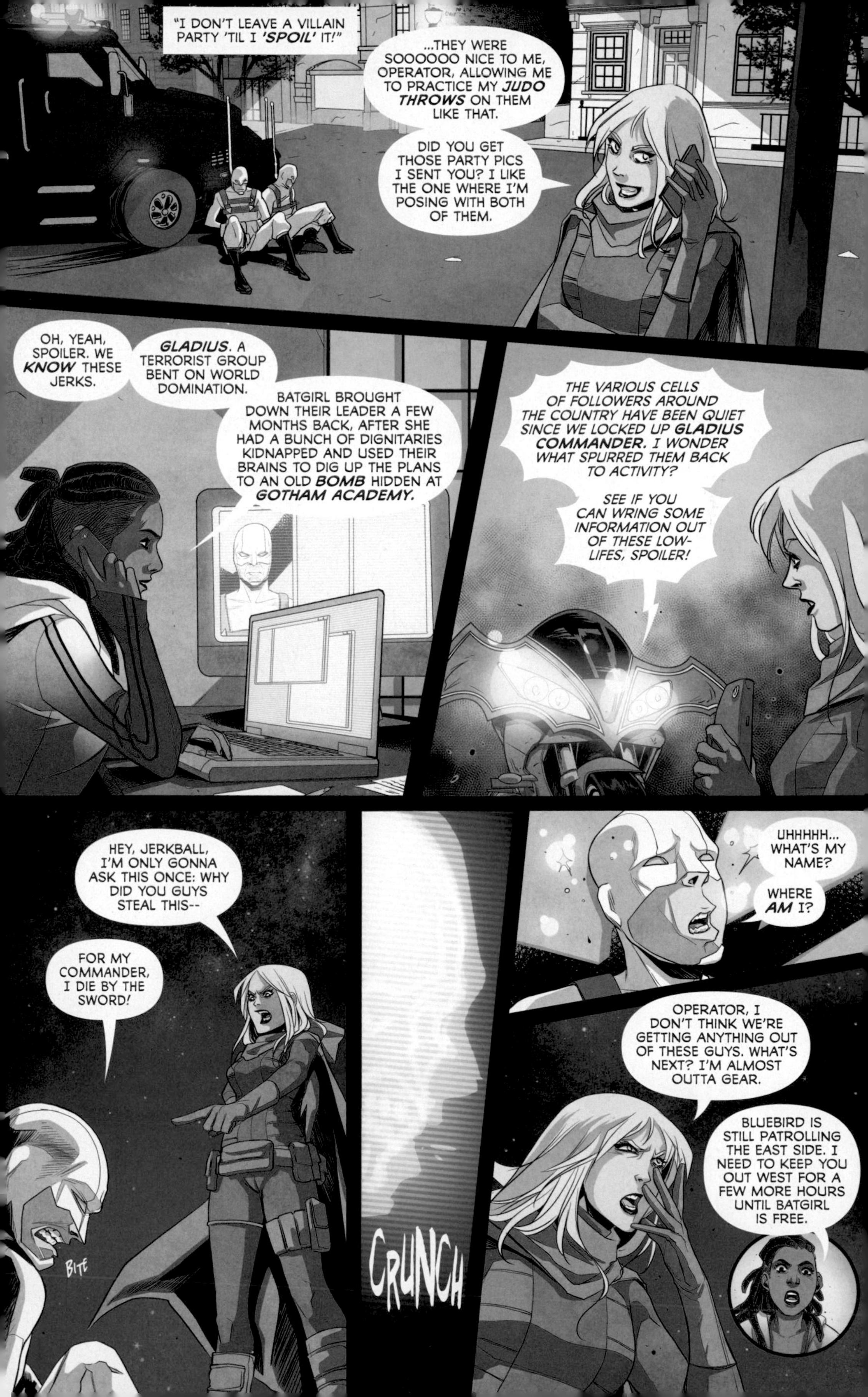
"I DON'T LEAVE A VILLAIN PARTY 'TIL I 'SPOIL' IT!"
...THEY WERE SOOOOOO NICE TO ME, OPERATOR, ALLOWING ME TO PRACTICE MY JUDO THROWS ON THEM LIKE THAT.
DID YOU GET THOSE PARTY PICS I SENT YOU? I LIKE THE ONE WHERE I'M POSING WITH BOTH OF THEM.
OH, YEAH, SPOILER. WE KNOW THESE JERKS.
GLADIUS. A TERRORIST GROUP BENT ON WORLD DOMINATION.
BATGIRL BROUGHT DOWN THEIR LEADER A FEW MONTHS BACK, AFTER SHE HAD A BUNCH OF DIGNITARIES KIDNAPPED AND USED THEIR BRAINS TO DIG UP THE PLANS TO AN OLD BOMB HIDDEN AT GOTHAM ACADEMY.
THE VARIOUS CELLS OF FOLLOWERS AROUND THE COUNTRY HAVE BEEN QUIET SINCE WE LOCKED UP GLADIUS COMMANDER. I WONDER WHAT SPURRED THEM BACK TO ACTIVITY?
SEE IF YOU CAN WRING SOME INFORMATION OUT OF THESE LOW-LIFES, SPOILER!
HEY, JERKBALL, I'M ONLY GONNA ASK THIS ONCE: WHY DID YOU GUYS STEAL THIS--
FOR MY COMMANDER, I DIE BY THE SWORD!
BITE
CRUNCH
UHHHHH... WHAT'S MY NAME?
WHERE AM I?
OPERATOR, I DON'T THINK WE'RE GETTING ANYTHING OUT OF THESE GUYS. WHAT'S NEXT? I'M ALMOST OUTTA GEAR.
BLUEBIRD IS STILL PATROLLING THE EAST SIDE. I NEED TO KEEP YOU OUT WEST FOR A FEW MORE HOURS UNTIL BATGIRL IS FREE.

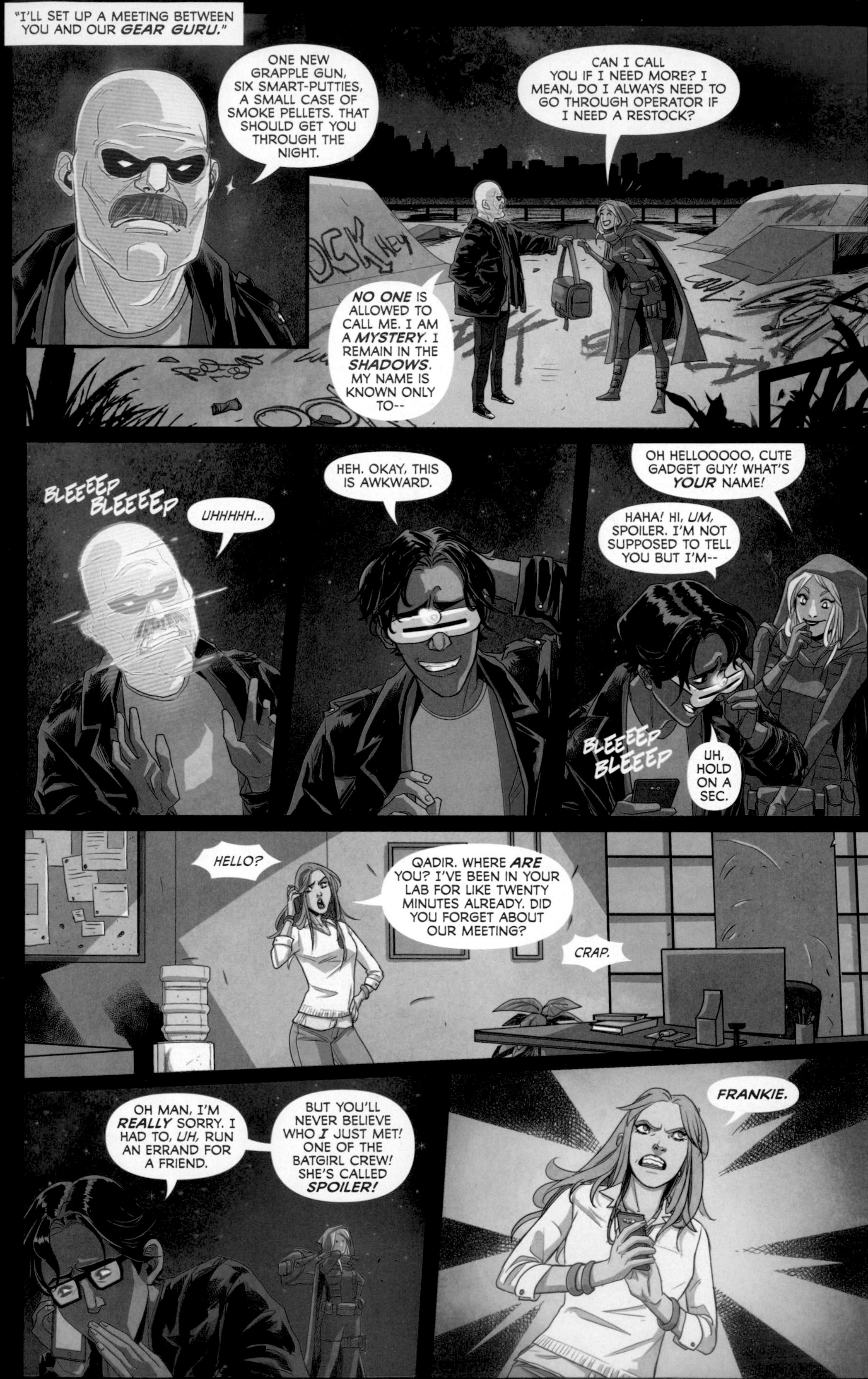
"I'LL SET UP A MEETING BETWEEN YOU AND OUR GEAR GURU."
ONE NEW GRAPPLE GUN, SIX SMART-PUTTIES, A SMALL CASE OF SMOKE PELLETS. THAT SHOULD GET YOU THROUGH THE NIGHT.
CAN I CALL YOU IF I NEED MORE? I MEAN, DO I ALWAYS NEED TO GO THROUGH OPERATOR IF I NEED A RESTOCK?
NO ONE IS ALLOWED TO CALL ME. I AM A MYSTERY. I REMAIN IN THE SHADOWS. MY NAME IS KNOWN ONLY TO--
BLEEEEP BLEEEEP
UHHHHH...
HEH. OKAY, THIS IS AWKWARD.
OH HELLOOOOO, CUTE GADGET GUY! WHAT'S YOUR NAME!
HAHA! HI, UM, SPOILER. I'M NOT SUPPOSED TO TELL YOU BUT I'M--
BLEEEEP BLEEEP
UH, HOLD ON A SEC.
HELLO?
QADIR. WHERE ARE YOU? I'VE BEEN IN YOUR LAB FOR LIKE TWENTY MINUTES ALREADY. DID YOU FORGET ABOUT OUR MEETING?
CRAP.
OH MAN, I'M REALLY SORRY. I HAD TO, UH, RUN AN ERRAND FOR A FRIEND.
BUT YOU'LL NEVER BELIEVE WHO I JUST MET! ONE OF THE BATGIRL CREW! SHE'S CALLED SPOILER!
FRANKIE.

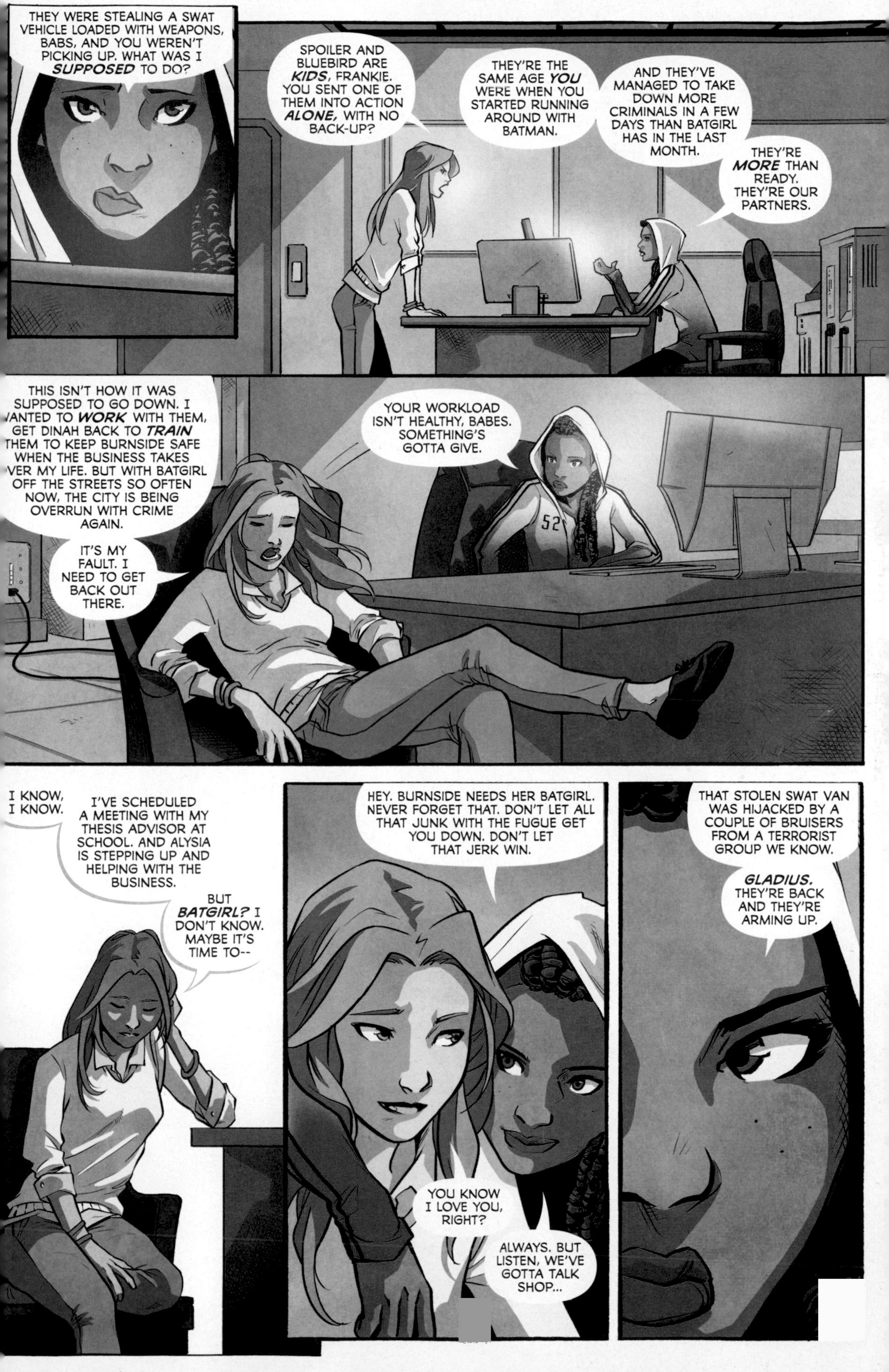
THEY WERE STEALING A SWAT VEHICLE LOADED WITH WEAPONS, BABS, AND YOU WEREN'T PICKING UP. WHAT WAS I SUPPOSED TO DO?
SPOILER AND BLUEBIRD ARE KIDS, FRANKIE. YOU SENT ONE OF THEM INTO ACTION ALONE, WITH NO BACK-UP?
THEY'RE THE SAME AGE YOU WERE WHEN YOU STARTED RUNNING AROUND WITH BATMAN.
AND THEY'VE MANAGED TO TAKE DOWN MORE CRIMINALS IN A FEW DAYS THAN BATGIRL HAS IN THE LAST MONTH.
THEY'RE MORE THAN READY. THEY'RE OUR PARTNERS.
THIS ISN'T HOW IT WAS SUPPOSED TO GO DOWN. I WANTED TO WORK WITH THEM, GET DINAH BACK TO TRAIN THEM TO KEEP BURNSIDE SAFE WHEN THE BUSINESS TAKES OVER MY LIFE. BUT WITH BATGIRL OFF THE STREETS SO OFTEN NOW, THE CITY IS BEING OVERRUN WITH CRIME AGAIN.
YOUR WORKLOAD ISN'T HEALTHY, BABES. SOMETHING'S GOTTA GIVE.
IT'S MY FAULT. I NEED TO GET BACK OUT THERE.
52
I KNOW, I KNOW.
I'VE SCHEDULED A MEETING WITH MY THESIS ADVISOR AT SCHOOL. AND ALYSIA IS STEPPING UP AND HELPING WITH THE BUSINESS.
BUT BATGIRL? I DON'T KNOW. MAYBE IT'S TIME TO--
HEY. BURNSIDE NEEDS HER BATGIRL. NEVER FORGET THAT. DON'T LET ALL THAT JUNK WITH THE FUGUE GET YOU DOWN. DON'T LET THAT JERK WIN.
YOU KNOW I LOVE YOU, RIGHT?
ALWAYS. BUT LISTEN, WE'VE GOTTA TALK SHOP...
THAT STOLEN SWAT VAN WAS HIJACKED BY A COUPLE OF BRUISERS FROM A TERRORIST GROUP WE KNOW.
GLADIUS. THEY'RE BACK AND THEY'RE ARMING UP.

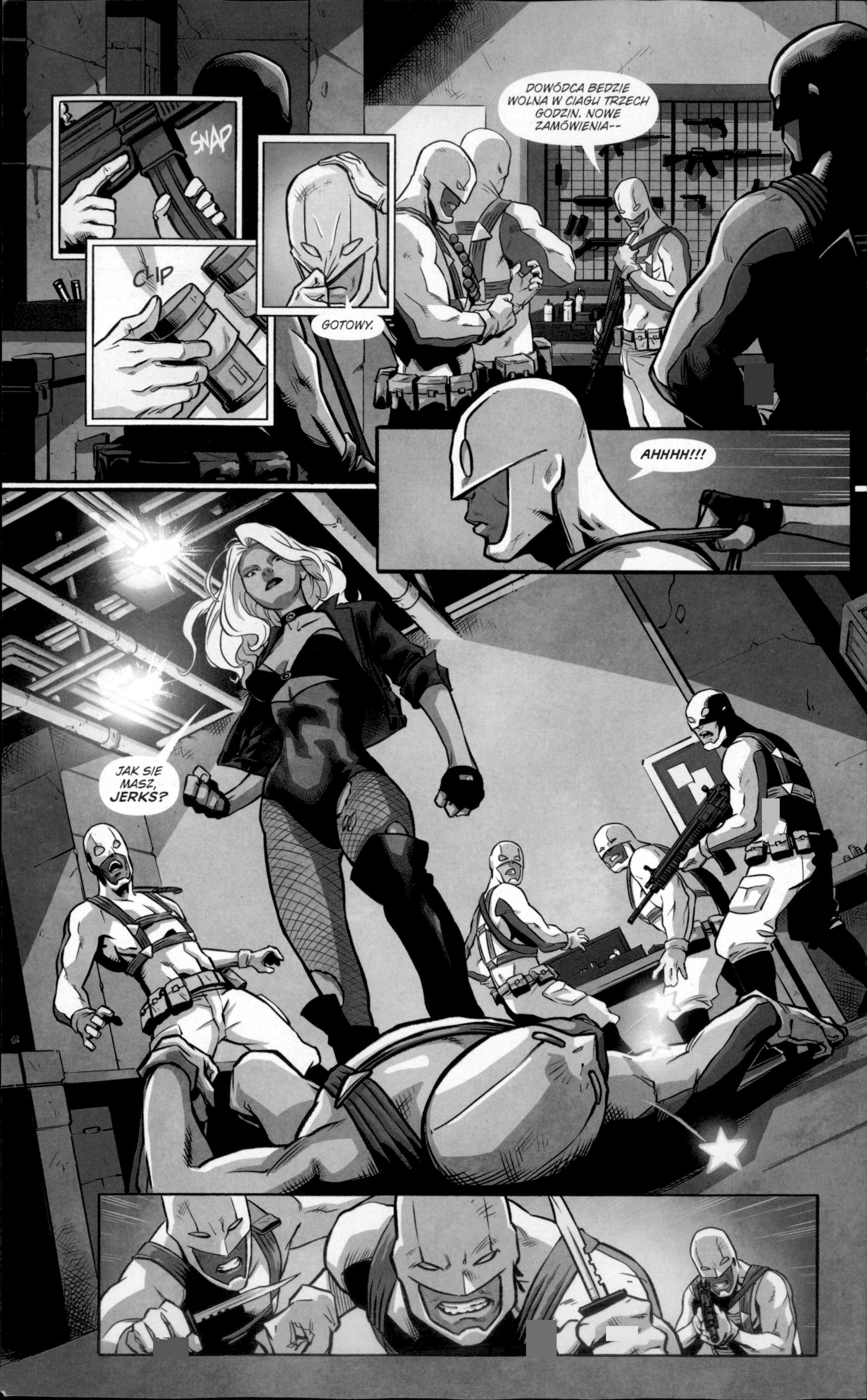
SNAP
CLIP
GOTOWY.
DOWÓDCA BEDZIE WOLNA W CIAGU TRZECH GODZIN. NOWE ZAMÓWIENIA--
AHHHH!!!
JAK SIE MASZ, **JERKS?**

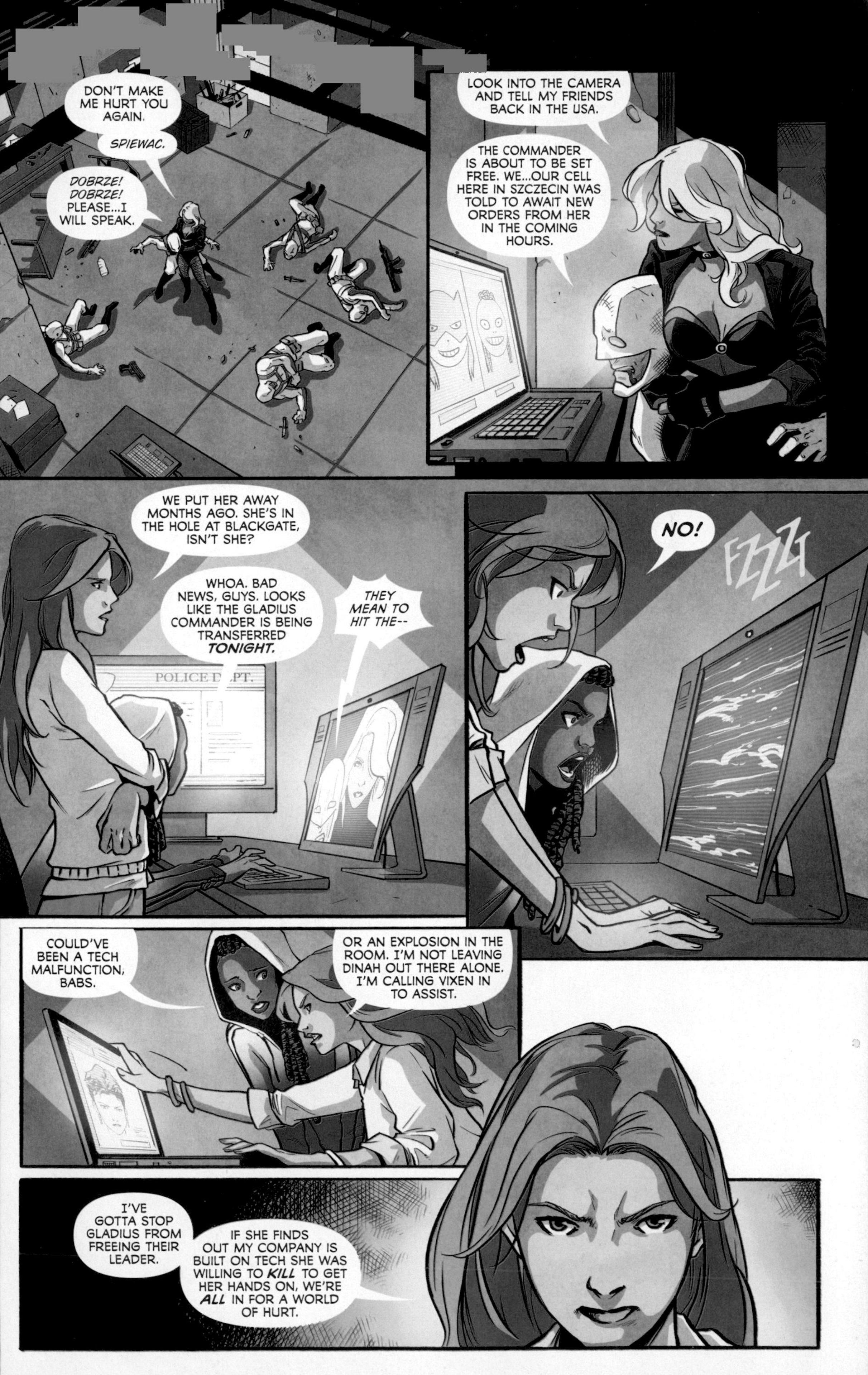

DON'T MAKE ME HURT YOU AGAIN.
SPIEWAC.
DOBRZE! DOBRZE! PLEASE...I WILL SPEAK.
LOOK INTO THE CAMERA AND TELL MY FRIENDS BACK IN THE USA.
THE COMMANDER IS ABOUT TO BE SET FREE. WE...OUR CELL HERE IN SZCZECIN WAS TOLD TO AWAIT NEW ORDERS FROM HER IN THE COMING HOURS.
WE PUT HER AWAY MONTHS AGO. SHE'S IN THE HOLE AT BLACKGATE, ISN'T SHE?
POLICE DEPT.
WHOA. BAD NEWS, GUYS. LOOKS LIKE THE GLADIUS COMMANDER IS BEING TRANSFERRED *TONIGHT.*
THEY MEAN TO HIT THE--
NO!
FZZZT
COULD'VE BEEN A TECH MALFUNCTION, BABS.
OR AN EXPLOSION IN THE ROOM. I'M NOT LEAVING DINAH OUT THERE ALONE. I'M CALLING VIXEN IN TO ASSIST.
I'VE GOTTA STOP GLADIUS FROM FREEING THEIR LEADER.
IF SHE FINDS OUT MY COMPANY IS BUILT ON TECH SHE WAS WILLING TO *KILL* TO GET HER HANDS ON, WE'RE *ALL* IN FOR A WORLD OF HURT.

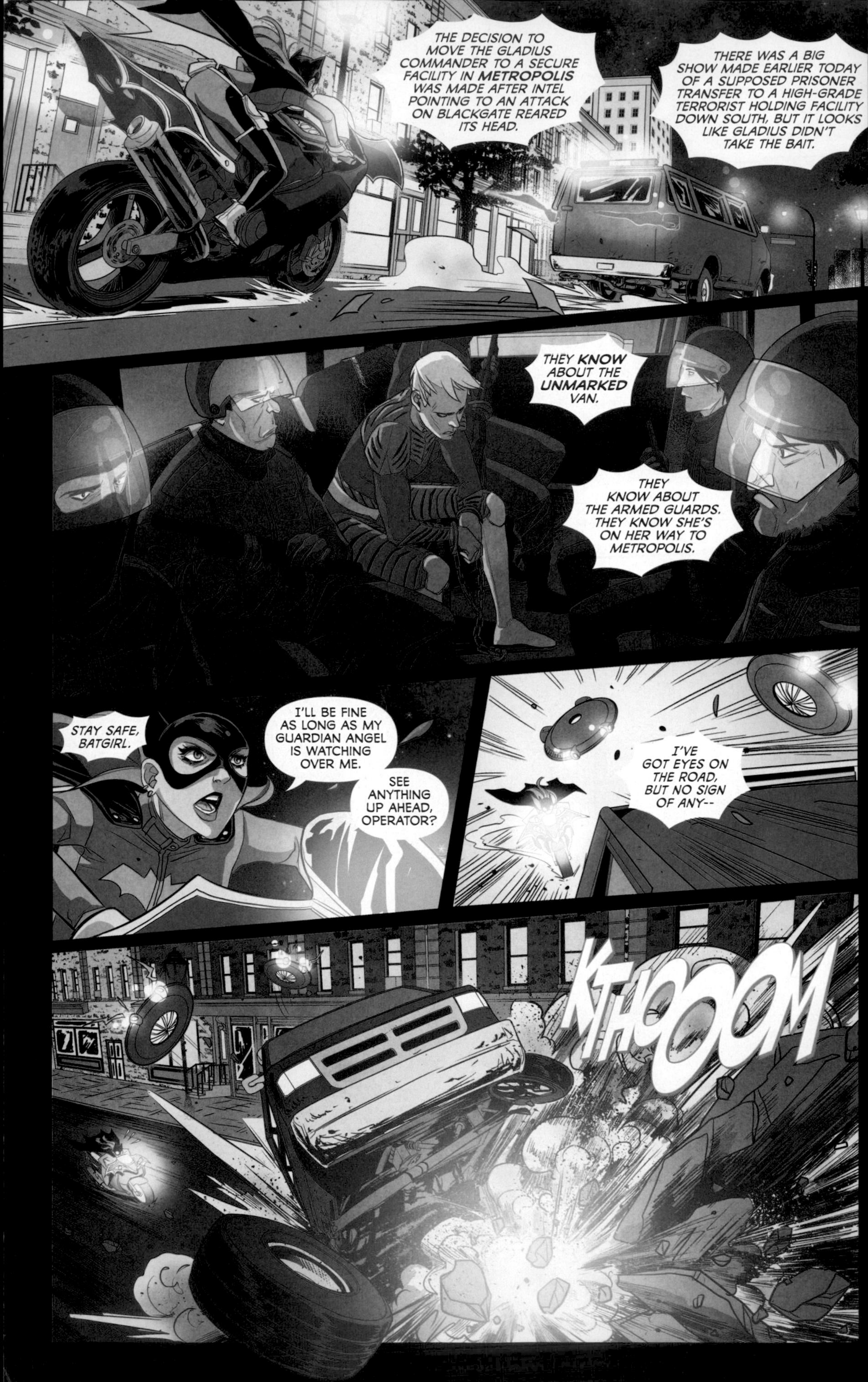
THE DECISION TO MOVE THE GLADIUS COMMANDER TO A SECURE FACILITY IN METROPOLIS WAS MADE AFTER INTEL POINTING TO AN ATTACK ON BLACKGATE REARED ITS HEAD.
THERE WAS A BIG SHOW MADE EARLIER TODAY OF A SUPPOSED PRISONER TRANSFER TO A HIGH-GRADE TERRORIST HOLDING FACILITY DOWN SOUTH, BUT IT LOOKS LIKE GLADIUS DIDN'T TAKE THE BAIT.
THEY KNOW ABOUT THE UNMARKED VAN.
THEY KNOW ABOUT THE ARMED GUARDS. THEY KNOW SHE'S ON HER WAY TO METROPOLIS.
STAY SAFE, BATGIRL.
I'LL BE FINE AS LONG AS MY GUARDIAN ANGEL IS WATCHING OVER ME.
SEE ANYTHING UP AHEAD, OPERATOR?
I'VE GOT EYES ON THE ROAD, BUT NO SIGN OF ANY--
KTHOOOM

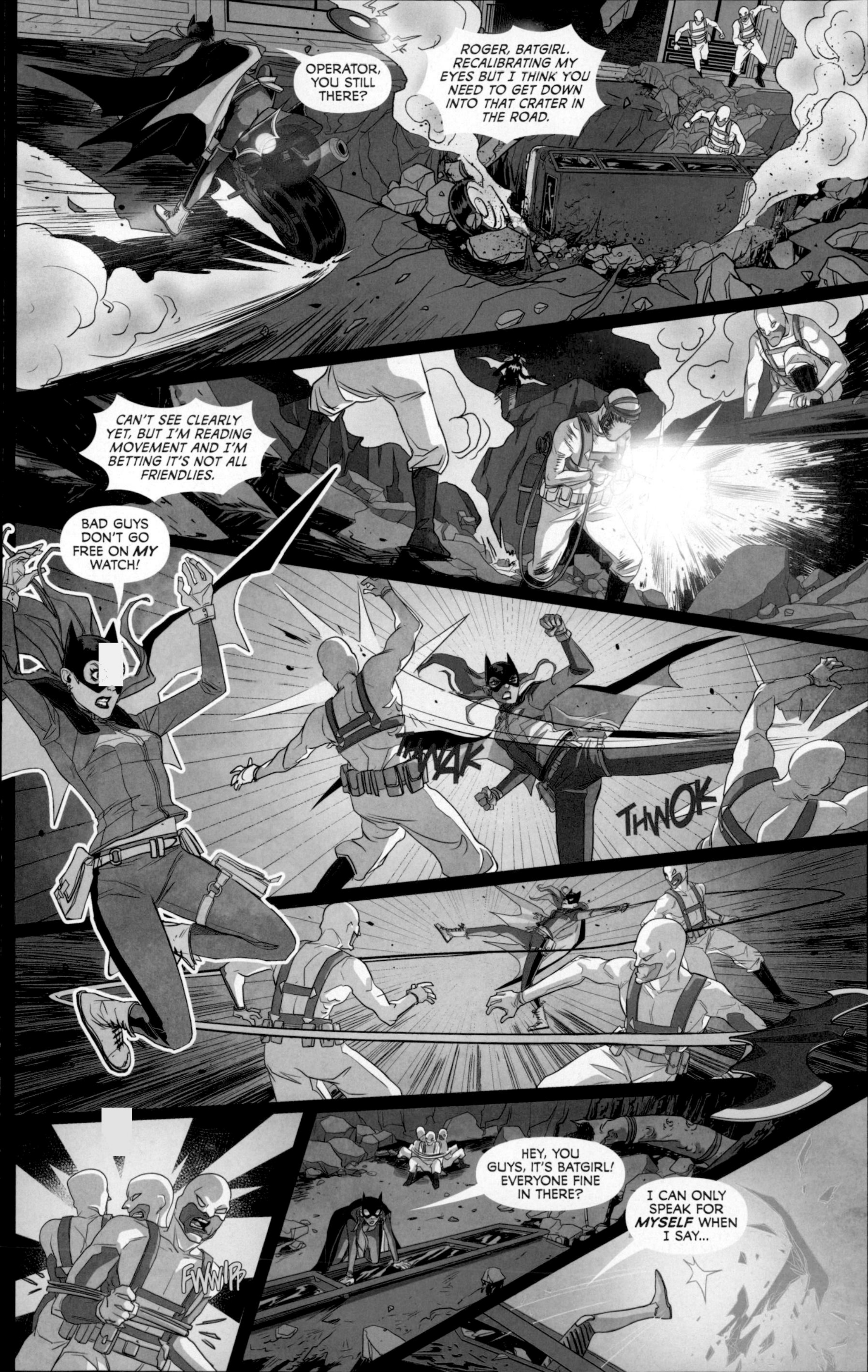
OPERATOR, YOU STILL THERE?
ROGER, BATGIRL. RECALIBRATING MY EYES BUT I THINK YOU NEED TO GET DOWN INTO THAT CRATER IN THE ROAD.
CAN'T SEE CLEARLY YET, BUT I'M READING MOVEMENT AND I'M BETTING IT'S NOT ALL FRIENDLIES.
BAD GUYS DON'T GO FREE ON MY WATCH!
THWAK
THWOK
FWWIPP
HEY, YOU GUYS, IT'S BATGIRL! EVERYONE FINE IN THERE?
I CAN ONLY SPEAK FOR MYSELF WHEN I SAY...

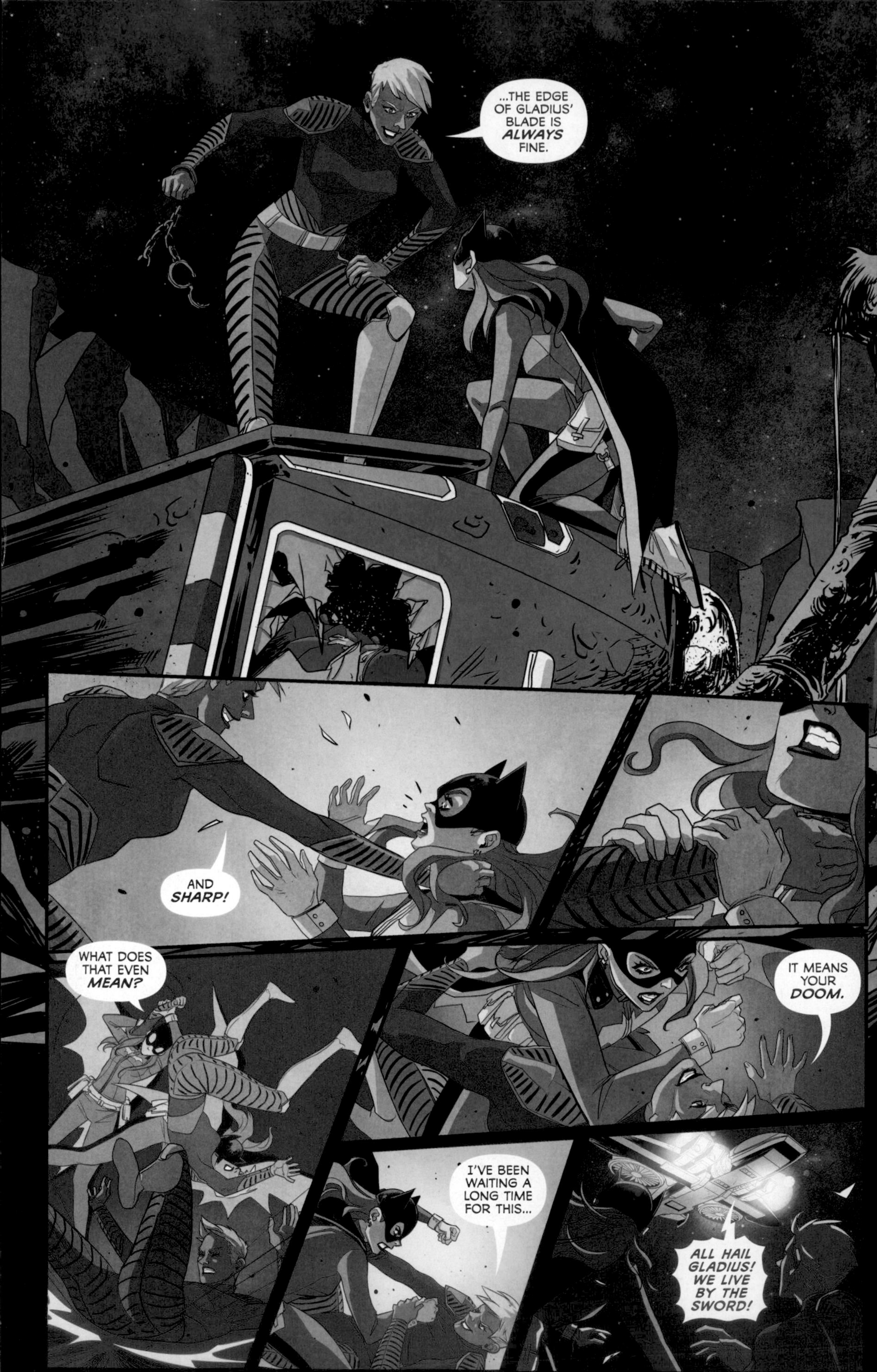
...THE EDGE OF GLADIUS' BLADE IS ALWAYS FINE.
AND SHARP!
WHAT DOES THAT EVEN MEAN?
IT MEANS YOUR DOOM.
I'VE BEEN WAITING A LONG TIME FOR THIS...
ALL HAIL GLADIUS! WE LIVE BY THE SWORD!

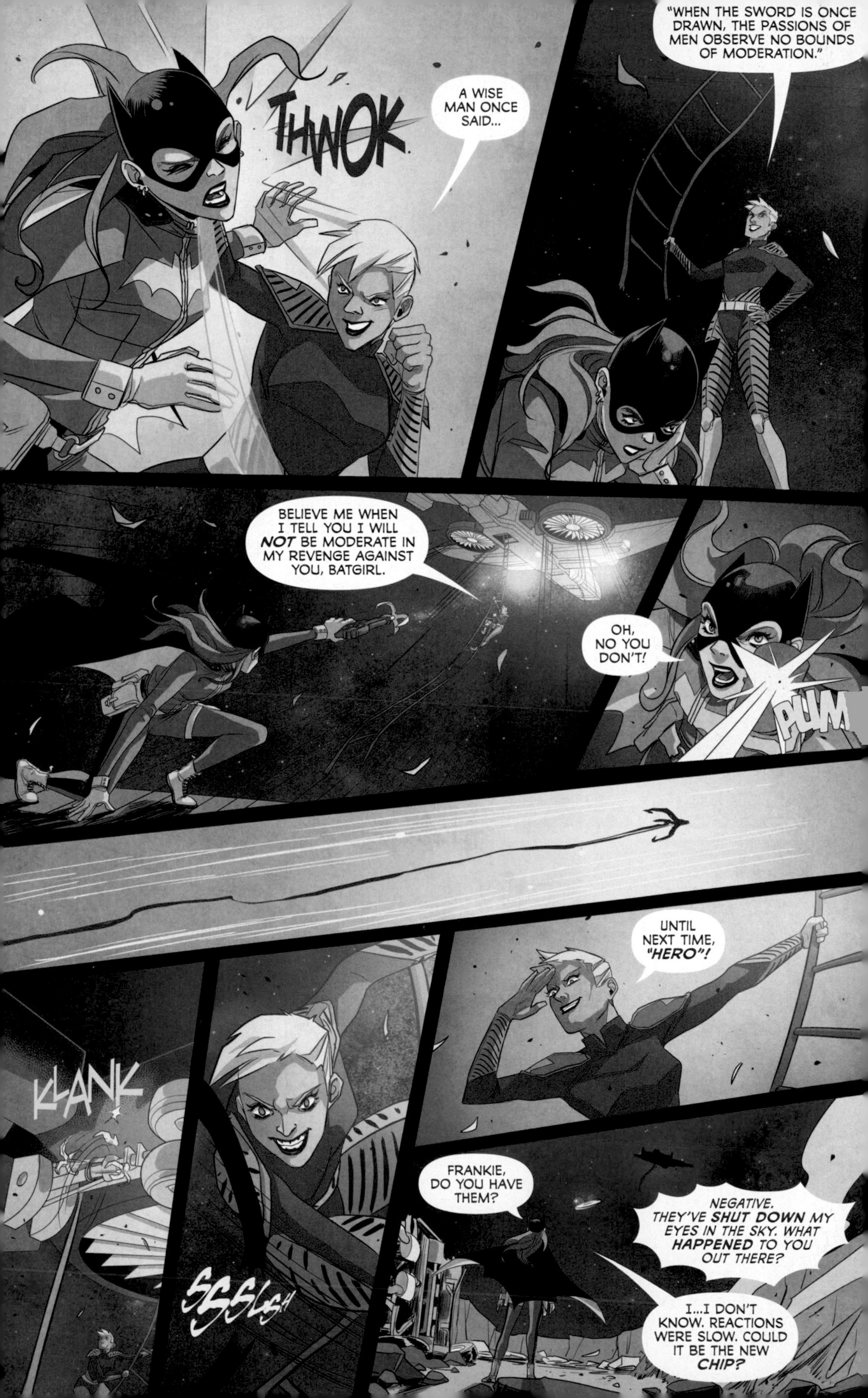
THWOK
A WISE MAN ONCE SAID...
"WHEN THE SWORD IS ONCE DRAWN, THE PASSIONS OF MEN OBSERVE NO BOUNDS OF MODERATION."
BELIEVE ME WHEN I TELL YOU I WILL *NOT* BE MODERATE IN MY REVENGE AGAINST YOU, BATGIRL.
OH, NO YOU DON'T!
PUM
UNTIL NEXT TIME, *"HERO"*!
KLANK
SSSLSH
FRANKIE, DO YOU HAVE THEM?
NEGATIVE. THEY'VE ***SHUT DOWN*** *MY EYES IN THE SKY. WHAT* ***HAPPENED*** *TO YOU OUT THERE?*
I...I DON'T KNOW. REACTIONS WERE SLOW. COULD IT BE THE NEW ***CHIP?***

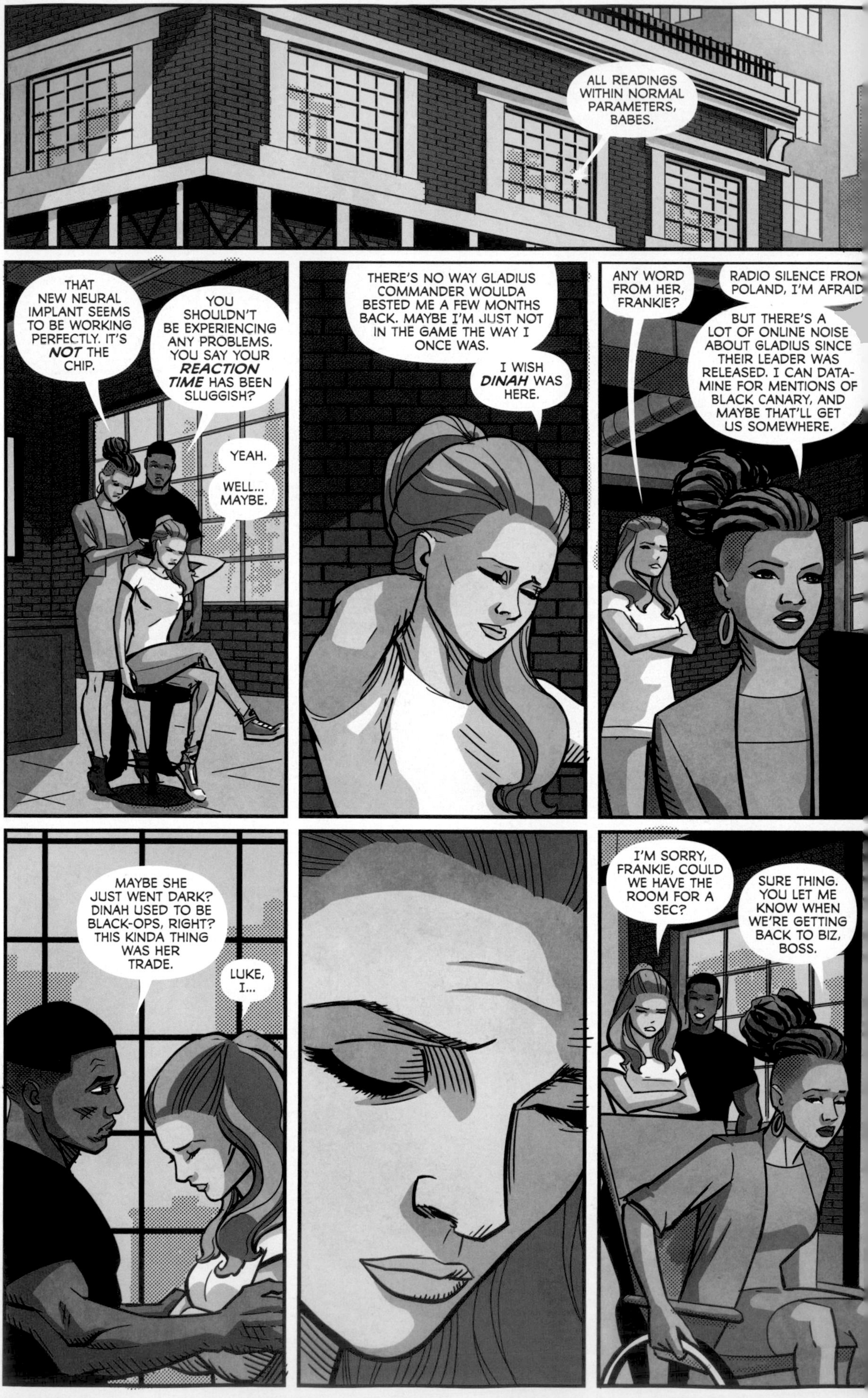
ALL READINGS WITHIN NORMAL PARAMETERS, BABES.
THAT NEW NEURAL IMPLANT SEEMS TO BE WORKING PERFECTLY. IT'S NOT THE CHIP.
YOU SHOULDN'T BE EXPERIENCING ANY PROBLEMS. YOU SAY YOUR REACTION TIME HAS BEEN SLUGGISH?
YEAH.
WELL... MAYBE.
THERE'S NO WAY GLADIUS COMMANDER WOULDA BESTED ME A FEW MONTHS BACK. MAYBE I'M JUST NOT IN THE GAME THE WAY I ONCE WAS.
I WISH DINAH WAS HERE.
ANY WORD FROM HER, FRANKIE?
RADIO SILENCE FROM POLAND, I'M AFRAID.
BUT THERE'S A LOT OF ONLINE NOISE ABOUT GLADIUS SINCE THEIR LEADER WAS RELEASED. I CAN DATA-MINE FOR MENTIONS OF BLACK CANARY, AND MAYBE THAT'LL GET US SOMEWHERE.
MAYBE SHE JUST WENT DARK? DINAH USED TO BE BLACK-OPS, RIGHT? THIS KINDA THING WAS HER TRADE.
LUKE, I...
I'M SORRY, FRANKIE, COULD WE HAVE THE ROOM FOR A SEC?
SURE THING. YOU LET ME KNOW WHEN WE'RE GETTING BACK TO BIZ, BOSS.

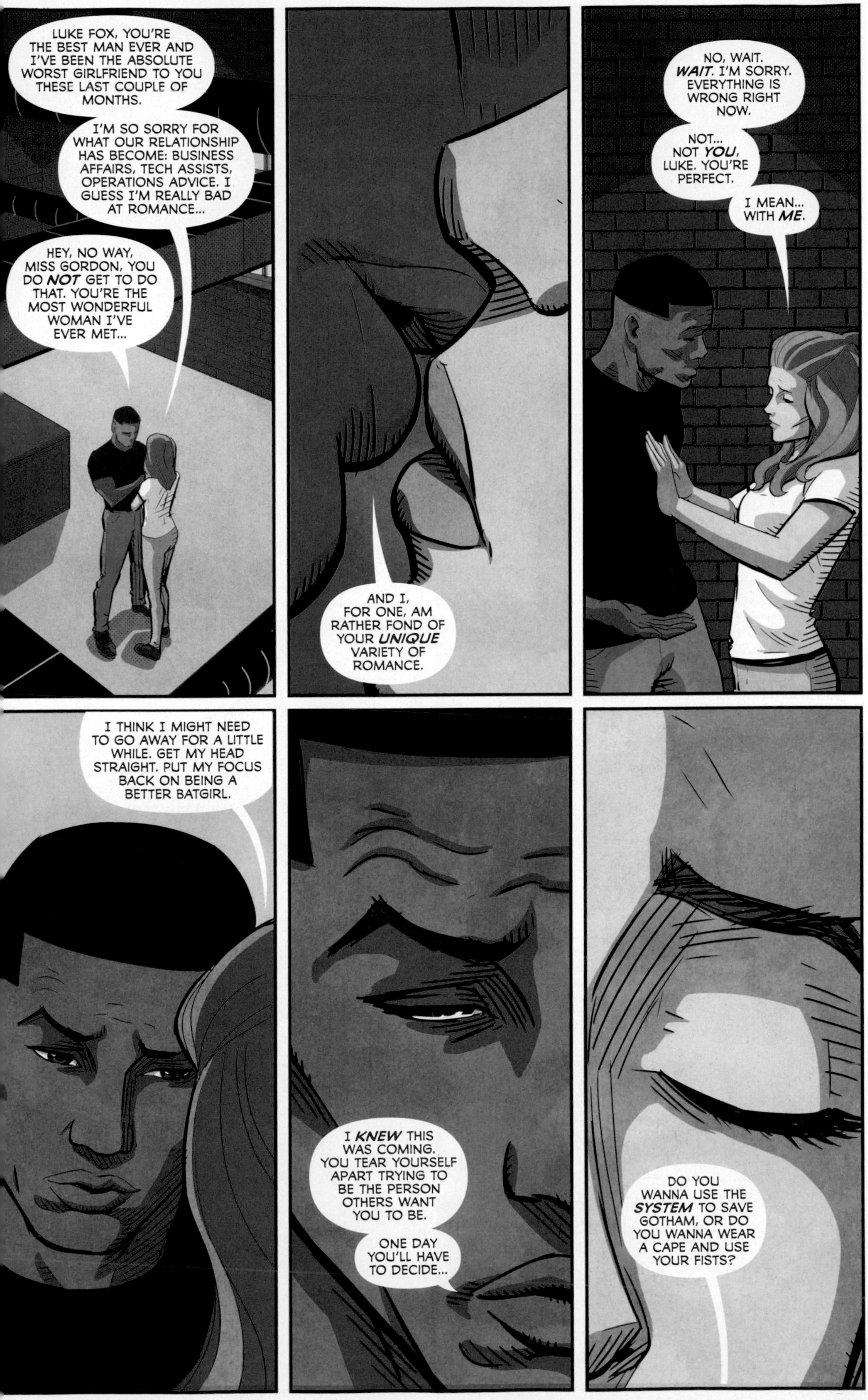
LUKE FOX, YOU'RE THE BEST MAN EVER AND I'VE BEEN THE ABSOLUTE WORST GIRLFRIEND TO YOU THESE LAST COUPLE OF MONTHS.
I'M SO SORRY FOR WHAT OUR RELATIONSHIP HAS BECOME: BUSINESS AFFAIRS, TECH ASSISTS, OPERATIONS ADVICE. I GUESS I'M REALLY BAD AT ROMANCE...
HEY, NO WAY, MISS GORDON, YOU DO *NOT* GET TO DO THAT. YOU'RE THE MOST WONDERFUL WOMAN I'VE EVER MET...
AND I, FOR ONE, AM RATHER FOND OF YOUR *UNIQUE* VARIETY OF ROMANCE.
NO, WAIT. *WAIT*. I'M SORRY. EVERYTHING IS WRONG RIGHT NOW.
NOT... NOT *YOU*, LUKE. YOU'RE PERFECT.
I MEAN... WITH *ME*.
I THINK I MIGHT NEED TO GO AWAY FOR A LITTLE WHILE. GET MY HEAD STRAIGHT. PUT MY FOCUS BACK ON BEING A BETTER BATGIRL.
I *KNEW* THIS WAS COMING. YOU TEAR YOURSELF APART TRYING TO BE THE PERSON OTHERS WANT YOU TO BE.
ONE DAY YOU'LL HAVE TO DECIDE...
DO YOU WANNA USE THE *SYSTEM* TO SAVE GOTHAM, OR DO YOU WANNA WEAR A CAPE AND USE YOUR FISTS?

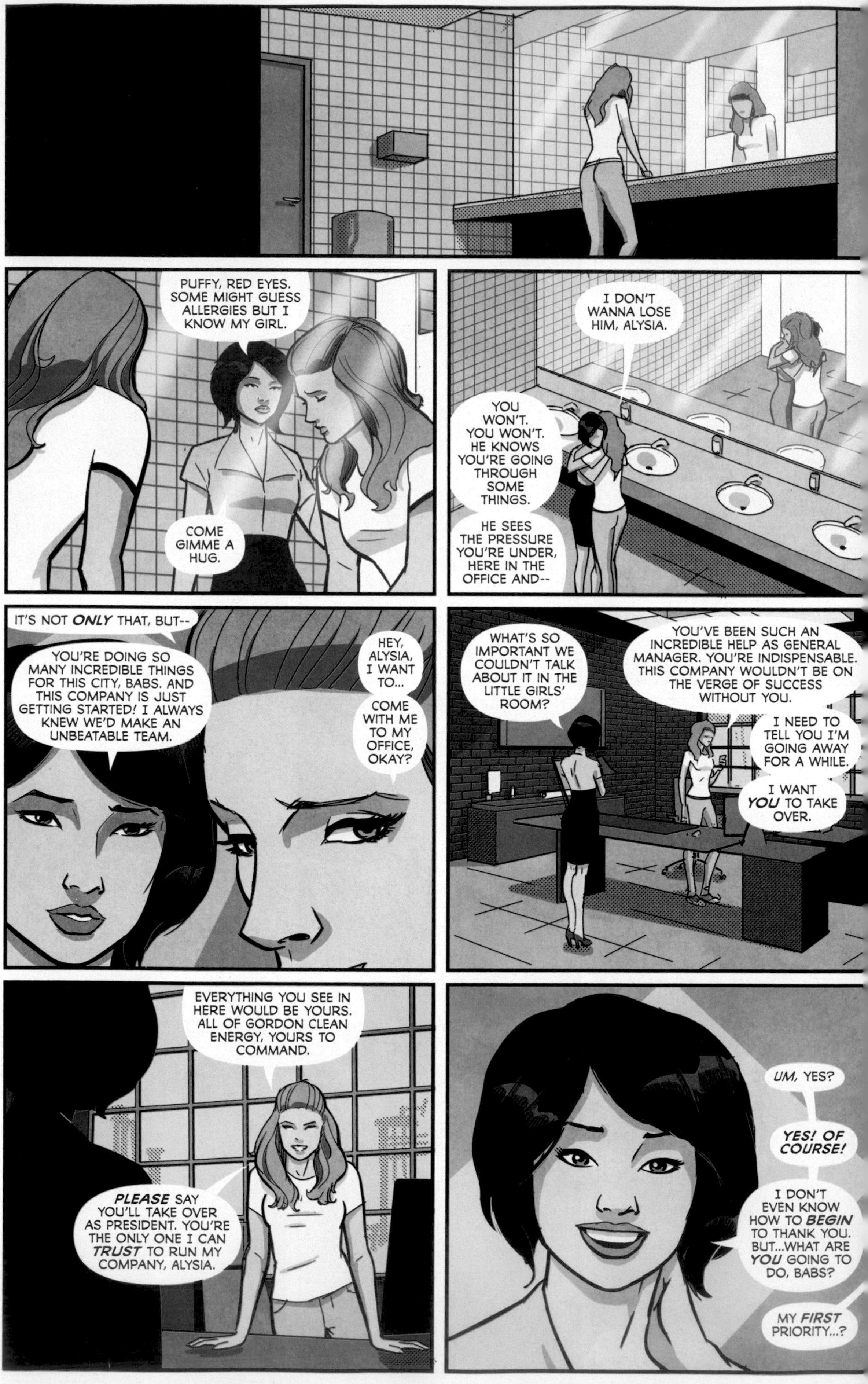
PUFFY, RED EYES. SOME MIGHT GUESS ALLERGIES BUT I KNOW MY GIRL.
COME GIMME A HUG.
I DON'T WANNA LOSE HIM, ALYSIA.
YOU WON'T. YOU WON'T. HE KNOWS YOU'RE GOING THROUGH SOME THINGS.
HE SEES THE PRESSURE YOU'RE UNDER, HERE IN THE OFFICE AND--
IT'S NOT ONLY THAT, BUT--
YOU'RE DOING SO MANY INCREDIBLE THINGS FOR THIS CITY, BABS. AND THIS COMPANY IS JUST GETTING STARTED! I ALWAYS KNEW WE'D MAKE AN UNBEATABLE TEAM.
HEY, ALYSIA, I WANT TO...
COME WITH ME TO MY OFFICE, OKAY?
WHAT'S SO IMPORTANT WE COULDN'T TALK ABOUT IT IN THE LITTLE GIRLS' ROOM?
YOU'VE BEEN SUCH AN INCREDIBLE HELP AS GENERAL MANAGER. YOU'RE INDISPENSABLE. THIS COMPANY WOULDN'T BE ON THE VERGE OF SUCCESS WITHOUT YOU.
I NEED TO TELL YOU I'M GOING AWAY FOR A WHILE.
I WANT YOU TO TAKE OVER.
EVERYTHING YOU SEE IN HERE WOULD BE YOURS. ALL OF GORDON CLEAN ENERGY, YOURS TO COMMAND.
PLEASE SAY YOU'LL TAKE OVER AS PRESIDENT. YOU'RE THE ONLY ONE I CAN TRUST TO RUN MY COMPANY, ALYSIA.
UM, YES?
YES! OF COURSE!
I DON'T EVEN KNOW HOW TO BEGIN TO THANK YOU. BUT...WHAT ARE YOU GOING TO DO, BABS?
MY FIRST PRIORITY...?

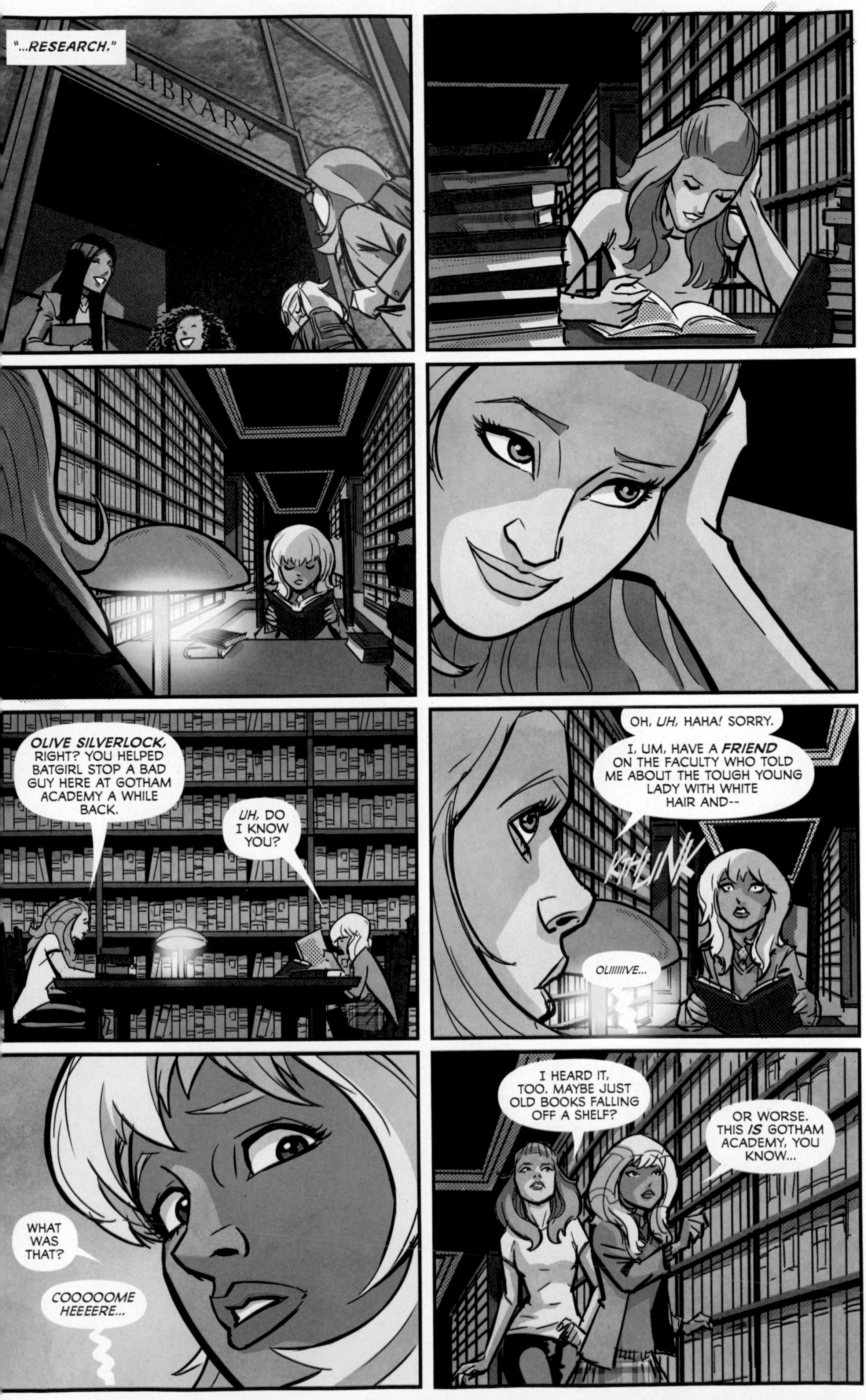
"...RESEARCH."
LIBRARY
OLIVE SILVERLOCK, RIGHT? YOU HELPED BATGIRL STOP A BAD GUY HERE AT GOTHAM ACADEMY A WHILE BACK.
UH, DO I KNOW YOU?
OH, UH, HAHA! SORRY.
I, UM, HAVE A FRIEND ON THE FACULTY WHO TOLD ME ABOUT THE TOUGH YOUNG LADY WITH WHITE HAIR AND--
KLUNK
OLIIIIIVE...
WHAT WAS THAT?
COOOOOME HEEEERE...
I HEARD IT, TOO. MAYBE JUST OLD BOOKS FALLING OFF A SHELF?
OR WORSE. THIS IS GOTHAM ACADEMY, YOU KNOW...

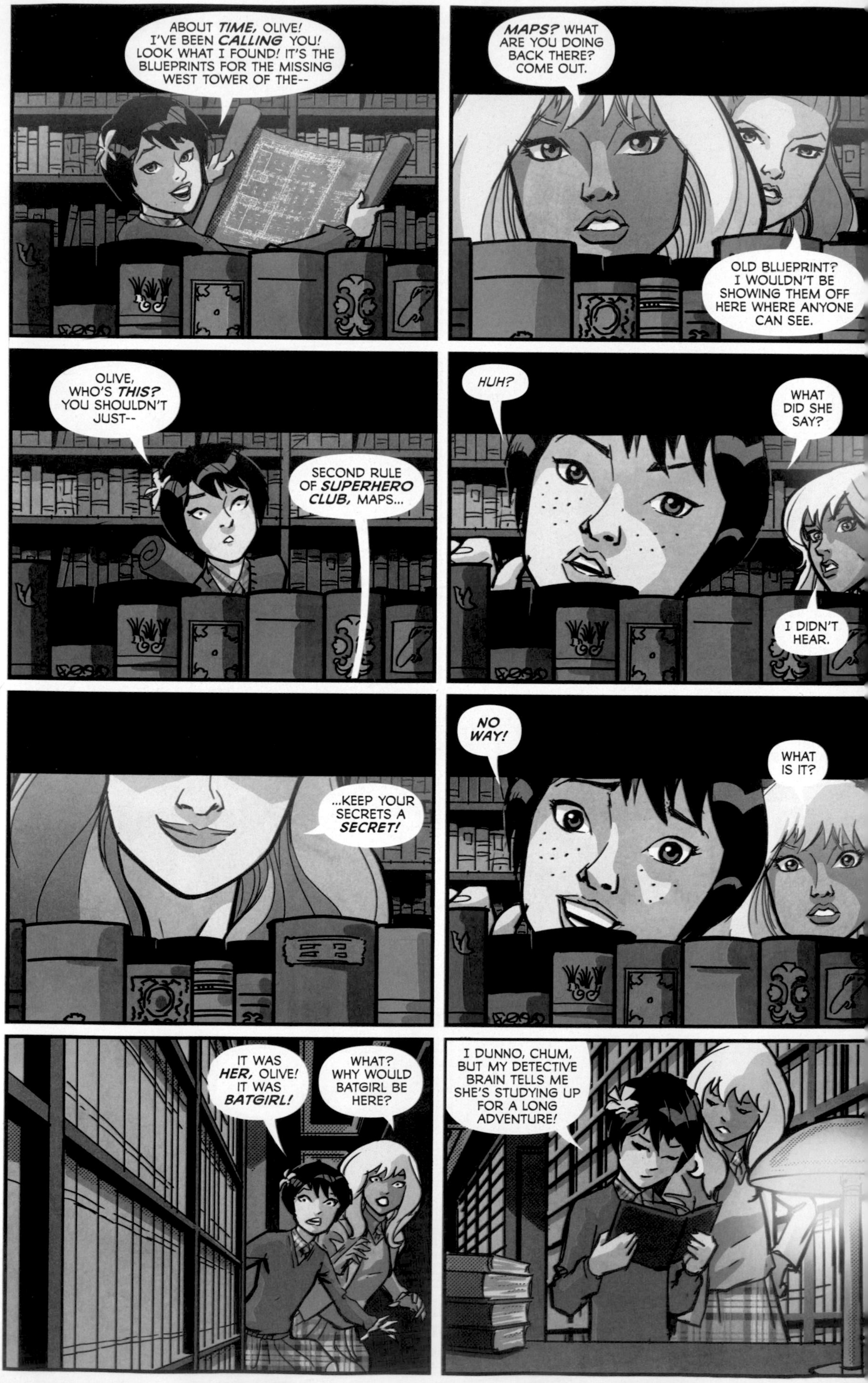
ABOUT TIME, OLIVE! I'VE BEEN CALLING YOU! LOOK WHAT I FOUND! IT'S THE BLUEPRINTS FOR THE MISSING WEST TOWER OF THE--
MAPS? WHAT ARE YOU DOING BACK THERE? COME OUT.
OLD BLUEPRINT? I WOULDN'T BE SHOWING THEM OFF HERE WHERE ANYONE CAN SEE.
OLIVE, WHO'S THIS? YOU SHOULDN'T JUST--
SECOND RULE OF SUPERHERO CLUB, MAPS...
HUH?
WHAT DID SHE SAY?
I DIDN'T HEAR.
...KEEP YOUR SECRETS A SECRET!
NO WAY!
WHAT IS IT?
IT WAS HER, OLIVE! IT WAS BATGIRL!
WHAT? WHY WOULD BATGIRL BE HERE?
I DUNNO, CHUM, BUT MY DETECTIVE BRAIN TELLS ME SHE'S STUDYING UP FOR A LONG ADVENTURE!

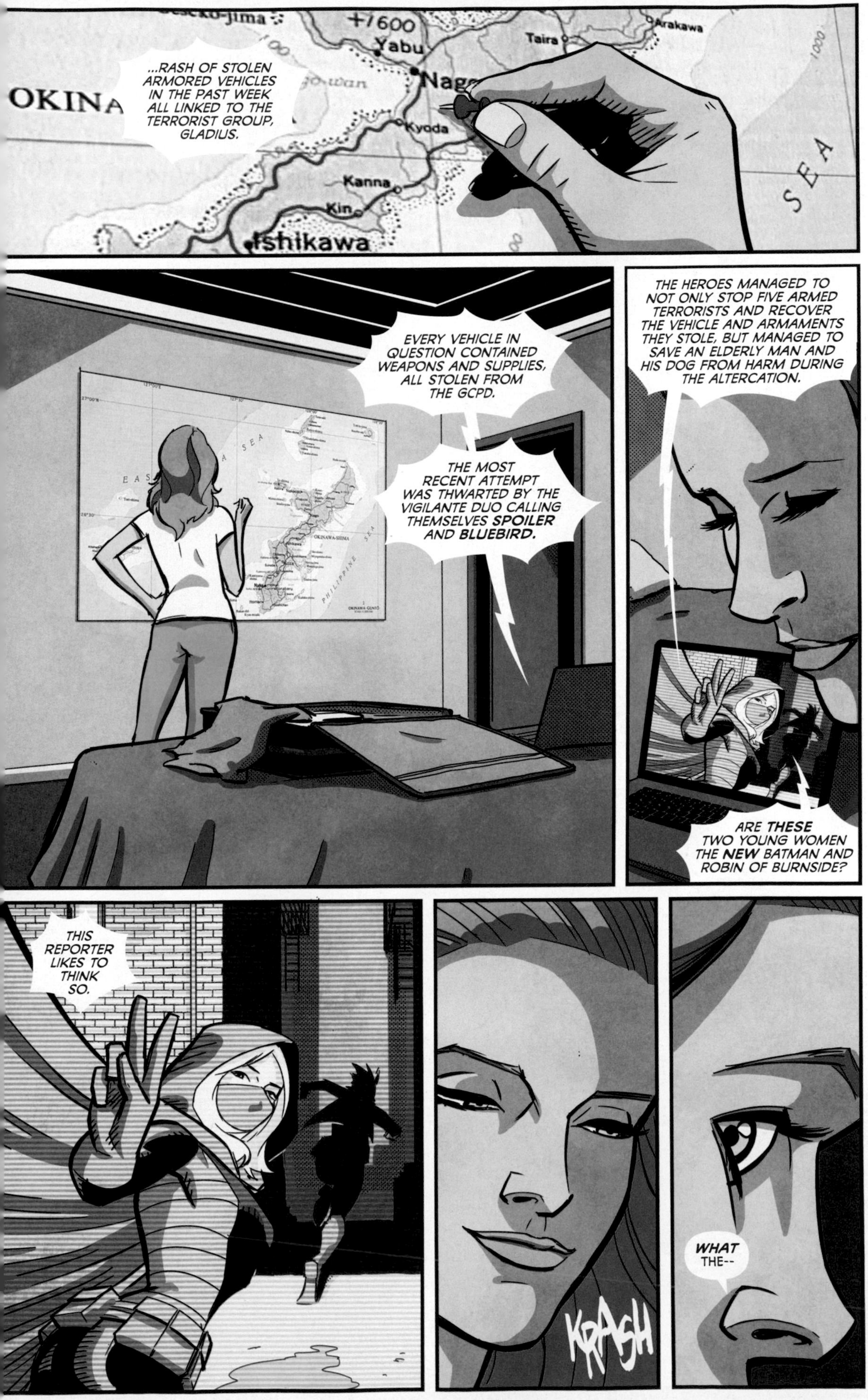
...RASH OF STOLEN ARMORED VEHICLES IN THE PAST WEEK ALL LINKED TO THE TERRORIST GROUP, GLADIUS.
EVERY VEHICLE IN QUESTION CONTAINED WEAPONS AND SUPPLIES, ALL STOLEN FROM THE GCPD.
THE MOST RECENT ATTEMPT WAS THWARTED BY THE VIGILANTE DUO CALLING THEMSELVES SPOILER AND BLUEBIRD.
THE HEROES MANAGED TO NOT ONLY STOP FIVE ARMED TERRORISTS AND RECOVER THE VEHICLE AND ARMAMENTS THEY STOLE, BUT MANAGED TO SAVE AN ELDERLY MAN AND HIS DOG FROM HARM DURING THE ALTERCATION.
ARE THESE TWO YOUNG WOMEN THE NEW BATMAN AND ROBIN OF BURNSIDE?
THIS REPORTER LIKES TO THINK SO.
KRASH
WHAT THE--

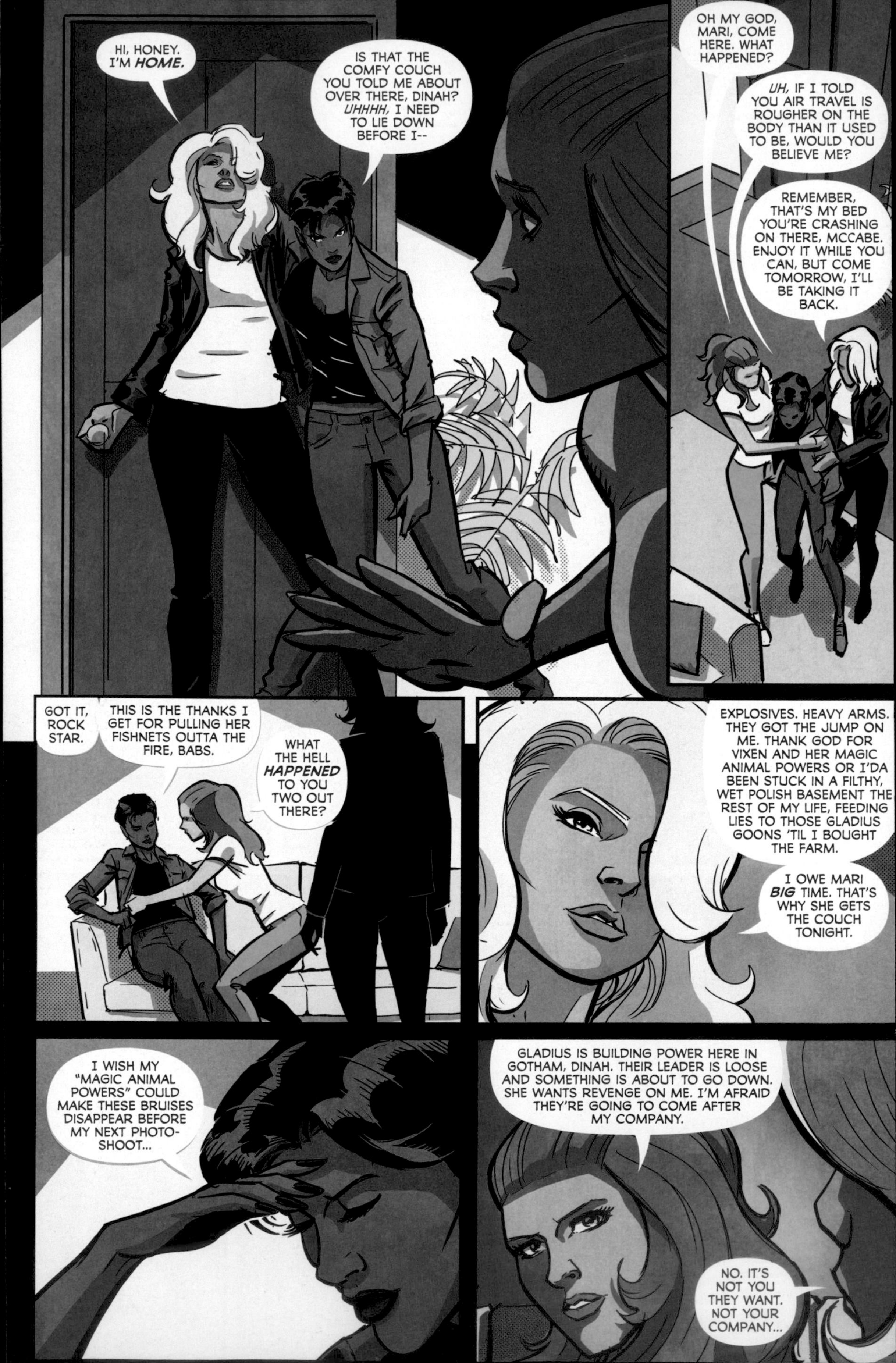
HI, HONEY. I'M *HOME.*
IS THAT THE COMFY COUCH YOU TOLD ME ABOUT OVER THERE, DINAH? *UHHHH,* I NEED TO LIE DOWN BEFORE I--
OH MY GOD, MARI, COME HERE. WHAT HAPPENED?
UH, IF I TOLD YOU AIR TRAVEL IS ROUGHER ON THE BODY THAN IT USED TO BE, WOULD YOU BELIEVE ME?
REMEMBER, THAT'S MY BED YOU'RE CRASHING ON THERE, MCCABE. ENJOY IT WHILE YOU CAN, BUT COME TOMORROW, I'LL BE TAKING IT BACK.
GOT IT, ROCK STAR.
THIS IS THE THANKS I GET FOR PULLING HER FISHNETS OUTTA THE FIRE, BABS.
WHAT THE HELL *HAPPENED* TO YOU TWO OUT THERE?
EXPLOSIVES. HEAVY ARMS. THEY GOT THE JUMP ON ME. THANK GOD FOR VIXEN AND HER MAGIC ANIMAL POWERS OR I'DA BEEN STUCK IN A FILTHY, WET POLISH BASEMENT THE REST OF MY LIFE, FEEDING LIES TO THOSE GLADIUS GOONS 'TIL I BOUGHT THE FARM.
I OWE MARI *BIG* TIME. THAT'S WHY SHE GETS THE COUCH TONIGHT.
I WISH MY "MAGIC ANIMAL POWERS" COULD MAKE THESE BRUISES DISAPPEAR BEFORE MY NEXT PHOTO-SHOOT...
GLADIUS IS BUILDING POWER HERE IN GOTHAM, DINAH. THEIR LEADER IS LOOSE AND SOMETHING IS ABOUT TO GO DOWN. SHE WANTS REVENGE ON ME. I'M AFRAID THEY'RE GOING TO COME AFTER MY COMPANY.
NO. IT'S NOT YOU THEY WANT. NOT YOUR COMPANY...

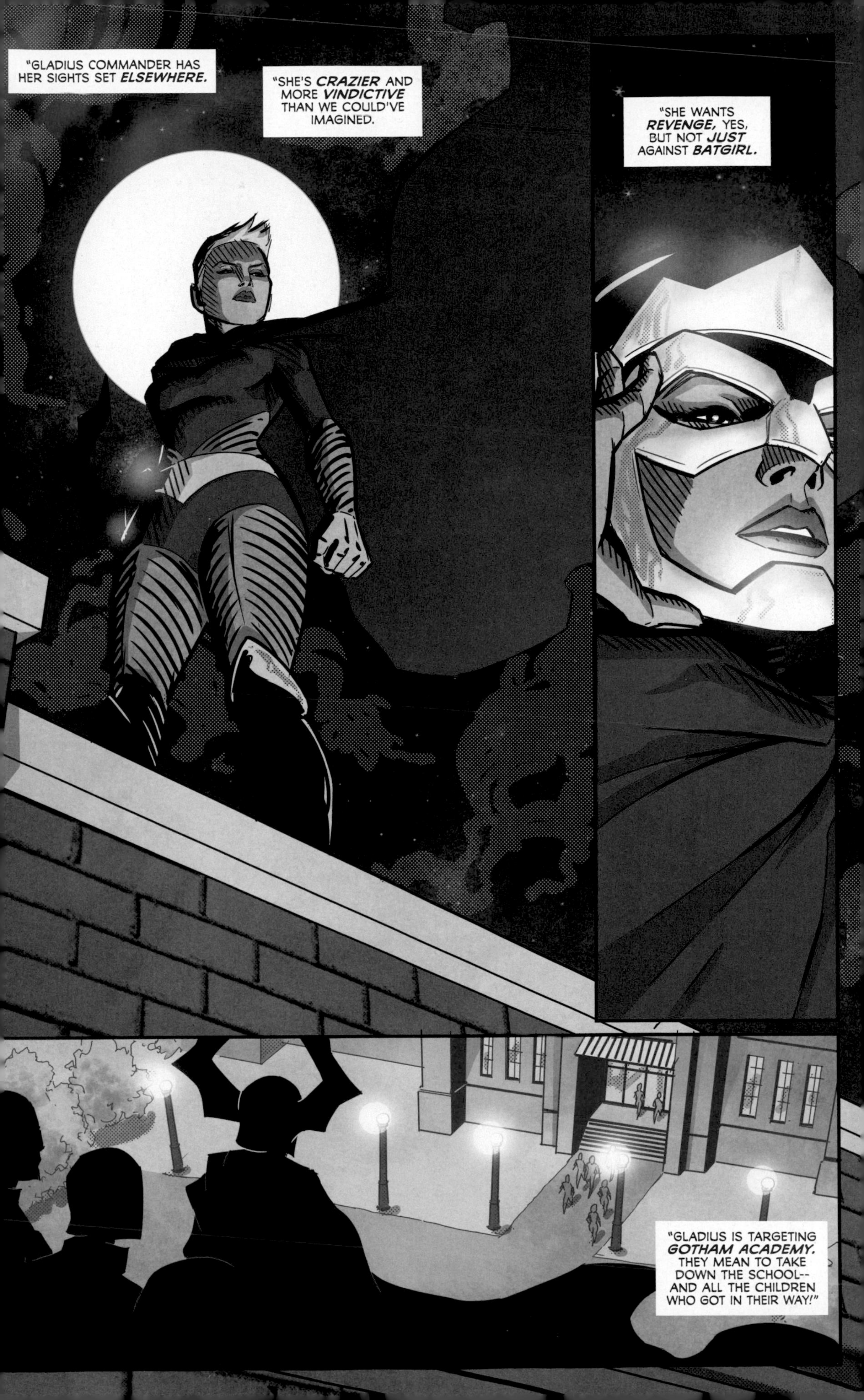
"GLADIUS COMMANDER HAS HER SIGHTS SET ELSEWHERE.
"SHE'S CRAZIER AND MORE VINDICTIVE THAN WE COULD'VE IMAGINED.
"SHE WANTS REVENGE, YES, BUT NOT JUST AGAINST BATGIRL.
"GLADIUS IS TARGETING GOTHAM ACADEMY. THEY MEAN TO TAKE DOWN THE SCHOOL-- AND ALL THE CHILDREN WHO GOT IN THEIR WAY!"

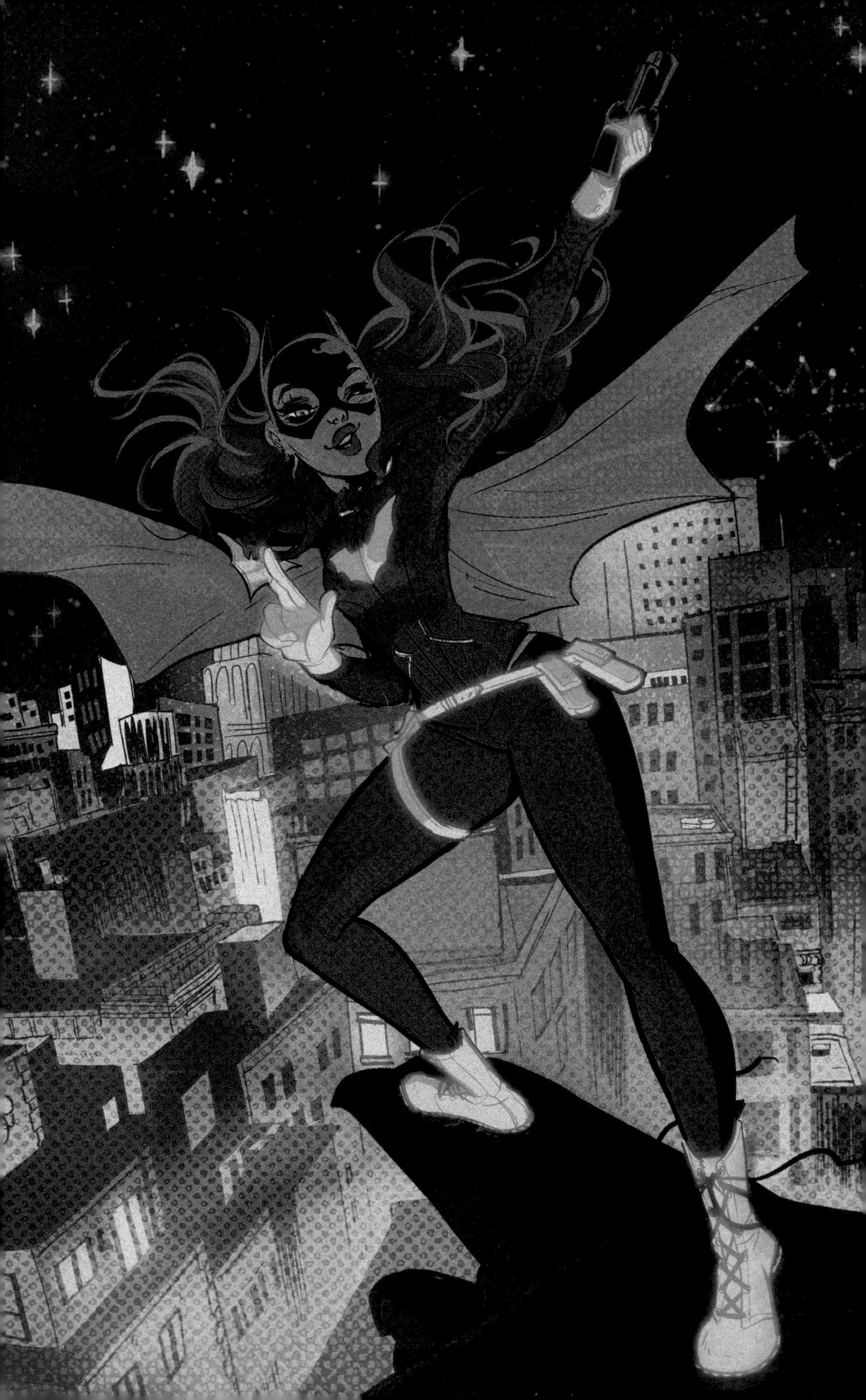

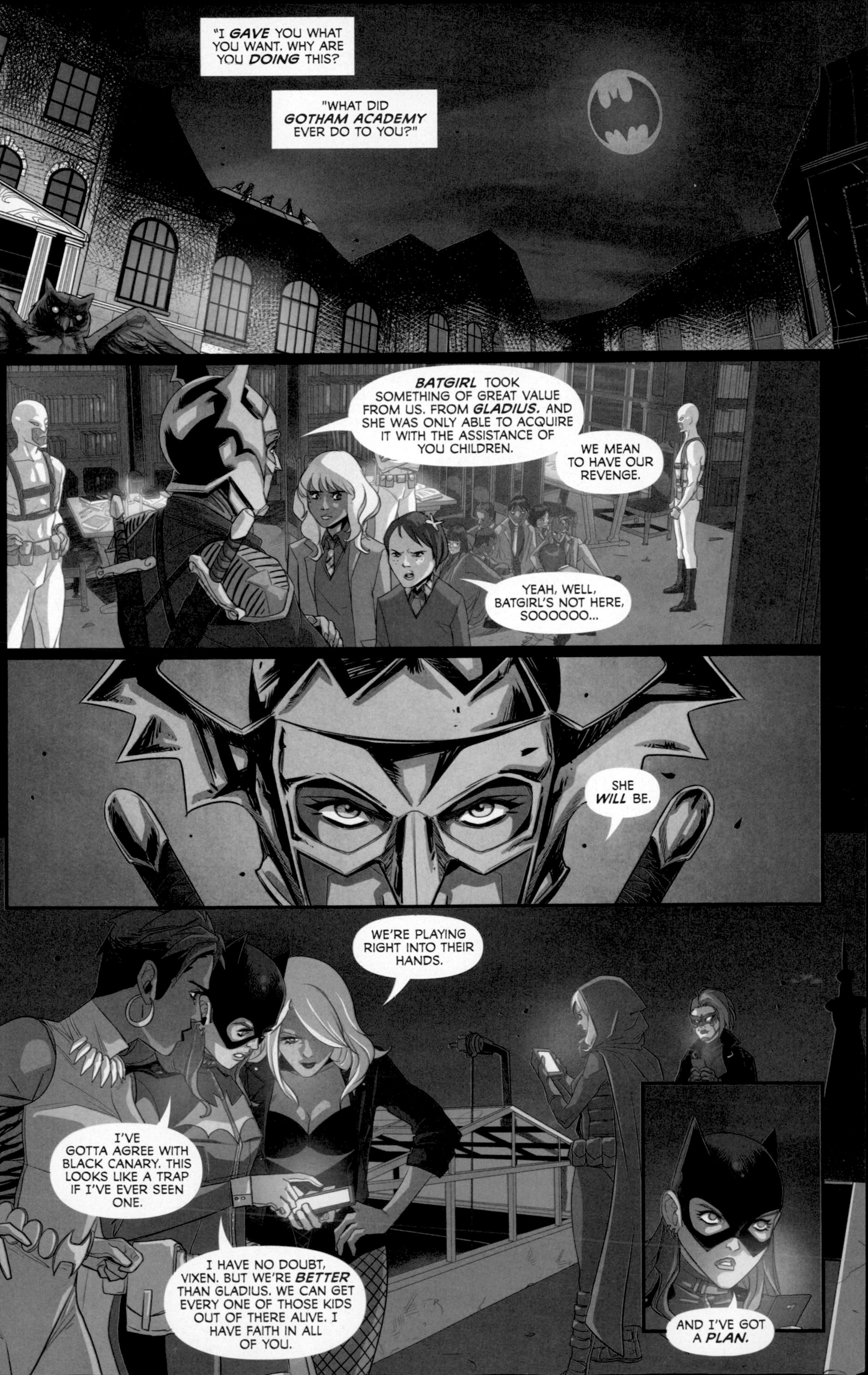
"I GAVE YOU WHAT YOU WANT. WHY ARE YOU DOING THIS?
"WHAT DID GOTHAM ACADEMY EVER DO TO YOU?"
BATGIRL TOOK SOMETHING OF GREAT VALUE FROM US. FROM GLADIUS. AND SHE WAS ONLY ABLE TO ACQUIRE IT WITH THE ASSISTANCE OF YOU CHILDREN.
WE MEAN TO HAVE OUR REVENGE.
YEAH, WELL, BATGIRL'S NOT HERE, SOOOOOO...
SHE WILL BE.
WE'RE PLAYING RIGHT INTO THEIR HANDS.
I'VE GOTTA AGREE WITH BLACK CANARY. THIS LOOKS LIKE A TRAP IF I'VE EVER SEEN ONE.
I HAVE NO DOUBT, VIXEN. BUT WE'RE BETTER THAN GLADIUS. WE CAN GET EVERY ONE OF THOSE KIDS OUT OF THERE ALIVE. I HAVE FAITH IN ALL OF YOU.
AND I'VE GOT A PLAN.

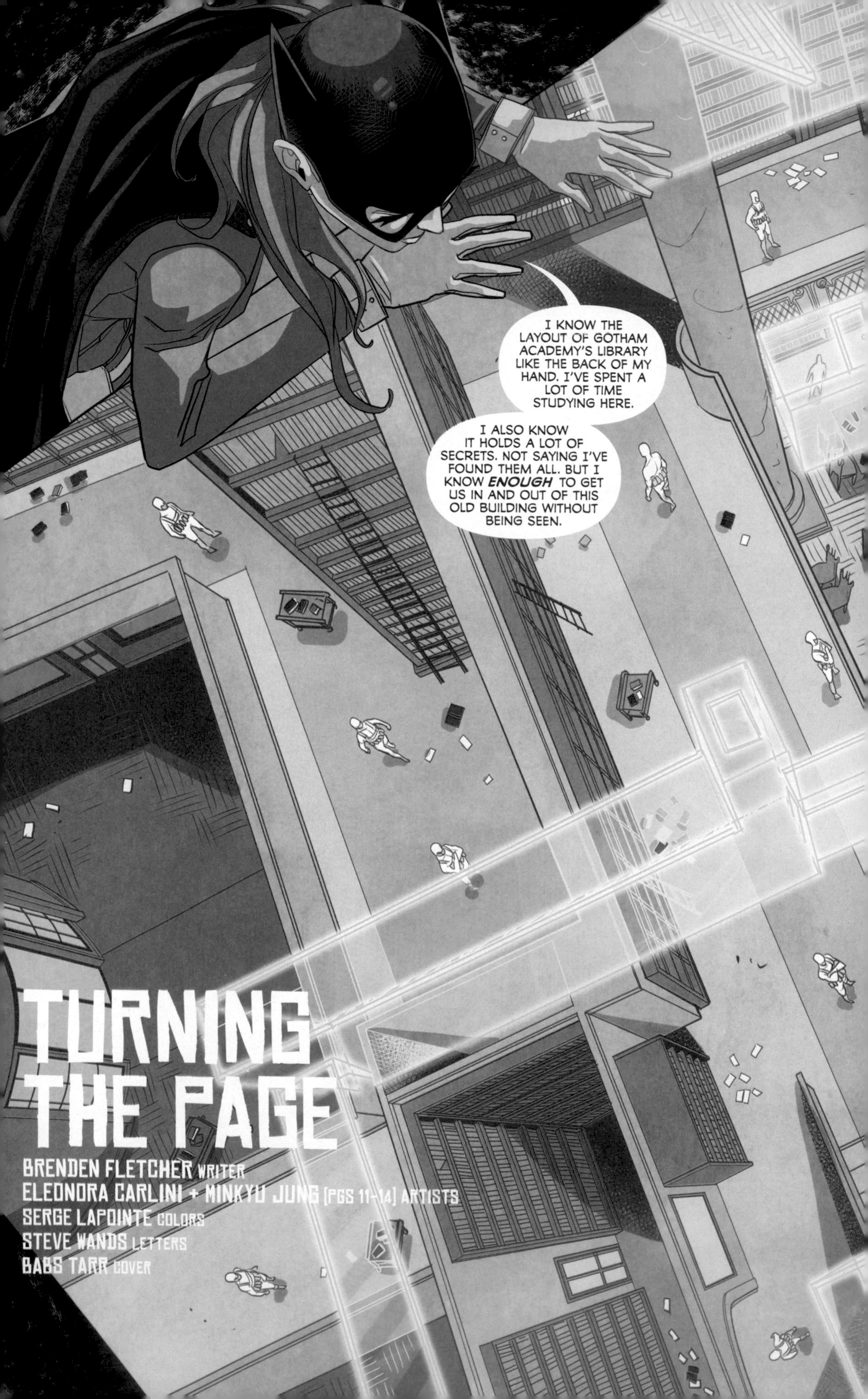
I KNOW THE LAYOUT OF GOTHAM ACADEMY'S LIBRARY LIKE THE BACK OF MY HAND. I'VE SPENT A LOT OF TIME STUDYING HERE.
I ALSO KNOW IT HOLDS A LOT OF SECRETS. NOT SAYING I'VE FOUND THEM ALL. BUT I KNOW ENOUGH TO GET US IN AND OUT OF THIS OLD BUILDING WITHOUT BEING SEEN.
TURNING THE PAGE
BRENDEN FLETCHER WRITER
ELEONORA CARLINI + MINKYU JUNG [PGS 11-14] ARTISTS
SERGE LAPOINTE COLORS
STEVE WANDS LETTERS
BABS TARR COVER

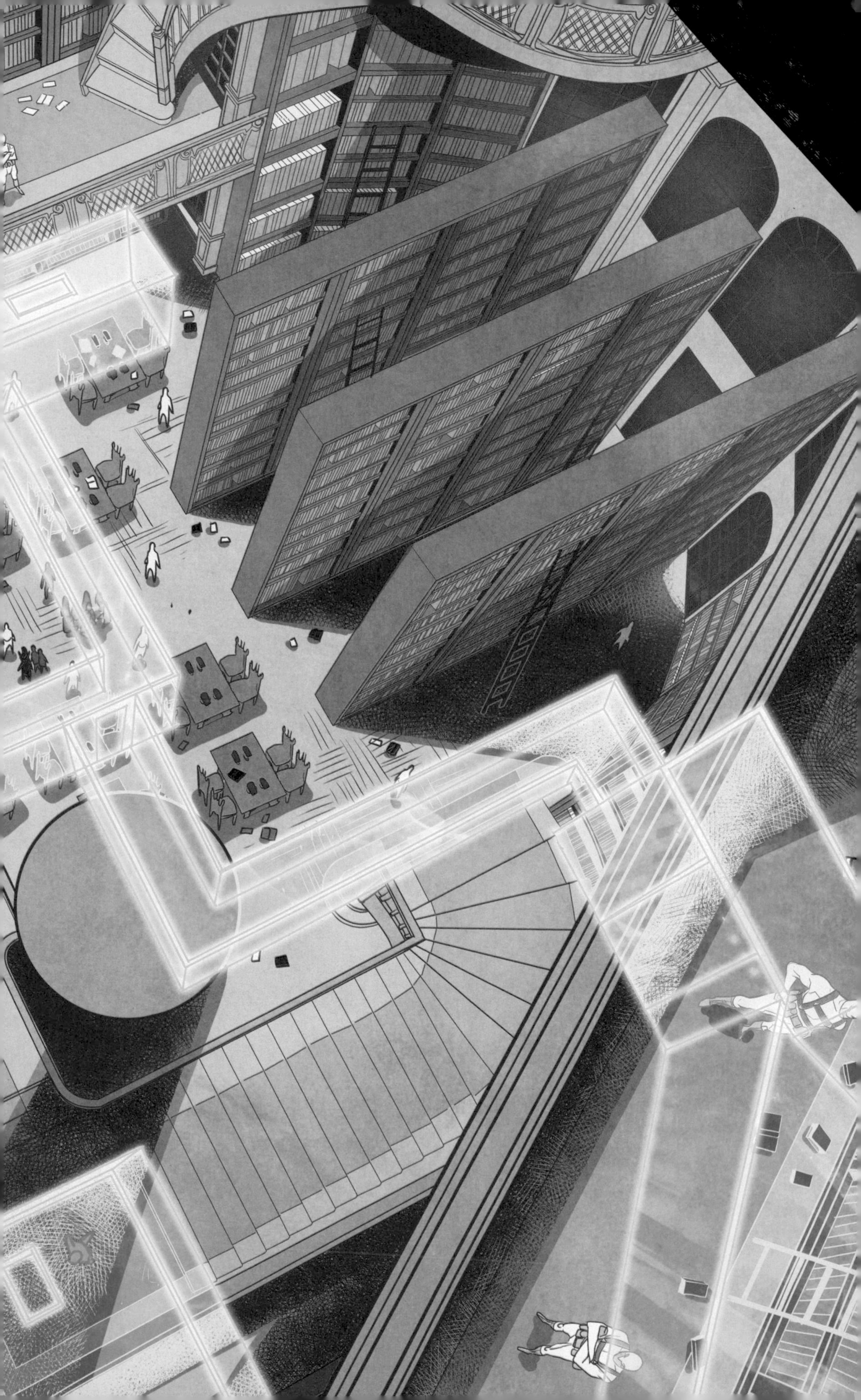

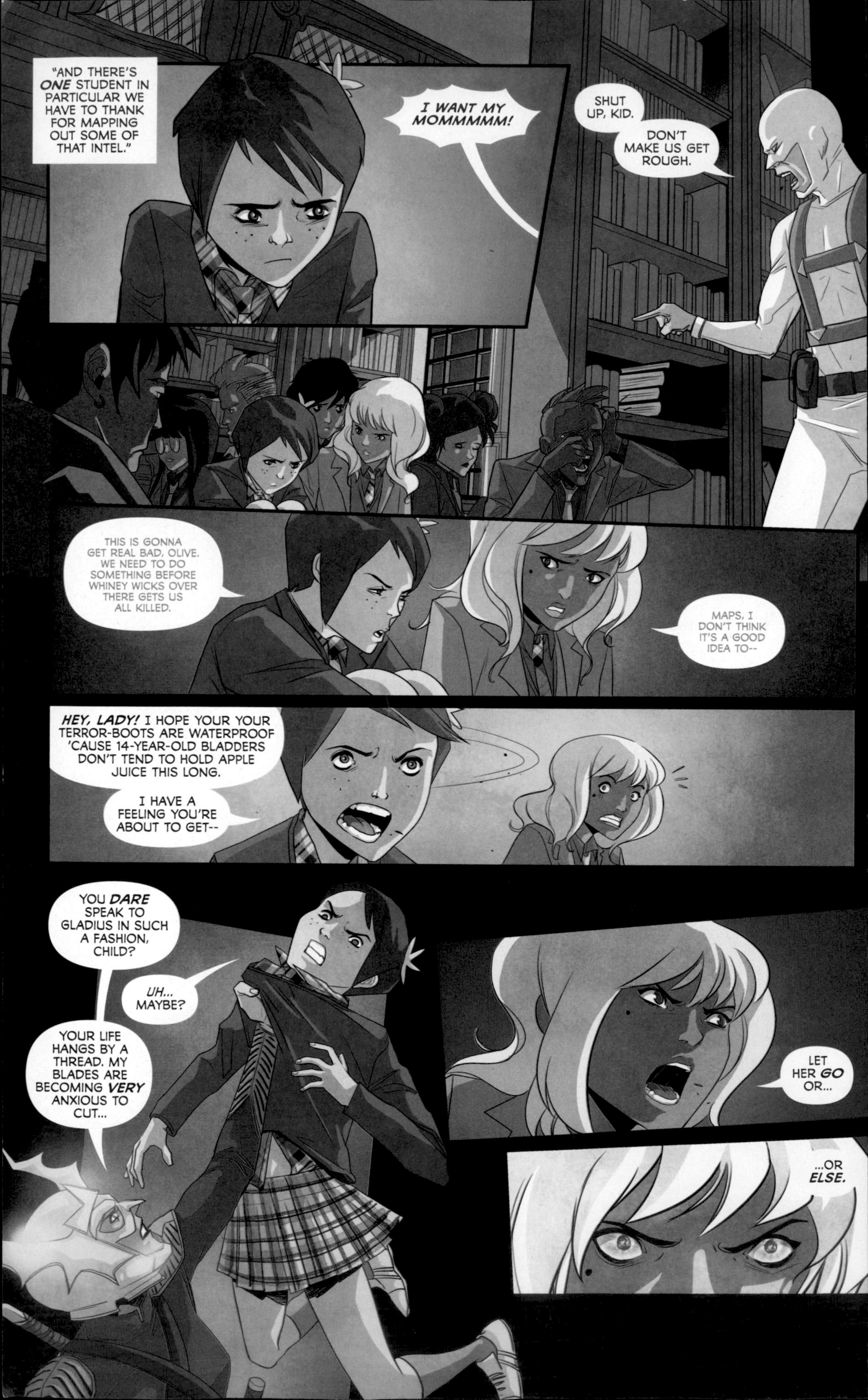
"AND THERE'S ONE STUDENT IN PARTICULAR WE HAVE TO THANK FOR MAPPING OUT SOME OF THAT INTEL."
I WANT MY MOMMMMM!
SHUT UP, KID.
DON'T MAKE US GET ROUGH.
THIS IS GONNA GET REAL BAD, OLIVE. WE NEED TO DO SOMETHING BEFORE WHINEY WICKS OVER THERE GETS US ALL KILLED.
MAPS, I DON'T THINK IT'S A GOOD IDEA TO--
HEY, LADY! I HOPE YOUR YOUR TERROR-BOOTS ARE WATERPROOF 'CAUSE 14-YEAR-OLD BLADDERS DON'T TEND TO HOLD APPLE JUICE THIS LONG.
I HAVE A FEELING YOU'RE ABOUT TO GET--
YOU DARE SPEAK TO GLADIUS IN SUCH A FASHION, CHILD?
UH... MAYBE?
YOUR LIFE HANGS BY A THREAD. MY BLADES ARE BECOMING VERY ANXIOUS TO CUT...
LET HER GO OR...
...OR ELSE.

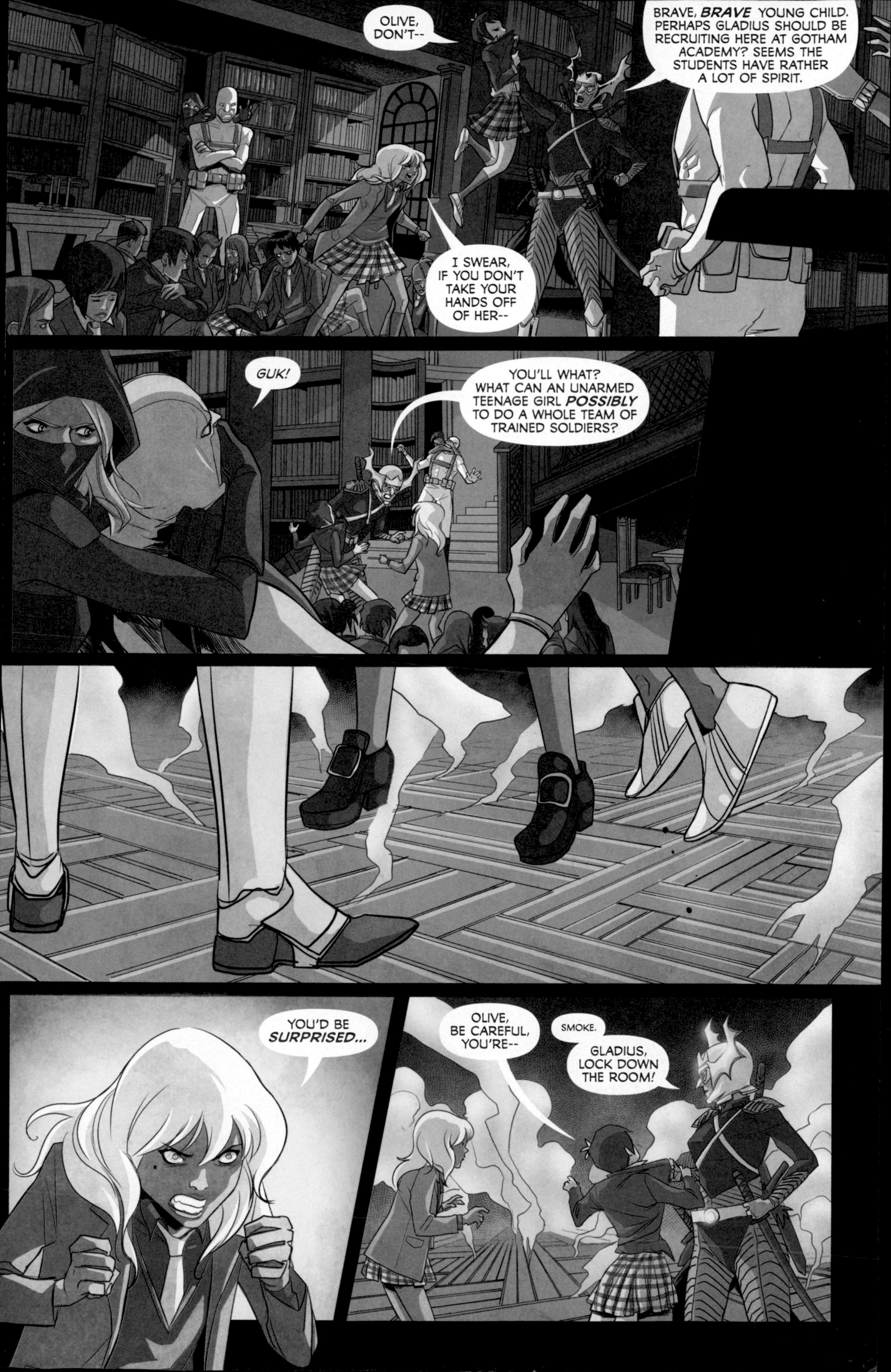
OLIVE, DON'T--
BRAVE, BRAVE YOUNG CHILD. PERHAPS GLADIUS SHOULD BE RECRUITING HERE AT GOTHAM ACADEMY? SEEMS THE STUDENTS HAVE RATHER A LOT OF SPIRIT.
I SWEAR, IF YOU DON'T TAKE YOUR HANDS OFF OF HER--
GUK!
YOU'LL WHAT? WHAT CAN AN UNARMED TEENAGE GIRL POSSIBLY TO DO A WHOLE TEAM OF TRAINED SOLDIERS?
YOU'D BE SURPRISED...
OLIVE, BE CAREFUL, YOU'RE--
SMOKE.
GLADIUS, LOCK DOWN THE ROOM!

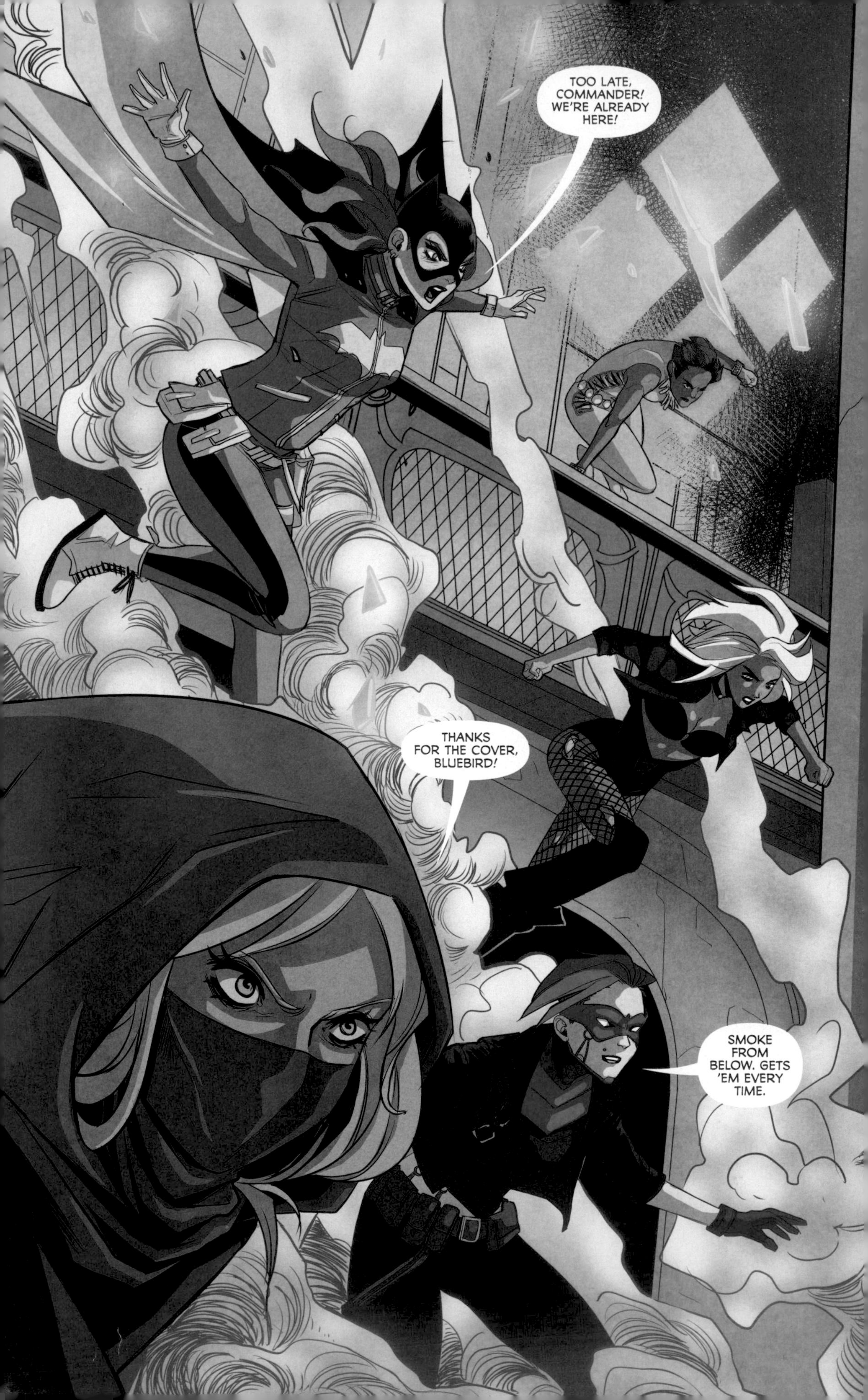
TOO LATE, COMMANDER! WE'RE ALREADY HERE!
THANKS FOR THE COVER, BLUEBIRD!
SMOKE FROM BELOW. GETS 'EM EVERY TIME.

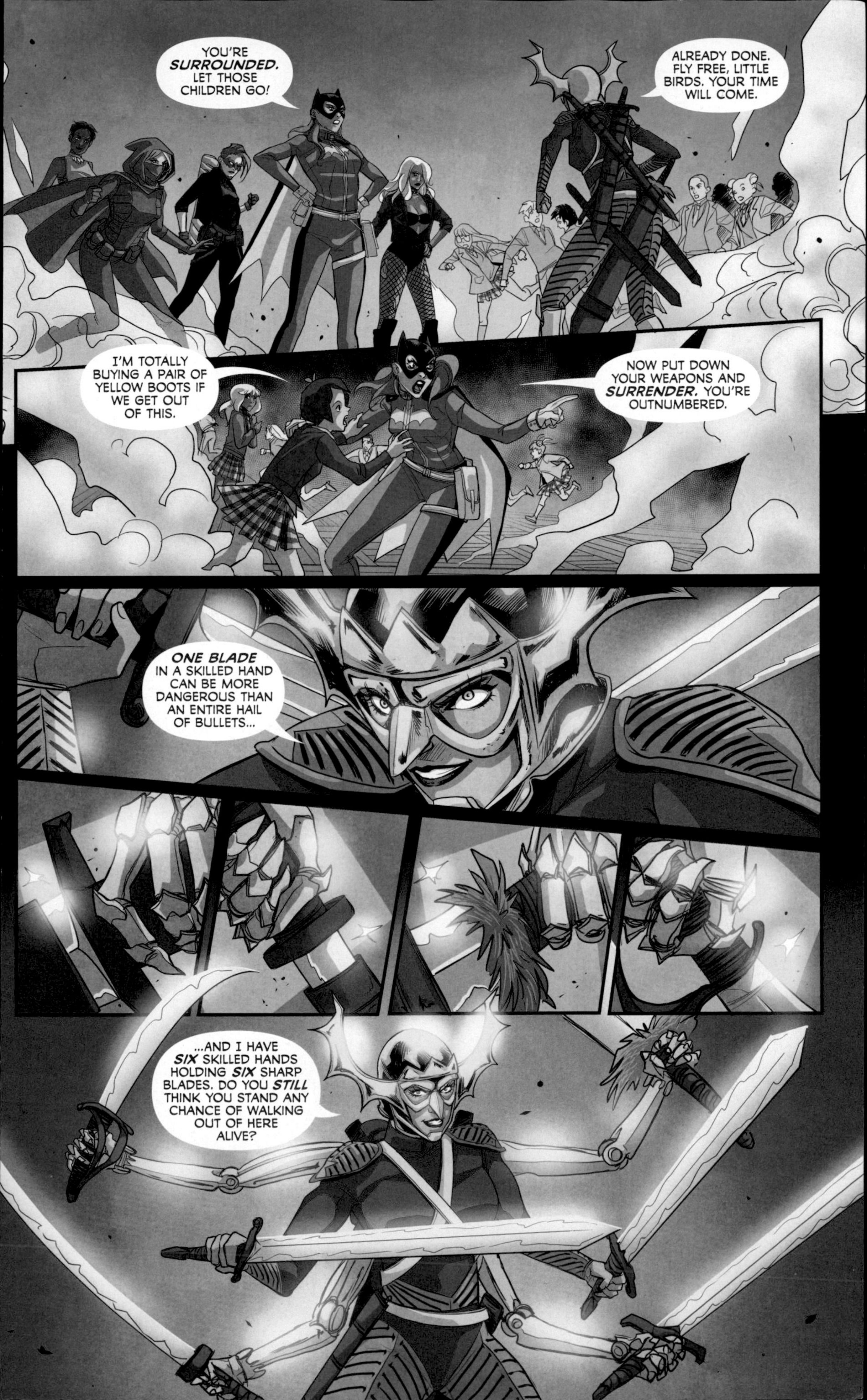
YOU'RE SURROUNDED. LET THOSE CHILDREN GO!
ALREADY DONE. FLY FREE, LITTLE BIRDS. YOUR TIME WILL COME.
I'M TOTALLY BUYING A PAIR OF YELLOW BOOTS IF WE GET OUT OF THIS.
NOW PUT DOWN YOUR WEAPONS AND SURRENDER. YOU'RE OUTNUMBERED.
ONE BLADE IN A SKILLED HAND CAN BE MORE DANGEROUS THAN AN ENTIRE HAIL OF BULLETS...
...AND I HAVE SIX SKILLED HANDS HOLDING SIX SHARP BLADES. DO YOU STILL THINK YOU STAND ANY CHANCE OF WALKING OUT OF HERE ALIVE?

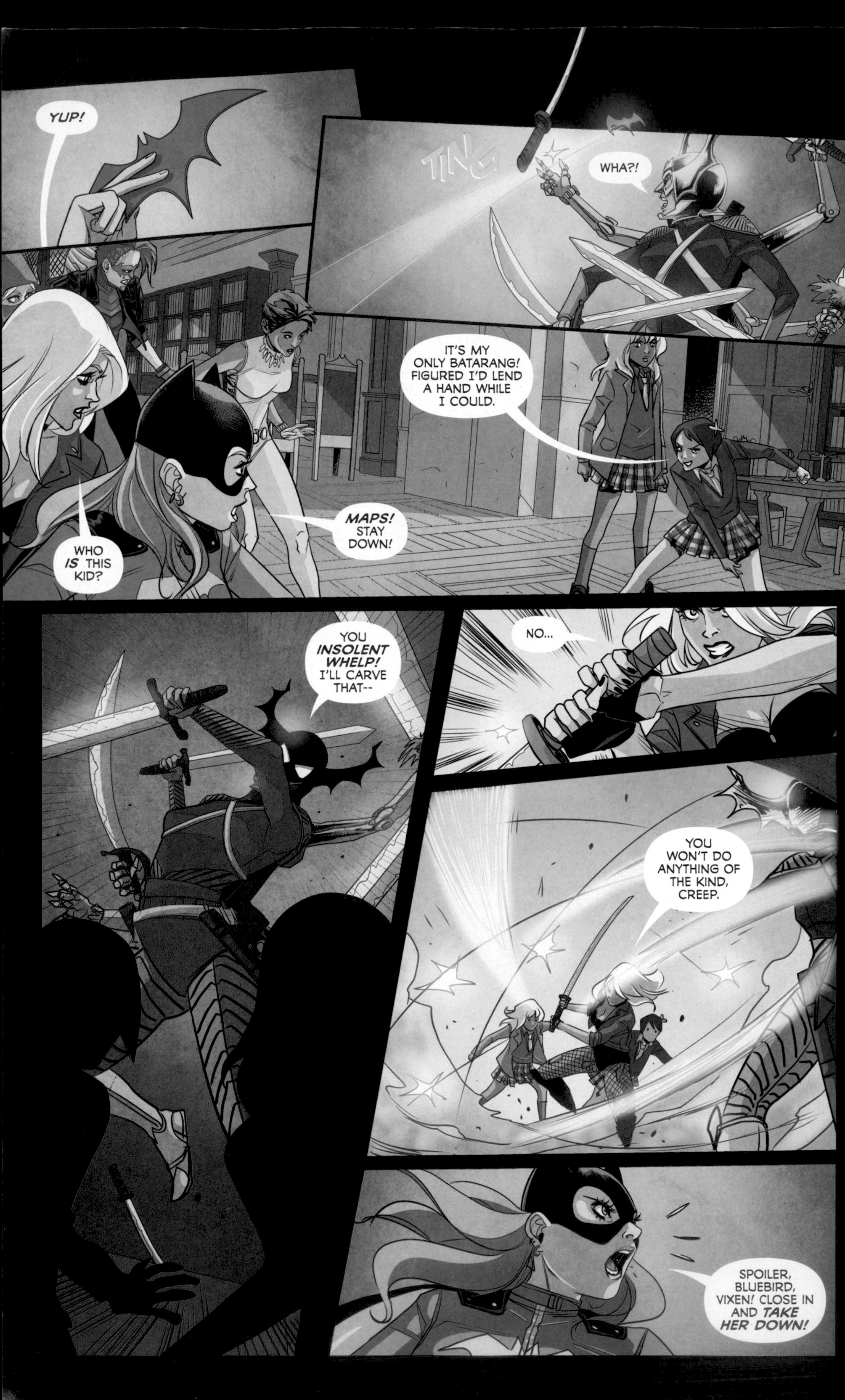
YUP!
TING
WHA?!
IT'S MY ONLY BATARANG! FIGURED I'D LEND A HAND WHILE I COULD.
MAPS! STAY DOWN!
WHO IS THIS KID?
YOU INSOLENT WHELP! I'LL CARVE THAT--
NO...
YOU WON'T DO ANYTHING OF THE KIND, CREEP.
SPOILER, BLUEBIRD, VIXEN! CLOSE IN AND TAKE HER DOWN!

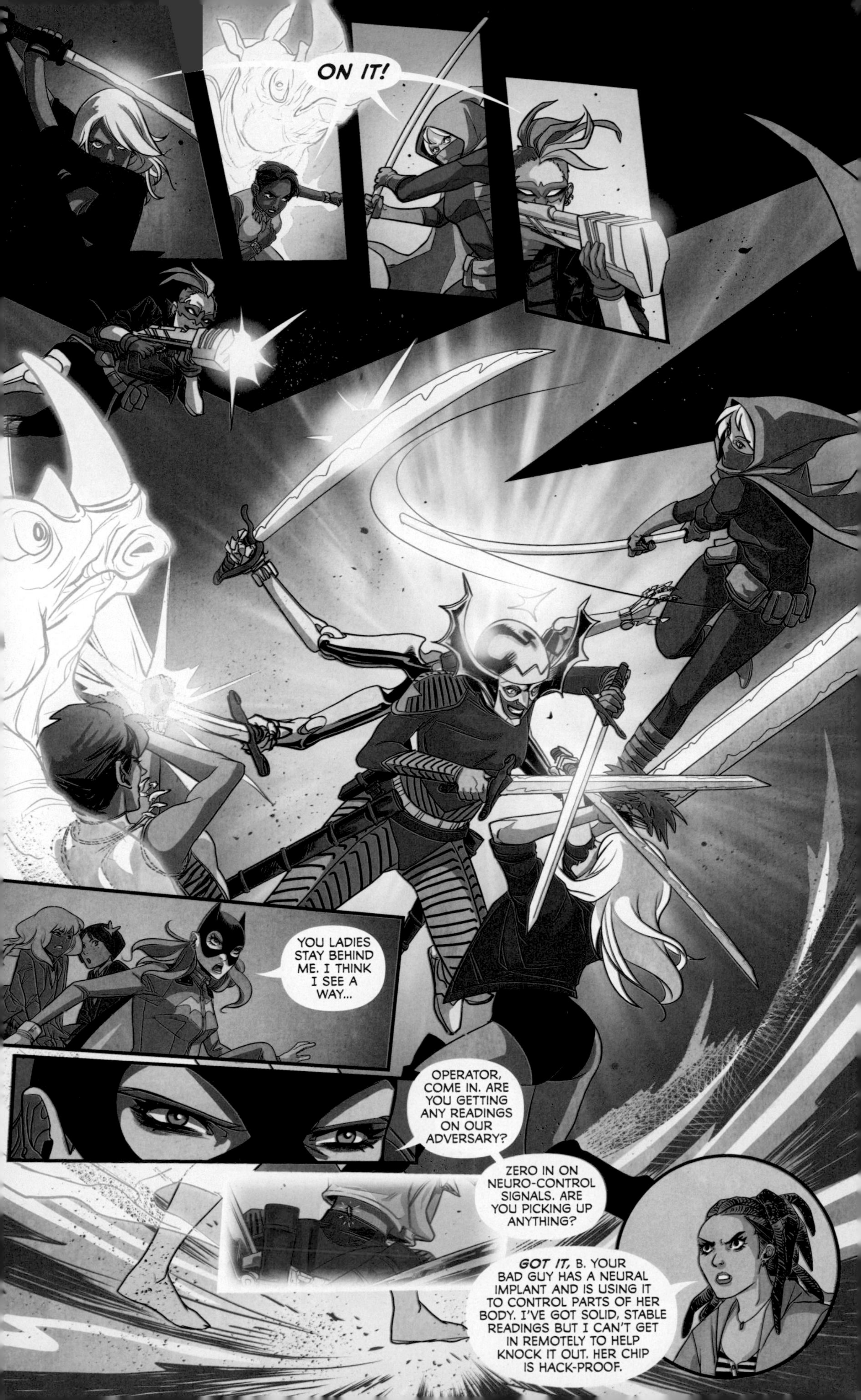
ON IT!
YOU LADIES STAY BEHIND ME. I THINK I SEE A WAY...
OPERATOR, COME IN. ARE YOU GETTING ANY READINGS ON OUR ADVERSARY?
ZERO IN ON NEURO-CONTROL SIGNALS. ARE YOU PICKING UP ANYTHING?
GOT IT, B. YOUR BAD GUY HAS A NEURAL IMPLANT AND IS USING IT TO CONTROL PARTS OF HER BODY. I'VE GOT SOLID, STABLE READINGS BUT I CAN'T GET IN REMOTELY TO HELP KNOCK IT OUT. HER CHIP IS HACK-PROOF.

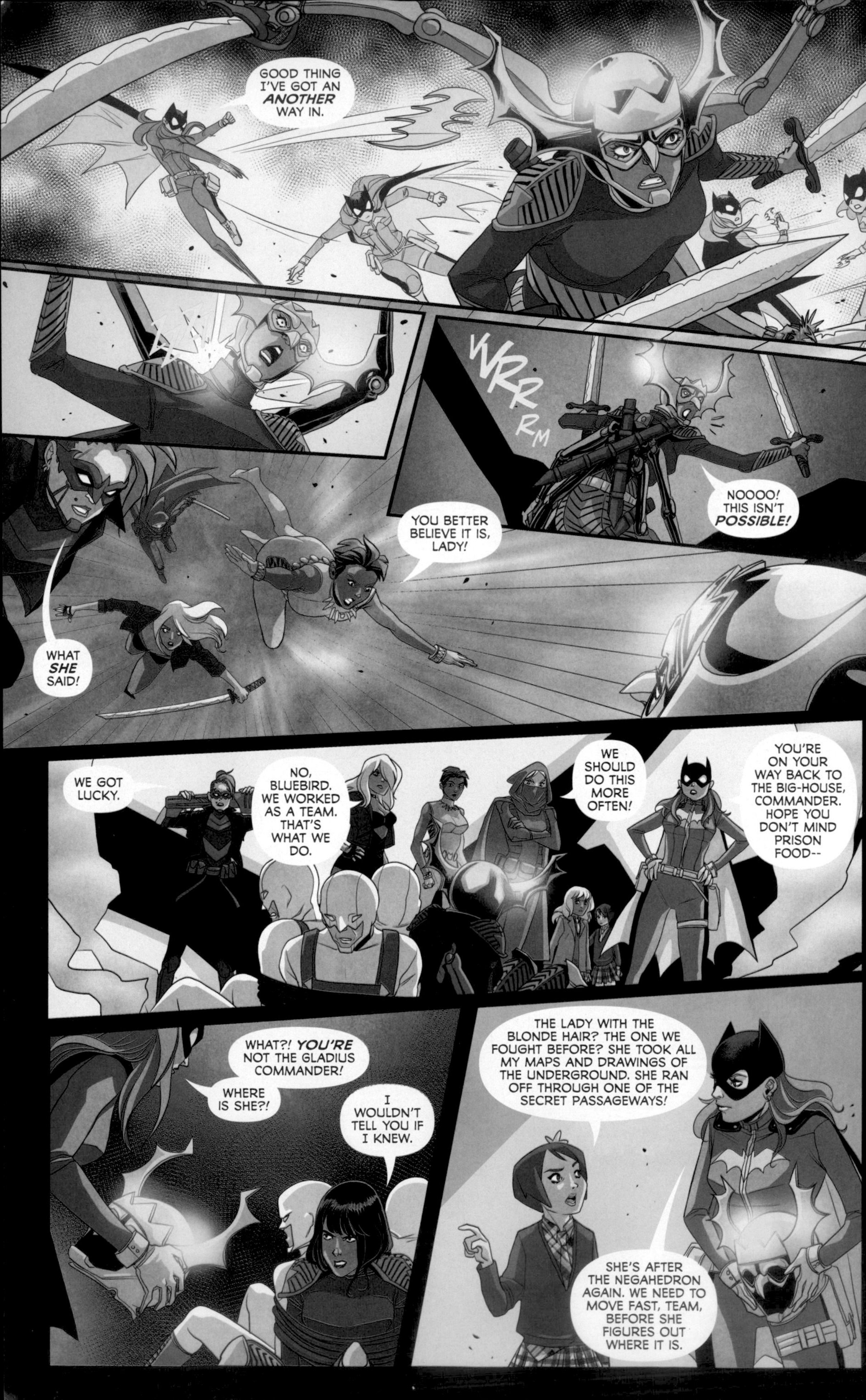
GOOD THING I'VE GOT AN ANOTHER WAY IN.
VWRRRM
NOOOO! THIS ISN'T POSSIBLE!
YOU BETTER BELIEVE IT IS, LADY!
WHAT SHE SAID!
WE GOT LUCKY.
NO, BLUEBIRD. WE WORKED AS A TEAM. THAT'S WHAT WE DO.
WE SHOULD DO THIS MORE OFTEN!
YOU'RE ON YOUR WAY BACK TO THE BIG-HOUSE, COMMANDER. HOPE YOU DON'T MIND PRISON FOOD--
WHAT?! YOU'RE NOT THE GLADIUS COMMANDER!
WHERE IS SHE?!
I WOULDN'T TELL YOU IF I KNEW.
THE LADY WITH THE BLONDE HAIR? THE ONE WE FOUGHT BEFORE? SHE TOOK ALL MY MAPS AND DRAWINGS OF THE UNDERGROUND. SHE RAN OFF THROUGH ONE OF THE SECRET PASSAGEWAYS!
SHE'S AFTER THE NEGAHEDRON AGAIN. WE NEED TO MOVE FAST, TEAM, BEFORE SHE FIGURES OUT WHERE IT IS.

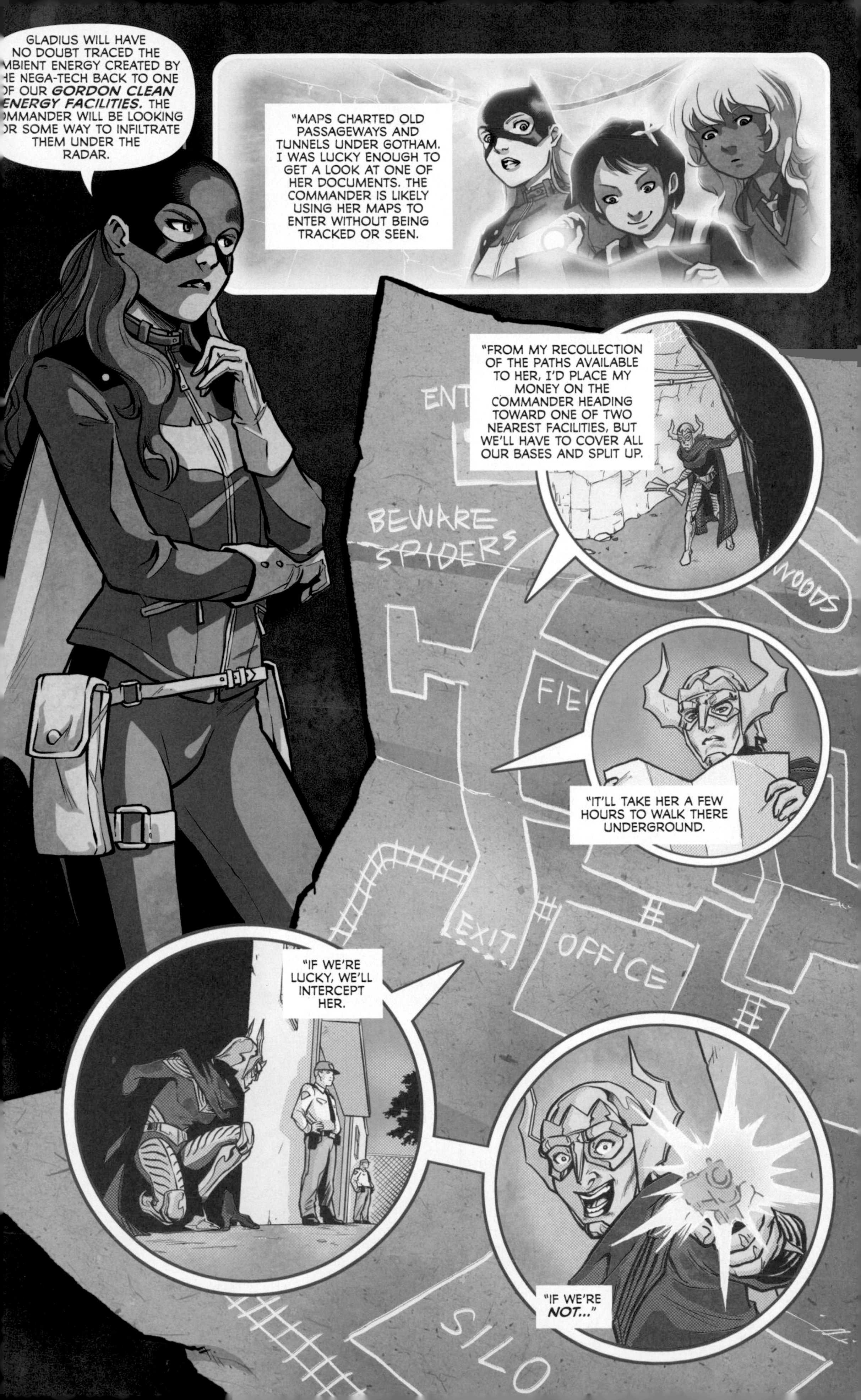

GLADIUS WILL HAVE NO DOUBT TRACED THE MBIENT ENERGY CREATED BY HE NEGA-TECH BACK TO ONE OF OUR ***GORDON CLEAN ENERGY FACILITIES.*** THE OMMANDER WILL BE LOOKING OR SOME WAY TO INFILTRATE THEM UNDER THE RADAR.
"MAPS CHARTED OLD PASSAGEWAYS AND TUNNELS UNDER GOTHAM. I WAS LUCKY ENOUGH TO GET A LOOK AT ONE OF HER DOCUMENTS. THE COMMANDER IS LIKELY USING HER MAPS TO ENTER WITHOUT BEING TRACKED OR SEEN.
"FROM MY RECOLLECTION OF THE PATHS AVAILABLE TO HER, I'D PLACE MY MONEY ON THE COMMANDER HEADING TOWARD ONE OF TWO NEAREST FACILITIES, BUT WE'LL HAVE TO COVER ALL OUR BASES AND SPLIT UP.
ENT
BEWARE SPIDERS
WOODS
FIE
"IT'LL TAKE HER A FEW HOURS TO WALK THERE UNDERGROUND.
EXIT
OFFICE
"IF WE'RE LUCKY, WE'LL INTERCEPT HER.
"IF WE'RE ***NOT...***"
SILO

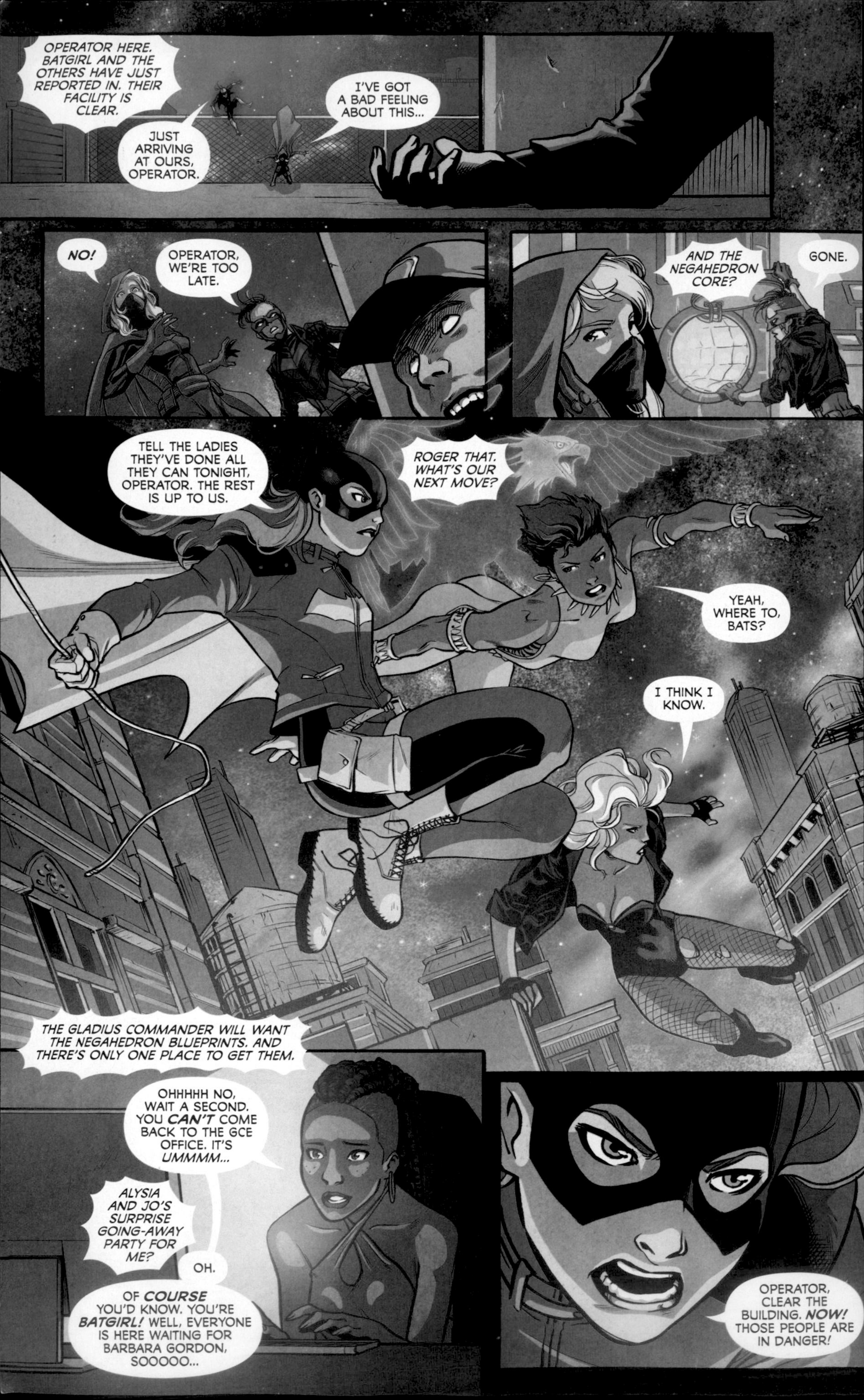

OPERATOR HERE. BATGIRL AND THE OTHERS HAVE JUST REPORTED IN. THEIR FACILITY IS CLEAR.
JUST ARRIVING AT OURS, OPERATOR.
I'VE GOT A BAD FEELING ABOUT THIS...
NO!
OPERATOR, WE'RE TOO LATE.
AND THE NEGAHEDRON CORE?
GONE.
TELL THE LADIES THEY'VE DONE ALL THEY CAN TONIGHT, OPERATOR. THE REST IS UP TO US.
ROGER THAT. WHAT'S OUR NEXT MOVE?
YEAH, WHERE TO, BATS?
I THINK I KNOW.
THE GLADIUS COMMANDER WILL WANT THE NEGAHEDRON BLUEPRINTS. AND THERE'S ONLY ONE PLACE TO GET THEM.
OHHHHH NO, WAIT A SECOND. YOU **CAN'T** COME BACK TO THE GCE OFFICE. IT'S *UMMMM...*
ALYSIA AND JO'S SURPRISE GOING-AWAY PARTY FOR ME?
OH.
OF **COURSE** YOU'D KNOW. YOU'RE ***BATGIRL!*** WELL, EVERYONE IS HERE WAITING FOR BARBARA GORDON, SOOOOO...
OPERATOR, CLEAR THE BUILDING. ***NOW!*** THOSE PEOPLE ARE IN DANGER!

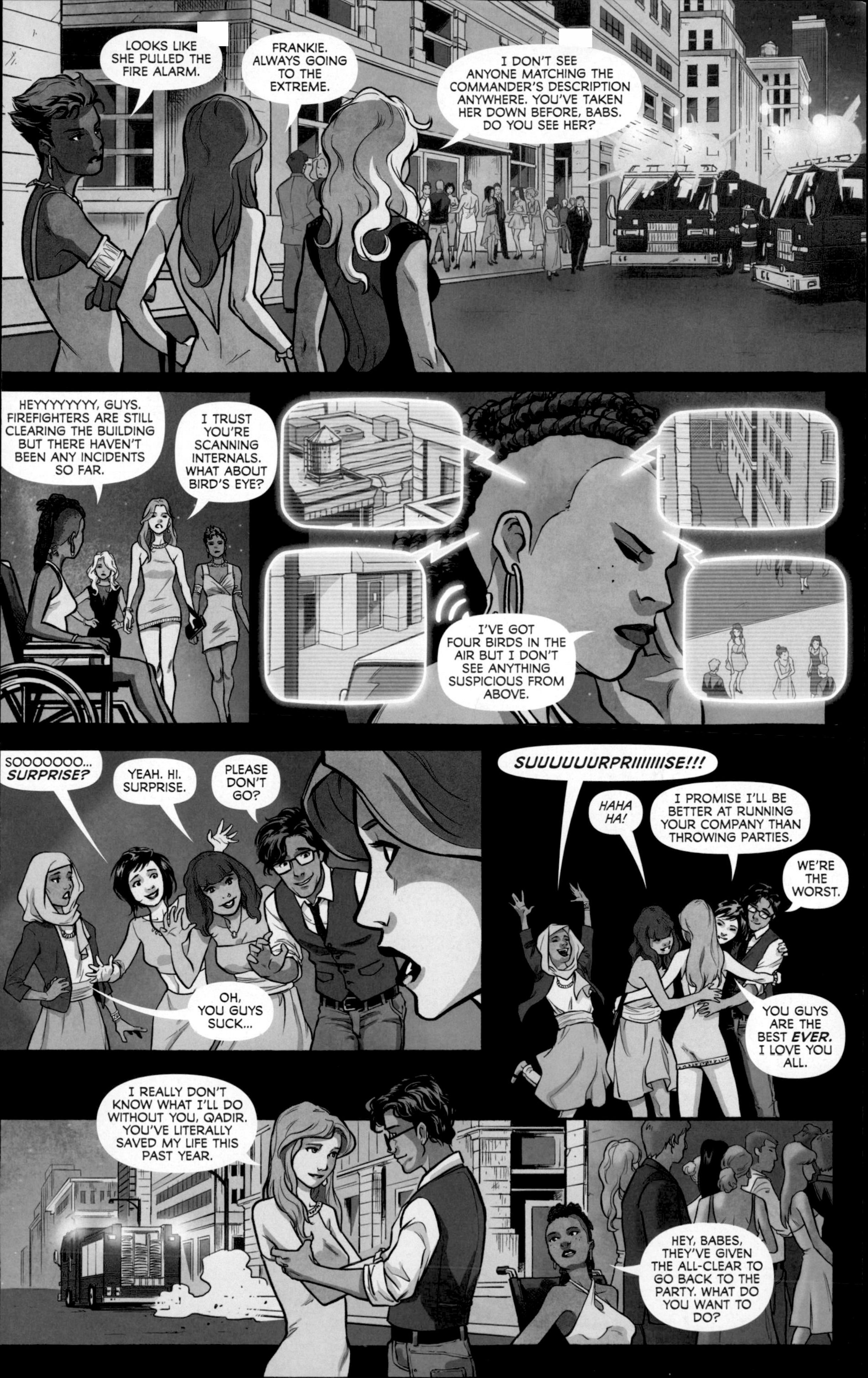
LOOKS LIKE SHE PULLED THE FIRE ALARM.
FRANKIE. ALWAYS GOING TO THE EXTREME.
I DON'T SEE ANYONE MATCHING THE COMMANDER'S DESCRIPTION ANYWHERE. YOU'VE TAKEN HER DOWN BEFORE, BABS. DO YOU SEE HER?
HEYYYYYYYY, GUYS. FIREFIGHTERS ARE STILL CLEARING THE BUILDING BUT THERE HAVEN'T BEEN ANY INCIDENTS SO FAR.
I TRUST YOU'RE SCANNING INTERNALS. WHAT ABOUT BIRD'S EYE?
I'VE GOT FOUR BIRDS IN THE AIR BUT I DON'T SEE ANYTHING SUSPICIOUS FROM ABOVE.
SOOOOOOO... *SURPRISE?*
YEAH. HI. SURPRISE.
PLEASE DON'T GO?
OH, YOU GUYS SUCK...
SUUUUUURPRIIIIIIISE!!!
HAHA HA!
I PROMISE I'LL BE BETTER AT RUNNING YOUR COMPANY THAN THROWING PARTIES.
WE'RE THE WORST.
YOU GUYS ARE THE BEST *EVER.* I LOVE YOU ALL.
I REALLY DON'T KNOW WHAT I'LL DO WITHOUT YOU, QADIR. YOU'VE LITERALLY SAVED MY LIFE THIS PAST YEAR.
HEY, BABES, THEY'VE GIVEN THE ALL-CLEAR TO GO BACK TO THE PARTY. WHAT DO YOU WANT TO DO?

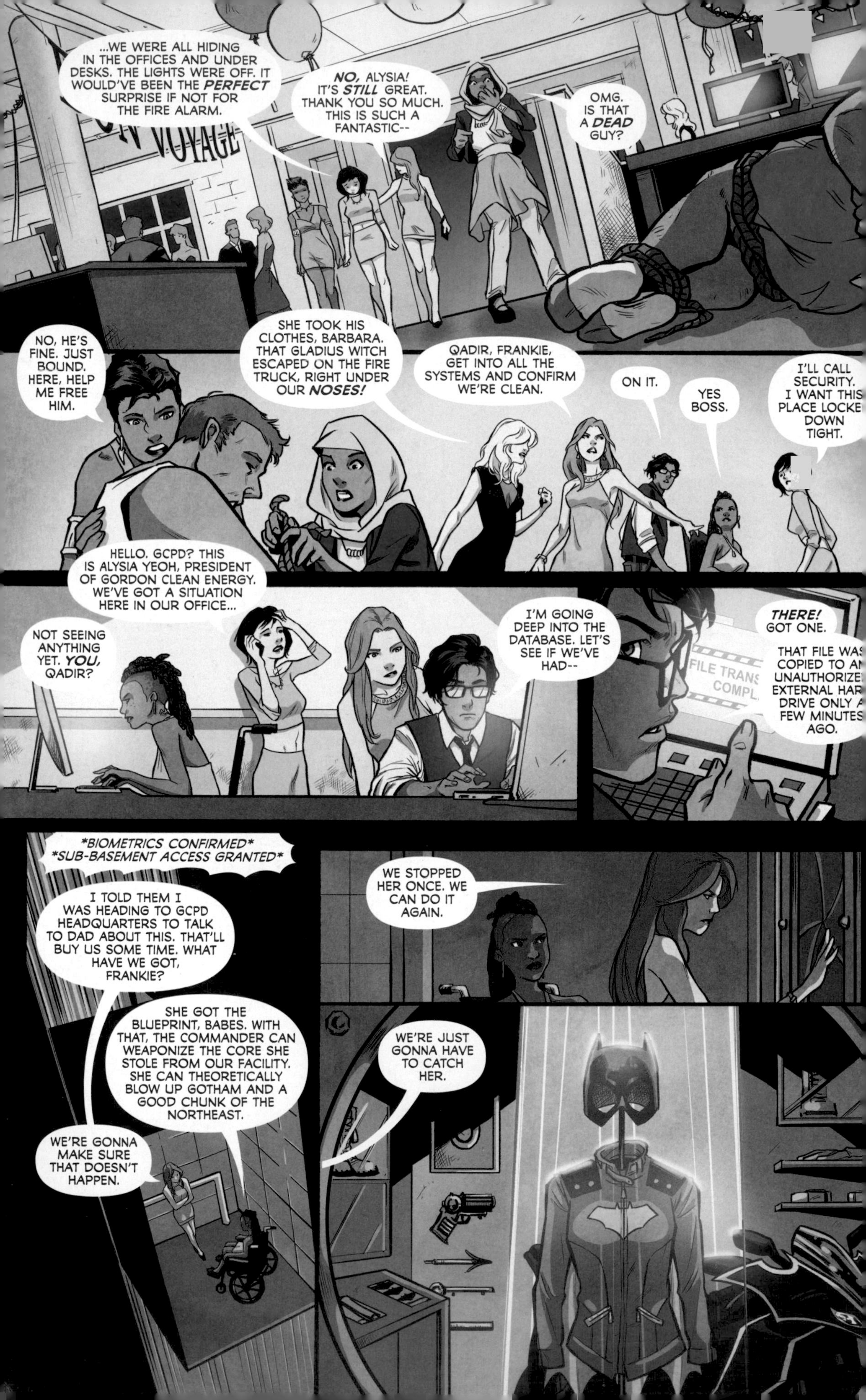
...WE WERE ALL HIDING IN THE OFFICES AND UNDER DESKS. THE LIGHTS WERE OFF. IT WOULD'VE BEEN THE PERFECT SURPRISE IF NOT FOR THE FIRE ALARM.
NO, ALYSIA! IT'S STILL GREAT. THANK YOU SO MUCH. THIS IS SUCH A FANTASTIC--
OMG. IS THAT A DEAD GUY?
NO, HE'S FINE. JUST BOUND. HERE, HELP ME FREE HIM.
SHE TOOK HIS CLOTHES, BARBARA. THAT GLADIUS WITCH ESCAPED ON THE FIRE TRUCK, RIGHT UNDER OUR NOSES!
QADIR, FRANKIE, GET INTO ALL THE SYSTEMS AND CONFIRM WE'RE CLEAN.
ON IT.
YES BOSS.
I'LL CALL SECURITY. I WANT THIS PLACE LOCKE DOWN TIGHT.
HELLO. GCPD? THIS IS ALYSIA YEOH, PRESIDENT OF GORDON CLEAN ENERGY. WE'VE GOT A SITUATION HERE IN OUR OFFICE...
NOT SEEING ANYTHING YET. YOU, QADIR?
I'M GOING DEEP INTO THE DATABASE. LET'S SEE IF WE'VE HAD--
THERE! GOT ONE.
FILE TRANS COMPL
THAT FILE WAS COPIED TO AN UNAUTHORIZE EXTERNAL HAR DRIVE ONLY A FEW MINUTES AGO.
BIOMETRICS CONFIRMED *SUB-BASEMENT ACCESS GRANTED*
I TOLD THEM I WAS HEADING TO GCPD HEADQUARTERS TO TALK TO DAD ABOUT THIS. THAT'LL BUY US SOME TIME. WHAT HAVE WE GOT, FRANKIE?
SHE GOT THE BLUEPRINT, BABES. WITH THAT, THE COMMANDER CAN WEAPONIZE THE CORE SHE STOLE FROM OUR FACILITY. SHE CAN THEORETICALLY BLOW UP GOTHAM AND A GOOD CHUNK OF THE NORTHEAST.
WE'RE GONNA MAKE SURE THAT DOESN'T HAPPEN.
WE STOPPED HER ONCE. WE CAN DO IT AGAIN.
WE'RE JUST GONNA HAVE TO CATCH HER.

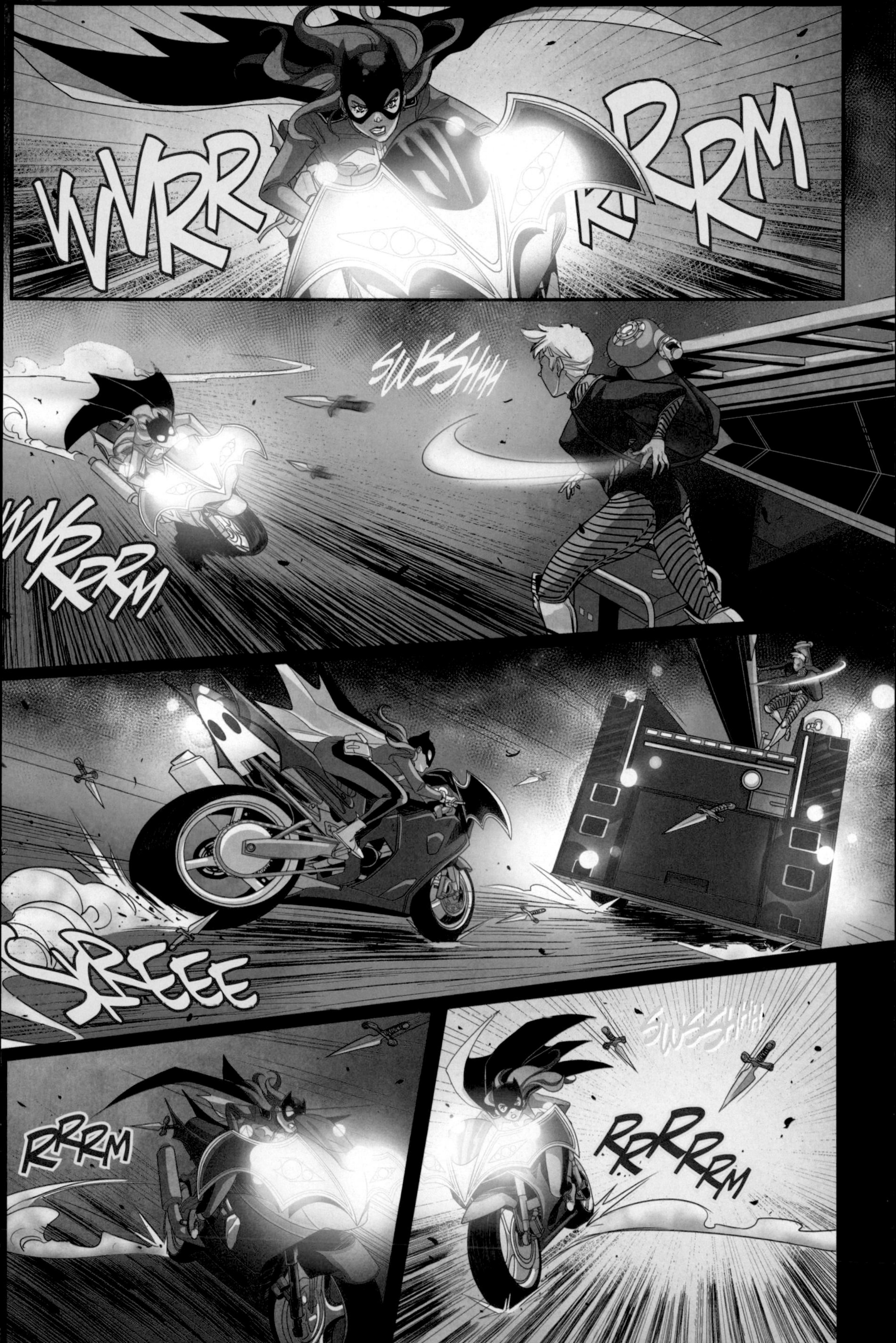
WWRR
RRRM
SWSSHHH
WWRRRM
SREEEE
RRRM
SWSSHHH
RRRRRM

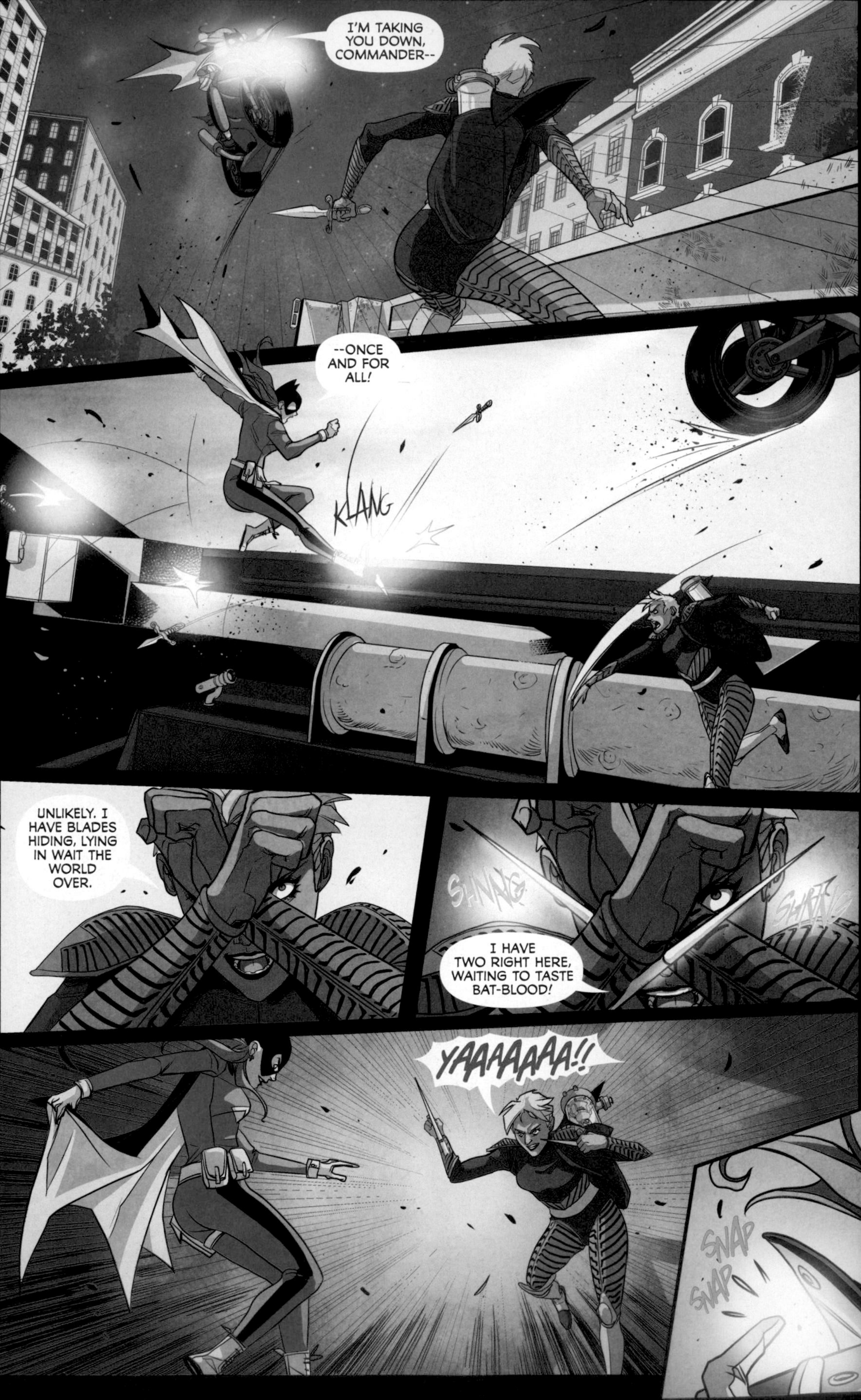
I'M TAKING YOU DOWN, COMMANDER--
--ONCE AND FOR ALL!
KLANG
UNLIKELY. I HAVE BLADES HIDING, LYING IN WAIT THE WORLD OVER.
I HAVE TWO RIGHT HERE, WAITING TO TASTE BAT-BLOOD!
YAAAAAAA!!
SNAP
SNAP

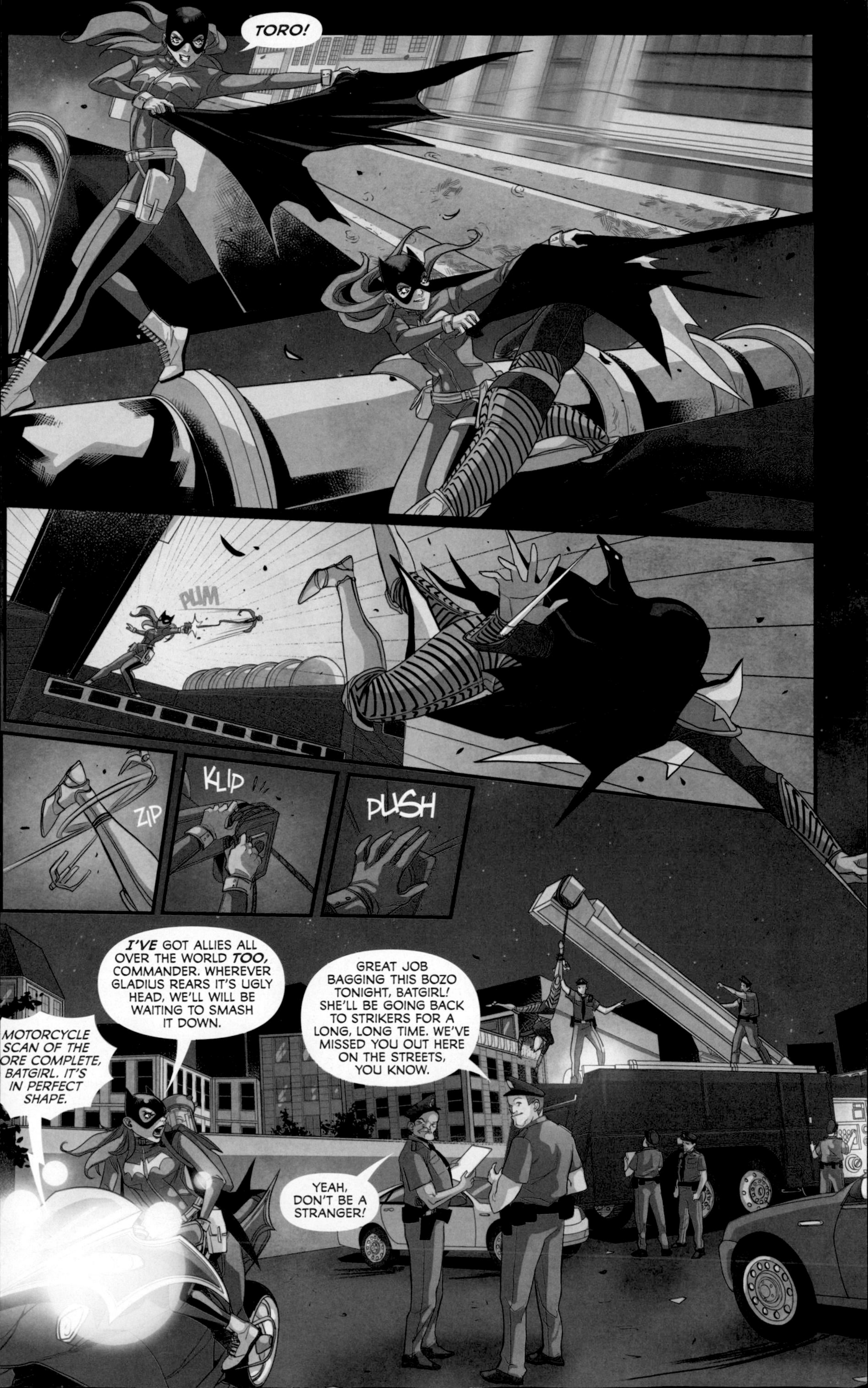
TORO!
PUM
ZIP
KLIP
PUSH
MOTORCYCLE SCAN OF THE ORE COMPLETE, BATGIRL. IT'S IN PERFECT SHAPE.
I'VE GOT ALLIES ALL OVER THE WORLD TOO, COMMANDER. WHEREVER GLADIUS REARS IT'S UGLY HEAD, WE'LL WILL BE WAITING TO SMASH IT DOWN.
GREAT JOB BAGGING THIS BOZO TONIGHT, BATGIRL! SHE'LL BE GOING BACK TO STRIKERS FOR A LONG, LONG TIME. WE'VE MISSED YOU OUT HERE ON THE STREETS, YOU KNOW.
YEAH, DON'T BE A STRANGER!

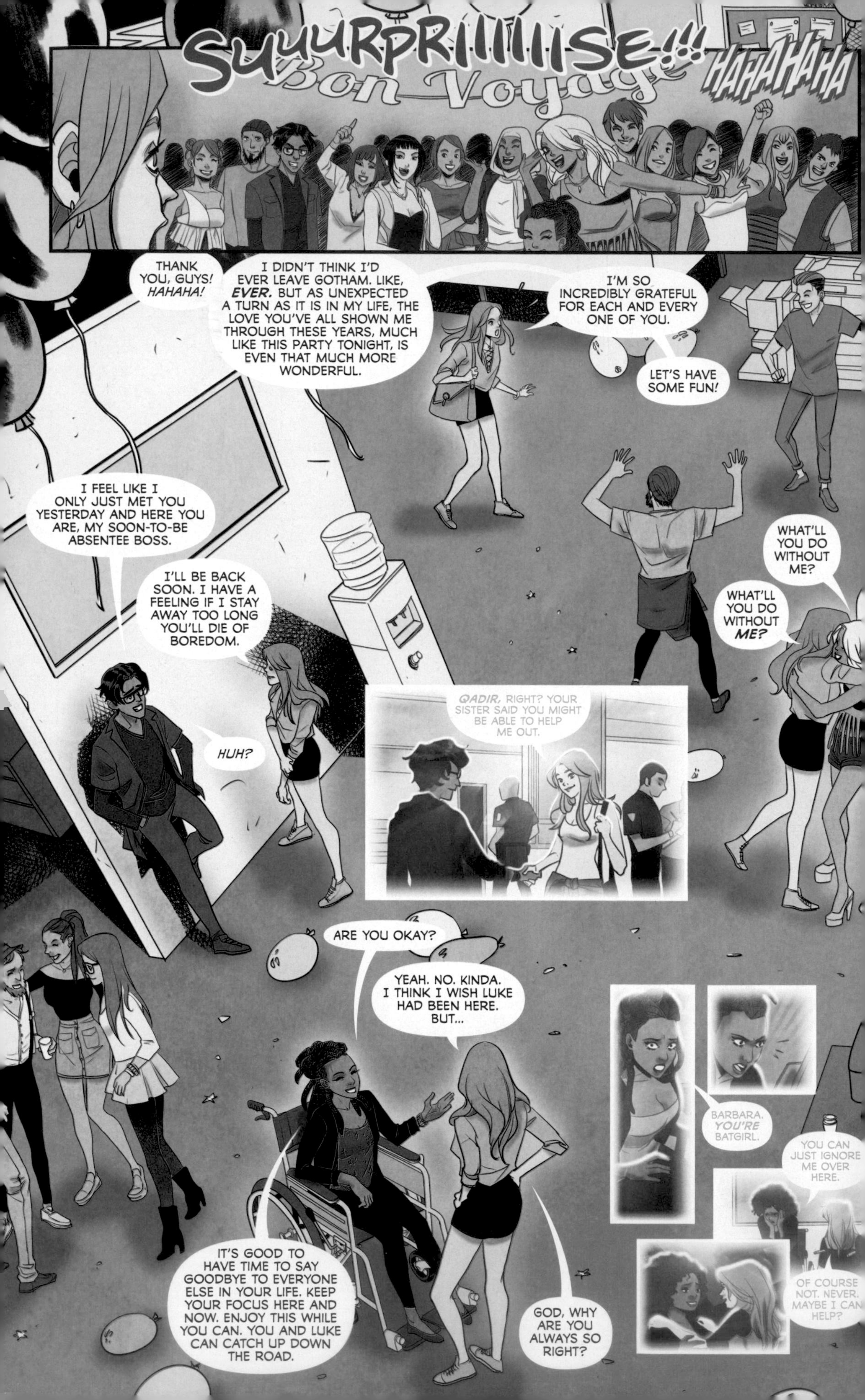
SUUURPRIIIIIISE!!!
Bon Voyage
HAHAHAHA
THANK YOU, GUYS! HAHAHA!
I DIDN'T THINK I'D EVER LEAVE GOTHAM. LIKE, EVER. BUT AS UNEXPECTED A TURN AS IT IS IN MY LIFE, THE LOVE YOU'VE ALL SHOWN ME THROUGH THESE YEARS, MUCH LIKE THIS PARTY TONIGHT, IS EVEN THAT MUCH MORE WONDERFUL.
I'M SO INCREDIBLY GRATEFUL FOR EACH AND EVERY ONE OF YOU.
LET'S HAVE SOME FUN!
I FEEL LIKE I ONLY JUST MET YOU YESTERDAY AND HERE YOU ARE, MY SOON-TO-BE ABSENTEE BOSS.
I'LL BE BACK SOON. I HAVE A FEELING IF I STAY AWAY TOO LONG YOU'LL DIE OF BOREDOM.
HUH?
QADIR, RIGHT? YOUR SISTER SAID YOU MIGHT BE ABLE TO HELP ME OUT.
WHAT'LL YOU DO WITHOUT ME?
WHAT'LL YOU DO WITHOUT ME?
ARE YOU OKAY?
YEAH. NO. KINDA. I THINK I WISH LUKE HAD BEEN HERE. BUT...
IT'S GOOD TO HAVE TIME TO SAY GOODBYE TO EVERYONE ELSE IN YOUR LIFE. KEEP YOUR FOCUS HERE AND NOW. ENJOY THIS WHILE YOU CAN. YOU AND LUKE CAN CATCH UP DOWN THE ROAD.
GOD, WHY ARE YOU ALWAYS SO RIGHT?
BARBARA. YOU'RE BATGIRL.
YOU CAN JUST IGNORE ME OVER HERE.
OF COURSE NOT. NEVER. MAYBE I CAN HELP?

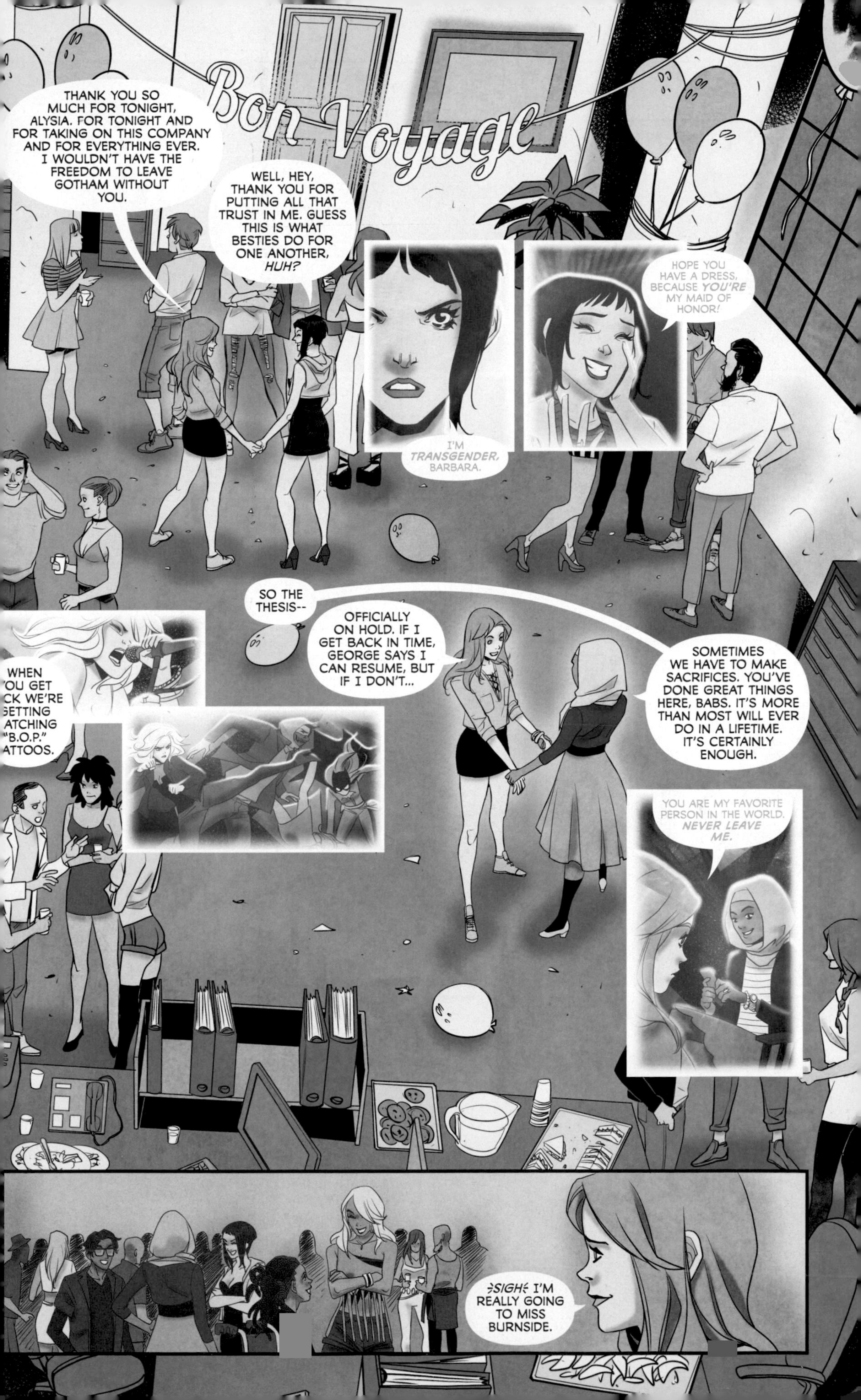
Bon Voyage
THANK YOU SO MUCH FOR TONIGHT, ALYSIA. FOR TONIGHT AND FOR TAKING ON THIS COMPANY AND FOR EVERYTHING EVER. I WOULDN'T HAVE THE FREEDOM TO LEAVE GOTHAM WITHOUT YOU.
WELL, HEY, THANK YOU FOR PUTTING ALL THAT TRUST IN ME. GUESS THIS IS WHAT BESTIES DO FOR ONE ANOTHER, *HUH?*
I'M *TRANSGENDER,* BARBARA.
HOPE YOU HAVE A DRESS, BECAUSE *YOU'RE* MY MAID OF HONOR!
SO THE THESIS--
OFFICIALLY ON HOLD. IF I GET BACK IN TIME, GEORGE SAYS I CAN RESUME, BUT IF I DON'T...
WHEN 'OU GET CK WE'RE ETTING ATCHING "B.O.P." ATTOOS.
SOMETIMES WE HAVE TO MAKE SACRIFICES. YOU'VE DONE GREAT THINGS HERE, BABS. IT'S MORE THAN MOST WILL EVER DO IN A LIFETIME. IT'S CERTAINLY ENOUGH.
YOU ARE MY FAVORITE PERSON IN THE WORLD. *NEVER LEAVE ME.*
SIGH I'M REALLY GOING TO MISS BURNSIDE.

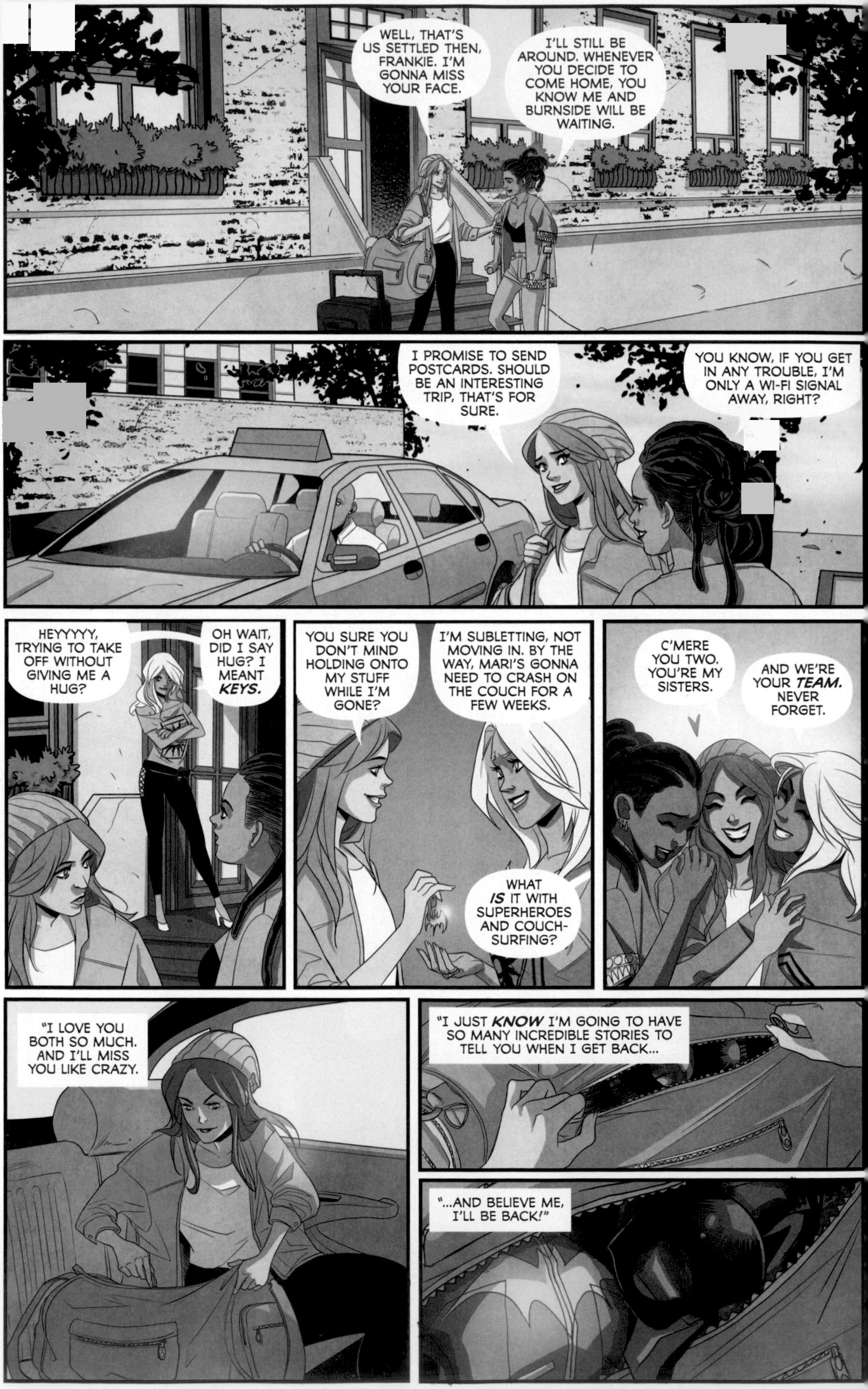
WELL, THAT'S US SETTLED THEN, FRANKIE. I'M GONNA MISS YOUR FACE.
I'LL STILL BE AROUND. WHENEVER YOU DECIDE TO COME HOME, YOU KNOW ME AND BURNSIDE WILL BE WAITING.
I PROMISE TO SEND POSTCARDS. SHOULD BE AN INTERESTING TRIP, THAT'S FOR SURE.
YOU KNOW, IF YOU GET IN ANY TROUBLE, I'M ONLY A WI-FI SIGNAL AWAY, RIGHT?
HEYYYYY, TRYING TO TAKE OFF WITHOUT GIVING ME A HUG?
OH WAIT, DID I SAY HUG? I MEANT *KEYS.*
YOU SURE YOU DON'T MIND HOLDING ONTO MY STUFF WHILE I'M GONE?
I'M SUBLETTING, NOT MOVING IN. BY THE WAY, MARI'S GONNA NEED TO CRASH ON THE COUCH FOR A FEW WEEKS.
WHAT *IS* IT WITH SUPERHEROES AND COUCH-SURFING?
C'MERE YOU TWO. YOU'RE MY SISTERS.
AND WE'RE YOUR *TEAM.* NEVER FORGET.
"I LOVE YOU BOTH SO MUCH. AND I'LL MISS YOU LIKE CRAZY.
"I JUST *KNOW* I'M GOING TO HAVE SO MANY INCREDIBLE STORIES TO TELL YOU WHEN I GET BACK...
"...AND BELIEVE ME, I'LL BE BACK!"

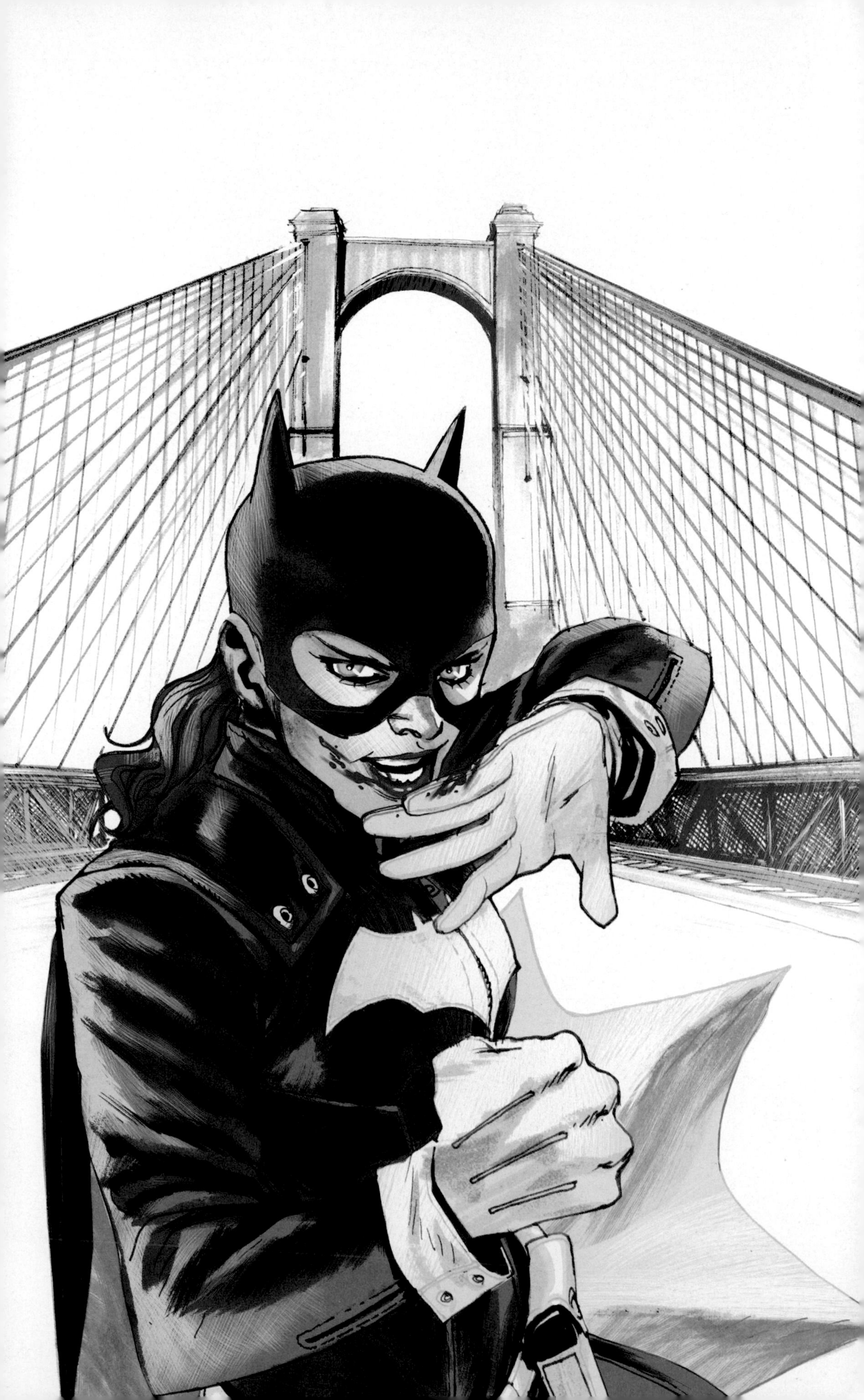

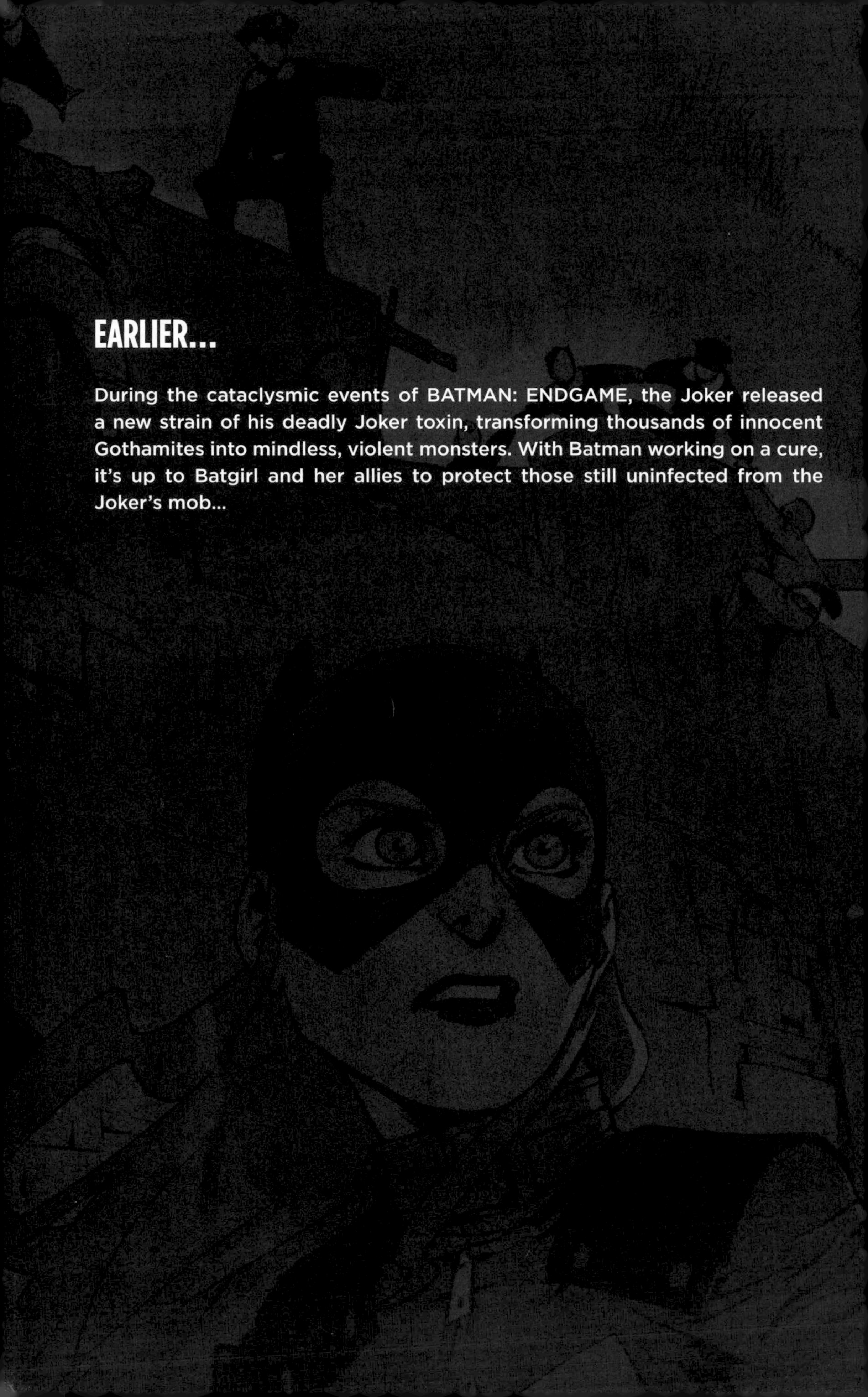

EARLIER...

During the cataclysmic events of BATMAN: ENDGAME, the Joker released a new strain of his deadly Joker toxin, transforming thousands of innocent Gothamites into mindless, violent monsters. With Batman working on a cure, it's up to Batgirl and her allies to protect those still uninfected from the Joker's mob...

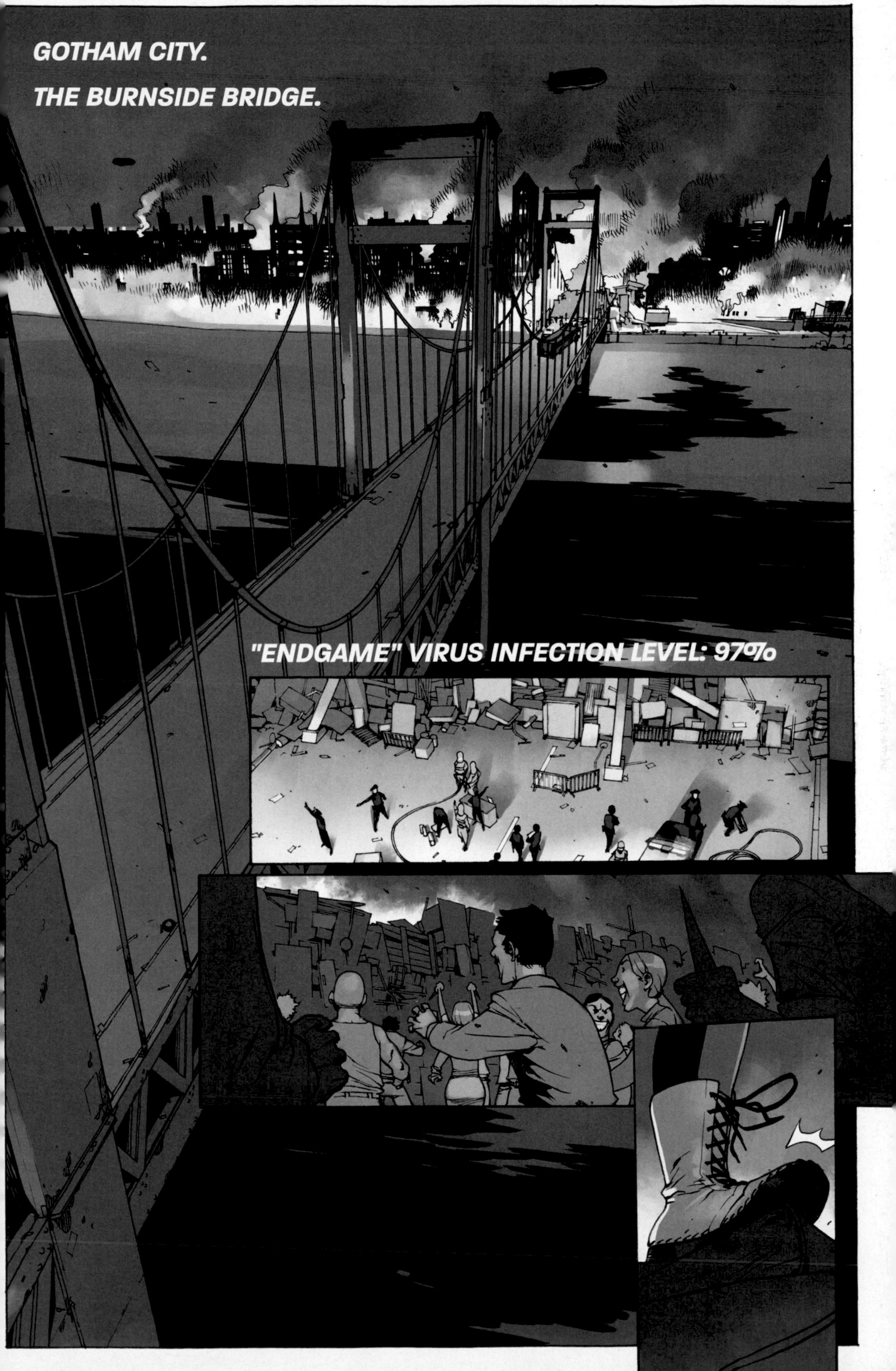
GOTHAM CITY.
THE BURNSIDE BRIDGE.
"ENDGAME" VIRUS INFECTION LEVEL: 97%

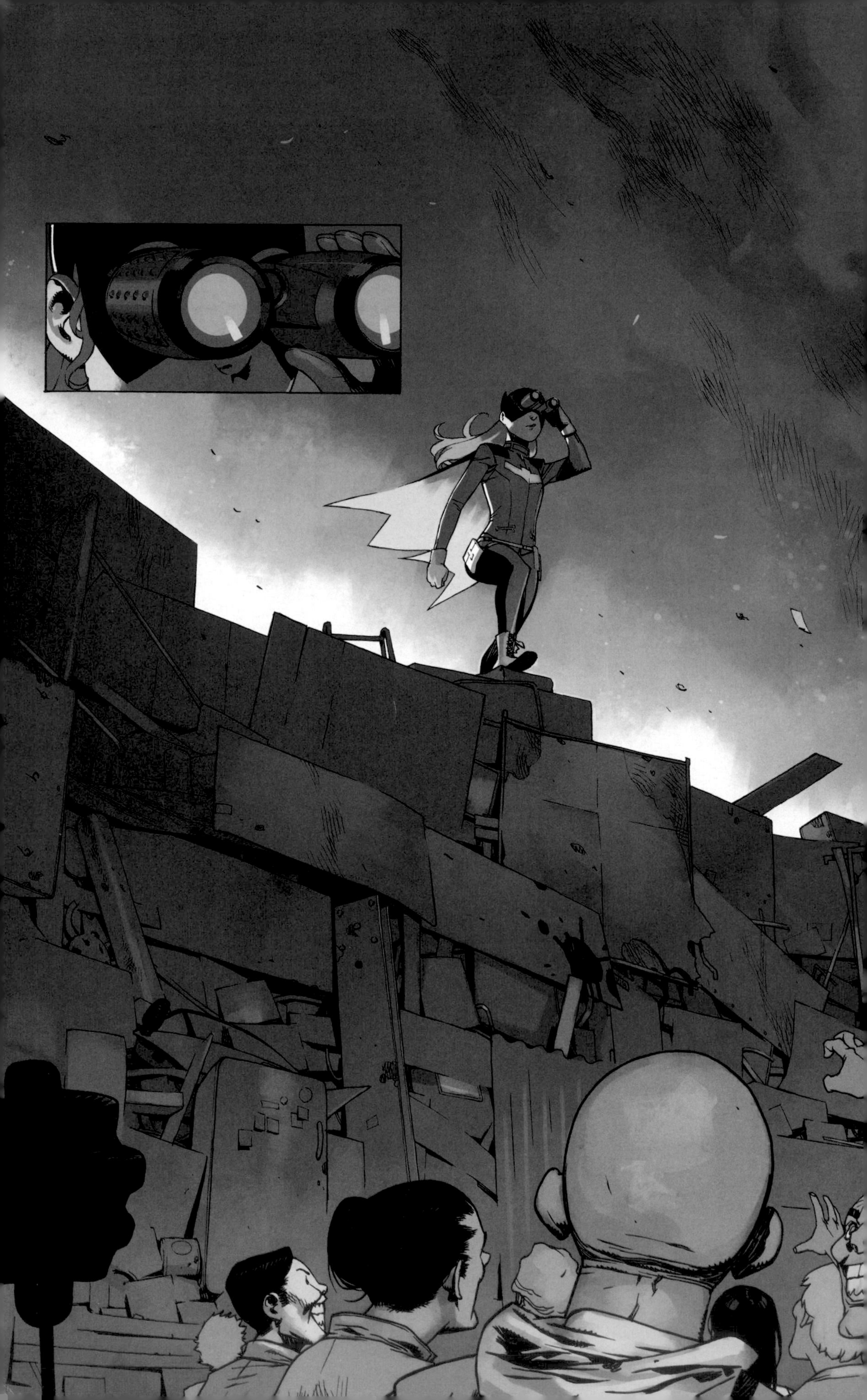

CAMERON STEWART &
BRENDEN FLETCHER writers
BENGAL art & color
JARED K. FLETCHER letters
RAFAEL ALBUQUERQUE cover

THE BATTLE FOR THE BURNSIDE BRIDGE

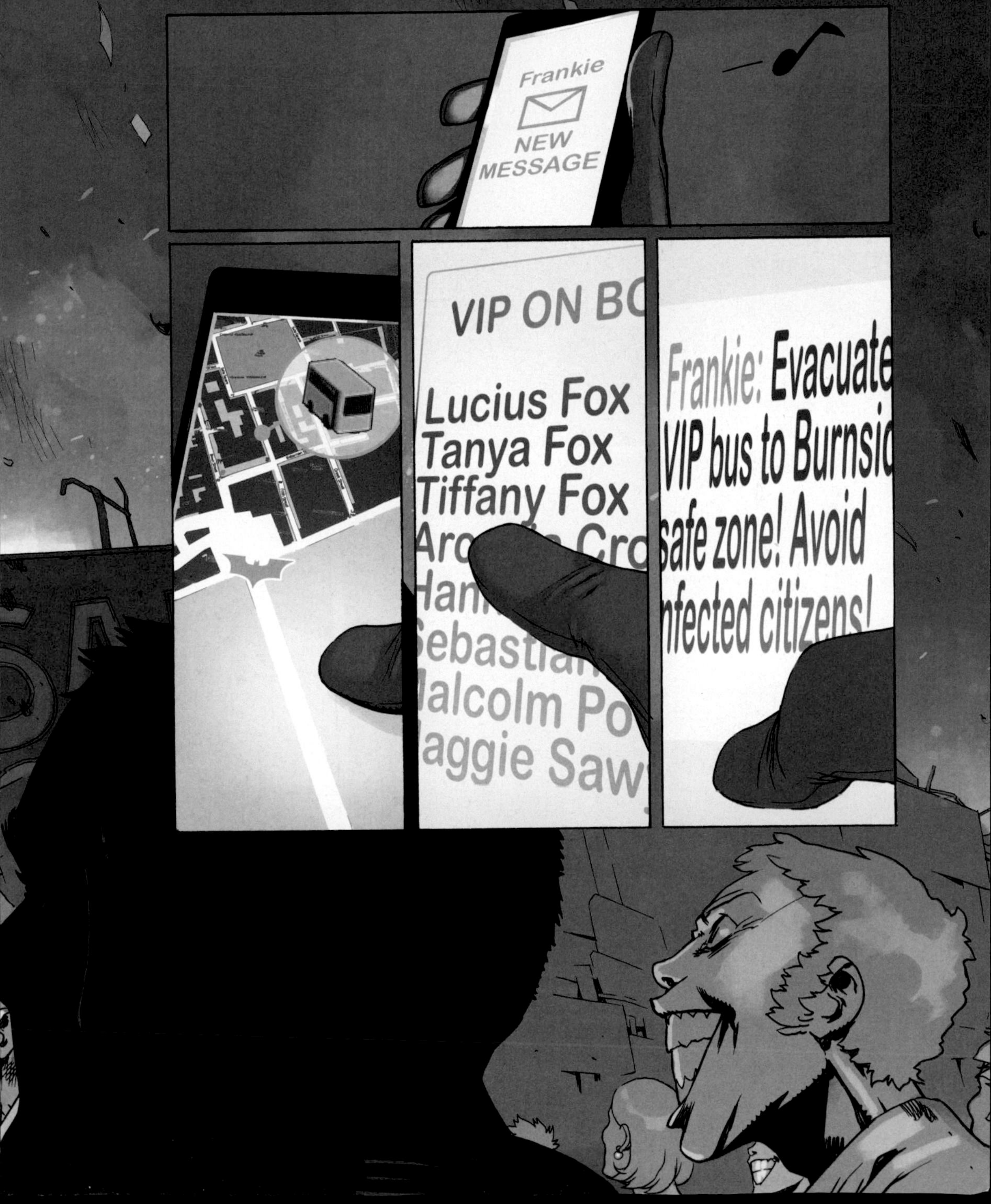
Frankie
NEW MESSAGE
VIP ON BO
Lucius Fox
Tanya Fox
Tiffany Fox
Frankie: Evacuate
VIP bus to Burnsid
safe zone! Avoid
nfected citizens!

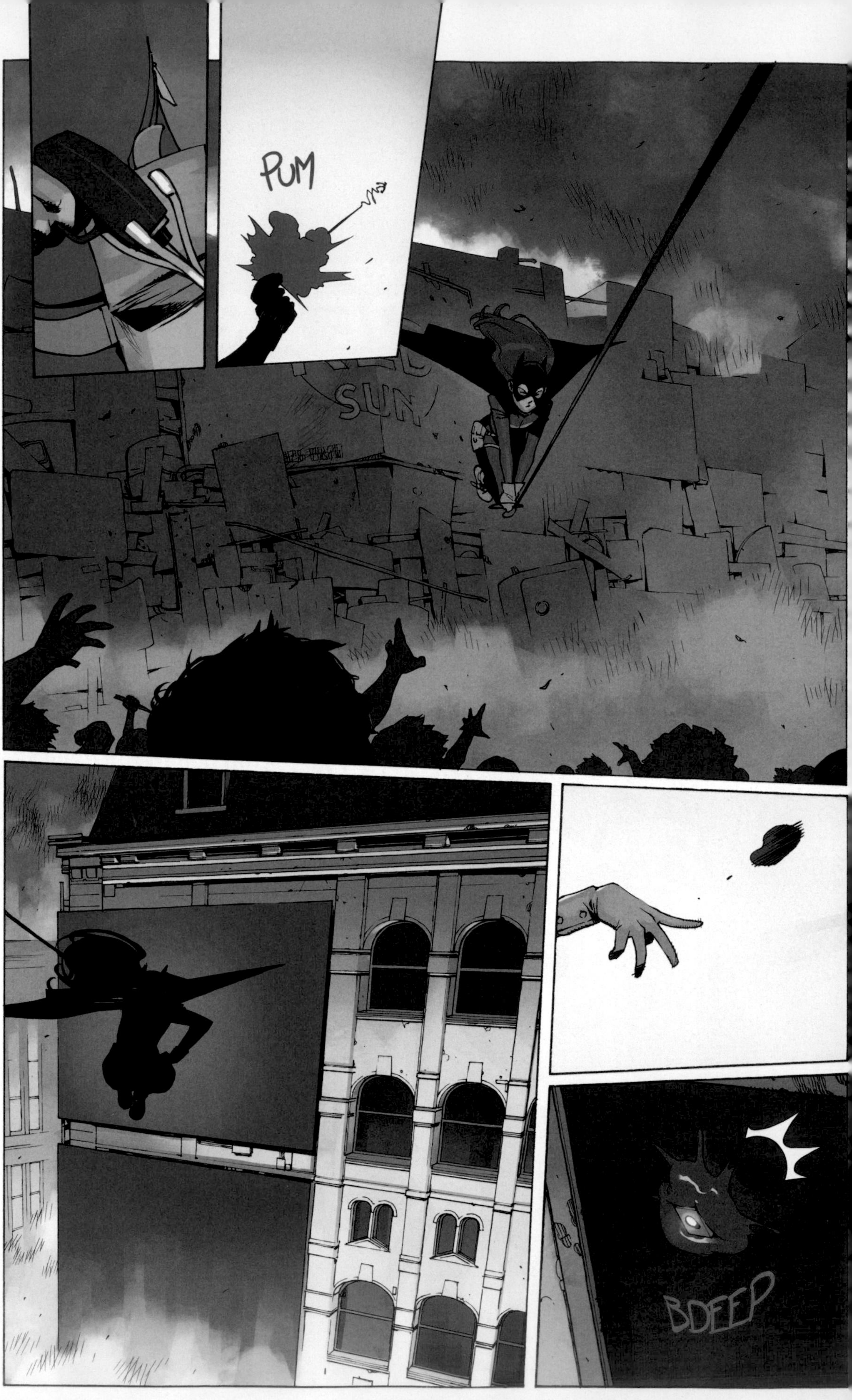
PUM
SUN
BDEEP

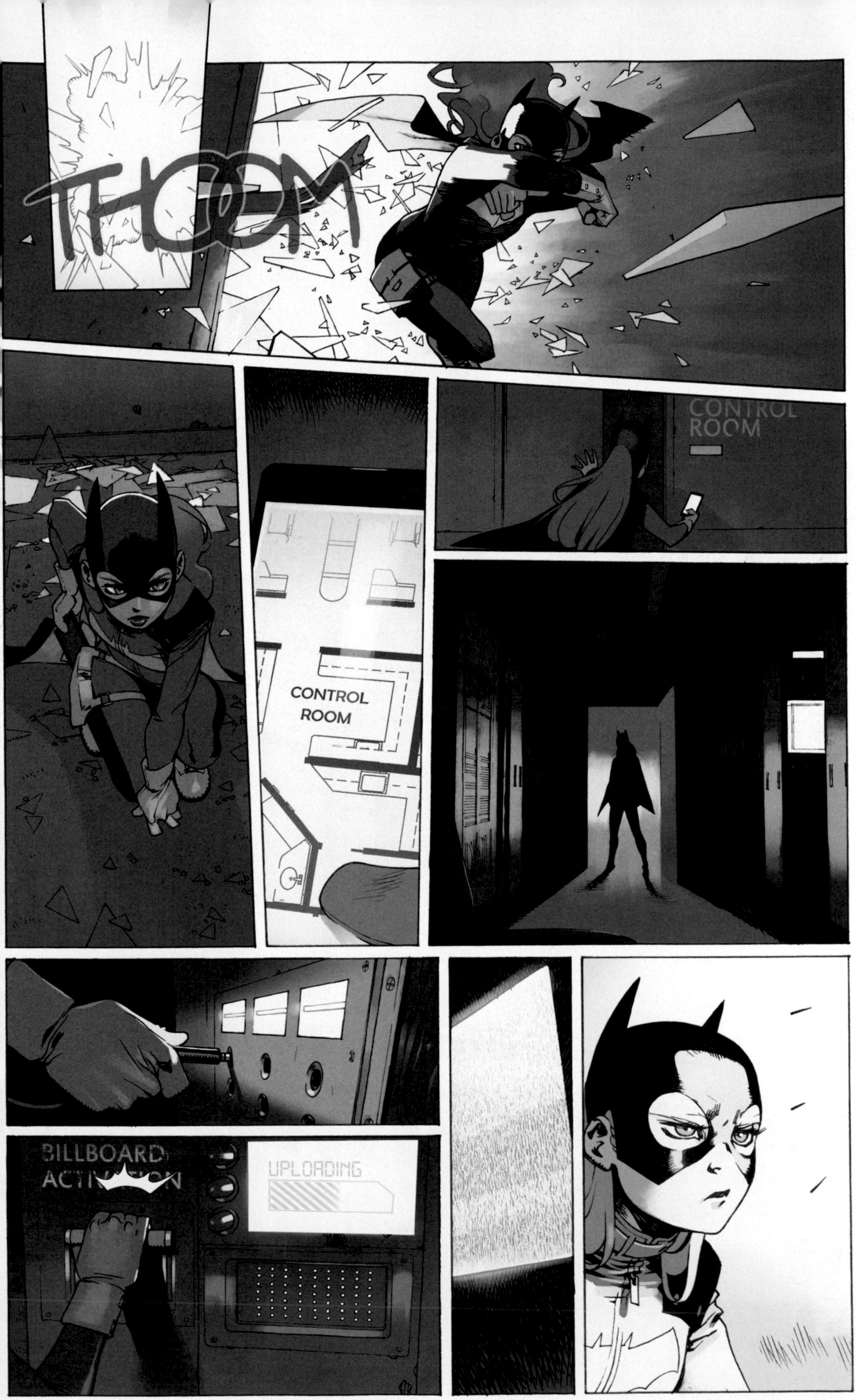
THOOM
CONTROL ROOM
CONTROL ROOM
UPLOADING

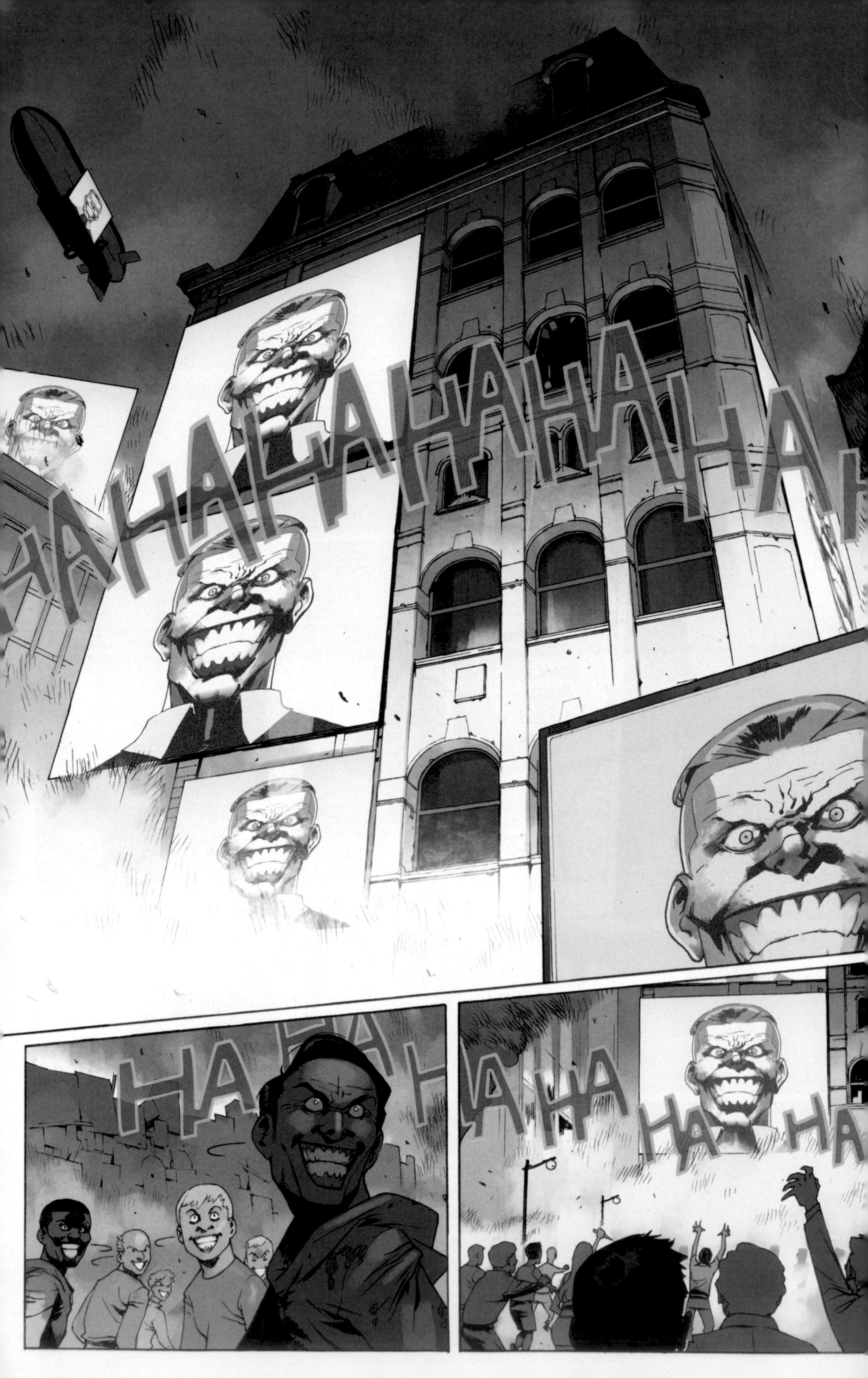

HAHAHAHAHAHAHA
HAHA
HAHA
HAHAHA

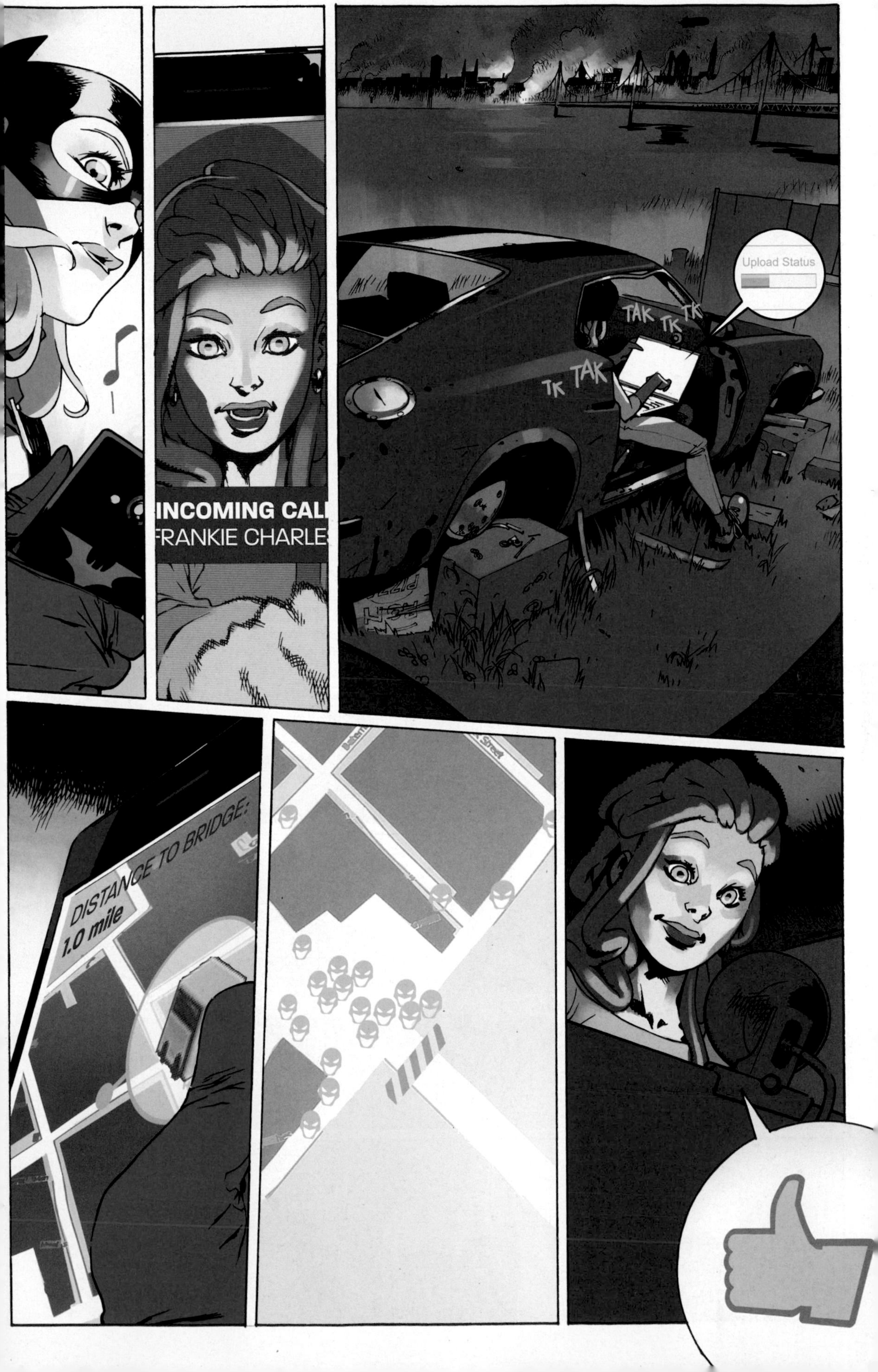
INCOMING CALL
FRANKIE CHARLES
Upload Status
TAK TK TK
TK TAK
DISTANCE TO BRIDGE:
1.0 mile

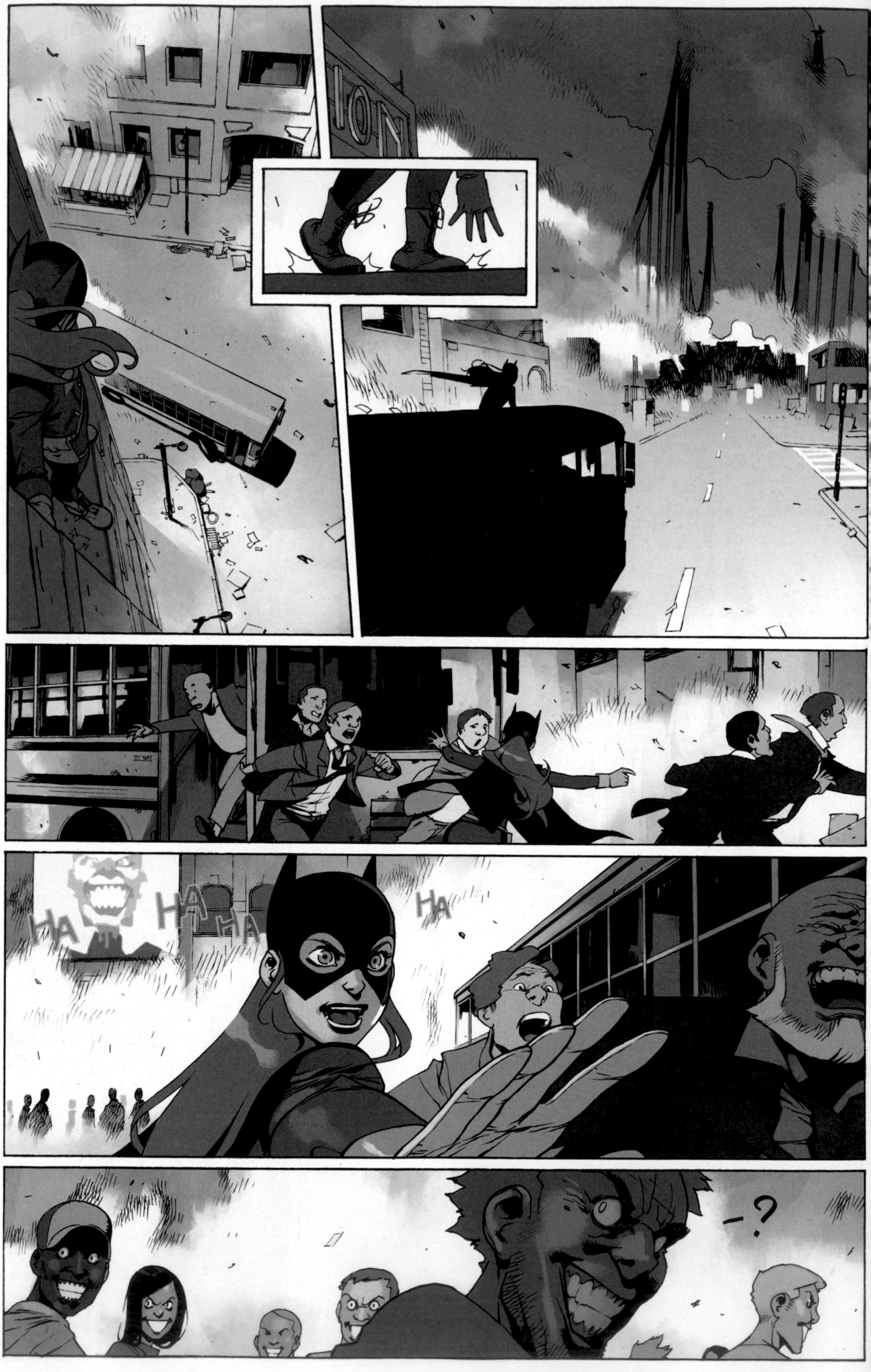
HA HA HA HA
HA
-?

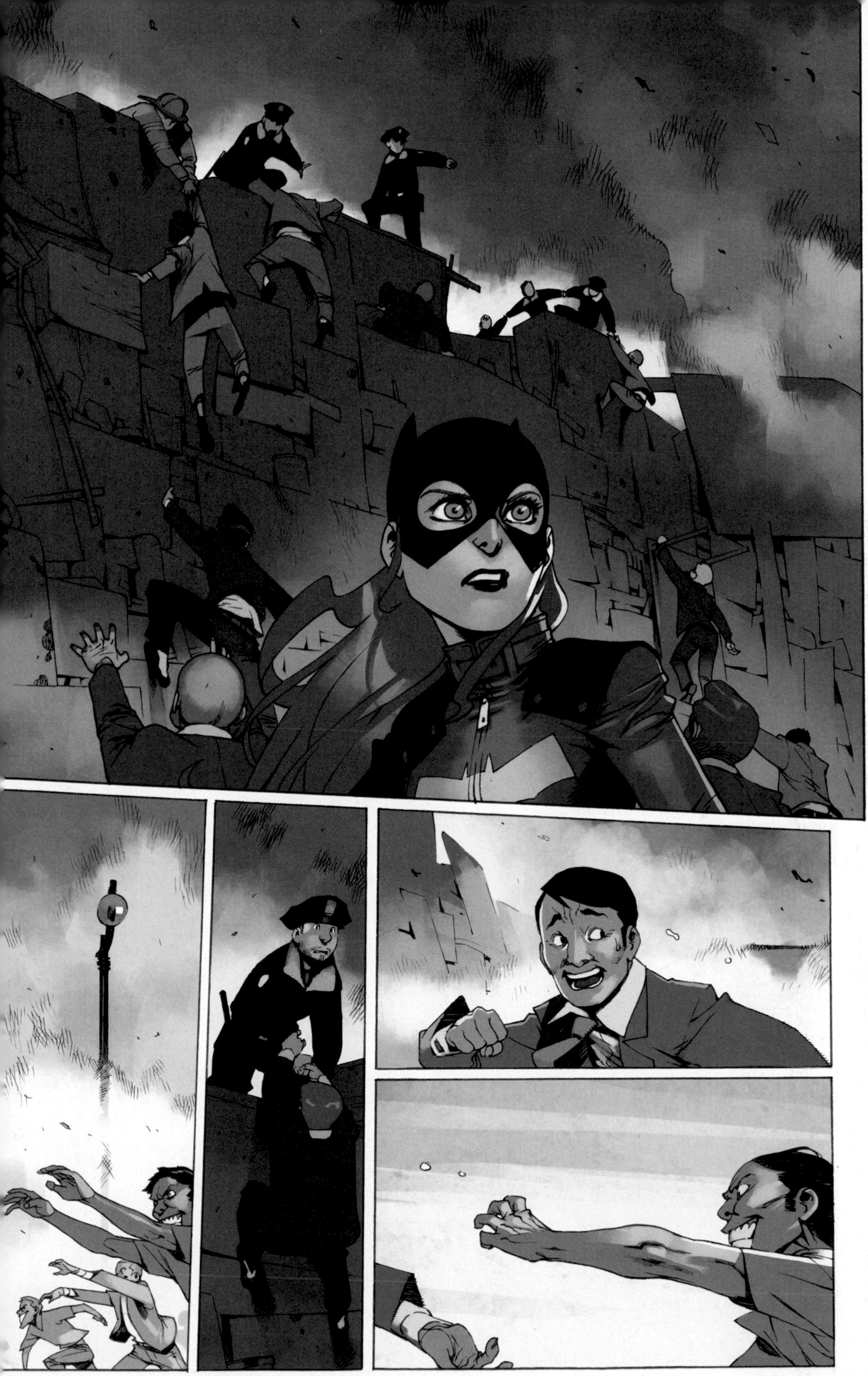

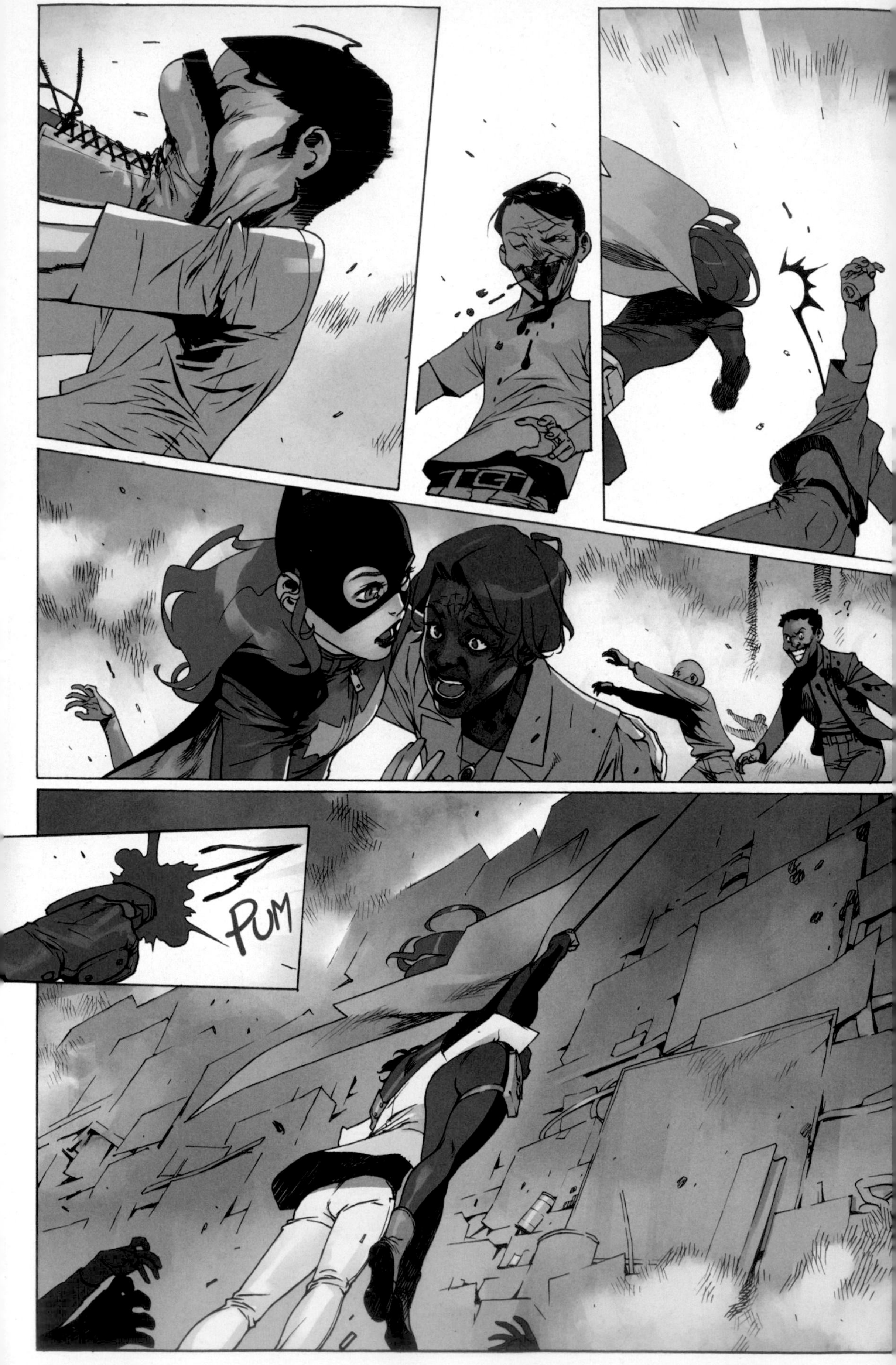
PUM

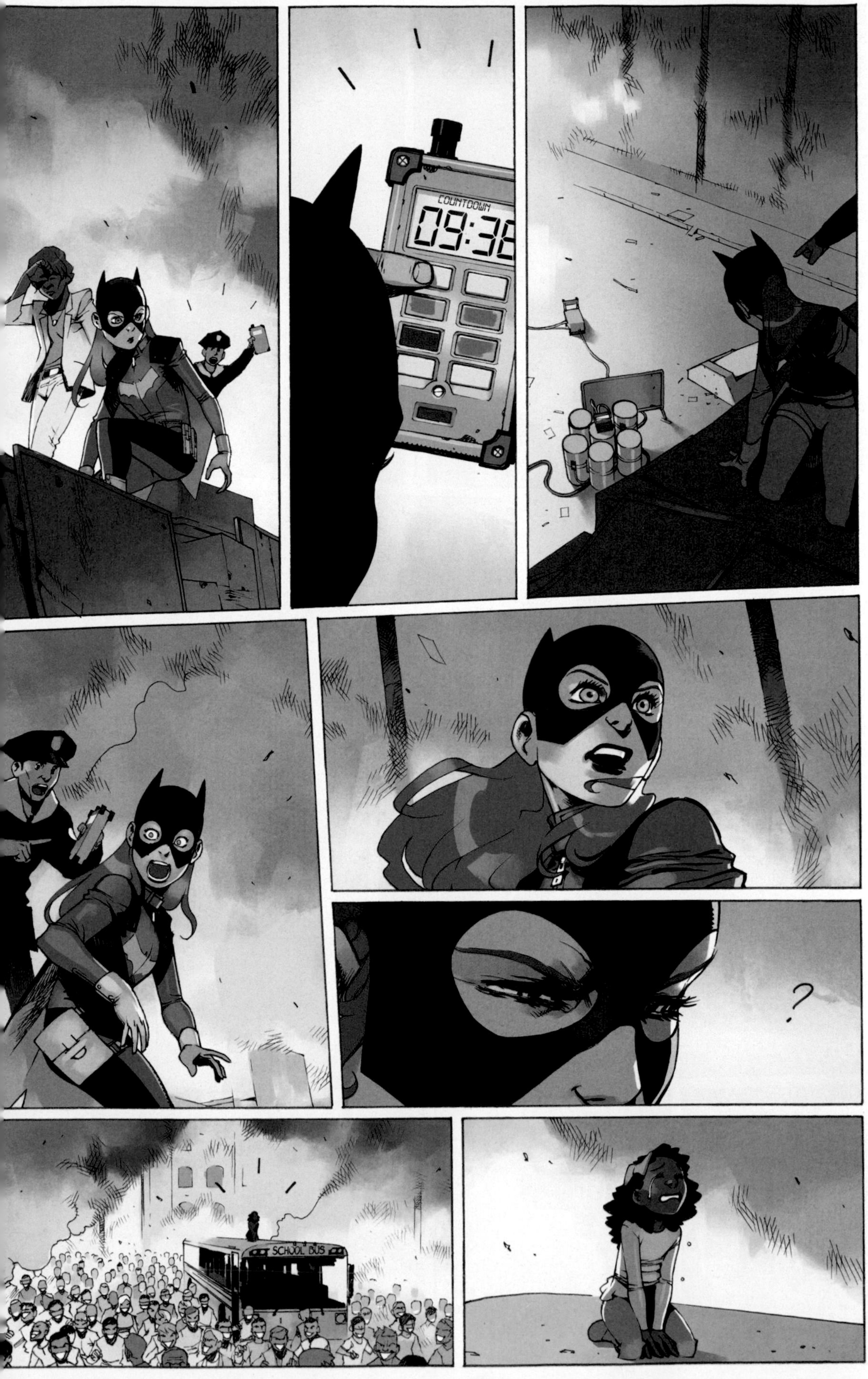
COUNTDOWN
SCHOOL BUS

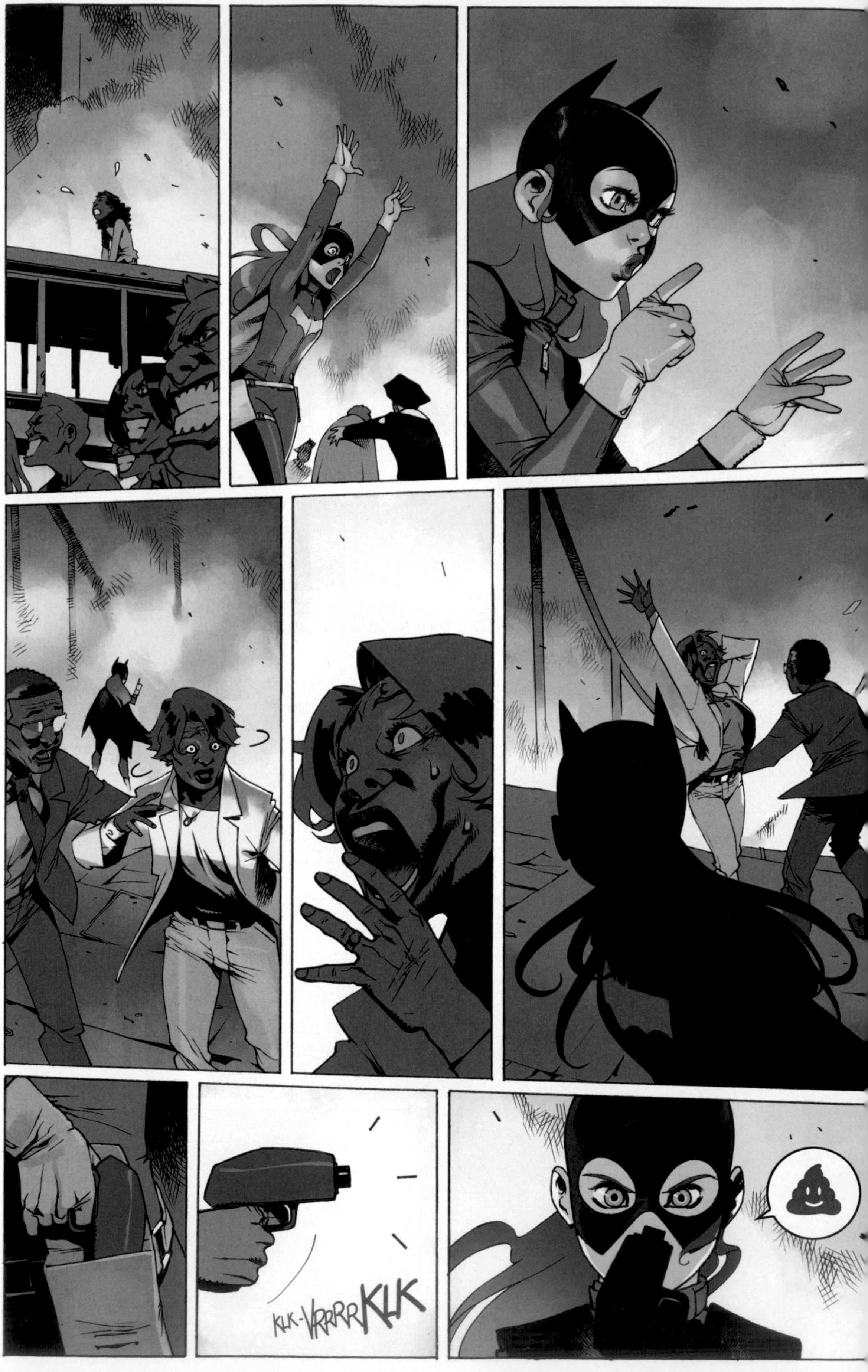
KLK-VRRRR KLK

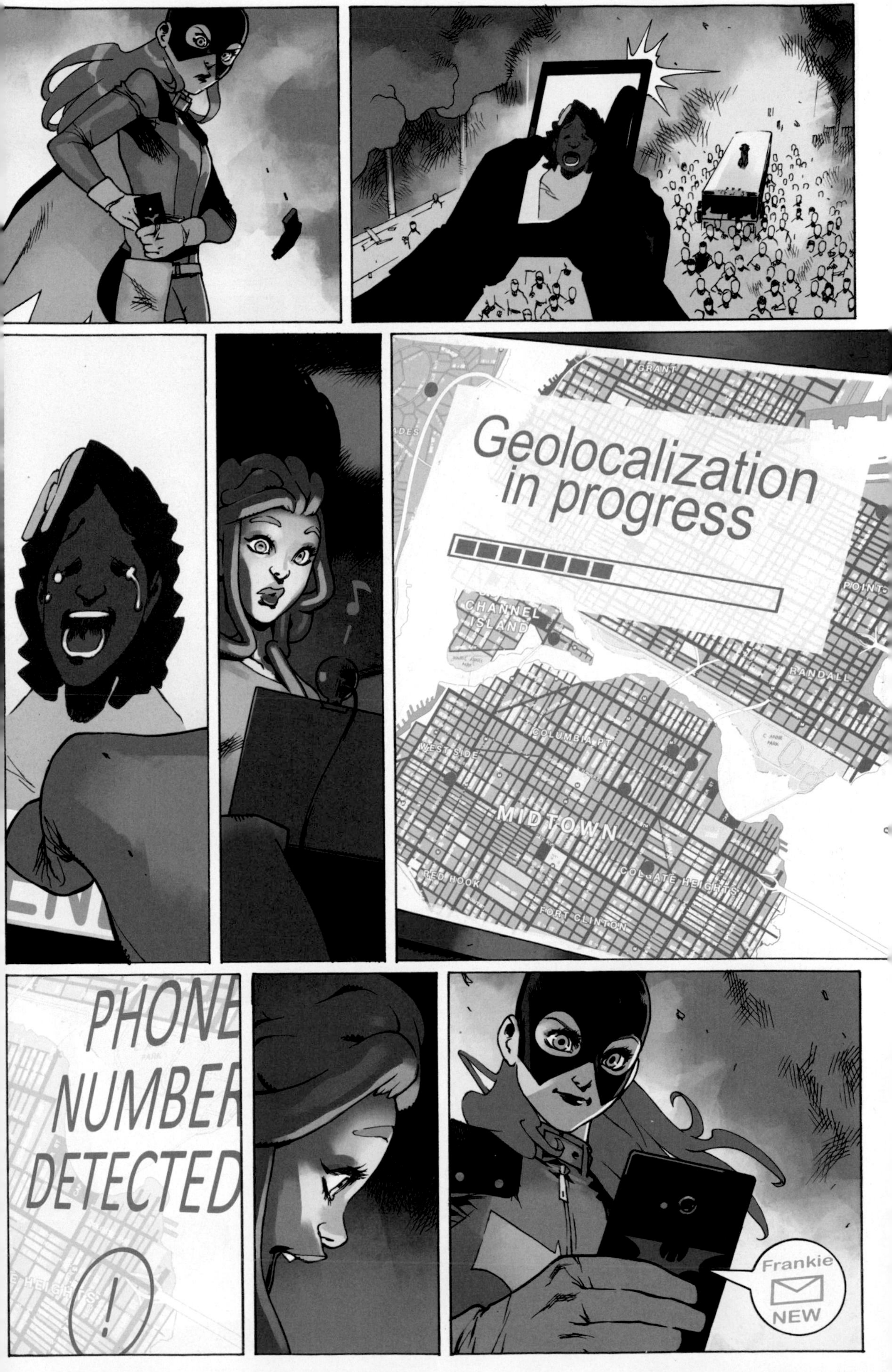
GRANT
Geolocalization in progress
CHANNEL ISLAND
POINT
RANDALL
COLUMBIA PT
WEST SIDE
MIDTOWN
RED HOOK
COLGATE HEIGHTS
FORT CLINTON
PHONE NUMBER DETECTED
!
Frankie
NEW

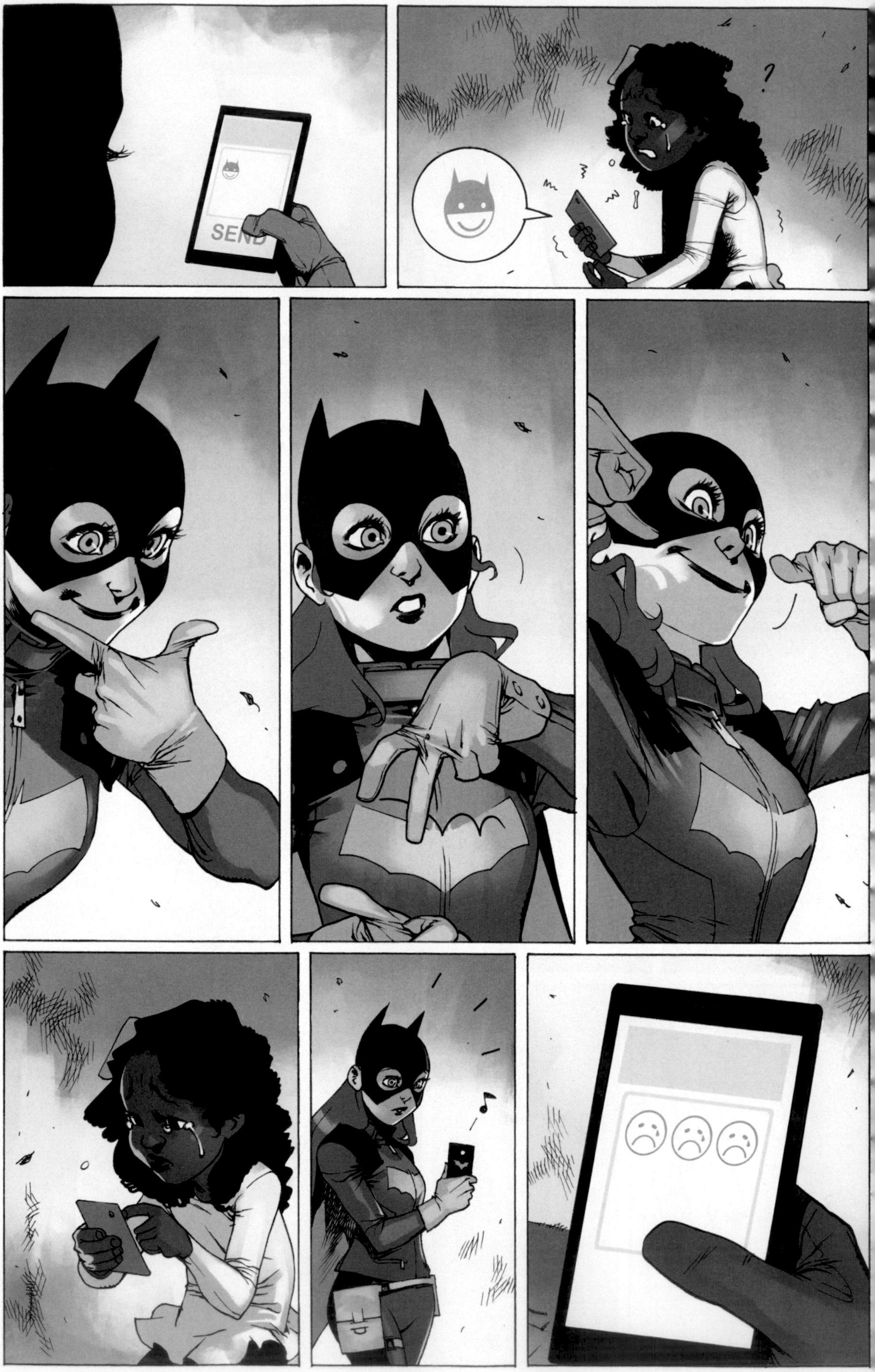
SEND

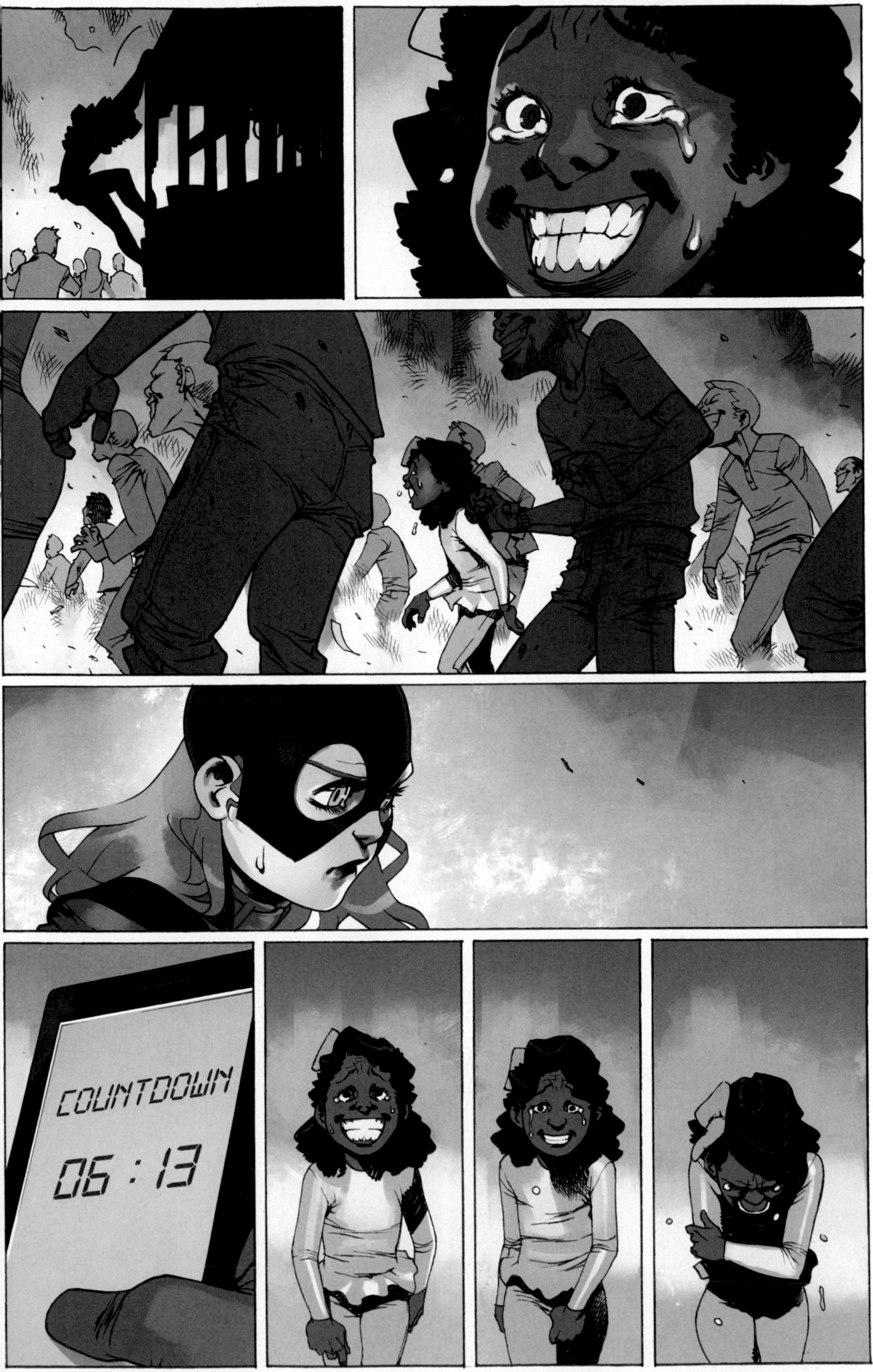
COUNTDOWN
06 : 13

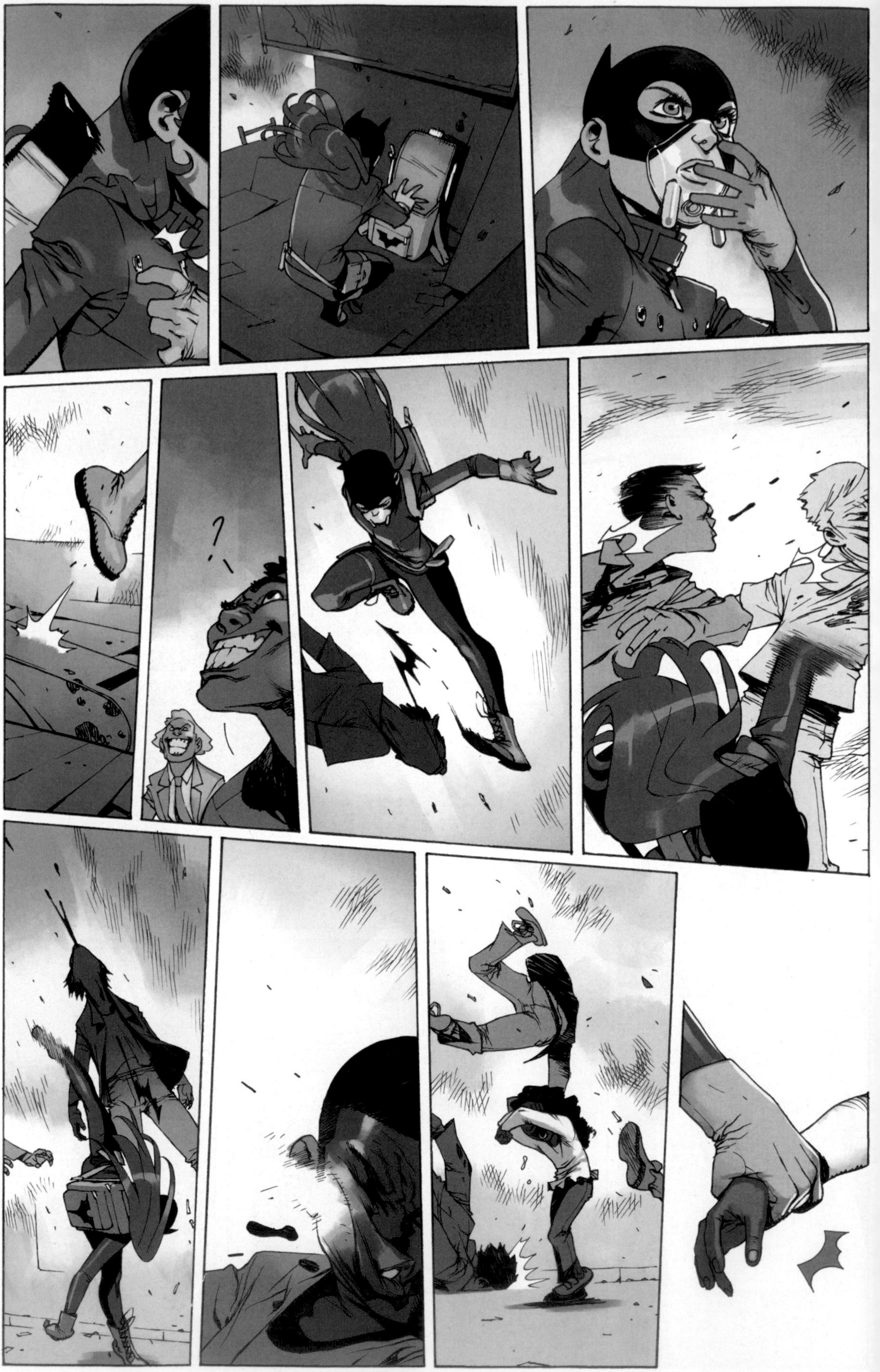

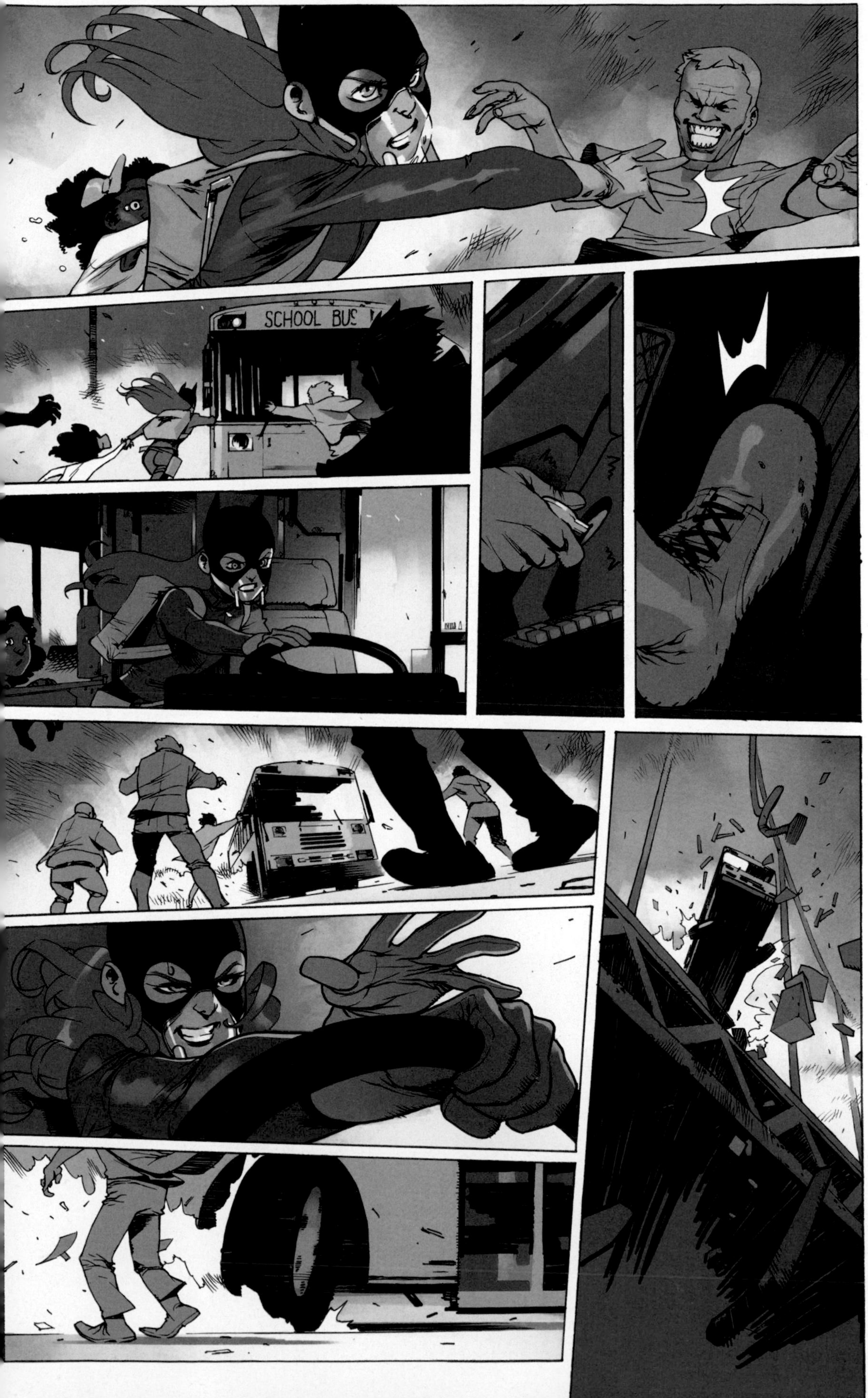
SCHOOL BUS

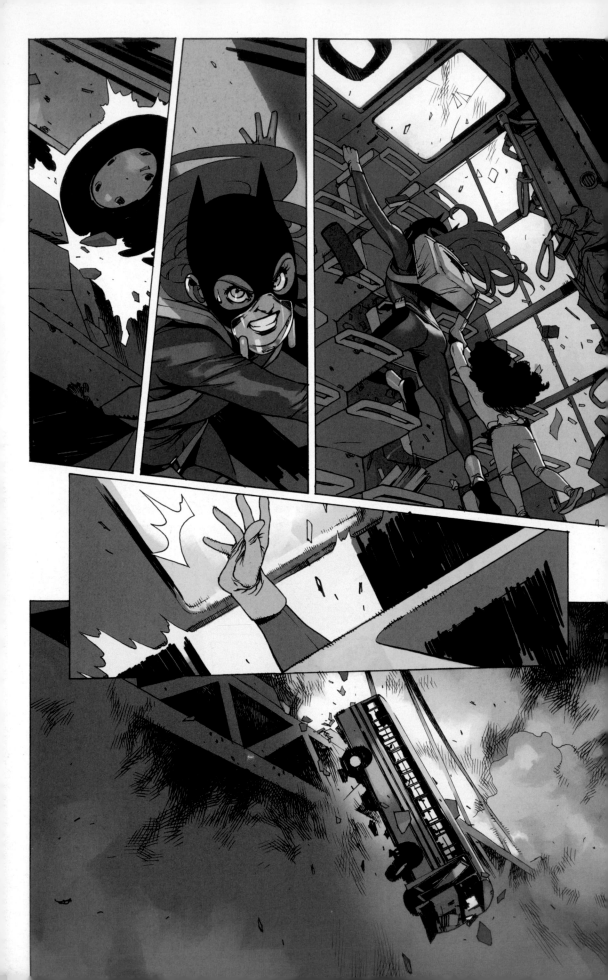

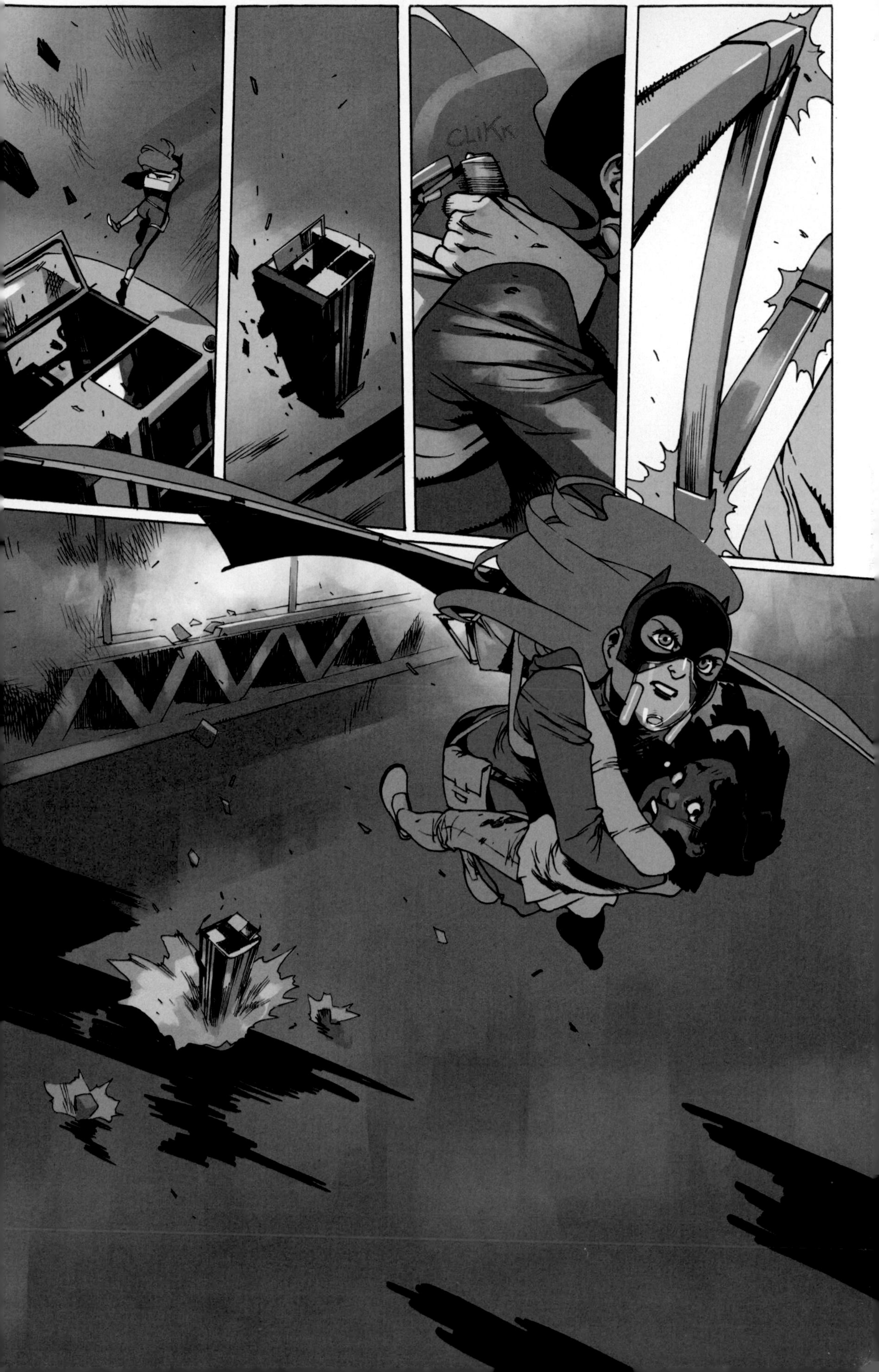
CLIKK

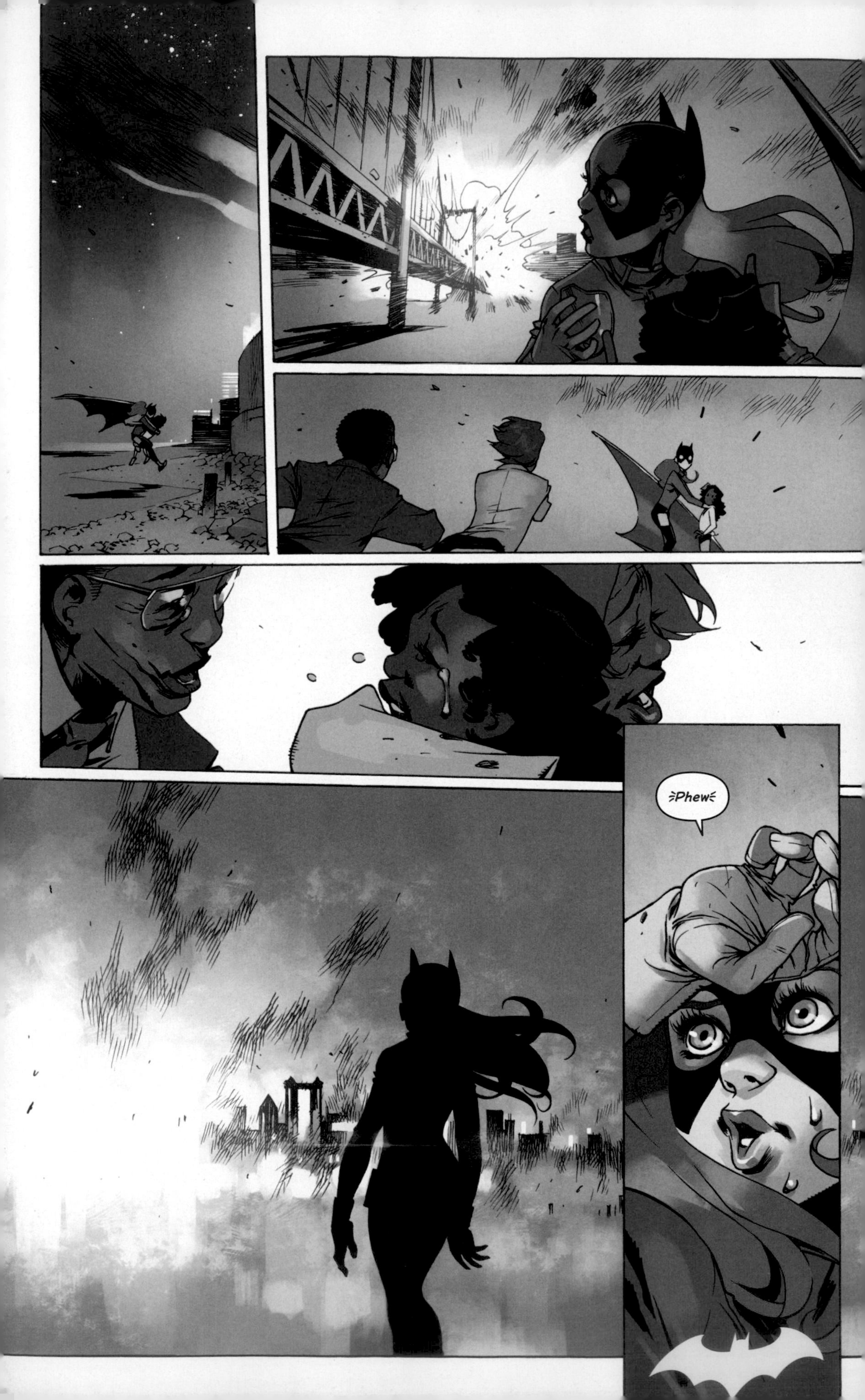
Phew

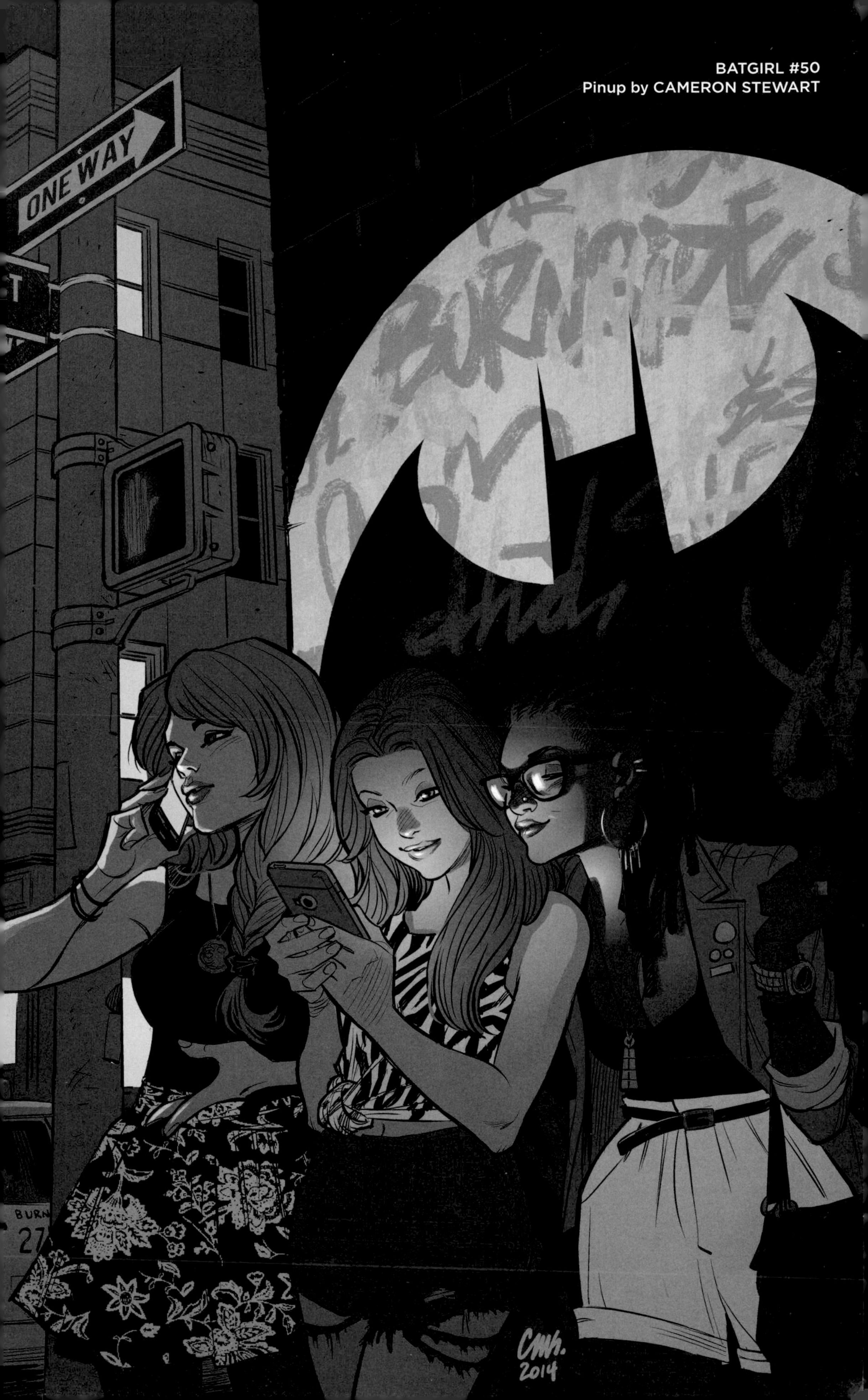
ONE WAY

BATGIRL #50
Pinup by CAMERON STEWART

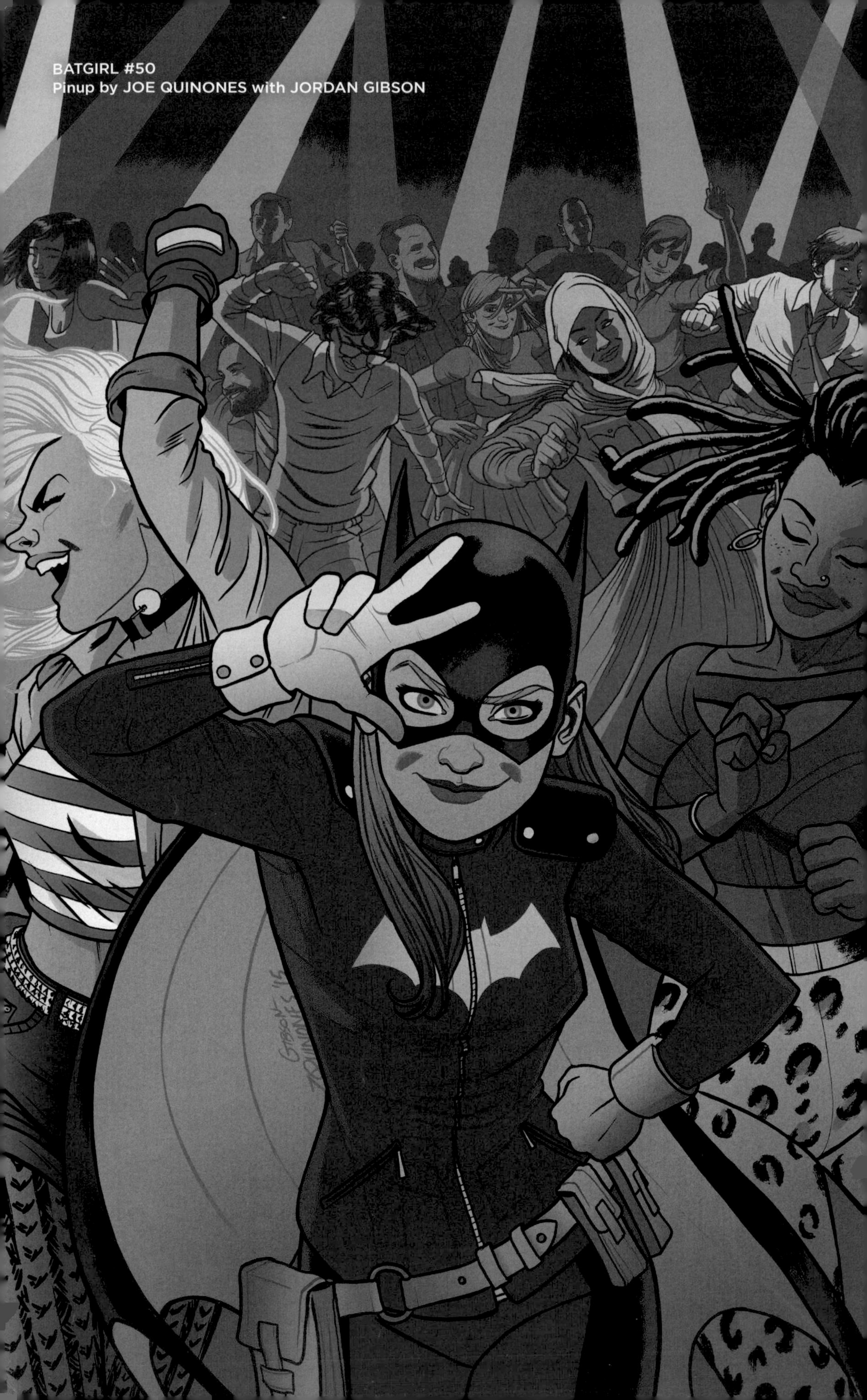

BATGIRL #50
Pinup by JOE QUINONES with JORDAN GIBSON

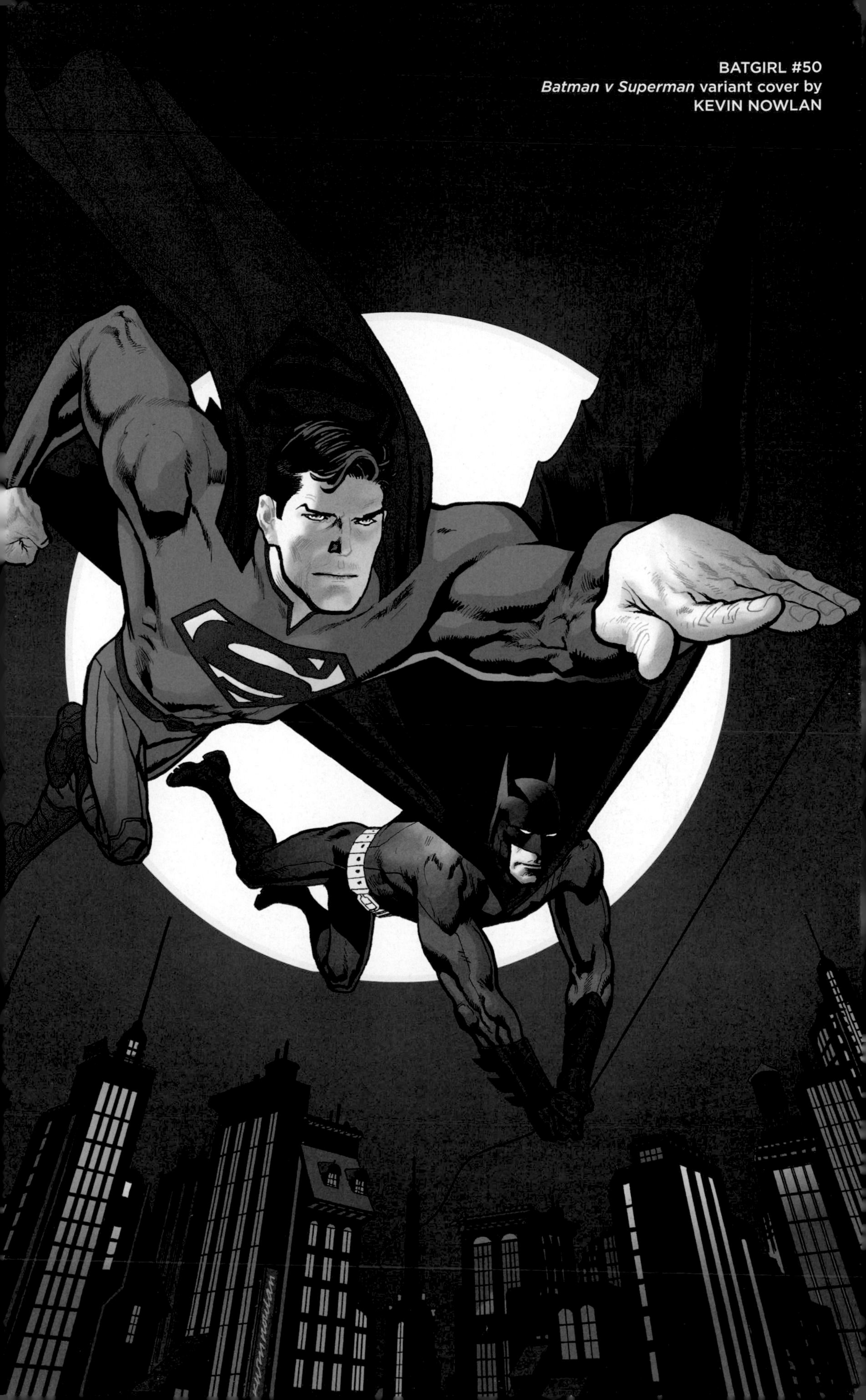

BATGIRL #50
Batman v Superman variant cover by
KEVIN NOWLAN

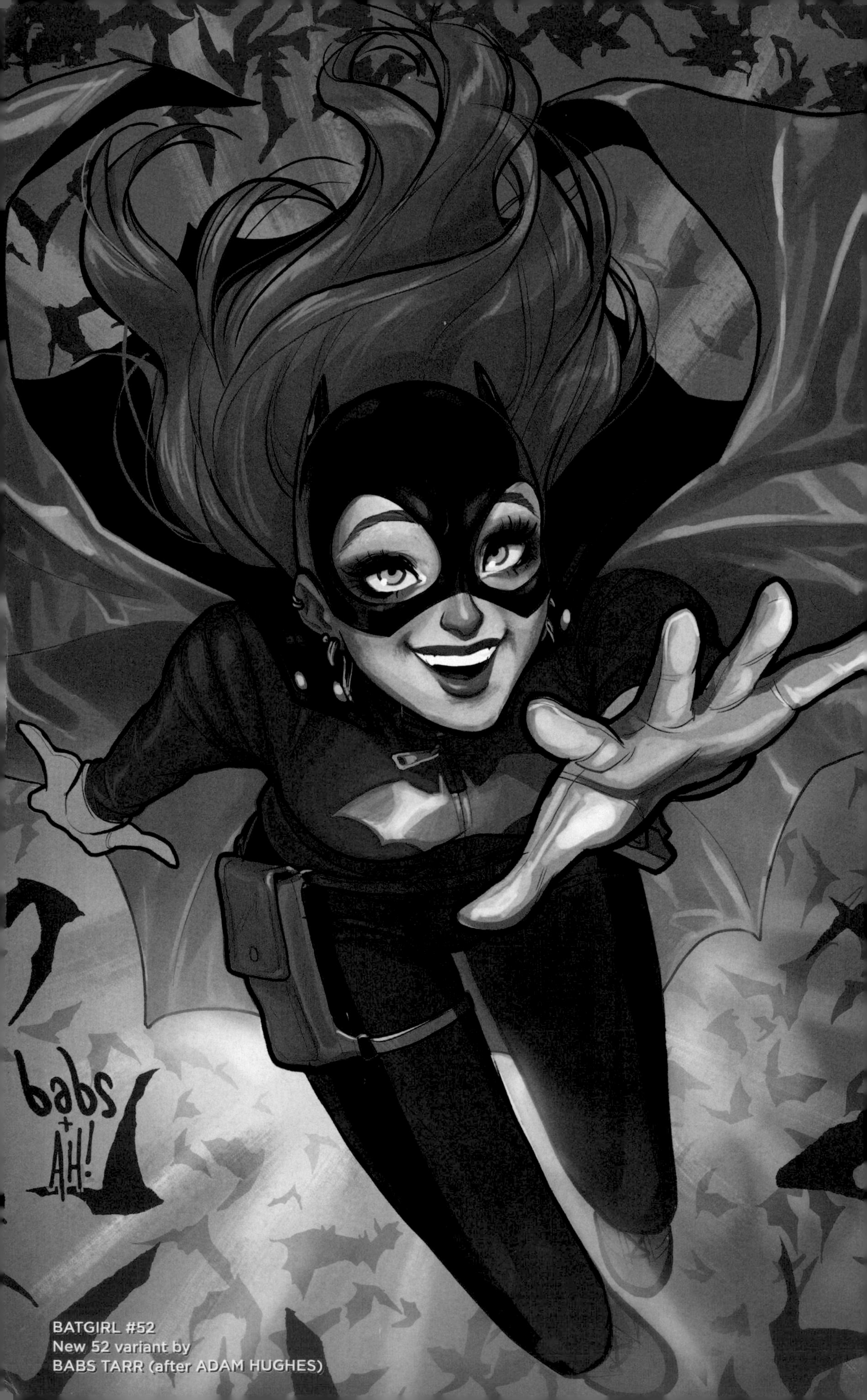
babs
+
AH!

BATGIRL #52
New 52 variant by
BABS TARR (after ADAM HUGHES)

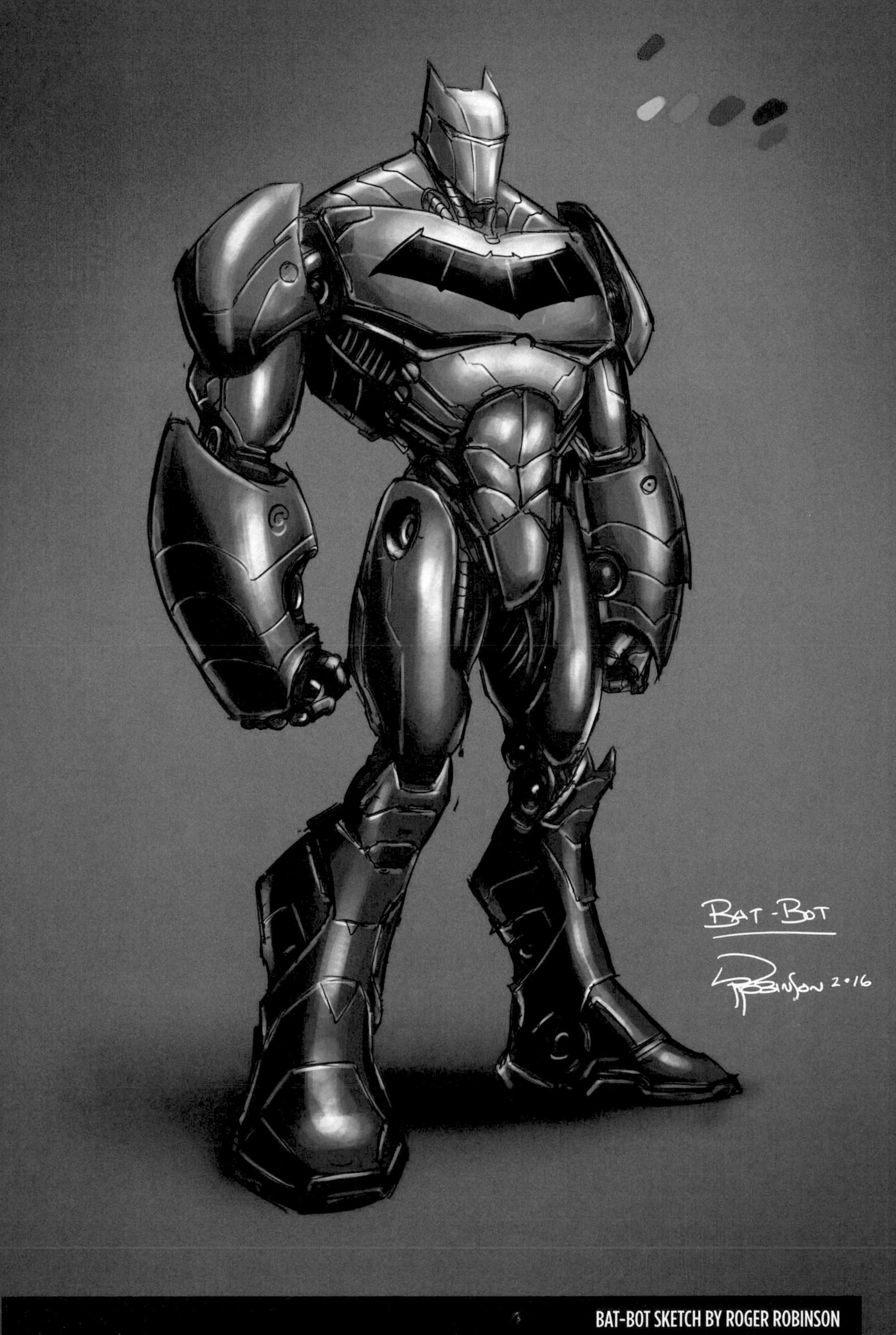
BAT-BOT
ROBINSON 2•16

BAT-BOT SKETCH BY ROGER ROBINSON

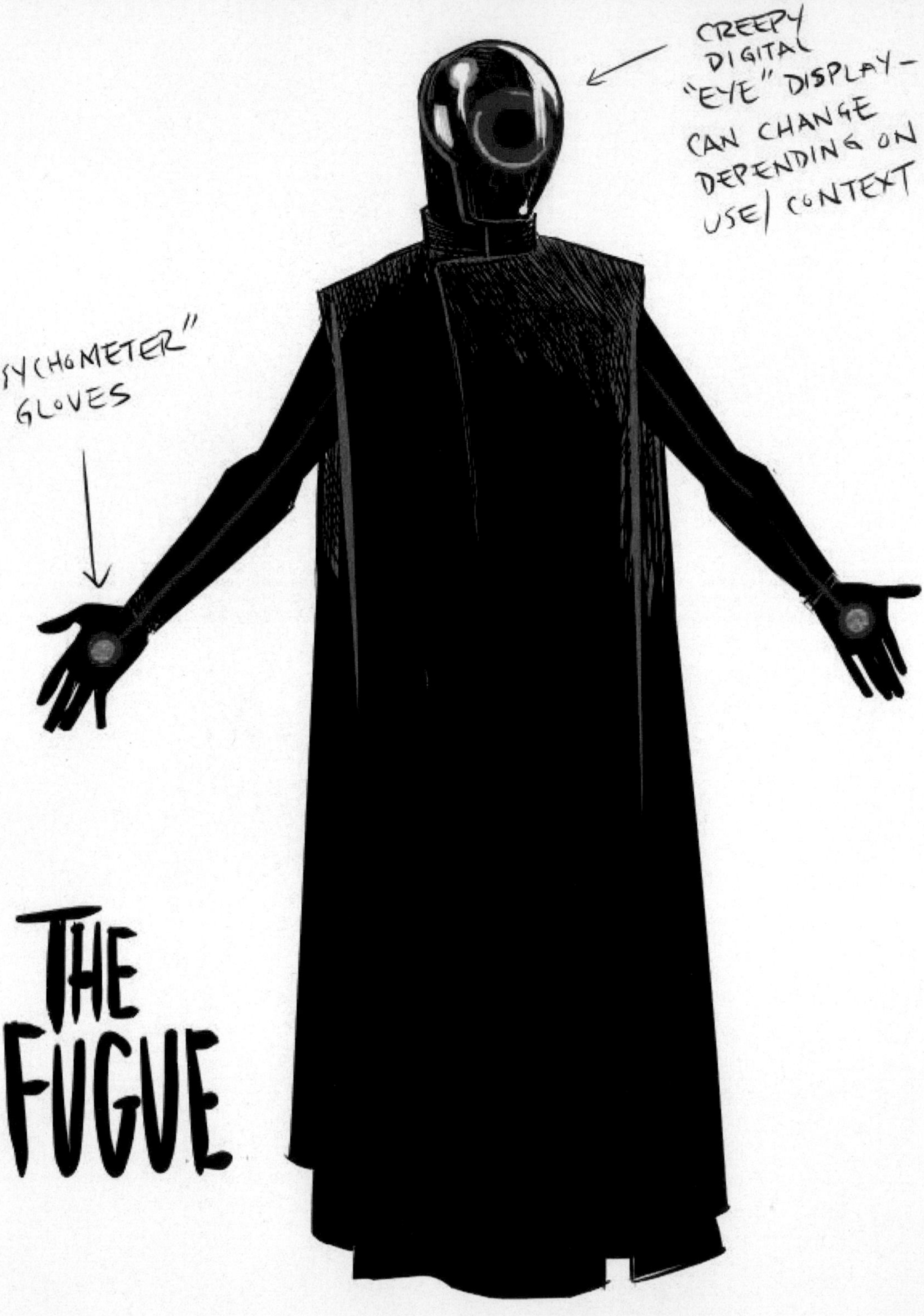

CREEPY DIGITAL "EYE" DISPLAY - CAN CHANGE DEPENDING ON USE/ CONTEXT
"PSYCHOMETER" GLOVES
THE FUGUE

CORPORAL PUNISHMENT (ORIGINALLY CALLED COUNTESS PAIN)
DESIGN BY BABS TARR

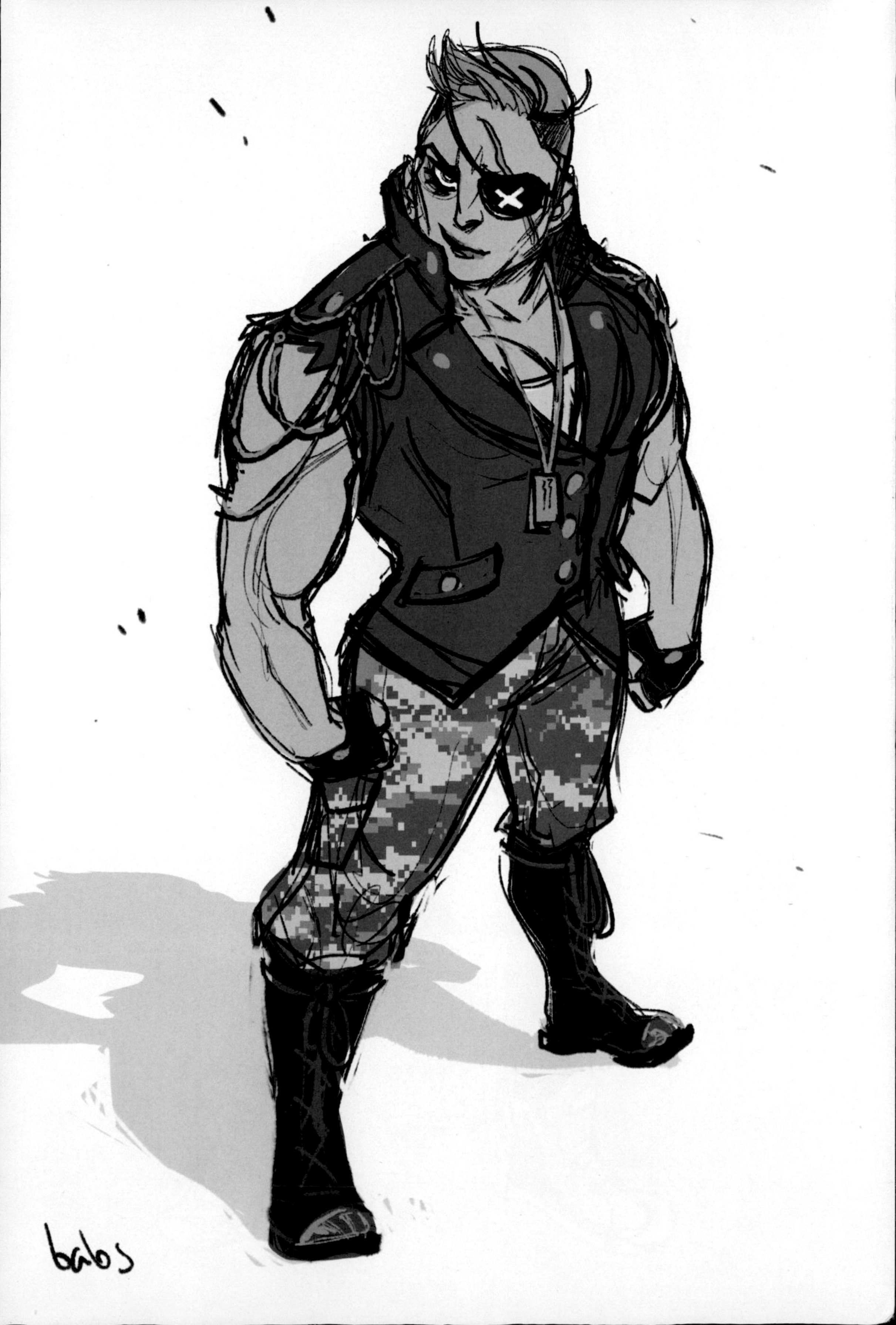
babs

MOKUGEKI DESIGN BY BABS TARR

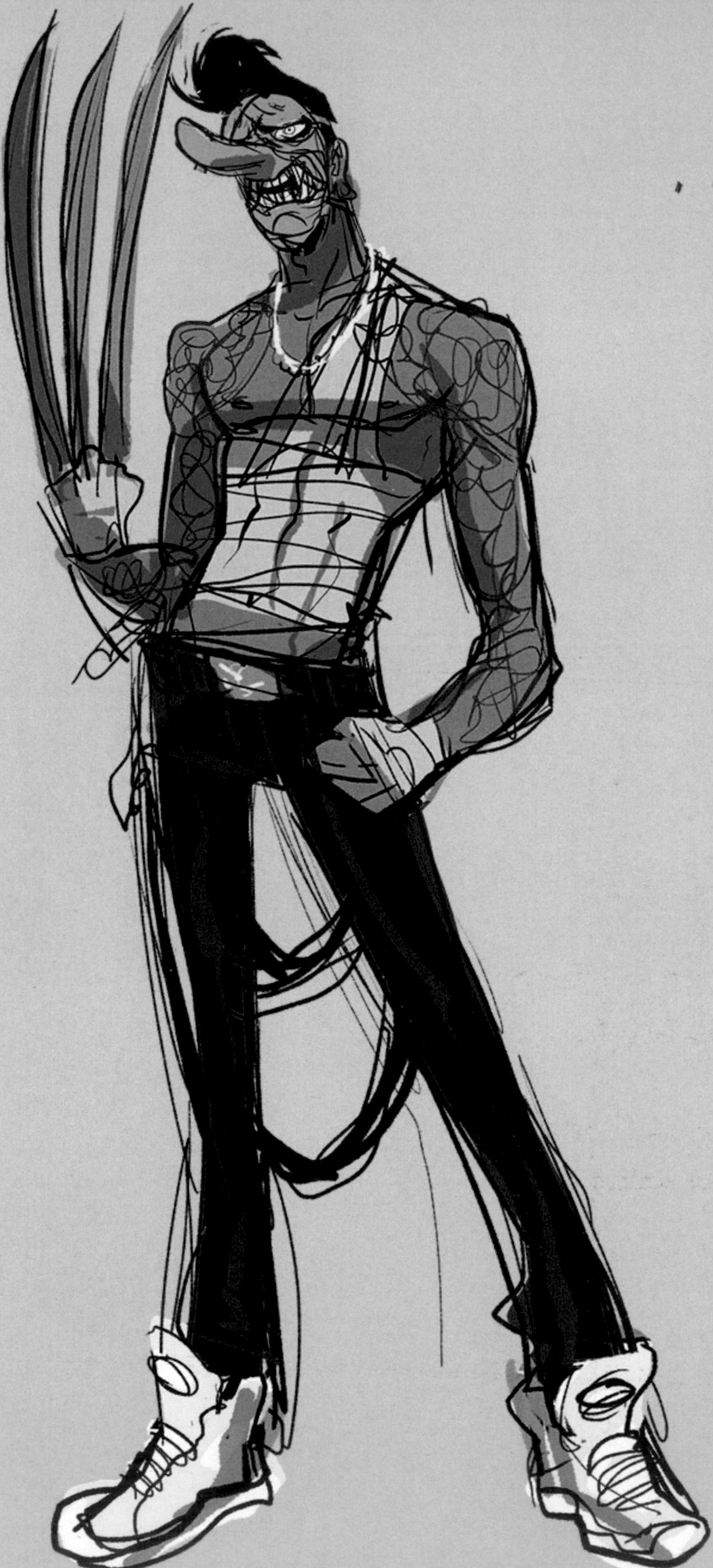